1

To Marguerite

AMERIKA

Paul Lally

— a fellow soul on the same happy journey —

love

Paul Lally

2015

3

4

I know not with what weapons World War Three will be fought,
but World War Four will be fought with sticks and stones.

- Albert Einstein

Courage is fear holding on a minute longer.
General George S. Patton Jr.

America didn't lose World War Two. We quit before it started.

What choice did we have?

After New York and D.C. disappeared beneath mushroom clouds, Hitler said Chicago was next, and then Boston, Philadelphia, Detroit, St. Louis - or so he claimed - when he delivered his ultimatum to President Perkins.

Unlike the rest of FDR's cabinet, Secretary of Labor Frances Perkins had been in Philadelphia the night of December 8, 1941, when Roosevelt addressed a joint session of Congress. For those of you too young to remember (or would just as soon forget), the Japanese had attacked Pearl Harbor the day before and broken the back of our Pacific Fleet, including our aircraft carriers *Lexington* and *Enterprise.*

Despite this near-fatal blow, America was not about to take it lying down. No sir, not anymore. Not after three long years of watching France, Britain, Russia, and China go down in flames while we stood on the sidelines cheering them on with lend-lease airplanes, tanks and ammunition.

The time had finally come for us to roll up our sleeves and fight for what was right.

Right?

Right.

And for good reason. For almost a decade, Japan had been carving out bigger and bigger chunks of real estate in China and Korea, while bowing and scraping and being polite about it all, but still killing tens of thousands of innocent civilians without batting an eye or shedding a tear.

But the day they bombed Pearl Harbor, Americans knew the Stature of Liberty would finally rise like the wounded giant she was, and with her blazing torch of freedom she'd start swinging.

Or so we thought.

Where were you the night FDR made his speech? My guess is you were among the tens of millions of Americans across the nation listening to their radios, waiting to hear the 'swoosh' of that fiery torch, right?

Me too, except I was stuck in Buenos Aires, and outraged like everybody else about Pearl Harbor. I promised myself the instant I got stateside, I'd take a furlough from Pan American Airways, enlist in the Army Air Corps and start shooting down every damn Nazi plane I could find.

Or so I thought.

FDR began his speech by saying 'On Sunday December 7th, a day that will live in infamy -' and the radio went dead. I thought it was mine. You thought it was yours.

We were both wrong.

Afterwards, they said ground zero had been a mile up Constitution Avenue. But the force of the atomic blast had been so powerful it could have been right on top of the Capital dome, which still looks like a giant hand punched it down and didn't bother being neat about it.

The only survivor was blind-lucky Frances Perkins, and according to the Constitutional line of succession, America's first woman was duly sworn in as president until full elections could be held in November. But presiding over what?

The twenty kiloton nuclear blast had turned senators and representatives into vapor as they sat in their historic, creaking chairs in the Capitol, listening to FDR's speech. Ditto the Supreme Court, all dressed up in their fancy robes and turned to ashes. The executive branch, too: President Roosevelt, Vice-president Garner, the cabinet members - the entire sitting body of the federal government gone in a millisecond flash of white light.

And don't forget Manhattan.

In that same millisecond, half of the island was gone with the wind, taking Wall Street along with it, including thousands of men and women who had been working night and day to get our country onto a war footing.

Think about it: In one stroke, Hitler pulled off a double play that left America staggering around like Goliath with his head cut off. A week later, when President Perkins signed the *Neutrality Act of 1941* into law, Adolf's double play turned into a home run.

Game over. Nazis take the World Series.

But seriously, what choice did Perkins have? Chicago? Boston? St. Louis?? If you were living in one of those cities you'd have agreed with her that hundreds of thousands - maybe millions - of innocent American lives, including yours, would be lost when the next wave of Nazi rocket-delivered atomic bombs started raining down from the sky, unless we agreed to their lousy terms.

What would you have done? What would I have done?

I don't know.

But what history will forever note is that President Perkins signed on the dotted line, and I for one don't blame her even though you may. Your privilege. It's a free country. But her call. She's president, and the way I figure it, lousy decisions come with lousy jobs.

By mid-August, 1942, eight short months after December's mushroom clouds, here's where we stood: Germany ruled Britain, France and the Netherlands, and had Russia on the ropes, ready to throw in the towel. Japan was raising hell all across the Pacific, taking what it wanted without asking. And the United States? We were as neutral and indifferent as Switzerland about the fascist darkness sweeping across the world.

Correction.

'Indifferent' is wrong. Stunned is more like it. Maybe even numb is better. But it's no surprise when you stop and think about what it was like back then: forty-eight governors had to appoint new members to congress, a temporary Federal government had to be established in Philadelphia, a supreme court had to be created, plus don't forget the thousands of layers of bureaucracy that had to be restored in order to run our country as a nation.

Nation? Who are you kidding? We were far from being a nation.

If you were around at the time, you know what I'm talking about. If you weren't, trust me - trust us - it's true. State governments were ruling their citizens like separate nations and who could blame them?

Oklahoma was talking to Indiana, Florida was doing business with Georgia; Pennsylvania was trading with Ohio - in short we were the 'States of America,' but not the United States anymore. The Nazi bombs blasted Abraham Lincoln's dream of union into forty-eight broken pieces.

Sure, prayer was still going on all across the land for that blessed day when we would re-unite as a people and rise up and do something about our dilemma. And even more prayers were being said for those millions suffering around the world while we sat on our neutral rear-ends from sea to shining sea, twiddling our thumbs and wringing our hands.

But prayer is one thing, action another.

Mine began on a boiling hot day in August, 1942 when my partner Orlando Diaz and I were nursing our beat-up, ex-Pan American Airways Sikorsky S-38 twin-engine seaplane from Providence, Rhode Island to our home base in Key West, Nicknamed *The Flying Slipper*, her long, slender, shoe-like fuselage was suspended from the wings and twin tails by struts and bracing wires. Ugly, you bet, but she flew like a dream – except today our dream had turned into a slow-motion nightmare.

Starting with her damned landing gear.

The amphibian S-38 can operate from both water or land because it has retractable landing gear. Problem was, when we took off from the runway in Providence, the right wheel stayed in the 'down-and-locked' position. Not the end of the world. All we had to do was re-lower the left wheel and return to the airport. Problem was, when we tried, it wouldn't go down.

So here we were, like a wounded duck, one foot up and one foot down, with no place to go but forward, in hopes we could figure out what the hell to do next.

And just as Orlando and I had figured out what, our nightmare got worse. We started leaking fuel.

A lot of it.

Orlando was a licensed A&P (airframe and power plant) mechanic, and while he loved airplanes and engines he hated to fly. So it became my job to scramble back into the passenger compartment and weasel my way out through the boarding hatch and onto the lower wing to figure out what the hell was going on.

Hard enough to do on the ground, try fighting an eighty mile-an-hour slipstream with a wrench in your hand. Meanwhile, Orlando, not a pilot in any way shape or form, sat in the co-pilot's seat, struggling to keep the wings level while praying in a booming voice that even I could hear outside, let alone God in the heavens:

'Almighty Father, look DOWN upon two sinners at one thousand feet and closing fast. Look down and hear our prayer, and give STRENGTH to Brother Samuel's hands so that he may STEM the mighty tide of gasoline

10

coming from number two engine. In your name I pray to DELIVER us from evil and the approaching earth below. Amen, halleluiah, and glory be thy everlasting name - and Brother Sam, I bet you ten to one it's a bad compression fitting.'

Like I said, Orlando was a hell of an A&P mechanic. A moment's examination revealed a loose fitting on the fuel line feeding our starboard engine.

'Bang it hard, brother' he said.

'I am.'

'Harder!'

My third whack loosened the off-center joint, and after two quick twists of the wrench, the compression nut seated and the spray of gasoline stopped.

And with that, the flow of adrenaline to my heart did too, turning my legs into rubber. Great. All I needed was to go sliding off the wing and down into the waters of Long Island Sound. At this altitude it would be like hitting concrete.

'Need a hand out here, brother.'

'Negative. Both on the wheel.'

I took a deep breath and slowly slid across the tightly-stretched wing fabric, being careful to place my shoes on the cross ribs, otherwise I'd rip holes in the doped fabric and end up looking like Buster Keaton in a silent movie, my legs wiggling in the air.

Just before I made the final move to the open hatch, I risked a downward glance. Even with both engines working we were still descending. Waves breaking along the Connecticut coastline, Orlando was singing some kind of hymn.

I shouted, 'Shut the hell up and give her more throttle and pull back on the wheel.'

In answer, the engines went to full power, the nose pitched up sharply and I began sliding. Only a last-second grab at one of the passenger windows saved me. The S-38 was so old and battered that the latch gave way and my fingers grabbed hold of the frame, stopping my forward motion. Even though I'm on the thin side, there's no way I could have squeezed myself through that small window.

But never underestimate the power of a descending airplane to create minor miracles, because I managed to squirm and squiggle my way back inside, vault over the battered, wicker passenger seats and head for the cockpit.

I dropped into the left hand seat. 'I've got the aircraft.'

'Amen, brother.'

I pulled the pin on the center-post control column, swung it over to my side, established a positive rate of climb and flew in silence for thirty seconds or so before I turned to Orlando and said casual-like, as though I'd just been out for a stroll,

'Let's give that landing gear a look-see, shall we?'

That's how airline pilots are. Calm. Cool. Collected. Especially when they're not.

Orlando knew how to play that game as good as me. 'Can't see why not.'

He bumped into me as he struggled out of the cramped cockpit. Not that the space was small, it's just that Orlando is big. If he weighs under three hundred pounds it's a miracle. And if any of that's fat it's a double-miracle.

I said over my shoulder, 'Think you can fix it?'

A toothy smile split his dark face like a sunrise. 'Ain't nothing I can't fix with two hands and the Lord's tool box.'

Hammer at the ready, he slid open a starboard passenger window and thrust his muscle-bound arm outside to do battle with the stubborn landing gear. For a long minute his prayers intermixed with his pounding. Then his deep-pitched voice cut above the roaring wind stream,

'When I shout 'down gear' you say a prayer and start cranking!'

'Roger.'

I can't tell you exactly where or when Orlando got this religion thing. The whole time we were kids growing up in Key West, playing in the alleys and on the wharves, he never used the word 'God' unless he was cursing me or somebody else - or something else - which was almost all the time.

We lived on opposite sides of the tracks - literally, because my father was an engineer on the Florida East Coast Railroad, running passenger trains back and forth from Miami to Key West. By contrast, Orlando's father lay in an unmarked grave somewhere down in Cuba, killed as a freedom fighter for *Partido Independiente de Color*.

Two years earlier, with a 'dead or alive' price on his head, his father had sent Orlando and his mom packing across the Florida Straits to Key West, where we fell in together and became thick as little thieves. When word of his father's death arrived, we became angry little thieves as well.

'Try it now!' Orlando boomed.

I grabbed the gear crank and started turning.

'Stop! Now go the other way!'

'Going the other way.'

'Stop!'

Orlando wedged his head and shoulders into the cockpit, huffing and puffing, his breath hot on my face, his fist the size of a small ham opened up to reveal a broken piece of metal.

'Hinge-pin snapped.'

'Can you fix it?'

He snorted like a bull. 'We'll figure out something.'

'You and the Lord?'

He gave me a long hard look, and then stomped off.

Most of the 'Conchs' - what we call Key West natives - frowned on this skinny little white boy playing with that chunky little black boy. Slavery was long gone in the south but not long forgotten. Even so, folks knew better than to cross swords with my mother, Rosie Carter, and dare tell her how to raise her boy. They wisely looked the other way while Orlando and I continued being black-and-white friends.

To boost my father's meager paycheck - he was just an engine hostler back when O and I first met - Rosie went to work in a cigar factory. If you remember Prohibition, you might remember that in the 1920s Key West had hundreds of them. Bad booze mixes with good cigars.

Anyhow, Rosie worked shoulder to shoulder with O's mom, Carlita, rolling cigar after cigar, hour after hour, day after day, and became fast friends. By the way, you become friends with my mother whether you like it or not. She has a way of making you feel like there's nobody in the world as interesting as you, while she looks at you with those cornflower-blue eyes of hers and smiles at what you're saying.

My late wife Estelle used to claim that I looked at her the same way Rosie did. I would always disagree, arguing that I was cantankerous, opinionated, bull-headed and cocky. But she'd wait me out, smiling, knowing that sooner or later I'd come to a sputtering stop and shrug my shoulders and surrender.

That's because my wife was one of the only people - aside from my mother - who saw the real Sam Carter gliding along beneath the hard-polished skin of 'Samuel J. Carter, Pan American Airlines;' a stiff, by-the-book, professional airman doing the job he'd trained a lifetime to do; bravely piloting flying boats in and out of harbors from Miami to Buenos Aires, and landplanes from Mexico City to Panama, day after day, week after week without a murmur of complaint; rarely seeing his wife and kids, and utterly determined to make captain even if it killed him, which in hindsight maybe would have been better, all things considered.

But it didn't happen that way. I'm here writing this down as living proof that what you think is going to happen in your life is just that, a thought. What really happens is what really happens.

And what happened to me is that the night the Nazis dropped their atomic bombs, my life basically vanished, including my job with Pan Am - courtesy of my own actions, let me state for the record. And now I was just a small time charter pilot flying a beat-up hangar queen, scrambling to make ends meet in between trying to pick up the pieces of my dream.

It sure as hell wasn't easy. Still isn't.

But that's not the story I'm telling now, with O and me in mid-air, trying to make a living in a new world not of our choosing – or any American's, for that matter.

Ever since the Neutrality Act, the Nazis had restricted civilian flights along the Atlantic coastline - only one of their many conditions. They had officials on the ground to enforce them, too. Not soldiers, of course. Helmets and hobnail boots would not have gone down well with the American public.

No, sir, these swastika-wearing bastards knew how to do things right by using 'Compliance Officers;' smooth-talking, diplomatic types in civilian clothes who just 'happened' to be stationed at key industrial sites across the United States to make sure our factories were turning out cars not tanks; washing machines not fighter airplanes. Nothing to aid the global war effort. No arms. No weapons. Just stuff and more stuff.

They even shipped over their own military aircraft to make sure we toed the line in the restricted airspace, using squadrons of top-of-the-line Messerschmitt Me-109's, the same plane that had helped win the Battle of Britain in 1940. But for their enforcement role in America, they painted the planes white. And the menacing, black iron crosses on their wings? A friendly green, instead, to make everything seem nice and innocent and diplomatic-like. But make no mistake, the planes carried twenty millimeter cannons and their pilots were more than happy to shoot you down if you flew into 'temporarily restricted airspace.'

Temporary, my ass.

Berlin calmly insisted these restrictions were 'dictated by current events and not to be considered permanent.' which was a nice way of saying, 'until you get your country up and running again, we're going to make damn sure you don't do anything stupid, like start a war. Because if you do we will hammer you flat the same way we're hammering Russia flat.'

And they were doing that in spades. At last report, Stalin was still alive and well, but like D.C. and New York, the city of Moscow was nothing more than a smoking nuclear crater. What was left of the Soviet government had retreated east behind the Ural Mountains, claiming they were merely re-grouping. But from what radio reports were saying - propaganda or not - Hitler was about to pull off what Napoleon had only dreamed about and God help the Soviet peasants who stood in the way of the SS Troopers goose-stepping eastward, where sooner or later they would shake hands with Imperial Japan.

Final score? Fascists: 1 -- World: 0.

In the middle of all this crap, here's what caught my attention. For some odd reason, Pan American Airlines was still flying airplanes, which surprised many people, but not me. I figured its president Juan Trippe had cut some kind of secret deal with the Germans that allowed his big silver birds to keep making money for his airline. That's how Trippe was.

'War? What war? Let's get down to business, boys.'

By contrast, American Airlines and United Airlines had had their wings clipped on all their coastal operations. Me? I had my wings taken away literally. But don't blame Pan Am. They prefer sober pilots in the cockpit and I had turned up drunk. Twice, actually. If I had been Trippe, I'd have pulled my wings too. But in my case, I handed them over before they lowered the boom. Regardless of what had happened to me to create this situation, no matter how justifiable my behavior, company rules were company rules and I had broken them.

On purpose.

'New York's coming up to starboard,' I shouted back to Orlando.

'Keep clear of it, you hear? It's still glowing.'

'You don't know what you're talking about. There's nothing there now but a big hole in the ground.'

'Better safe than sorry.'

He had a point. It had cost me five hundred dollars to bribe Air Compliance Control for our extended flight plan to Key West. I wasn't about to lose it by violating their precious airspace. I patted the polished oak control yoke. How many times in the past had my sweaty hands gripped this very wheel under very different circumstances?

This particular S-38, NC-6000, had a previous life before becoming a hangar queen for the Providence charter outfit, where I had bought her and changed her call sign to 'Carter Air 45.' She had once been the star performer of Pan American's fledgling airline service from Miami to Havana in the early 1930s. In her heyday, she had flown fun-seeking passengers, pockets full of gambling money, from Pan Am's Key West seaplane base down to swinging and swaying Havana for a fun-and-sex-filled weekend.

I know, because I was flying in the right hand seat and Captain Fatt, my mentor, the left.

Together we'd skim across the smooth waters, lift off and begun that familiar, slow, lazy climb to twenty-five hundred feet where we would weave in and out of the puffy cumulous clouds and make our way south across the Florida Straits. Weather permitting we could cover the ninety miles separating our two nations in less than an hour and deliver our passengers safe and sound to the Havana's Prohibition-free, bar-filled streets.

I glanced over at the empty co-pilot's seat and remembered a younger, happier Sam Carter sitting in that very same spot ten years earlier, hands in his lap, patiently waiting for Fatt to swing the wheel over to his side and say in his gravelly voice, 'You have the aircraft, kid.'

'I have the aircraft, sir.'

'Maintain your heading, I'm going back to mingle.'

And with that, he would heave up his bulk from the left-seat and ease back into the passenger compartment. Already snug quarters with seating for twelve, Fatt's presence made it burst at the seams. But happily so.

As I flew along, I would do my best to eavesdrop on his smooth banter, trying to learn his secret of mixing drinks for the passengers using the small bar built into the back of the bulkhead that separated the cockpit from the paying customers. The plane's original plans had called for isolating these two areas. But Juan Trippe understood the value of a captain mingling with his customers and modified it. Captain Fatt's dominating physical presence not only reassured them to the safety of aviation, it also guaranteed future flights would be booked on our small airline, not some rival.

Pan Am was tiny back in 1929 when I first started working there. Trippe had opened service out of Key West using under-powered Fokker Tri-planes, lots of prayer, and miles of baling wire. I joined them a few months later as an eager nineteen year-old radio operator, after lying that I knew all about it. But after studying my head off the night before my final interview, I managed to bluff my way through the tests the next day, and kept at it until I actually did learn Morse code and communicated with the Pan Am planes flying back and forth across the Straits carrying passengers and mail.

But I didn't want to pound a Morse Key the rest of my life. I wanted to fly. I already had my license. Against my father and mother's wishes, I had run away from Key West at seventeen to help build runways for the airmail routes. Along the way I got flying lessons here and there from airmail pilots who took my hard-earned money, stuffed me in the front seat of a beat-up Jenny J-4 biplane and showed me the difference between a slip and a crab, a bank and a turn until I finally got the idea and soloed.

Don't get me wrong. Saying you've soloed an airplane is like saying 'I took my first step.' There's a lot more to walking than that. And don't forget running, leaping, jumping and twisting. Flying's the same way; everything's new and different and scary, then you do it over and over again until it becomes second nature, and then disappears completely and your hands and feet and head and heart become one with the stick and rudder pedals and ailerons and elevator and you're no longer flying an airplane, you're just flying.

A big BANG from the back.

'Try it now,' Orlando shouted,

I cranked the landing gear handle. Something clicked, and the drawbars on both wings rose, lifting the wheel struts in turn, and the tires pivoted smoothly into the 'up' position.

'Perfect!'

'Now the other way.'

'You sure?'

'Trust in the Lord.'

I did as I ordered. They worked perfectly.

Orlando dropped down into the right seat. He stroked the chipped and battered instrument panel.

'Poor girl's been through a lot.'

I pointed down. 'So has New York.'

We were still well outside the 'No-Fly' zone, but even so, any minute I imagined Me-109's swooping down on us like greyhounds toying with a groundhog. I leveled off at two thousand feet. From here difficult to see much of the atomic bomb damage. The summer ground haze didn't make it any easier. But what I could see matched up with the devastating photographs and newsreels that had flashed across the nation during that terrible week. That had been in black-and-white. This was full color.

Right around 82nd street, you could see a radical change in the skyline. From the beginning of the Manhattan Island down to that spot, the shapes of various apartments and office buildings and skyscrapers reached upwards like so many different fingers and thumbs. But from 82nd street down to the Battery, like a giant foot had crushed everything flat. In a white-hot, shattering instant, the nuclear blast formed a crater a half-mile across and destroyed a full third of the island. Final casualty counts were over eight-five thousand dead and wounded. New Yorkers never saw it coming. Neither did Washingtonians. How could they?

Afterward the Nazis bragged how their two-stage A9-10 intercontinental rockets had performed flawlessly on their four-thousand mile, pre-emptive strikes. Newsreels showed simulated animation footage of the two-stage beasts lifting off their launch pads at Peenemünde. At sixty-thousand feet, the first stage burnt out and fell to the ground by parachute, while the second stage accelerated to over three thousand miles-an-hour and became a silent, nuclear-tipped poison dart.

'Time to be good citizens,' I said, and turned on the radio. For a moment I forgot the assigned frequency. Then it came to me, and with it a flash of anger at what I had to do. I let it pass before I keyed the microphone.

'New York Control, Carter Air four-five is with you at two thousand feet, heading two-ten degrees.'

Hiss, crackle; lousy radios. Then a German-accented voice, clipped and precise: 'Carter Air four-five, why are you not at your assigned altitude of three thousand meters?'

'In-flight emergency.'

A long hissing wait. 'You are declaring an emergency?'

'Negative. It's been resolved. Climbing to assigned altitude now.'

'Roger, maintain proper separation from no-fly zone, according to procedures.'

'Affirmative.'

'Be advised your approved flight plan closes at--' the voice paused. I could almost hear the chromium steel gears meshing in his Nazi brain as he performed the calculation. 'Zero-two hundred hours tomorrow.'

I felt like somebody had punched me. 'My flight plan was approved for twenty-four hours. You cut it in half.'

'That is the plan I have before me.'

'With all due respect, there's been a mistake. I can't fly non-stop to Key West, Florida. That's over sixteen hundred miles from here. I have to refuel, I have to sleep.'

'You will land your aircraft on or before zero-two hours hundred tomorrow morning. If you wish, you may re-apply for an additional flight plan to continue your journey. New York Control, out.'

I stared at my microphone as if the Nazi was going to climb out of it, give me a 'Heil Hitler' salute and click his heels to seal the deal.

Orlando said, 'If it's any help, I can fly while you sleep.'

'You'll have to. Those lobsters go out at noon tomorrow.'

'Want me to take over?'

I thought about his earlier handling of the controls. 'Not yet. Let me think this through.'

The first lesson I learned from Captain Fatt when he taught me to fly the S-38 was that if I got myself back on the ground safely, the passengers behind me would too - which meant I didn't have to over-think about being responsible for their lives.

'We're in this together, kid,' he said. 'And it'll all come out right in the end if you keep your eye on the runway ahead, not the runway behind.'

Our current 'runway' was in Key West, Florida, and I had to get there practically non-stop before my flight plan expired. If we were still in the air when it happened, an escort of Messerschmitt's would be sitting on our tail within minutes; their cannons armed and gun sights hot. That's how organized these people were in their so-called 'compliance' duties. It made me mad, but it also made me scared.

What kind of world were we living in?

I re-worked the numbers: our plane's range was roughly seven hundred miles a leg, but since we had easily lost a third of our fuel because of that crappy compression joint, we would have to make the hop in three jumps, starting with a re-fueling stop somewhere north of Baltimore. Then on to Savannah, Miami, and finally home.

It would take thirteen hours of steady flying. Not impossible. My time as a first officer in Pan American's four-engine *China Clippers* involved Pacific Ocean over-water flights much longer than that on a regular basis. But we had relief crews to spell us every four hours like they do on ocean liners.

Not this time.

Just me and the control wheel and a ham-fisted mechanic who could hold the plane at altitude if I fell out of my seat from exhaustion. But no way was that going to happen. Not on my watch.

'Where's that coffee?'

Two sips later, the caffeine jolt rippled through my system and my lips literally tingled. 'Tell me again where you learned how to make this stuff.'

'Mama's recipe.'

'Which is?'

'A secret.'

'C'mon.'

Orlando rubbed his heavy jaw and smiled. 'Let's just say there's a little something extra in it.' He raised his cup, which looked like an acorn in his enormous hand. 'Here's to Carter Aviation. Long may it prosper.'

'Amen to that.'

We both sipped.

I raised my cup in return. 'Death to the Nazis.'

'Hallelujah to that.'

The weather forecast called for CAVU - ceiling and visibility unlimited - from Providence south as far as Washington, D.C. But after that things got iffy. Two days ago a low pressure system had shouldered its way across the plains and bucked up flat against a high pressure system stretching from Louisiana to Ohio. The resulting clusters of thunderstorm cells were now marching their way southeast. My original flight plan would have let me slide past unscathed as they worked their way off the North Carolina coast and out to sea. But with the Nazis cutting my flight plan in two, it would be a race against bad weather that I knew we couldn't win.

If worse came to worse, we could always put down on either water or land, now that Orlando had the gear working. But just to be sure, I cycled it up and down.

Orlando grinned and patted instrument panel. 'What's it like to fly this old bird again?'

'Same tricks, just older, that's all.'

'Was this the very plane where...' he wiggled his eyebrows suggestively. I knew what he was driving at, and for some ridiculous reason I felt myself blushing. 'As a matter of fact it was.'

'So, the newlyweds really...?'

'I don't know. We pulled the curtains.'

It had been a last minute, weekend charter job, just two months after I got Pan Am pilot's wings. A wealthy real estate speculator had married a chorus girl half his age. She wanted a honeymoon in Havana. He bought up all twelve seats on the plane, had four of them removed and a divan installed, plus a champagne bucket, a cooler filled with hors de oeuvres that, after we landed, I noticed hadn't been touched. But the bride sure had, because halfway to Cuba, Captain Fatt and I thought we had hit a rough patch air turbulence that made our plane buck and swerve. A quick peek through the curtains confirmed that the disturbance was coming from the busy newlyweds in the back blissfully consummating their vows at four thousand feet and climbing.

Orlando said with a wink, 'Maybe we could build us a little side business.'

'How could a man of God say such a thing?'

'I'm a part-time preacher but a full-time businessman. We could make us some good money while we're at it. In fact, I know some folks might be interested.'

'Forget it. We're staying on this side of the law.'

He saluted me. 'Aye, aye, Captain Sam. You're the boss. Me? I'm just the worker bee.'

'Like hell you are. You own a third of this company, like me and Rosie.'

'Your mother is a fine woman.'

'She is that.'

'And bless her heart for taking care of Abby the way she does.'

Eight months ago, I had stood on the porch of my mother's house, hand poised over the door, not wanting to knock. The awful news about my wife and baby was still on my side. My mother and my ten year-old daughter Abby were on the other. And then I knocked.

Orlando's meaty hand blocked my forward view. 'Baltimore Harbor Airport at your ten o'clock.' His thick finger tapped the fuel gauge. 'Just in time. We're sitting on empty.'

I throttled back and began our descent. The 'Flying Slipper' was easy to fly, but not so easy to land. Her long, duckbill-shaped nose obscured forward vision and I smiled, thinking about my dad leaning out his locomotive cab window, trying to see past the engine's long boiler to the track ahead. Same deal, different kind of 'train.'

But by applying opposite rudder to my ailerons and skewing the plane into a sideways slip I could catch quick glances of the approaching water surface, adjust accordingly, and then swing her nose back to center.

'There's our mighty clipper fleet,' Orland said.

'Not ours anymore.' I snapped.

It broke my heart to see Pan American's big beautiful Boeing 314 flying boats gleaming in the late morning sunshine. Had things turned out differently, I would have been down there flying one, instead of up here like a kid looking through the window of the candy store.

Orlando said, 'Mighty pretty birds. How do they handle?'

'How would I know?'

He snapped his fingers. 'That's right, you were going to fly them but never did. I forgot that part of your sad story.'

'The hell you forgot, you know all about it.'

One of the clippers was moored alongside the boarding dock, waiting for her outbound passengers for Europe. While Pan Am's Orient operations had been cut short by Pearl Harbor, Trippe's other routes were still working, and the big Boeings were making two and three trips a week to Lisbon, Portugal, and from there to points north, south and east via Lufthansa, the Nazi's civilian airline.

The flying boat's broad upper wing surfaces had been painted orange-red to aid search aircraft in case she came down in the ocean - which would never happen, of course. The plane could fly on two of her four big, beautiful sixteen hundred horsepower Wright radial engines without missing a beat.

The recently-arrived inbound Clipper from Europe, now perched on a beaching cradle, was slowly being winched up onto dry land for a lightning-fast, twenty-four hour turnaround. A swarm of mechanics climbed over and around her like ants on a sugar cube. The triple-rudder tail of yet a third Clipper peeked out of the immense hangar built to accommodate these brand-new giants of the sky.

'Carburetor heat on,' I called out.

Orlando just sat there.

I nudged him. 'Pull out those two red knobs up there.'

'Sorry.' He yanked out the knobs.' Affirmative, carb heat on.'

'You're one hell of a co-pilot.'

'After today, the Lord is your co-pilot. I'm spending the rest of my life on the ground fixing things like He intended.'

I throttled back to twenty-three hundred RPM and began a slow right turn to enter the downwind leg.

'Get on the horn and announce our arrival.'

Orlando dialed in the correct frequency and keyed the microphone. 'Baltimore Harbor Tower, Carter Air four-five requests landing permission, water.'

An American voice answered in a rich, Baltimore accent that warmed my heart. 'Carter Air four-five you are cleared to land sea lane one. Wind zero-two-eight degrees at five. Caution, military traffic your three-o'clock, taking off to the south.'

In answer, two white Luftwaffe compliance fighters zoomed almost straight up into the sky to our right, climbing north, not even bothering to give us the once-over.

'Somebody's been a bad boy,' Orlando said into the microphone. 'And they're gonna' get spanked with twenty-millimeter.'

The air controller said, 'Be advised Carter Air four-five, the walls have ears.'

Orlando said, 'Roger, lips are hereby zipped.'

I began a steep turn to our base leg, and satisfied the water surface was clear of debris, turned final.

'See how the landing buoys seem to be coming straight at us?'

'I do.' Orlando said.

'If you're too low, they'll drift upward in your line of sight. Too high and they'll drift beneath. We're a little low, so watch what I do.' I goosed the throttles a touch. 'See? That brings them back to the center.'

'I'll be darned,' Orlando said. 'They did.'

'I'll make a pilot of you yet.'

'Dream on.'

I imagined the S-38 sliding down a silver wire to a fixed landing spot on the water surface. With little or no wind, the harbor water had barely a ripple, which was great for ships making their way across its glassy surface, but a depth-perception nightmare when landing a seaplane. That all-important last twenty feet or so is impossible to judge correctly. By contrast, when landing on water with some chop, you get your aircraft down to about thirty feet or so, cut power, apply full elevator, let her sink, and she'll stall just above the waves, your hull will hiss as it touches the water, and you're home at last, safe and sound, easy as pie.

But not on this glassy-smooth water that was getting closer and closer. Out of the side of my eye I saw a moored Boeing Clipper flash by and my heart skipped a sad beat.

Then a small jolt and shudder as the S-38's keel touched the water and spray wiped out what little vision I had over the nose. I had to rely on my side vision to keep her tracking straight.

'Whatever you do, don't reduce power, keep flying her just in case she wants to skip back into the air - see that? That's just what happened. Hold back pressure on the wheel and fly her back down again until she settles. Let the speed fall off to under fifty, and then you can relax. Got it?'

Orlando laughed. 'Got most of it, until she bounced. I don't know what the hell you did you get her back down.'

'I prayed.'

Re-fueling would be the easy part. Taxiing the plane to the dock to do another story. Not because of the wind or water conditions, but because I would have to taxi in front of the *Yankee Clipper* moored to the dock. As I drew abreast, eight men in dark blue uniforms with gold buttons and starched white caps marched in perfect unison down the loading dock toward the plane. The familiar flight ritual I had performed a thousand times had begun once again for these lucky guys. Once the captain and crew were on board, a bell on the dock would chime twice and the well-heeled, privileged passengers would board as well.

I looked away - unfortunately straight into Orlando's eyes.

'Know any of the boys?' he said.

'Williamson the navigator and Heath, the co-pilot. We flew the Caribbean Division together.'

'Why don't you wish them *bon voyage?*'

'You don't know when to stop, do you?'

'Lancing a boil eases the pain, brother.'

'I'm not hurting.'

Orlando shook his head, said nothing and turned away. I could never lie to him and get away with it, not when we were boys, not now either. I yanked back on the throttles; the S-38 wallowed forward and came to a bobbing stop. I popped open the side window, leaned out, cupped my hands and shouted,

'Hey, Tommy, bring me back some single malt, will you?'

The flight team kept marching along, but Tommy Heath shot a glance my way. He checked his smile, rolled his eyes toward the captain, indicating he was a hard-ass, and then nodded slightly.

Dick Williamson's face brightened in recognition too, but he kept in character as he followed the crew onto the wing sponson, and entered the aircraft the last in a line of tin soldiers, just like I had done countless times in the past.

But 'tin generals' is a better word for a Boeing clipper crew. These were hand-picked veterans who'd worked their way up Pan Am's tortured chain of seniority to finally arrive at the very top, ready to serve the public by flying the largest plane in the world all over the world.

The *Yankee Clipper* still had her all-silver paint job. But my blood pressure went up by twenty points when I saw that *LUFTHANSA* had replaced the *Pan American Airways System* lettering along the upper fuselage. And my pressure went up another ten points when I saw the red-banded swastikas painted on her triple-tail rudders. Even though a Pan Am crew was flying her, she belonged to Berlin.

'Trippe doesn't give a damn if he gets dollars or *Deutschemarks*, as long as money pours into his hot little hands and his deep pockets.'

'That's no way to talk about an old friend.'

'Not anymore.'

The boarding bell gonged, and the knot of people waiting on shore slowly untangled and became a long stream of neatly-dressed passengers walking singly and in pairs along the well-maintained dock.

'Easy to spot the Nazis, ain't it?' Orlando said.

Most of the passengers walked with the casual, relaxed gait of the privileged class who could afford this expensive airborne ocean crossing, but five or six of them, despite their civilian clothes, had a peculiar, almost clipped way of moving more associated with a parade ground than wooden planks.

'Who do they think they're fooling, dressed like that?' I said.

Orlando chuckled. 'Why don't you shout *Sieg Heil* and see what happens.'

I almost did, but thought better of it. Still, the idea of was tempting, so I cupped my hands, leaned out and shouted, '*Wiedersehen Scheisskopf!*"

One of them looked up sharply, but just as he did, I firewalled the throttles and the engines roared in response, kicking up a rooster tail of spray as we shot forward, heading straight for the refueling dock. Infantile, I know, even dangerous to call him a 'shit head.' But when you're powerless against the bad guys, sometimes the only way to preserve a shred of integrity is to do something stupid and then get the hell out of Dodge before they catch you.

I'm here to say we made it out of Dodge without getting arrested for insulting our 'compliance partners.' As we reached our cruising altitude of three thousand feet, Orlando said, 'Do you think they'll report us?'

'They saw our tail number. Probably will.'

'And?'

'And by the time the paperwork makes its way up and down the Nazi chain of command, we'll be long gone and happy in Key West, flying lobsters and passengers to our hearts content.'

'Hope you're right.' He leaned forward and cupped both his ears. After a long, analytical moment he said, 'Engines sound okay.'

'What did you do to them when I was fueling?'

'Laid hands over their sorry cylinders.'

After all the fuss the S-38 had given us at the start, she was now performing the way Sikorsky had designed her. With her engines humming in perfect synchrony and my hands in my lap, I didn't need to touch the control wheel. Properly trimmed, she kept her heading and altitude perfectly. Some planes need hands-on attention every minute you're in the air, while others just want to fly, and the less you interfere with your clunky wheel and rudder adjustments, the happier they are and the sweeter they behave.

I repeated Captain Fatt's familiar phrase, 'She'd just as soon you stay on the ground and she'll go flying by herself.'

That's what he had told me the day he finally let me take the wheel of the Pan Am Fokker T-1 Monoplane. When Juan Trippe hired me on as a radio operator, I lied about knowing Morse code. But I had also lied about my age too. Don't get me wrong. Truth is always better than fiction. But I was young and desperate, and my lies were just my way of keeping my hopes alive until I could match them up with reality.

And the reality was that from the very beginning I wanted to fly, and the instant I could weasel my way into Fatt's favor and get some lessons, I did just that. He loved good cigars, and my mother rolled the best at *Key West & Havana Cigar Company*. Thanks to her and Carlita, I made sure the good captain had an unlimited supply of their *Maestro* brand.

I patted my right shirt pocket and felt the familiar shape of the same cigar. I don't smoke any more, but I still carry one as a good luck charm. Not that it had worked worth a damn over the past year, but I wasn't about to give up the tradition. But unlike me, Orlando was puffing away on a cigar the size of a small baseball bat.

'Where do you get those things?' I said.

His lips rose into a sweet smile but he said nothing.

'They sure as heck don't come from Key West – Havana is it?'

He shook his head. 'A secret.'

'Tell me.'

'If I did, it won't be a secret.'

'Then at least crack your window. You're killing me with that smoke.'

The engine noise swelled to a roar when he slid up the window, and I took the opportunity to scan the instruments: oil pressure fine, manifold pressure in the green, altimeter at a rock-steady three thousand feet and airspeed locked in at one hundred-ten mph indicated. But according to my dead reckoning, we had a headwind that would bring us down to about one hundred knots true airspeed or less. I did the math and figured we would reach Key West a little after midnight. Not great for a night's sleep, but plenty of time to get ready for the first paying flight of *Carter Aviation, Inc.* I liked how the name rolled off my tongue. It sounded impressive, even though our company was far from it.

Eight months ago I had been wearing the dark-blue uniform of a Pan American Airways captain and flying the prestigious Caribbean route. Today I was muscling a twin-engine amphibian piece of junk and praying it would stay in one piece. All because of what I saw approaching to my starboard. Without thinking I banked to a new heading that would take us closer.

Orlando realized what I was doing and jumped as if shocked. 'Brother, you best bring us back on course right now.'

'I just want to see.'

'They almost nailed us in New York. Don't push your luck.'

'I'll be careful.'

Orlando folded his thick arms across his chest; a sure sign he wasn't getting through to me. And he was right. But he wasn't giving up yet.

'You've still got a little girl and your momma, too. They're waiting for us in Key West.'

I ignored him and put the plane into a shallow bank to the right, and the green, tree-lined horizon obediently tilted to reveal a distant view of Washington D.C. According to zoning laws, no buildings could be taller than U.S. Capitol, except the Washington Monument.

Before the 'war that wasn't,' whenever I'd fly into the city, the visual effect at altitude suggested that someone had applied a giant flatiron to a normal sized city and squashed everything flat. Except of course, for the slender-spired Washington Monument that resembled a giant index finger pointing to the sky as if to say, 'Here is the Capital of the United States of America.'

But eight months ago that finger had snapped in two from the fury of an atomic blast. Today, the upper half of it lay crumpled on the ground in a tumbled heap of limestone blocks. The remaining stump stood in mute testimony to our broken nation. They had plans to re-build it. But so far nothing had happened.

'Like a tombstone.' I said.

Orlando folded his arms tighter.

'Fifteen thousand people gone in less than a second.'

'Sam, don't do this. You're just -'

'One minute alive and breathing and the next, burned as crisp as a -'

'You couldn't have done anything.'

'How do you know?'

'Nobody could. The bomb went off and everybody died. That's what happened and you know it.'

'Estelle and Eddy were down there. I wasn't.'

I eased up on the throttles and let the plane sink into a shallow glide. The distant blur of buildings grew more distinct. So did the vast bomb crater just south of the U.S. Capital. Southwest Washington had borne the brunt of the initial blast. That's where my wife and son had been staying with her parents. They'd travelled up from Miami to celebrate the birth of her sister's first baby. A family affair all around - except for me.

'I should have been there.'

'Can we discuss this outside their airspace?'

'Screw them, they don't own this country, we do.'

'They damn well own this part of it and we're inside it.'

'I want to see their graves.'

The slanting summer sunlight created a deep shadow inside the bomb crater. Even though eight months had passed, the devastation looked like it happened yesterday. For a mile and a half in all directions from the epicenter, nothing remained but scraps of what used to be buildings. Partial sections of the more substantial stone structures like the National Archives and Department of Commerce were still standing, but their empty windows and mounds of rubble marked them as memories not realities.

Somewhere beneath the shattered wood, steel and stone of what used to be 1207 Perry Place, SW, Estelle and Eddie lay buried in her parents' vaporized house. No bodies had been recovered that close to the epicenter.

'Let us pray for the departed,' Orlando said softly.

'Let us pray for vengeance first.'

Orlando tossed his cigar stub out the window and slammed it shut. 'To everything there is a season, Brother. Our time will come.'

I opened my mouth to say something hateful, just as a thundering blast of noise screamed overhead. A blur of white wings, a green Nazi cross, and our world turned upside down as the S-38 nearly flipped over in the prop wash from the compliance fighter.

'Bastard!'

I applied full power, leveled my wings and lowered her nose to regain control. Just in time, thank God, before another roar and another blast from the fighter's wingman doing the same thing, and ending with a triumphant Immelmann turn to the left that brought him high above us, heading in the opposite direction, whereupon he promptly turned again and took up station about five hundred feet above.

His wingman drew up alongside my port wing. Flight goggles, helmet and a white silk scarf obscured most of the pilot's face. He pointed at me, and then to the ground. The universal meaning was all too clear but I refused to play along. I smiled and waved back.

Orlando grunted, 'We're in it now, brother, up to our ears.'

'Not if I can play stupid we aren't.' I waved harder and tried to make my smile seem genuine.

The sound of his twenty millimeter nose cannon stopped my bright idea dead in its tracks. Golden-red tracers flashed across the afternoon sky like tiny comets, each round capable of blowing our engines to bits.

Orlando shouted, 'I told you we-'

'-shut up and pray.'

The Nazi's wingman dropped down to join us just off our starboard wing like a Berlin bookend. When he lowered his landing gear the meaning was clear: 'follow me to the ground or be shot down.' To confirm this, our radio came alive with a crisp, female German-accented voice that said, 'Unidentified aircraft, this is Washington Control. You have violated restricted airspace. We are vectoring patrol aircraft your vicinity. Hold position until they arrive.'

I keyed the microphone. 'Too late, *Fraulein*. They're already shooting at us.'

'Say again last?'

'I said, we surrender, we're coming down.'

Terrorism is the best political weapon for nothing drives people harder than the fear of death.
- Adolf Hitler

'Papers,' the Nazi official snapped.

I played it stupid. 'Huh?'

'Your documents, a passport, some means of identification.'

He stood up from his desk and marched around to face us. He wore a dark grey suit, white shirt and black tie. But I bet you even money his SS uniform wasn't far away, probably hanging in his closet, waiting for the victory parade down Pennsylvania Avenue, so that he could goose step past the rubble of the White House along with the rest of his skull-and-bones buddies.

I fished for my wallet and nudged Orlando. 'Got anything that says who you are?'

He drew himself up sharply and stuck out his chest. 'I am Orlando Diaz, a United States citizen.' He turned to our inquisitor. 'And who are you to speak to us in such an insulting manner?'

Orlando's response took the official by surprise so much that he automatically answered, 'Hauptman Ritter, assistant commandant of Washington Regional Air Traffic Compliance Center.'

I stuck out my hand. 'Glad to meet you Mr. Ritter. I'm Sam Carter, and let me say right up front that me and Orlando are mighty sorry we flew into your airspace. We got to talking about some fishing we got planned, and before we knew it your boys were up there shooting at us like we were some kind of enemy. Must admit it came as quite a surprise. Yes, sir, it did.'

Ritter stared at my hand but didn't take it. Not a good sign. But I kept up my hillbilly routine, because I didn't know any other way to escape this brightly-lit office situated off a long corridor that connected to a dimly-lit room filled with Nazi air controllers keeping the restricted skies over Washington, D.C. clear of commercial air traffic like ours.

Only moments ago we had landed at National Airport, three miles south of ground zero. Even at this distance, their main hangars had been severely damaged from the blast and the control tower taken out completely. In its place, the *SS Waffen* had installed a Luftwaffe mobile field tower.

And that's what I saw when I banked the S-38 into her final approach. Just as I flared for landing, the two Me-109s who had jumped us did a double victory roll overhead and went back on patrol. Arrogant bastards. But truth be told, fighter pilots are tough, wiry, clever and competitive, no matter their nationality. I ought to know. I've gotten in arguments with enough of them and some fights with a few and never came out a winner.

I held out my well-worn pilot's license to the official. 'Will this do?'

Ritter examined it, jotted something on a piece of paper with his gold-tipped ink pen, and handed it back.

He glared at Orlando. 'And you?'

'Like I said, mister.' Orlando spread open his huge hands, palms up, like pink catchers' mitts. 'I'm an American.'

He frowned. 'You are a Negro.'

'So?'

'I want proof of your identity!'

He shrugged. 'I got me a birth certificate floating around back home somewhere, if that's what you mean.'

Ritter's eyes tightened. 'Don't play the fool with me.'

'Oh, surely I ain't, sir.' Orlando rummaged in his pants pockets and proceeded to play it even more stupid. 'Lemme, see if I gots anythin' else that might hep you out.'

He pulled out a penknife and a handful of change and placed them on the desk. Then a tightly-rolled wad of fifty-dollar bills.

'Couldja' hold this please? Almost a thousand dollars. My life savings.'

Without blinking his cold gray eyes, Ritter took the money and hefted it. 'Why don't you keep this in a bank?'

Orlando laughed. 'Ever hear of the Depression?'

Ritter brightened. 'Ah, yes. The Jews and their banks. They nearly did America in.'

'And you're doing us in instead,' I said without thinking.

He shot me a look. I kept my face neutral and said, *'Deutschland über Alles'*, isn't that the song you guys sing all the time?'

'Germany truly is over all.'

Ritter smoothly slipped Orlando's roll of bills into his pocket. 'I think you gentlemen have learned that lesson firsthand today. Haven't you?'

'Yes sir, Mr. Ritter,' Orlando said. 'We surely have, haven't we, Sam?'

His face was impassive, but still waters run deep with that man.

Ritter returned to his desk, sat down and pressed a button on a small speaker. 'Escort the prisoners out.'

'Jawohl, Kapitan.'

'Prisoners?' I said. 'Now, wait just a second.'

Ritter smiled. 'Don't worry Mr. Carter. It's just a formality while you are under our jurisdiction.' He patted the bulge of money in his pocket.

'The moment you lift off from the runway, you will be free of that term.'

Two tough-looking, bullet-headed men entered the office wearing civilian clothes just like Ritter, but if they weren't SS troopers I'll eat my hat. To their credit they didn't handcuff us, but I felt them on my wrists just the same. As much as I hated it, I shook hands with Ritter.

'Sorry about what happened. I promise it will never happen again.'

Ritter took it. 'We all make mistakes.'

'Even Nazis?'

He laughed at my little joke and waved us out.

I expected to leave the building and head over to the apron where our S-38 sat waiting for us to continue our journey south. Instead they marched us down a set of stairs, then along a darkened corridor, and brought us to a halt in front of a holding cell.

'What the hell's going on here?'

The first thug said, 'We need to get your release papers.'

'Then get them. We'll wait out by the plane.'

The second thug said softly, 'Sorry, sir. Regulations. It won't be long, I assure you.'

Even though his face was kind and reassuring, I didn't like the smell of this. From the look on Orlando's face, neither did he. But we had no choice in the matter. When in Nazi-land, you do as the Nazis do. So in we went.

The door clanged shut and sure as hell, 'a few minutes' turned into an hour, then two, and then four. Repeated shouting and banging on the bars brought no response. Even Orlando bellowing his demands in his preacher-sized voice made no difference. Sometime around midnight a man brought food to our cell. He refused to answer any questions. Just shoved the metal trays through the slot provided. Two sausages swam in some kind of tan-colored cream sauce, surrounded by boiled potatoes and pale green peas. Orlando picked up a potato, examined it, and dropped it. 'I bribed that son of a bitch for nothing.'

'Eat up,' I said. 'We need our energy to figure out how we're going to get out of this mess.'

'All because you... because...' Orlando stumbled to a stop.

'Because I wanted to see their graves?'

Like a light switch, his angry face softened into sadness, he closed his eyes and nodded.

'Sweet Estelle and baby Eddie. May they rest in everlasting peace, Amen.'

'Amen.'

'And while you're at it Lord, grant us the wisdom to figure out how to get out of this pickle Brother Sam got us into.'

I dreamed Estelle was running ahead of me, but no matter how loud I shouted, she wouldn't stop. My daughter Abby held baby Eddie in her arms and cried, 'Hurry, Daddy, hurry, she's getting away!' But the faster I ran the softer the ground became and I kept falling to my knees. I tried shouting again, but nothing came out.

'Mr. Carter.'

The deep male voice was soft, yet insistent and I awoke to see a weary-looking, round face of a balding, middle-aged man with friendly blue eyes behind glittering glasses bending over me, and it all came back in a rush: getting jumped by the Nazis, forced to land in Washington D.C. and now stuck in jail.

The cell door was open behind him. But he read my mind and pressed down on my shoulder. 'You are free to go. Mr. Diaz, too. There's been a terrible mistake and I'm here to apologize.'

'Who are you?'

'Max Bauer.'

He nudged Orlando, who woke with a jump and Bauer leaped back as if shot. For an overweight middle-aged man he had the grace of a bull fighter dodging Orlando's horns. Bauer re-adjusted the fit of his full-length grey leather jacket, smoothed his lapels, and then beamed at my partner.

'Good morning Mr. Diaz. I won't ask if you slept well. These cells are notorious in that department.'

'I repeat, who are you?'

'My official title *is Sturmbahnfüher der Polizei fur Geheime Staatspolize*. But I much prefer Max.'

'What's that mean in English?'

'I'm what you Americans call a 'cop.''

'And?'

'And I have just finished arresting *Herr* Ritter for placing personal greed before the needs of the Third Reich, '*Heil Hitler*,' and all the attendant praise therein for our brave leader in Berlin.' His face grew hard. 'Ritter will get ten years at hard labor if I have anything to say about it. And I most certainly do.'

He dug into his coat pocket and pulled out Orlando's wad of fifty-dollar bills. 'It's taken me six months to catch that snake in the grass with his hand in the till, and today was the day, thanks to you.'

He handed Orlando the money. 'My apologies to you, sir. This should never have happened.'

Still half-asleep, 'The Bull of Key West' pocketed it without saying a word.

Undaunted, Bauer continued 'Your plane has been fueled and serviced at our expense, including adjusting a faulty fuel connection on your number two engine, and an issue you had with your landing gear. I also had your flight plan modified and extended to reflect your unfortunate detention here. And finally, as a courtesy, we have breakfast waiting for you in our cafeteria. American bacon and eggs I'm told, plus a box lunch for you to take with you on your trip to Key West where your daughter and mother, I'm most certain, nervously await.'

'How do you know all this stuff?'

'Once the Gestapo intelligence machine gets up and running, it's a marvel to behold. And run it did late last night when your name came across the wires and onto my desk.'

He referred to a small index card. 'You have very detailed employment records with Pan American Airways, including your untimely dismissal. That event, coupled with records of your bereavement in losing family members on the December 8th attack on Washington D.C. makes for a very clear picture of one Samuel J. Carter, except I don't know what your middle initial stands for.'

'Why the hell should I tell you?'

He grinned. 'My guess is that it's 'John' because that was your father's name. An engineer on the Florida Coast Railroad, it says here.'

'What else does it say? Like how many times I take a crap?'

'Nothing more actually, other than the name of your daughter, Abigail, and her age.' He tucked the card away. His smooth face softened slightly. 'I have a family too.'

He hesitated and I stared at him, wondering where this fat German cop in a grey leather trench coat was going with all this chatter.

'Two boys. They're grown and in the service of their country; one in the Wehrmacht, the other the Luftwaffe, and I fear for their safety every minute of every day. But you have already suffered what I only fear. The loss of your wife and son, and I am deeply sorry that happened.'

I wanted to punch him in his prissy little mouth, but the sincerity in his voice stopped me cold. I know the ring of truth when I hear it, so I muttered, 'Thanks.'

'May this war end soon,' he said.

'It never even started here.'

'True.' He took off his glasses and rubbed the bridge of his short nose.

'But it rages everywhere else. If only Russia would fall, I do believe that der

Führer would end things once and for all.'

'England will keep on fighting.'

He smiled as though I were a two-year-old. 'You know that cartoon where the big man places his hand on the little man's head who's trying to punch him? That's Germany and England at the moment. Churchill can plot and plan all he wants to up in Canada while the King and Queen drink their afternoon tea with him and listen to him go on and on about fighting on the beaches when they return. But the truth is, England is no longer a nation, it is an idea.'

'Don't tell them that.'

He replaced his glasses. 'Don't worry, I won't. The Gestapo has enough criminals for me to chase that will keep me busy for years.'

'Minus *Herr* Ritter, of course.'

He laughed, his teeth were slightly pointed. 'Why is it that people never think other people might be watching them? Especially when they're breaking the law.'

'Were you always a policeman?'

'You mean before...'

'Yes.'

'A police inspector in Heilbronn, Germany. South of Heidelberg. Do you know of it?'

'No.'

'No matter. It is a small, sleepy town with sleepy citizens and I loved working there. But when Hitler came to power the nation woke up, and so did Heilbronn. Because of my experience and my knowledge of English I was made a Gestapo officer in their International Division. That, more or less, brings me to our present moment.'

'Could you have stayed on in Heilbronn?'

'I would have preferred to, but as *der Führer* commands, so must his citizens obey.' He clicked his heels slightly and smiled. 'Now then, just this final detail.' He pulled out a sheet of paper. 'If you two gentlemen would sign here, you can be rid of me at long last.'

'This is the catch, right?' I said.

'I'm not familiar with that idiom.'

'The part in your little fairy tale where we sign the papers but then end up in prison for the rest of our lives for some obscure reason.'

'I don't know what you're talking about. This is a Form 40-78, Personal Property Release form. It's quite standard.'

I looked at it. 'It's all in German.'

'*Natürlich.*'

'It could be something completely different for all I know.'

'Yes it could be, but it's not. You can trust me on that.'

'Can I?'

He drew himself up and frowned fiercely. 'Mr. Carter you are pissing up the wrong tree.'

I smiled. 'Where did you hear that one?'

He looked flustered. 'I can't remember.'

'You mean 'barking up the wrong tree.''

'*Ja, das is richtiger!*'

I exchanged looks with Orlando. He smiled and shrugged.

'Okay I'll sign.'

When I finished, I handed Orlando the pen and he did the same. When he finished he said softly, 'The Lord is my shepherd, I shall not want.'

Bauer tucked the signed form into his jacket. 'And we shall dwell in the house of the Lord forever.'

'You know scripture?'

He winked. 'Don't tell the Gestapo.'

The box lunch the Nazis packed for our flight home was even worse than the meal we got in jail. And their bacon and egg breakfast? If you like your eggs cooked about twenty minutes and your bacon warm, slippery and half raw, right up your alley. Still, the cook who made it for us beamed at her accomplishment, and who was I to fault her for trying to make American food? I mean, she didn't start the war, she was just a German civilian who'd came over with the troops and was doing her humble job.

I keyed the microphone. 'Key West tower, Carter Air four-five is with you, requesting runway and wind.'

Orlando beamed. 'Home sweet home at last.'

At last was right. Twelve hours overdue, but if my calculations were right, Mike Beamer's lobsters were just arriving at the airport. With luck, Carter Aviation was going to pull a rabbit out of the hat and start earning some money. It had better. Our first loan payment was due in less than two weeks.

'Carter Air four-five, be advised compliance aircraft landing naval air station. Report visual.'

Two familiar white airplanes, toy-sized at our altitude of two thousand feet, were on final approach for the Key West Naval Air station, two miles off our starboard wing. Key West's smaller civilian airport lay three miles dead ahead.

'Have visual, will comply.'

Orlando said, 'Those Luftwaffe boys are everywhere ain't they?'

Like National Airport in Washington, the Key West Naval Station had been designated a 'Compliance Base of Operations,' which meant regular patrols of German fighters zoomed in and out, while our U.S. Navy fighters sat on the tarmac, lashed to their tie downs like so many doomed butterflies.

This particular military 'no-fly zone' extended in a two-hundred mile radius to encompass the Florida Straits and Cuba, and up north well past Miami. With the airspace neutralized by fighter planes, Nazi U-Boats completed the compliance choke hold by patrolling the coastal waters.

If a submarine captain suspected an American vessel of violating the Neutrality Act, he'd send over a boarding party to check its manifest. If they found anything illegal, a spread of well-aimed torpedoes would send the ship to the bottom. They sank five ships early on, but nothing for the past four months. No surprise there. Torpedoes have a funny way of convincing skippers not to go where they don't belong.

I felt a flash of panic. 'Key West Tower, do you have my flight plan on file? They were supposed to send you an updated version.'

'Roger, we got it a couple of hours ago, and you're cleared to land runway one eight, wind two-four-zero at ten.'

The airport came into view and I smiled like seeing an old friend. I had grown up in Key West and had watched it grow from a small, sleepy grass strip to the long, paved runway that it is today.

'Carter Air four-five on final.'

The crosswind nudged me sideways and I crabbed slightly to keep the runway numbers planted on my windscreen. Any minute now the S-38's long snout would block my forward vision, an annoyance that grated on my nerves every time I landed or took off.

'I don't know how ducks do it,' I said. 'Flying with their damn bills stuck out there in front.'

'They ways of the Lord are past knowing.'

'Thanks for clearing that up for me. Gear down.'

'Nazi-repaired gear coming down.'

That cop Bauer was right; from the smooth clicking coming from either side, the mechanism was working perfectly. The Nazi mechanics really had fixed the gear.

Two hundred feet...the small blue and white shack attached to hangar number two, housing *Carter Aviation*, flashed past and the blur of a small figure running toward the taxiway. No time to wave, just time enough to feel my heart lift in warm happiness at seeing my daughter Abby again. One hundred feet...fifty...cut the throttles. Get ready to swing the nose out of the sideways crab and flare for landing.

'Lord you are the wind beneath our wings,' Orlando droned.

'Please shut up.'

Just above stall speed now, needed to make my control movements big and bold as she flirted with the idea of not flying anymore. Her right wing began lifting into the wind, and I corrected, bringing her level just as she broke into a stall a few feet above the runway and stopped flying. The tires squeaked and spun into life, and at the same instant her steel tail skid touched the concrete and began screeching like a thousand banshees. I swung quickly off the runway onto the grass and the noise dropped off to a muffled rumble. The S-38, an amphibian, had been built in a time when dirt runways were common. Not anymore.

'We've got to retrofit a tail wheel. That skid won't last the week.'

'I'll get on it the minute you get back from your run,' Orlando said.

I taxied alongside the deserted runway. This time last year, Key West Airport and Key West Naval Air Station had been two competing bee hives with civilian and military aircraft filling the skies day and night. Today a ghost town.

Orlando pointed out the side window. 'Ground crew at your ten o'clock.'

Ten-year old Abby stood there, face dead serious, hair tucked beneath a Brooklyn Dodgers baseball cap, outstretched arms holding two red flags as she gave me the 'Continue approach' signal. I applied a touch of power. The closer I got, the higher she raised the flags, until, just as my wheels reached the exact spot, she expertly snapped the flags into an 'X' over her head. I hit the brakes, and killed the engines.

She went from poised ground crew to little kid ran over to the cockpit. I managed to slide open the side window just in time for her to leap halfway inside for a hug.

'Did you get lost, daddy?'

'Very funny.'

'You were supposed to be here yesterday.'

'Uncle O and I got a little tied up.'

'Grammy was worried.'

'What about you?'

'Not a bit.'

'Truth?'

A beat. Her brown eyes as wide as Estelle's and just as beautiful. 'A little toward the end. But mostly not. Where's my stay-at-home gift?'

I fished inside my jacket pocket and pulled out a small red lobster with the words, *Souvenir of Cranston, Rhode Island* painted on its tail.

Abby made a face. 'Daddy, we have tons of lobsters in Florida. Mr. Beamer has a whole truck of them waiting for you.'

'Pull on its tail.'

She gave me "the look," but then did so and a tinny-sounding, mechanical voice inside said, 'Let go my tail.'

She exploded into laughter, and pulled it again.

'Try mine.' Orlando reached over his enormous fist and opened it to reveal a grey clam with the same words painted on its shell.

Abby opened the clam and the same voice shouted, 'Clam up!'

She screamed with glee. 'How do they do that, Uncle O?'

'When you're done playing with them, we'll find out.'

'Let's find out right now!'

I could already see the two of them, foreheads touching, like consulting surgeons over a patient, as they dissected the lobster and clam mechanisms to see what made them tick. Abby's knack for mechanics and Orlando's skills made these two dangerous.

'Later,' I said. 'We've got lobsters to fly and Uncle O has an engine to fix, don't you, reverend?'

'I do, indeed.'

A month ago, we had bought a junked Wright Radial two thousand for parts. It would come in handy for scavenging, now that we had a plane to go along with it.

Abby said, 'Can I fly right seat?' Her face was hard to resist.

'You remember up from down, port from starboard?'

'Don't insult me, daddy.'

'Okay, then Officer Carter, let's get those lobsters loaded!'

Rosie supervised the loading with the same precision as when she rolled cigars; no wasted effort, delivering maximum product in minimum time. Me? I was happy to be taking orders instead of giving them.

'Don't face the crates outward,' she bossed. 'Alternate back and forth. They fit better that way.' She used a short piece of line to lash the crates together. 'Give me another crate. We haven't got all day.'

It had taken Orlando, me, Abby, and Lobster Mike, only a few minutes to unbolt the light wicker passenger seats and store them in the hangar. In their place bright yellow-painted crates took up every available inch in the fuselage. Filled with squirming sea-green lobsters, Key West's best of the best, they soon would be on their way to Miami where ten restaurants eagerly waited.

Stooped over in the cramped space, Lobster Mike and I manhandled last of the crates forward to where Rosie impatiently waited.

Mike said, 'Thought I was gonna' be stuck with all these critters and no place to sell them.'

Rosie said, 'Hurry up, you two, this ain't a tea social.'

Abby called out from the cockpit, 'Daddy, can I do pre-flight?' Her headphones practically swallowed up her entire head.

Rosie said, 'You are NOT going to let that girl fly right seat.'

'Why not? She knows the controls.'

'She's ten years old, that's why.'

'I was ten when I wanted to fly.'

Her face grew serious. 'That was then, this is now.'

I lowered my voice. 'Look, mom, we're starting over, okay? And the two of us need to talk. This will be a good time.'

'In a plane at two thousand feet?'

'Absolutely. If she gets mad, where's she going to go?'

My mother tensed her lips, locked in thought, and then quickly nodded her assent. I'll give Rosie credit: when comes time to change airports, she'll kick rudder so fast it'll make your head spin. Pop was completely the opposite. Sure, he'd change course eventually, but he'd keep considering and re-considering the alternatives long after the change had been made. I suppose that's why he made such a good railroad engineer. He needed to keep his eye on the track ahead, and the track behind as well.

Not me.

As a pilot, all I ever cared about was the next airport, and the one after that. Where I just took off from was instant history. Let other people sort out what was left behind. Not this time, though. Today I had to go back, pick up the pieces with Abby and try to make sense of what was left of our family.

We lifted off Runway two-six, just after four o'clock in the afternoon. Full gas tanks, engines purring, landing gear working, ceiling and visibility unlimited, Abby in the right seat and Lobster Mike's cash-in-advance paid cargo in the hold. Life was good.

If everything worked according to plan, we'd make Miami in two hours, unload the lobsters dockside, re-fuel and be back in Key West in time for supper. But rarely does anything happen that way with me. And especially not when I'm operating a machine with tens of thousands of parts, any one of which could and often would go wrong. But so far, so good as we leveled off at two thousand feet.

I pulled out the locking clip on the control wheel and swung it over to Abby. 'You have the aircraft.'

'I have the aircraft, sir.'

I could barely hide my smile at her serious face when she nodded, crisply repeated the ritual-like response, opened her small hands and gripped the large wooded control wheel. But she held it with a light touch. Fingertips. Sign of a good pilot.

'Rudder pedals okay?' I said.

'Affirmative.' She tapped the wooden blocks I'd strapped onto the pedals so her short legs could reach them.

'Maintain a heading of zero-six-zero degrees, altitude of two thousand.

Keep an eye out for other aircraft, and holler if you need me.'

'Roger, zero-six-zero degrees, two thousand feet, and watch out for bogies.'

I laughed, 'Where'd you pick that up?' She shrugged. 'I forget.'

'C'mon, which radio show?'

Another shrug. 'Terry and the Pirates. They're shooting down bogies all the time.'

'Haven't heard them for a while.'

'It's such great show. When I grow up I want to be an air pirate just like them and shoot down Nazis. They're so mean.'

'That's for sure.'

Our nation's forty-eight states were on their own. Some of them defiantly flew their state flags over the stars and stripes to protest to the 'cowardly Neutrality Act.' Texas was one, Louisiana another. More and more each day it seemed.

'Back soon.'

I clambered over the small partition separating the cockpit from the passenger compartment to check out my mother's tie downs - not that I needed to. She came from a long line of Key West 'wreckers;' men who ever since the seventeenth century had made a living salvaging the remains of storm-wrecked ships in the Florida Straits. No surprise that each of her knots was perfect, just like her cigars. I pumped up pressure in a small tank filled with sea water and waved the spray nozzle back and forth over the squirming lobsters. Their rubber- banded claws clicked like castanets in their fury at being trapped in a cage.

'I know how you feel, fellas.'

Abby shouted, 'Traffic, ten o'clock high.'

'Look again. This is a no-fly zone except for us.'

'But I see it, Daddy!'

Seconds later I saw it too, a big, beautiful Pan Am Sikorsky S-40 flying boat about a thousand feet above us, on the same course, her four engines throttled back to lose altitude without causing a drop of gin to spill in the cocktails the passenger were no doubt enjoying.

This must be Pan Am's twice- daily Havana/Miami Flight, right on schedule and earning another hefty chunk of money for Juan Trippe and company. Unlike the Baltimore-based Boeing 314 Clippers painted in Lufthansa colors, the S-42 still had its Pan American Airways lettering. I couldn't begin to imagine the deal Trippe had cut with the Nazis to keep his airline going, but the man never did business with anybody unless a hefty chunk of cash led in a straight line from the signed contract to his bank account.

Back in the early-30s, our Miami/Havana flight had been one of my first regular assignments as a 'Pilot-in-Training,' the term Pan Am gave their new-hires. Fortunately I got promoted to the engineering side soon after and lost that designation. Then I transitioned to navigator and then finally to the cockpit as first officer. All new-hires went this same route; step by step, job by job, up the long ladder to the left seat. Nobody ever just walked in and took over as captain. Pan Am's Chief Engineer André Preister saw to that.

I first met that stiff-necked, bald headed, tight-fisted, hard-headed Dutchman when I was nineteen. I was working the radio night shift one night when Orlando dropped by for a visit. My job in the operations hut involved very little work on this particular night because weather had delayed the Havana takeoff.

I had been sitting doing nothing for two solid hours waiting for the Morse code signal from the airplane telling me they had finally lifted off. Once that happened, I would stay busy transmitting and receiving position reports all along the ninety-mile route separating Key West from Havana. But at this rate it looked like it would never happen.

At the time, Orlando worked at the Key West docks as a marine engine mechanic laboring in the hulls of smelly old fishing boats, making sense of their beat-up engines and barely getting paid. Since I spent my nights here, we didn't see each other as much as we used to when we were kids. I remember that particular night saying something to him like, 'Ninety miles from here to Havana is nothing. I could piss that far.'

Orlando's booming laughter made me laugh too.

Preister's voice cut through us like a saber. 'Vatt iss so funny?' He stood in the doorway, short and stern, his small eyes blinking rapidly in the bright light. He pointed accusingly at Orlando. 'Who iss diss?'

'My friend, Mr. Diaz.'

'No visitors on duty, Mr. Carter. You know dat iss the rule. Get out now Mister Diazzzzz.'

I thought fast. 'But sir, Orlando wasn't here to visit. He was here to see you about a job.'

'A yob?'

I exchanged a wordless glance with Orlando. He squinted ever so slightly, our silent signal that meant 'go for it,' so I continued quickly, 'Mr. Diaz one of the best mechanics in Key West, sir. And since you fired Mr. Brewster the other day, I thought maybe you could find time to…'

Preister said, 'I haff already five egg-sellent candidates.'

'But none of them are as good Mr. Diaz.'

'Vy you say diss?'

'I've seen him raise engines from the dead. Like Lazarus in the bible. In fact, I sometimes call him Jesus - just kidding, of course - but it's true.'

'Vatt is true?'

'The marine engines he works on are beat up, worn out pieces of junk when he gets his hands on them, but a few hours later they're running like new. Show him your hands, O.'

Orlando spread open his hands. The imbedded grease stains traced a complex map upon his pink palms.

'If he laid his hands on four-oh-six's engines in hangar two, I bet you they'd start working for a change.'

Preister frowned. 'Nussing will make dem work right. I am sending dem back to Wright.'

Orlando said, 'Mind if I take a look first, sir?'

'Deez are airplane engines, not boats.'

'Beg pardon, sir, but a bad engine's a bad engine. Let me take a look. If I get 'em going you hire me, if I don't, you don't. My work won't cost you a penny. It's on the house.' Orlando's smile lit up the room. 'How's that sound?'

Preister took the measure of this towering giant. Orlando was only nineteen years old like me, but he looked a lot older. Maybe the lateness of the hour or a sudden flash of insight, but whatever the reason the Dutchman dropped his customary rod-up-his-ass attitude and said, 'Hangar two. You come back in morning.'

'If you don't mind, sir, I'll start in right now.' He raised his eyebrows. 'You haff tools?'

'I'll get 'em.'

When dawn broke the next day, the birds were singing, and so were the engines on NC 406. Orlando was hired, and he stayed with Pan Am until the day I got fired.

At the time of my disgrace, he said to me, 'You need me more than they do.'

'For what?'

'For *Carter Aviation*. We can't have an airline without a licensed mechanic.'

'We?'

He took my hand in his callused and scarred mitt and shook it.

'Us.'

Abby watched in silence as the Pan Am S-40 grew smaller and smaller, easily traveling fifty knots faster than us.

'Were they fun to fly?' she said.

'Fun and hard. Lots of moving parts, both on the ground and in the air.'

The wake of the plane caused some mild turbulence that Abby handled easily. She patted the control wheel. 'Nice having you here instead of there.'

'Good.'

'You were never home before. Just mommy and me all the time – I mean, before Baby Eddie came. We never EVER saw you.'

'Not true. I was home plenty of times.'

She shook her head. 'Not enough.'

'I had to make money to buy food and clothes for the family.'

46

She shook her head in disagreement, but didn't say anything. Instead, she looked out her side window. 'If you follow the railroad tracks, isn't that the same course to Miami?

I let her change the subject. 'More or less, yes.'

'Then why don't we? Mail plane pilots flew the rails all the time.'

'They did, but what do you do when it's cloudy and you can't see the ground?'

She sighed and tapped the compass. 'I guess you follow this. But it's not as much fun - tell me about Pop-Pop.'

'You know the story.'

'I like hearing it when I can see the railroad tracks where it happened.'

'Watch your heading. We've drifted five degrees.'

She tapped the rudder pedals. 'Sorry.' Then she grinned. 'Pop-Pop didn't have to worry about compasses. He just rode the rails.'

My father, John Carter, had worked his way up from a hostler servicing Florida East Coast engines in Miami, to fireman when they extended the line down to Key West. He met my mother there, and when he got promoted to road engineer, they married and that's when I was born.

'It didn't happen on a day like this,' I said.

'A terrible hurricane. High winds, rain, the worst weather they'd seen in ten years.'

'Who's telling this story?'

'Sorry.'

'The Labor Day Hurricane of 1935 was heading straight for the Middle Keys just as Pop-Pop was finishing up his Key West-Miami run. He heard about it and volunteered to run a rescue train down there to save the track workers.'

'Islamadora!'

The small town slowly drifted by below, nestled in a pearl-like string of keys. Even six years later, it still bore the scars of the hurricane's path.

'Did Pop-Pop drown?'

'Most likely.'

She shivered. 'Water over the tracks, people stranded everywhere, including the men on the bridge, right?'

'During the depression FDR sent men across America to bridges, highways, schools, swimming pools. About six hundred men, mostly World War One army vets, were working in Islamadora when the hurricane hit.'

'Just as Pop-Pop got there with his rescue train.'

'Some say the wind was over two hundred miles an hour. The first storm surge scoured the town clean of everything; palm trees, houses, people, you name it, gone for good.'

'But it didn't blow over the train.'

'Too heavy. If Pop-Pop had stayed inside with the fireman, he would have probably survived.'

'But the soldiers were too scared to come out of their barracks, right?'

'Pop kept blowing the train whistle for them to find their way to the train, but they stayed put. So he went outside to fetch them. The fireman said Pop-Pop managed to lead the first bunch back to the train. Then headed back to get the rest. That's when the second storm surge hit and swept away the building and everybody inside it.'

'A wall of water.'

'Over four hundred folks drowned that day.'

'Would have been more without Pop-Pop helping, right?'

I thought of the letters mailed to my mother after the funeral. Some crudely-spelled, others more eloquent, but all of them praising my father's train for having saved their lives and expressing condolences that he lost his life in doing so.

The Hurricane of 1935 not only killed hundreds of people, it also killed the Key West extension of the Florida East Coast Railroad. With miles of track washed into the sea and hundreds of bridges and causeways gone for good, the railroad ended its thirty-year adventure and sold its right-of-way to the state to build highways instead.

'Pop-Pop was a hero,' Abby said.

'For sure.'

'I want to be a hero too, some day.'

'You can't decide something like that.'

'Why not?'

'Because history picks its heroes. Not the other way around.'

'Doesn't make sense.'

'A hero is someone who does something ordinary in extraordinary times - like when Pop-Pop went out and led those men back to the train. It's really an ordinary thing when you think about it, but he did it with the wind blowing and the rain coming down in buckets and the water rising all around him. Even with all that scary stuff happening, he just went ahead and did it.'

'While that old fireman hid in the locomotive.'

'Don't blame him. You weren't there to see what happened.'

She scowled. 'If I'd been there, I'd have gone out with Pop-Pop to save those men. And maybe I could have saved him too.'

'Maybe so.'

'I know so.'

She clenched her jaw, looked straight at me and her brown eyes seemed to darken. 'And if I hadn't been sick and stayed with Grammy that night, maybe I could have saved Mommy and Baby Eddy. But they're dead, and it's all because of the Nazis, they're worse than any damn hurricane!'

She pulled the release pin and swung the control wheel over to me. 'I don't want to fly anymore.'

She sat there, arms folded, head down and frowning while I corrected our course and re-trimmed the flight controls. I finally said, 'If I hadn't been out on my trip, maybe I could have saved them too.'

'But you were, and they died and why did you go, Daddy? Couldn't you have said 'no' just once?'

I bit back the truth and lied, 'It was my job, honey. I had to.'

She folded her arms tighter. 'If that's what it's like to have a job, I'm never going to have one as long as I live.'

'What are you going to do to stay alive?'

'Be like you and Uncle O.' She patted the armrest. 'Have my own airplane and fly lobsters and stuff.'

'Then it's time you start learning what it takes to do just that.' I swung the controls back. 'You have the aircraft.'

I expected her to smile, but she sat up and looked straight at me, her face serious, and in that instant I saw Estelle looking at me instead. I wanted to look away but couldn't.

'I have the aircraft, sir,' she said.

After our Miami delivery, Abby slept all the way home to Key West, despite the constant engine roar. Been that way ever since she was a baby. Sleeps through anything. No need to tiptoe. Just bang and clang and she'll snooze away. Her sleep, minus the serious face, seemed sweet and simple. I wished she could stay that way forever. But too much had happened in her short life to think that could ever be.

Had I been like this at ten? I think so. In fact, I think all kids are, but grownups don't realize it. To them we're in a state of unending bliss, when in fact we're living in a jungle filled with wild beasts, and it's up to the grownups to help us make it out alive. And if they can't help us, then at least, please get the hell out of our way.

I tugged Abby's seatbelt tighter and then and contacted Key West tower. As the operator rattled off the landing information, I throttled back and entered the downwind leg of the landing pattern.

As usual, I was the only thing flying in the sky, but not forever. I had twenty-nine days left on the Nazi's 'Limited Commercial Flying Permit.' After that I had to come up with another thousand dollars up front, and five hundred more in under- the-table bribes to extend it another ninety days. The boys from Berlin were making a mint off private airlines like mine trying to make a living up and down the east coast.

I knew damn well that shipping Mike's bi-weekly lobster catch was never going to keep Carter Aviation in the air. I had to hustle fishing charters and critical-cargo companies if I wanted to survive.

Thank God -- and thank Rosie for having taken out ads in the Miami and Jacksonville newspapers at her own expense - because she had landed a three-day, island-hopping, fishing charter for next week. Probably some real estate lawyer from Jacksonville and his cronies.

I could see them now: cigar- smoking, whisky-drinking, well-heeled 'sport fishermen' strutting their way onto the plane, all decked out in their outfits, ready to drink and cuss and lie like Hemmingway. Fine by me. I'd fly them to kingdom come if they wanted to, as long as they paid me for doing so.

Just as I began my final turn to line up with the runway, my heart stopped: a bright red, Beechcraft Staggerwing soared off the runway and headed straight for me like a rocket. For some inexplicable reason, the sleek, blunt-nosed executive biplane had taken off downwind instead of upwind and was on a direct collision course.

I firewalled the throttles, banked hard left and shouted into my mike, 'Beechcraft, break right, break right!'

Abby woke with a start and started screaming as the high-powered airplane blasted past us in a shuddering roar, oblivious to my radio message.

Within seconds, nothing remained except its dwindling red and green wingtip navigation lights fading in the dusk sky.

A tight voice broke the silence. 'Carter Air four-five, be advised aircraft your immediate vicinity.'

'That bastard almost hit us. Which runway did you give him?'

A long pause.

'Two-six.'

'He damn well used the opposite end.'

'We'll file a report.'

The image of the sleek, high-priced aircraft flashed through my mind. Most likely belonged to some steel or oil tycoon.

'Fat lot of good that'll do.'

By the time we taxied up to the ramp, dusk had surrendered to nighttime. Our landing lights picked out the small shack attached to the small hangar that I leased from the airport. I wouldn't park the plane inside tonight, because Orlando had filled the floor with parts of the engine he was overhauling. Not to worry. The Florida night air was surprisingly sweet and clear, the moon bright, and conditions perfect for sleeping beneath the wing under the stars. And that's just what I intended to do; like back in the old days when I was learning to fly by following barnstormers.

As my engines rattled to a stop, the office door banged open and Rosie hurried toward me. Her face looked more serious than I wanted at this hour.

Abby leaped over onto my lap, slid down the window and shouted,

'Grams, I flew all the way to Miami!'

Rosie tried to look interested but failed. 'Good for you, dear.'

'And I slept all the way back, except for when that crazy bastard almost hit us.'

'Uh huh,' she said distractedly.

'Something the matter?' I said.

She shrugged. 'Yes and no. We have visitors.'

'Nazis?'

'A woman. I know I've seen her someplace before - and a man. They just came in on that Beechcraft.'

I felt a quick stab of anger. 'They came to apologize, I hope.'

'Actually, they want to talk to you. About a charter.'

'As long as it doesn't conflict my fishermen gig, I'll fly them anywhere.'

'It won't, I'm sure. It's just that...' She trailed off, folded her arms, pursed her lips and paused.

'What's wrong, Grams?' Abby said.

'Nothing, dear.'

I patted Rosie's shoulder. 'Grams is just having one of her premonitions, honey. Fasten your seatbelt.'

'I can't help it if I get these feelings.'

'Think they're good for the money?'

'They have cash and will pay up front.'

'Then I can't help it if I get the feeling that if we don't pay our bills, Carter Aviation is out of business.'

I unfastened my seatbelt. 'Tell them to meet me over in the hangar. I'm going to check up on Orlando.'

My business partner had spread out the spare engine like a vast, unfinished jigsaw puzzle across the hangar floor: manifolds, pistons, rods, exhaust ports, reduction gears. To the unpracticed eye like mine, utter chaos, but to Orlando, it made perfect sense. Ever since we were boys he had torn apart clocks, radios, fans, and small engines and put them back together again. Nothing had changed, just bigger stuff.

'What's your best guess?' I said.

He straightened up from where he'd been working on a piston. 'Three, maybe four hours.'

'To put all this back? Not a chance.'

'It's easy when you know how everything fits - lobsters get there okay?' I patted my shirt pocket. 'Our first payday.'

He lifted the heavy piston in salute. 'Here's to many more.'

'We might have another one sooner than you think. Rosie said some folks want a charter.'

'That so?'

'Captain Carter?'

The woman's voice drifted from the shadows of the hangar, low and melodious. I turned but saw nothing. The single light bulb above Orlando's work space created a small pool of light. Beyond that, darkness.

'That's me,' I said into the void. 'But it's Mister Carter, not captain. And you are?'

'Ava James.'

She walked into the light and my mouth went dry. It's one thing to see a movie star on the screen, but to see one in person is unnerving. At least for me. All I could do was mumble like an idiot, 'I... I saw you in *Ceiling Zero*, with Jimmy Cagney and Pat O'Brien. You were great.'

She smiled and brushed back a strand of reddish-blonde hair. 'Thanks, but the pleasure was all mine. Quite an honor to work with those two.'

She stopped in front of me and I was surprised at her height.

'Jimmy Cagney's not that tall,' I said. 'How did you... I mean, what did you...'

'Mr. Cagney stood on his toes a lot.'

'Never would have known.'

She raised her eyebrows. 'Movie magic, Mr. Carter.'

She half-turned and said over her shoulder. 'Are you going to spend the rest of your life in the shadows? Get the hell out here.'

A short, egg-shaped man scurried out of the darkness into the light, eyes bright, hand extended, hair slicked back and smiling like there was no tomorrow.

'Didn't want to spoil your entrance, darling. Never would, never could.'

I took his small, pudgy hand; like shaking hands with a dishcloth.

'Name's Nathan Siegel, I'm Ava's agent, but everybody calls me Ziggy. You can too, Mr. Carter - and who might this gentleman be?'

Orlando wiped the grease from his hand and took Ziggy's. 'Orlando Diaz.'

'What a handle! I could get you movie work with a name like that.'

'I prefer planes.'

'In pieces or all together?'

The Bull of Key West just stared.

'A joke, kid, a joke. Pay me no mind. I come with the furniture in the mighty House of Ava James.'

Ava's slightly hooded eyes lowered. 'One of these days you're going to talk yourself off a cliff.'

'True. Don't doubt it. Probably happen.'

'And I won't be there to catch you.'

'True. Don't doubt that either.'

She turned back to me. 'I have a proposition, Mr. Carter - Mr. Diaz, too.'

'Wrong word choice,' Ziggy said quickly. Don't you mean -'

A sharp uplift of her chin 'Don't tell me how to run a scene, okay?'

'Sorry, kid. I'm a sphinx. Lips zipped. Promise.'

He stuck his hands in his pockets and rocked up and down on his heels, a perpetual motion machine.

'I'm listening,' I said.

'Have you eaten dinner, Mr. Carter?'

'No?'

'It's always good to talk business on a full stomach, and I haven't eaten since - since when, Ziggy?'

'Chicago. That's where we refueled. Noon or so. You had half a sandwich, I had a...'

Ava rode over his endless answer and said to me, 'Your mother said the *Blue Heaven* was a nice place to get a bite.'

'Not for us,' I said.

'Why not?'

'Because...' I stopped.

'The color of my skin,' Orlando added. 'The Conchs, God bless their white hides, don't like colored folks like me eating in their fancy restaurants.'

Ava shrugged. 'So where can we get something to eat without that kind of crap on the menu?'

Orlando smiled. '*Sugar Cane Club's* got pretty good chow.'

Ziggy said, 'White folks allowed?'

'The right kind.'

The chubby agent straightened up. 'I can assure you we're more than that. We're the best. In fact, just the other day, I was saying to -'

'Knock off the sell job,' Ava said. 'You've got to forgive Mr. Siegel, gentlemen. Agents can't stop selling. Especially this one. Even does it in his sleep.'

'How would you ever know, darling?' he leered.

She rolled her eyes, patted her small wine-red shoulder purse and said.

'My treat. Times wasting. Let's go.'

In all the years I'd been coming to the *Sugar Cane*, I never knew exactly what it looked like on the inside. Mostly because the cigarette smoke and dim lighting made everything look sort of vague. Liquor helped, too. But if you ever go there, don't order something called the 'Sugar Cane Special.' Take it from me, it's special all right. The next morning your head will feel like a sack of hammers.

Ziggy ordered one, even though I warned him not to. Orlando did too, but he can hold his booze as good as his bible lessons. I figured Ziggy wanted to impress us. Be one of the gang.

The three-piece combo was playing the intro to *The Man Who Got Away*. The vocalist stood in the small spotlight waiting for her entrance, shoulders swaying to the beat. The place was half-empty and wouldn't get busy until later.

Ava glanced at the menu, put it down and smiled brightly at Orlando.

'What do you recommend, Mr. Diaz?'

'Fried chicken and gravy's as good as it gets.'

'You're on.'

Ziggy said, 'Is it kosher?'

Ava's eyes locked on target. 'Who writes your material?'

'I do, darling.'

'That's what I thought.'

I felt like I was watching a movie, having the real Ava James sitting across from me, exchanging snappy lines back and forth with Ziggy. The way she talked, the way she held her shoulders and fiddled with her drink, reminded me of a scene she and Cagney did in Ceiling Zero. I did my best to make conversation.

'So, Miss James, what movies have you been in lately?'

Her face tensed and right away I knew I'd said something wrong.

Ziggy gulped his drink and leaned forward. 'We're in between pictures at the moment...sorting through scripts... trying to make up our mind. Not easy. Lots and LOTS of options.'

'Cut the hot air, you little sap,' Ava said. 'What Ziggy means is that I haven't worked for over a year. In Hollywood, that's as good as dead and buried.'

Ziggy would not be derailed. 'Wait until Warner Brothers hears my latest. It's the perfect story of boy meets girl.'

'What my agent isn't saying is that I can't get arrested in Hollywood.'

'Why not?'

She looked away. 'Nice voice. She been here long?'

Orlando said. 'Two years almost.'

I said, 'Orlando's in love. The fallen woman scenario appeals to his preacher values.'

Orlando looked pained. 'How can a woman who sings like an angel be fallen?'

Ava brightened. 'You two seeing each other?'

'Sometimes.'

'What's her name?'

'Jasmine.'

'Nice.'

I said, 'Tell her what you do on your dates.'

He looked away and then back again. 'We read scripture together.'

Ziggy gulped, his eyes widened and he started coughing.

Orlando glowered, 'What's wrong with that?'

Ava said, 'Yeah, what's wrong with that?'

'Nothing at all. This drink's like a stick of dynamite.'

A long silence. Jasmine's velvety voice handled the lyrics like a sad confession. I felt nervous, on edge, so like a jerk I said, 'You didn't answer my question. Why won't anybody hire you?'

She hesitated. 'Walked out on a film.'

Ziggy squirmed. 'Let's not get into that just now, shall we, darling? How about another round? My treat. Love this stuff.'

'Do you mind motor-mouth?' Ava said, 'I'm talking with Mr. Carter.'

'Call me Sam.'

'Ava.'

'Okay.'

She smiled, drained her glass and put it down.

'Long story short: mother lives in New Orleans, she had a stroke last year, nobody worth a damn to take care of her, so I walked off the set, headed home and did it myself. Took me almost a year to get her back to normal. She's doing pretty well now.'

Ziggy said, 'All it cost was your career.'

'Lousy movie anyhow. Annie Sheridan got roped into it after I left.'

'What's it called?' I said.

'*Dark Surrender*. Seen it?'

'No.'

'Don't. Even with Annie in it, it's a stinker.'

56

Jasmine finished her song to scattered applause, Orlando's the loudest. She smiled and gave a shy, half-wave to him and then slipped into the shadows.

Our meal arrived, and the next half-hour was spent, heads down as we tucked away chicken and gravy, greens, and biscuits, all washed down with ice cold beer.

Ziggy finished first. 'I haven't eaten this good since I left Brooklyn.'

I said, 'How long ago was that?'

'Fifteen years ago this month. That's when I headed west to make my fortune.'

Ava said, 'And here you are in Key West eating chicken with an unemployed actress. Some fortune, huh?'

Ziggy touched her arm. 'For better or worse, richer or poorer, in sickness and in health. Besides, what goes down must come up. And it will, I promise you.'

'Unless mother gets sick again and they won't let me out of my contract to take care of her.'

'We'll make that a pre-condition.'

I said, 'You did the right thing. Taking care of her, I mean.'

'Sometimes I wonder...' A long pause. She nibbled a piece of dry biscuit. 'Maybe I could have arranged my exit with a little less drama.'

Ziggy said, 'Throwing a lamp at Jack Warner was bad enough, but a lamp in his own office.'

'Would have thrown a brick if I had one.'

'I'll pack one in your purse for next time.'

'If there ever is a next time.'

'Trust me, there will be.'

Ava laughed. 'Who are you kidding? Those Hollywood boys are running scared. Ever since America went neutral, Berlin's been on their case to tell their story to America. Where else but Hollywood, and who else but a bunch of Jewish studio heads who have relatives they're holding hostage in Europe?'

'Will they do it?' I said.

She smiled. 'If it means somebody you love lives instead of dies, what do you think?'

I let that pass and said, 'Do you miss it? The movies, I mean?'

'Sure I do. What's better than getting paid to make-believe?'

'Lots of things. Flying an airplane, hunting, fishing, taking care of someone who needs help, like you did.'

She shrugged. 'I'm the one who needs it this time around.' She leaned forward and said softly, 'That's why I came here to see you and Mr. Diaz.'

'How so?'

She lowered her voice. 'I'm looking for buried treasure.' She reached inside her small red leather purse and pulled out an envelope. 'See for yourself.'

I did.

'Count it.'

Ten crisp one-hundred dollar bills.

'You just print these?'

'Very funny. Take a look at what else is there.'

At first I thought it was yellowed leather, the way it felt in my hands, smooth and flat. And then it dawned on me.

'Is this what I think it is?'

'Open it,' Ava said.

The light was dim. A thin tracery of what looked like a diagram of some kind. Dotted lines here, faint printing there.

'Recognize the island?' she said.

'No.'

'You've flown over the Dry Tortugas a zillion times and you don't remember seeing that one?'

'Islands come and go down there. Storms bury them and bring them back.'

She leaned forward until her head was almost touching mine as we both looked at the map. She smelled of cocoanut and mint. I don't know if it was perfume or just her.

I slid the map over to Orlando, who examined it carefully, and then said, 'This could be off Loggerhead Key.'

'No way, there's nothing there but Fort Jefferson.' Ava said, 'We won't know for sure until we get there.'

I laughed. 'This is like a movie where a gorgeous women gets two unsuspecting suckers to help her look for buried treasure.'

Ziggy jumped into the conversation. 'Funny you should say that. It's going to be a feature film one of these days, except Humphrey Bogart will play your part and Paul Robeson will play Orlando - providing there's a happy ending of course. Hollywood loves happily-ever-after's and so do I.'

58

'Be quiet and eat, will you?' Ava said.

Her long, red, fingernail traced the dotted line on the map until it stopped over a lopsided circle with an 'X' through it.

'Right there. Guaranteed.'

'This map's for real? Not some movie prop?'

'It's real and your money's real. One thousand bucks to fly us down there. After we find the treasure, you get another thousand for your efforts and maybe a bonus if you're nice. Deal?'

'What if you don't find it?'

'We will.'

'I'm warning you that island could be long gone.'

'It's not.'

'How do you know?'

'Trust me.'

'Charter a boat, it's a lot easier – and cheaper.'

'And slower, and more people, too - besides, you come highly recommended.'

'By who?'

She leaned back slightly. 'What's with the twenty questions? Are you a cop?'

'Just curious. Who told you about Carter Aviation?'

'Ever read the newspapers?'

She pulled out a tattered clipping: One of Rosie's ads in the Miami papers.

'Do we have a deal or don't we?'

I regarded her outstretched hand.

Orlando said, 'Manna from heaven, brother. Count me in.'

I said, 'What are you going to do with the gold, if you find it?'

She looked at me like I was crazy and she was right. Stupid question, but I like asking them to keep the air clear. Her movie-star beauty shifted to utter seriousness.

'Use it for a very worthy cause.'

'Which is?'

'Ask that after we find the gold - that is, if you're in. Are you?'

I smiled at the image that flickered through my mind of pirates, doubloons, palm trees and cutlasses. 'Isn't this how Treasure Island starts? The old pirate shows the kid the map, and away he goes. Long John Silver, Ben Gunn. Great movie.'

Ava folded the map and put it away. 'That was make-believe, this is real. In or out?'

We shook hands all around. Her cool, thin fingers gripped mine with surprising strength and I gripped back.

Be where your enemy is not.

- Sun Tzu

Promptly at five A.M. the next morning, Ava and Ziggy showed up.

Their battered pickup truck was loaded with camping equipment, digging gear, tie-down cables, and enough food to last a week. Ziggy's pith helmet hat two sizes too big and his safari jacket a size too small.

Ava was a different story. How she made plain khaki slacks and a checked shirt look glamorous at that hour was a mystery. She'd tied back her long auburn hair with a plain yellow scarf but even that looked stylish.

'You look like Katherine Hepburn.'

'Kate wouldn't be caught dead in this. She's a class act.'

'You look fine to me.'

Ava touched her hair and grinned. 'Thank you, captain. C'mon Zig, lend a hand.'

'Where'd you get your rig?' I said to him.

'An outfitter in Hollywood.'

'You lugged it all the way here?'

He tapped his helmet and grinned. 'All the way from tinsel town.'

The loading went quickly with the four of us working like a team. Just as the sun cleared the hangar roof, the S-38 was loaded, fueled and ready to go. I leaned out the cockpit window and shouted at my sleepy lineman. The fire extinguisher wand in Abby's hand was almost as tall as she was. She had insisted on seeing us off, and besides, she knew her business.

'Clear left.' I shouted.

'Clear left.'

I primed number one engine and pressed the starter. The polished metal propeller turned slowly at first, then faster and faster as the engine groaned, sputtered and coughed into life, sending out clouds of blue exhaust smoke.

Ava said from the co-pilot's seat, 'Lights...camera...action.'

She'd asked if I wanted company up front. I wasn't about to turn down a movie star sitting in the right hand seat.

Ziggy's muffled voice shouted from somewhere in the back, 'Hey, what kind of theater is this? Where's your popcorn?'

Number two engine shuddered as the pistons began firing in turn. As I brought it up to its assigned RPM, the clatter quickly smoothed into a steady roar.

'Sounds sweet,' Orlando shouted.

Did a quick instrument check; engines in the green, oil pressure steady, cylinder head temps fine; pre-flight finished, ready to taxi.

'Key West tower, Carter Air four-five requesting permission to taxi active.'

I glanced at Ava, hands in her lap, feet flat on the floor, clear of the rudder pedals, just like I told her. She caught my eye and lifted her hands like she was handcuffed. 'Don't worry, won't touch a thing.'

'Carter Air, you're cleared to taxi three-six.'

'Three-six, Carter Air.'

I leaned out the window and nodded to Abby, who brought both her arms straight up, and then lowered her left one to direct me toward the taxiway. I blew her a kiss. She scowled, too intent on her job to acknowledge fatherly affection. I stuck my fingers in my mouth, stretched my cheeks into a rubbery grin and wiggled my tongue. That made her laugh and roll her eyes.

I mouthed over the engine roar, 'See you soon.'

She nodded and smiled.

'Nice kid,' Ava said.

'Thanks.'

'Nice dad, too.'

'Not really.'

'A man who makes a face like that can't be all bad.'

From three thousand feet the Florida Keys are just like the postcards say, 'An emerald necklace floating on blue-green velvet.' But even prettier in person.

Heading south from Key West you pass smaller islands; Crawfish Key, Man Key, and Ballast Key. Few folks live there, mostly snakes, lizards, turtles, and alligators, all of which would prefer you never set foot there, leaving them free to run wild and chase and catch and eat each other in an endless cycle of kill-or-be-killed.

When Orlando and I were kids, we'd go with my dad on fishing trips around these lesser keys. Back then, we needed a strong male bearing down on our rambunctious lives and he was more than happy to oblige. Being fatherless, Orlando needed this even more than me.

But the minute pop left on his three-day trips for the railroad, it was an open invitation for Orlando and me to head out on 'trips' of our own. Most were innocent, like stealing candy from drug stores or lobsters from the fishermen's traps. For us it wasn't the deed that gave us pleasure, but the getting away with it that made it fun.

Nothing could beat running like the wind with an angry grownup chasing after you, except maybe vaulting over a high wooden fence you knew would stop that grownup cold. And the sheer, exhilarating feeling of laughing so hard you couldn't breathe, when we would arrive home unscathed. Now O and I were off on another adventure. How it would turn out was anybody's guess.

Ava tapped me on the shoulder just as we broke free of a line of clouds gathering into a thunderhead. 'Is that what I think it is?'

'U-boat.'

Three thousand feet down, the enemy submarine's bow and stern waves made twin V-shapes on the glassy-smooth sea.

'Wish to hell it were one of ours,' I said.

'One of these days it will be.'

'Not any time soon. Florida's going to secede from the Union. And they're not the only ones. Georgia and North Carolina are voting for it faster than when they repealed Prohibition.'

I put the plane into a shallow left bank for a closer look at the submarine, but careful to stay near the clouds. My Nazi-issued charter certificate allowed me a lot of freedom as to when and where I could fly. But flying this far south of Key West could need some heavy explaining if we got caught.

Ava unbuckled her seatbelt and leaned over my shoulder to look out the window. Wisps of auburn hair tickled my face.

'Sorry,' she said.

'That's okay.'

'Bastards. Just who do they think they are?'

'The winners.'

'Not if Russia stays in the fight.'

'Don't see how when Stalin's on one side of a mountain scared to death and Hitler's on the other with an atomic bomb.'

'So, why hasn't he dropped it yet?'

I didn't have an answer. All I could think of was the *Unterseeboot* below, sweeping the Florida Straits of contraband shipping the same way the Yankees did during the Civil War to choke off French and British supplies to the Confederacy.

Ava said, 'Why isn't he submerged?'

'Faster on the surface. Can see farther too.'

She went back and buckled in. 'I still can't believe it.'

'That we gave up?'

'Yes.'

'The president got caught between a rock and a hard place.'

'She should have told Hitler to go to hell.'

'And where would Miami be today? And Chicago, and St. Louis? And the people who live there? I'm thinking hell.'

She didn't say anything.

I was about to press my point even further, when suddenly the plane began vibrating like mad. My first instinct was to back off power, which reduced it somewhat, but not completely. Ava and I exchanged a long look, but to her credit she didn't say a word. Orlando was beside me in an instant.

'This bucket of bolts will not leave us alone,' he said.

'Any ideas?'

'Prop maybe. Throttle up, one at a time.'

The vibration increased, so I backed off, which helped, but the hands of the altimeter kept slowly unwinding.

Orlando said, 'Can you put her down?'

'If I have to, but I don't want to near that sub. They'll toss us on board and send our plane to the bottom.'

I tested the controls, first ailerons then rudder. No problems. All gauges in the green. The only thing not working was the radio for some reason.

Puzzling.

'It's not the engines, it's something else,' I said. 'Feels like something's screwy in the tail assembly. Do me a favor, stick your head out the boarding hatch. Tell me what you see.'

Orlando turned to go as I began a slow descending turn to the left. If we had to land, I wanted it to be as far away from the sub as possible on the slimmest of hopes that their lookouts wouldn't see us.

Ava read my mind. 'Any way we can hide down there?'

'Their lookouts probably spotted us a long time ago. Nazi sailors have sharp eyes.'

A sudden blast of noise as Orlando opened the rear boarding hatch. Seconds later, he came thumping up to the cockpit. 'Center tail brace broke clean in two.'

'That explains the radio gone. Did we lose the generator?'

'Hanging on by a wire. But those side braces are shaking us to pieces.'

'Can you break them off or bend them back?'

'It can be done.'

I knew what that meant. 'Sit here and keep her wings level like we did before.'

I started getting up.

'Don't bother, captain,' Ava said crisply, 'I have the aircraft.'

'Huh?'

Instead of answering, she deftly pulled the release pin from the control column, swung it over to her side and maintained a perfect heading.

'You fly?'

'Who do you think brought in that Beechcraft last night?'

'You?'

'Affirmative.'

'Who flew it out? He almost killed me.'

'The new owner - now get back there and fix this bucket of bolts. Orlando, hold his feet.'

No time for twenty questions. We were going down fast.

I cautioned, 'Watch your elevator trim. She'll go tail heavy on you when I start climbing around out there.'

'No kidding.'

'Keep her just above her stall speed of fifty knots. Otherwise the wind will blow me off, then where will you be?'

'Don't want that to happen.'

'You sure you can fly this bird?'

She ignored me, her stiffened shoulders and firm grip on the controls answer enough.

As I scrambled past the camping gear, Ziggy pulled me to his ashen face. 'Where you going?'

'Out.'

'You don't have a parachute.'

'Don't need one. I'm coming back.'

He shut his eyes and shook his head. 'I knew it was going to end like this.'

Orlando slid open the passenger boarding hatch and fastened the small step ladder in place.

I shouted to be heard over the roaring wind. 'Once I'm up, hold onto my ankles and I'll work my way down.'

He held up a pair of pliers. I pocketed them, tightened my belt, buttoned my collar button and climbed into the howling wind stream.

The S-38 has a forest of struts and braces designed to hold her wings, engines, and tail together like a complicated 'cats' cradle,' with intersecting wires and braces to keep everything in correct aerodynamic tension.

I could see at once what had happened: the big 'V' shaped strut that leads from the rear tip of the fuselage, up to each of the tail booms was still intact. But the horizontal braces halfway up had snapped in two. The broken pieces, each attached to its respective strut, fluttered and spun and moaned, making the entire tail vibrate in sympathy.

'Let go my feet,' I shouted.

Belly-down, I slid along the curved back of the fuselage until I reached the base of the V strut. I grabbed it and pulled myself up until I stood with the wind tearing at my back. The small, propeller-driven generator that powered our radio, normally attached to the center of the horizontal brace, spun around in the slipstream like a dervish. Without the radio we were sunk.

It took me three lunging tries, but I finally caught hold of the wire, reeled it in, snipped it free and stuffed it inside my shirt, wincing as the small propeller blades dug into my chest.

The plane nosed up slightly as Ava applied trim to balance my movement. She was doing okay, but with the engines throttled back we were still descending. I was afraid to look for the U-Boat.

It took me longer than I planned, but I finally managed to bend each brace back upon itself and then around each of the struts. They still rattled and moaned, but the vibration stopped. The V strut looked like it could hold fine on its own until we got back home, as long as I didn't play fighter pilot.

I started making my way back to the hatch, my shoes slipping and scrabbling on the fuselage until I touched Orlando's outstretched hand. He yanked me inside like a hooked fish. I headed for the cockpit and strapped in.

Moments later we were safely above the clouds, the U-Boat somewhere far behind, and the Dry Tortugas just coming into view on the horizon.

I said to Ava, 'Why didn't you tell me you knew how to fly?'

'You didn't ask.'

'Multi-engines?'

'Enough to get rated.'

'Not bad.'

A tight smile. 'Thanks.' She wiggled the control wheel. 'You want her back?'

'Keep her for a while. Where'd you learn?'

'You won't believe me.'

'Try.'

'Amelia Earhart.'

'You're right, I don't.'

'It's true. They hired her as a consultant for *Ceiling Zero*. We hit it off like sisters. Always wanted to fly, so she took me up one day.'

'How was it?'

'She's good, Sam, very good.' Ava hesitated. 'That is, until she went down.'

'Think she and Noonan are still alive?'

She shook her head. 'It's been over four years. Flying's a dangerous job.'

'So I've heard.'

Back in 1937, Amelia Earhart and her navigator Fred Noonan had disappeared somewhere in the vast Pacific during their second attempt to fly around the world. The whole world had searched for them, or so it seemed. Navy ships, airplanes, ocean liners, tramp steamers, the works. It's hard to lose dreams. Harder still when we lose the dreamers.

'I knew Freddie Noonan,' I said. 'Taught me navigation when he was with Pan Am in the early 30s. He ran their school.'

'How was he?'

'The best, like Earhart.'

67

'What went wrong, do you suppose?'

A thousand things can go wrong when you're flying from A to B: Winds aloft, temperature change, unreported turbulence, lightning strikes, hail, icing, and all you've got is a lousy map, a pair of dividers, a bubble octant to shoot the stars - providing you can see them - and a lot of prayer, providing you believe in God. But I don't know of any pilot, when the world's turning upside down and he doesn't know how to get it upright again, won't pray to a power greater than his own to save his sorry hide.

Everybody in the world knew about Amelia Earhart's fateful flight. I tried to imagine my own version of the story, where Freddie Noonan, a tall, dark-haired, brooding kind of guy, hunched over his map inside that tiny Lockheed *Electra*, maybe his hands shaking from having one too many-- although I never believed that about him - and he brushes back his lanky black hair that keeps falling across his forehead and blocks his view of the vast, blank, blue space of the Pacific Ocean, while he desperately searches for Howland Island; a dot that says it's there, but it's not.

'How long did you fly with her?' I said.

'Five, maybe six times, until I got the hang of it.'

'What was she like?'

'Like you. Quiet, all business. More serious than she needed to be, but considering what she was doing, maybe that's the way you professional pilots are.'

I thought about Captain Fatt, who had taught me the art of flying Pan Am clippers. 'Not all of them.'

We flew for a while in silence. The engines droned in perfect synchronization. Once again I admired Orlando's talent as an aviation mechanic. Before he quit Pan Am to team up with me, he had risen to become Assistant Chief of Maintenance, Caribbean Division. A lofty title, he often reminded me. He had thirty guys working for him, and every last one of them would have killed for Orlando because every morning he showed up in the hangar wearing spotless clean coveralls, and walked out every night as tired and grease-covered as the rest of them.

'Earhart taught you how to fly. That's something, alright.'

'Just the basics. When the production wrapped, she went her way and I went mine. Took lessons at a field near L.A. Soloed. Got my ticket a month later. Then my instrument rating and multi.'

'A Beechcraft Staggerwing is a lot of airplane.'

She laughed. 'You're telling me. When that big fat radial engine first fired up, I thought, dear God, what have I done?'

We laughed at that.

I said, 'It's a beautiful piece of workmanship,'

'Custom built. Leather seats, cruises at two hundred, lands at fifty like an eagle coming home to roost. I named her *Sweet Surrender*.'

'Must have cost a fortune. Twenty thousand new I read somewhere.'

'Movies pay a decent wage.'

'Providing you're a star.'

'Was, you mean. I sold that plane for a song.'

A long silence.

She sighed. 'You do what you gotta' do sometimes.'

'But if you find the gold you can buy it back again.'

She brightened. 'So you don't think I'm crazy?'

'Didn't say that.'

'Even if we do find the gold, I . . .' She fell silent.

'If we find the gold, what?'

'You ask too many damn questions.'

I gave up and used binoculars to scan the seven-island chain of the Dry Tortugas that began peeking through the broken cloud cover.

'You said to the west of Loggerhead Key?'

'That's what the map says.'

From two thousand feet the keys look insignificant. From the ground too, for that matter. Middle Key, a narrow spit of sand and scrub, is often awash in the summer. Loggerhead Key, the bottommost island, is larger and holds the Coast Guard lighthouse. Garden Key, the largest island in the group, is the site of Fort Jefferson. The six-sided brick monster of a fort with eight-foot thick walls was built back in the 1840s to protect the Straits of Florida, but never used because the real enemy, malaria, kept killing its occupants.

The wind and sea constantly alter the keys' shapes; one year here, the next year gone beneath the waves, the following year back again. Hurricane winds can scour a key smooth of all vegetation in an instant, but Mother Nature always fights back, and scrub and underbrush can re-appear within months. In Orlando's words, 'The Lord giveth and the Lord taketh away.' But I say Mother Nature's the one doing it, not the Lord; yielding abundance and plenty and then desolation and destruction.

The Dry Tortugas are a fisherman's paradise with yellowtail and snapper practically jumping into your boat. Tarpon, too, if you have the right rig to catch them. And when you get tired of fishing, you can look down into the crystal clear water and admire the rainbow-colored angel fish, wrasses, and sergeant majors swimming in and around the reef.

When Orlando and I came here fishing with my dad, I would often go diving and see them first hand. Orlando, for all his athletic skill and strength, barely knew how to swim. So, while he and my father sat in the boat swapping lies, I'd put on my homemade goggles, strip down to my shorts and go swimming. I always carried a knife with me, just in case I met up with something that wanted to eat me.

But in all the years I did this, I never met a predator other than myself. Luck played a part too, I know, but Captain Fatt taught me that luck is something you can count on in the cockpit when you're in a jam and everything else has failed. But if that fails, then - and only then - you pray for a miracle.

'Do me a favor and circle around the fort,' I said. 'Keep us at about five hundred feet.'

'What for?'

'The first officer never questions the captain.'

She grinned. 'I didn't realize I got promoted.'

'Anyone who can fly a Staggerwing, can fly this old bird.'

She laughed, and gently banked the plane over the six-sided fort. It rotated beneath our gaze.

'That a moat around it?' Ava said.

'Breakwater. Keeps the waves from chewing up the walls.'

'That thing's gigantic.'

The fort's brick walls, dotted with hundreds of gun ports, enclosed a vast parade ground. Where once Union artillery soldiers marched past their commanding officer in proud review, a small forest of fully-grown cocoanut, date palm and butternut trees filled the deserted space. The silent, majestic, deteriorating structure, long gone to seed, spoke of a time when Fort Jefferson was one of the greatest construction projects of the ages.

I said, 'Took sixteen million bricks to build it.'

'It's in the middle of nowhere.'

'Geographically yes, strategically, no. And every brick brought in by boat. Tons of flagstone, timber, and nails, plus slave labor from Key West to do all the work. And when done, the Yankees aimed four hundred-fifty smoothbore cannons out of those gun ports down there.'

'Ever see action?'

'Never. Rifled cannon put it out of business. You fire one of those into brick, and no matter how thick, it crumbles like sand. The Army declared it obsolete right after the Civil War began and then abandoned it a few years later. Now it's a national monument - hold it, there he is. I knew he'd hear our engines.'

A small figure dressed in white stood watching from a corner parapet, his hand shading his eyes from the hot sun.

'Throttle back for just a second and keep her wings level.'

When the noise abated, I slid open the cockpit window, cupped my hands and shouted, 'Ahoy, Billy, it's Sam!'

The figure stiffened, and then started waving furiously, his voice faint and faraway. I waved back, Ava throttled up and we continued flying south.

'That's Billy Button. Runs the place. President Roosevelt made Fort Jeff a national monument in the mid-thirties, Billy pulled the right strings and got himself appointed director. He's all alone down there. Just the way he likes it.'

'I'd go nuts.'

'He doesn't. Supply boat comes down once a week. He goes back on it and blows off steam in Key West.'

'He can just leave?'

'In the summer it's so hot nobody in their right mind comes down here except fisherman.'

'And treasure hunters like us. The map says it's five miles due west of Loggerhead Light.'

Just as she said this we flew over the black and white lighthouse. Perched on the edge of a three-quarter mile long key, the black and white striped landmark lay due south of Fort Jeff. By day, the one hundred fifty-foot high stone structure was a silent reminder that from here north, America began. By night, its three-million candlepower light warned ships of the perils of the reefs as they sailed north out of the Gulf of Mexico to continue up the Atlantic seaboard or head east to war-torn Europe - providing they carried no contraband. The five unfortunate ships the U-Boats torpedoed right after the Neutrality Act seemed to be keeping the other dogs at bay.

I said, 'Back in the old days, wreckers used to sneak down here and douse that light in hopes of causing a shipwreck.'

'Did it work?' Ava said.

'Many a fine house was built in Key West on the profits from salvaging those wrecks. My great-grandfather's for instance, except he was one of the honest ones.'

'You sure about that?'

'No.'

We laughed.

Ava said, 'What a life that must have been. It'd make a hell of a movie. John Wayne would fit the part like a glove.'

She was right: I could see movie images of salvage men tumbling out of bed in the middle of the night, horns blaring, running to launch their sloops and cutters into the teeth of a storm that had trapped some unfortunate three-mast barquentine, her holds full with valuable cargo and foundering on the reefs.

Whatever wrecker got there first laid claim to the hull and owned it outright, and in turn would divvy up the spoils with his fellow wreckers according to a strict method of accounting.

Many a ship's captain tried to ward off these wolves by refusing to leave. Some even tried the old trick of leaving a dog or cat on the wreck, claiming still living creatures were still on board. But the wreckers would grab the pet, heave it in overboard, roll up their sleeves and get down to the perilous work of lugging casks of wine, whiskey, lard, and whale oil out of the dark, water-filled holds that threatened to flood at any moment. They'd winch off cargoes of prime building lumber, bundles of silk, muskets, gunpowder, men's suit coats, ladies shoes, herds of goats, even cattle sometimes - and haul it laboriously back to Key West to sell it to an eagerly waiting market.

I said, 'Did this imaginary buried treasure of yours come from a wreck?'

A long pause. 'From a mutiny. And it's not imaginary.'

'Tell me what you see out there.'

She lifted herself up from her seat so as to be able to see over the S-38's long snout. 'Nothing.'

'We've come five miles, almost six now.'

'Keep going. It's out there.'

'I've been down here a lot and never saw it.'

'Ever flown out this particular course?'

She had me there. All the flying I'd done had been in and around Fort Jeff, and to be honest, the occasional key that I saw could well have disappeared in the next storm, so I never bothered.

'Knock, knock,' Ziggy said.

'Who's there?' Ava said.

'Delores.'

She sighed in surrender. 'Delores who?'

'Delores my shepherd, I shall not want.'

'We're busy. Go sit down.'

Instead, he wormed his way further into the cockpit. 'I tried that on Orlando. He didn't think it was very funny either.'

I said, 'Orlando's a preacher.'

'On the level?'

'Not ordained, but he does it part-time. Has a flock of folks who favor the way he sees the Lord.'

'Maybe he could pray for us to find the island.'

'It'll take a miracle.'

'No it won't. Ava tapped me on the shoulder. Check your eleven o'clock.'

Just off to port, a tiny, emerald green dot of scrub and tree-covered land floated in the middle of nothingness. The three of us crowded the window to stare at the approaching vision.

Ava said, 'Land ho.'

Ziggy whispered, 'Treasure Island.'

For a Florida key that wasn't supposed to be here, it was amazing to behold: a half-mile long, maybe, a quarter mile wide, the kidney-shaped island had substantial scrub and brush, which meant it had been around for some years. Why hadn't it been on the maps, I don't know, and it's not worth discussing here. Maps are a sore spot to flyers and navigators. The better they look, the less you trust them.

I slowly circled at five hundred feet while Ava took turns comparing the real thing to the treasure map in her lap.

'Shape's about the same. Not exactly, but close.'

'Where is 'X' marks the spot'?'

'According to this, a little beyond the scrub line on the westward side. Just up from the beach. See it?'

'Affirmative.'

In addition to a small beach, a narrow, curving spit of sand continued out into the water, providing a slight lee that would smooth the waters and help our landing.

'Good a place as any to set her down,' I said.

'Will you anchor in the water?'

'Only if the sand won't hold us, but it should. These tires are good and fat.'

Just as I said this, Orlando called out from the cabin. 'I don't think we need to unpack the raft, cap. That sand looks pretty firm to me.'

As always, Orlando and I were on the same frequency.

'I'm starving,' Ziggy said.

'Ignore him,' Ava said. 'He always gets hungry when he gets excited.'

'You should have seen me when you got the part in *Angels with Dirty Faces*.'

'I did, and don't remind me.'

Orlando leaned into the cockpit. 'Tell me something, Is Humphrey Bogart as mean as he looks?'

Ava said, 'A pussy cat. Or at least he was last time I saw him.'

'He handles a Tommy gun like he'd been doing it all his life.'

'Good actors make you believe in things even when they don't.'

I said, 'Like hunting for buried treasure?'

Her jaw muscles tensed but her smile was bright. 'Let's land this bucket of bolts and get rich quick.'

Our adventure almost ended before it began. Just as I flared for a landing Orlando shouted, 'Power!'

I instantly firewalled the engines. We'd been together too long for me to question his booming voice. Ava's sharp intake of breath cut through the sudden roar as I pulled up in a sharp climbing turn to the right.

'What'd you see?'

'Line of coral, just off the end of the spit.'

'I see it now. Didn't before.'

'Wind must have been blowing just right to ripple the water. Nobody could.'

He was just being nice, of course. An idiot could have seen that coral. But I didn't because instead of being a pilot, I had been <u>acting</u> like one instead, to impress Ava. Why? Don't ask me because I don't know. Maybe her being a beautiful movie star made me act like an idiot. Why else would I have made such a big deal of fussing with the throttles, fiddling with the controls, all official-like? Why else would I have blabbed on and on about how tricky it is to land on water, and how you have to keep a sharp eye out for hidden obstacles, like coral reefs.

I let my breath out as we completed our three hundred-sixty degree turn and lined up again for a landing, one that would carry us far clear of the menacing coral.

'That was close,' Ava said. 'I never saw it.'

'Me either.'

'Thank God for Orlando. How do you suppose he saw it?'

'For one thing, he didn't have this nose to fight with. Can't see a damn thing over it.'

A lame excuse, I know, but all I could think of at the moment, especially since the embarrassing truth was not something I wanted to share with Ava for fear of her laughing at me.

So this time around I became a pilot instead, and the landing was textbook. So was taxiing up to the beach line where I lowered the gear, gave a quick burst of power to get us moving and we rolled up onto the hardened sand like one of Pan Am's regular stops. All that was missing was my uniform.

I cut the engines. After they clattered into silence I said, 'Last stop, Treasure Island, everybody out.'

The mid-morning sun was merciless as we unloaded the gear and set off in search of Ava's buried treasure. The island had looked tiny from the air, but on foot a different story as we slogged through the soft, dry sand up to the brush line and then stumbled into the prickly underbrush.

Ava said, 'I figure it's about two hundred yards from here. See where those two palm trees line up over there? It's fifteen paces south from the second one.'

I said, 'Got your compass?'

'Yes, do you?'

'Affirmative.'

I patted the familiar lump in my right pants pocket, and then thought about her five hundred dollars cash, safe and sound back in the office. No matter what happened, I was ahead of the game.

'Lead on, Captain Kidd.'

Orlando helped Ziggy navigate through the chest high bushes, but it wasn't easy and the huffing, puffing little agent complained constantly as he dodged the sharp thorns.

Finally I said, 'Pretend you're an actor in *Treasure Island*.'

'I'd rather be watching it with popcorn instead.'

After a half-hour's struggle, we arrived at the palm tree in question and compared both of our compasses to determine south.

Ava took a few steps, turned and said, 'I wonder how long a stride it was back then.'

I said, 'I'm tall, Ziggy's short. We'll do it together and average the distance.'

With Ava counting the paces, Ziggy and I started shoulder to shoulder and I soon outpaced him. When we both stopped, she picked a spot that averaged where each of us had ended, and with her heel, made a crude 'X' in the hard-packed sand.

Her eyes danced with excitement. 'Curtain up.'

We worked in teams of two: Ziggy and me then Ava and Orlando. Our first hole took about an hour. We managed to get six feet down before we hit water. The second took longer. The third, where Ziggy had stopped, took the longest. We didn't talk much. What was there to say? Just bend and dig, bend and dig.

Orlando and Ava were at it when sea water began seeping into the hole again.

'Nothing here either,' he said.

Ava didn't answer. She kept studying the map, brows furrowed, mouth pursed in thought. The sun, now moving into late afternoon, ducked behind a rising line of darkening cumulus.

I pointed to the sky. 'I suggest we set up camp before the storm hits.'

She said, 'What storm? It's beautiful out.'

'In about a half hour it won't be.'

She stared into the empty hole. 'I'm not happy about this.'

I studied her map. The drawing, though faint, was straightforward: two palm trees. Direct line, fifteen paces south from the second one. Child's play.

'Close, but no cigar.'

Ava said, 'The only way to know for sure is to dig a five foot trench all the way along that line.'

'By hand? It'll take forever.'

She put her hands on her hips. 'So?'

'So, I'm a pilot, not a ditch digger.'

'Fine. Ziggy and I will do it. You and Orlando can sit on your lazy asses and watch us count gold coins and know that you'll not see a single one of them.'

'How do you know they're coins?'

A tiny hesitation. She glanced at the map. 'I'm assuming they are. Maybe pearls and diamonds, too.'

'You've got to be kidding.'

She threw down the shovel. 'Listen, captain, if I were kidding you'd be laughing about now, wouldn't you?'

'Yeah.'

'Well, are you?'

'I'm about to laugh at how stupid this is. Four adults digging in the sand like kids, pretending we're going to find buried treasure.'

She snatched the map back. 'Your problem is that if you don't see it you don't believe it.'

'So?'

'When I believe it, that's when I see it.'

'Who's right so far?'

She poked my chest. 'You are. But we're not done yet, not by a long shot.'

A distant rumble of thunder cut off my wise guy response. Instead I said, 'I suggest we continue this discussion after the storm.'

She spun around, picked up her shovel and stomped off.

Florida thunderstorms in August are not what you experience if you live in say, Virginia or Tennessee or Iowa. When they hit down here, it's the one time I'm transported back to the inner wilds of Brazil, or Venezuela, or any of the South American countries I flew for Pan Am. Rain there is more solid than liquid. Sure, you can walk through it and fly through it, but the sheer force of it slamming into you or your airplane makes you think twice before doing so.

I've had engines drown when flying through a heavy thunderstorm cell. I've been right side up one second, and upside down the next from the winds packed inside their dark grey hearts. Snow I can handle but rain I respect.

That's why when we got back to the beach, I realized it was too late to pitch any kind of camp. We had to take shelter inside the plane. Good thing we did, because Orlando and I barely had time to lash the wings to the dead man tie-downs we'd dug in the sand before the storm hit.

We tumbled inside just as the cold spatters began multiplying like angry hornets until they became a steady, drumming roar on the cabin roof. The stuffy, humid heat of the day surrendered to cold gusts of wind dumping down on us from tens of thousands of feet in the air.

Ziggy shivered. 'I can't remember when I've had a more wonderful time.'

'Did anyone ever tell you, you talk too much?' Ava said.

'My mother and you.'

The four of us huddled in the cabin, me perched on a food crate, Orlando on the floor, Ava and Ziggy in the two wicker passenger seats. The drumming sound of the rain on the roof made conversation impossible. Maybe that was providential. Each of us had plenty to think about.

As for me, I spent time on what I call 'connecting the dots.' It's a mental exercise I do that helps me find order in the midst of a problem that seems to be happening because of random occurrences, but in fact is not.

It saved my life more than once in a plane when, in the midst of some heart stopping crisis I was able to solve things smoothly and efficiently, because I could quickly connect the dots between whatever the emergency was at the moment, straight back to its originating source and take action.

For example, a failing engine could be traced to a lack of oil. Cut power, feather the prop, and re-trim the aircraft. Problem solved. A tail-heavy plane that won't climb is traced to a screwed-up loading. Apply power, maintain altitude, and if impossible, start looking for a place to land. And make it FAST.

In this manner I connected the dots between leaving Providence, Rhode Island in a beat-up seaplane, getting forced down in Washington and spending the night in a Nazi jail. Then I continued skipping from one dot to the next until I arrived here, staring at Ava James' neatly arranged tennis shoes she'd taken off to dry.

Everything looked normal, but I could feel trouble brewing. Something in the way she sat there, shoulders back, hands in her lap, made me think she was waiting for something I couldn't see, but I sure could feel it. Time to connect some more dots.

'So how'd that gold get here in the first place?' I said.

She glanced at me, and then looked away. 'They buried it.'

'I mean the story behind it.'

She shook her head. 'When you see it, you'll believe it, remember?'

'Be nice. I'm trying your way for a change.'

She gave me sharp look, took a deep breath and said, 'Let me just say this; when we find it, it's going to change a lot more lives than mine.'

'How?'

She examined her fingernails instead of saying anything more.

'Cat got your tongue?' I finally said.

'No, it's just that I've got orders to do this the way it's been planned. I can't change it.'

'Orders? What are you talking about? What plan?'

Ziggy interrupted. 'Your honor, what my client is trying to tell the court is that she can't spill the beans until certain conditions are met. Like finding the gold, for instance, right, darling?'

She nodded.

'And if we don't?' I said.

Ava said, 'Then you fly us back to Key West, and you and everybody else in America lives happily ever after underneath Nazi hobnail boots.'

'Do you really believe that?'

'If I didn't, I wouldn't be sitting here, soaking wet, looking for that god-damned gold.'

'This has got something to do with the war?'

She turned into a sphinx.

I said, 'We're going to find that gold. I know it.'

She leaned forward and gave me the once over. 'Change your mind?'

'No, but I'm acting like it.'

After the storm passed we pitched camp near the plane. Tents for Ava and Ziggy, Mosquito netting over the wing for Orlando and me. And while Ziggy was all thumbs trying to pitch tents, he made up for it by being a great firewood scrounger, arriving with generous armload of twigs and thick roots.

Within minutes he had coaxed the wood into flame, and soon had it hot enough to make a bed of coals. Meanwhile Orlando and I went off to catch some fish. Not two minutes after casting our lines baited with shrimp, he got a strike.

'Hallelujah,' he said softly.

The reel screeched as the fish took hold and started fighting. But it didn't last long. Never met a fish that could beat Orlando. I waded out into the shallow water to net it.

'Let it go, brother,' he said. 'Bonefish.'

'How can you tell?'

'By feel.'

'No way.'

'Want to bet?'

'No.'

Moments later the silvery bonefish lay twisting in the net. One of the best fighters around, but terrible eating. Orlando grabbed it by the gills while I removed the hook. The fish flashed away into the shallow blue waters.

'Wished they tasted as good as they looked,' Orlando said.

I examined the low-lying brush and palm trees that dotted the beach line. 'What's with this place? I've never seen it on a map.'

'Keys come and keys go.'

'Look at the size of it. Something this big belongs on a map.'

'Not on any I've ever seen.'

'Except Ava's.'

'The Lord giveth and the Lord taketh away.'

I cast my line into the water. 'Let's hope he gives us a real Treasure Island.'

Orlando didn't say anything. Instead he busied himself opening a can of sardines.

'That trick never works,' I said.

'Never works for you, you mean.'

He took two sardines, broke them in two, rubbed them in the palm of his hands and then swished his hands in the water.

He crooned, 'Come and get it, little friends.'

Then he baited his hook with a whole sardine and smoothly cast it nearly on top of mine.

'Find your own place,' I grumped.

'Don't worry, won't be here but a minute.'

Five minutes later, a pile of plump mangrove snappers lay flopping and twisting on the beach, their coppery-red skin the color of the sunset now blazing in the western sky. Unable to resist the sardine oil, they had struck Orlando's line almost immediately. So fierce was the feeding frenzy that even I managed to land a few.

The trick to catching snapper is to not set the hook when the fish first bites. If you do you'll be looking at an empty hook. Instead, slowly lift the line, tempting the fish to attack it even harder. And if you're lucky, it will.

We cleaned and dressed the fish in the seawater.

I said, 'Know any scripture for helping us find buried gold?'

Orlando thought for a moment. 'How about 'Thou shalt not steal?''

'This isn't stealing, it's finding.'

'That gold belongs to its rightful owner, not us.'

I grabbed a clutch of fish and stomped away, saying over my shoulder, 'Don't you ever stop preaching?'

He just smiled and kept working.

To my surprise, Ziggy was as good a cook as he was making a fire. I was going to rustle up a simple camp supper, but when he caught sight of our fish, he clapped his hands with glee and took charge. Before we knew it, we were eating herb-crusted, baked fish, spring potatoes, and fresh corn. And just before we started he scampered off to a shady spot and dug up two bottles of white wine he'd had cooling there. He even brought wine glasses and poured like a *sommelier*.

'Compliments of the house,' Ziggy said.

Ava lifted her glass. 'To buried treasure.'

We drank.

Ava lifted her glass again, her face suddenly somber in the flickering firelight. 'To the United States of America. May she triumph and prosper over all adversity.'

'Amen and alleluia,' Orlando said.

The hard and hopeless work of the day soon gave way to the pleasure of Ziggy's perfectly cooked meal and crisp white wine. We ate in happy silence; the best compliment you can give a chef. While we finished off the second bottle of wine, the clear night sky filled with stars.

I broke the silence. 'Storm brought some good weather behind it.'

'Billions of stars,' Ava said.

I pointed out the ones used for navigation: blue-white Sirius, bright yellow Capella, Cassiopeia, and the North Star.

'How do you keep track of them all?' she said.

'Same way you remember your dialogue. Practice.'

'Running lines is a lot easier than taking a star sighting in the middle of the Pacific,' she said.

'I've done it many a time.'

'Ever get lost?'

'Sure.'

'What'd you do?'

'Figured it out. Otherwise we'd end up in the drink.'

'We're flying blind now.'

'Not finding it, you mean?'

She nodded.

By now Orlando and Ziggy were rigging the tents for sleep. I took a deep breath and said quietly, 'Does finding this have to do with that toast you made about the United States?'

To her credit, only her eyes gave her away. 'You're getting warmer.'

'Spill the beans.'

'Rules are rules, captain.' She stood up and brushed sand off her beautiful bottom. I confess I didn't look away.

'We start again at first light,' she said.

She thrust her shoulders back, rolled her neck and then, like a panther stretching after a meal, she bent over in a smooth motion of touching her toes and groaned.

'I am so out of shape it's a crime.'

'You don't look it.'

She punched my arm lightly. 'You don't look it either.'

'Trust me, there's not a joint that's not aching.'

Sleep came fast. One moment I was staring at the night sky through the mosquito net, the next, oblivion. What woke me up I'll never know. All I remember is that the stars re-appeared, only this time the familiar ones had moved slightly because of the earth's rotation. I raised up on an elbow. My motion awakened Orlando instantly, who slept as lightly as a cat.

'What's wrong?' he whispered.

'Heard something. I'll be back.'

I slipped out of the netting we'd rigged beneath the plane's wing and made my way up the beach to Ava and Ziggy's tents pitched near the brush line. Both were closed and dark. The fire was long dead and all I could hear was the soft lapping of water on the beach. Then I heard the other sound again. I followed it into the underbrush and came upon the path that led to where we'd been working during the day. The sound grew louder as I grew closer, and within minutes I spotted Ava digging furiously, some distance away from where we had failed.

'What's going on?' I said.

She kept digging and said, 'I'm kicking myself for not figuring it out.'

'Figuring what out?'

'The map was reversed. On purpose. To trick us. And it sure as hell did. This is where they buried it all along. I just know it.'

A loud thump instead of the scratchy sand sounds.

'My God!'

The hole was about three feet deep. I grabbed a shovel and joined her in clearing away the remaining dirt. The faster we worked the faster she talked.

'I was looking at the map in front of the fire after Ziggy turned in. I put it down to do something, and then picked it up again and got confused. The handwriting didn't make sense, and then realized I was looking at it from the other side. Look. Like this.'

She pulled out the map. Her small penlight wavered and wobbled as she shined it from behind. 'I didn't think anything of it. Went to sleep, but then woke up suddenly and it came to me. The words are reversed.'

'So?'

'Look at the very bottom. On this side it looks like waves around the island, right? Like squiggles. But what does it look like on your side?

The shadow of Ava's finger traced the spot in question. I looked closer. 'It says 'TURN OVER MAP'.'

She laughed. 'And I did, and they buried it here. The treasure's here!'

I played her penlight over the surface of the dirt-covered chest. Three feet wide by four feet long. How deep, I didn't know yet.

'We need help,' I said. 'I'll be back.'

I returned with Orlando, some rope and sleepy, complaining Ziggy. 'This couldn't wait until morning?'

Ava had already widened the hole considerably. She stared into it, her arms folded, head bowed.

'What's wrong?' I said.

She didn't say anything. Just handed me her penlight and pointed. I played the beam over sand and rocks at first, and then a skeletal hand and a scrap of cloth poking out from the side of the hole.

Ziggy said, 'Tell me this is a bad dream.'

I said, 'They must have killed one of their own.'

Ava said softly. 'Dead men tell no tales.'

I carefully covered the hand with a shovelful of sand. 'Rest in peace, old fellow.'

Working in somber silence, we widened the hole around the chest, being careful not to disturb the dead man's resting place. Then we dug down three more feet before we reached the bottom of the chest. If filled with gold coins it would weigh a ton. Fortunately we had brought along a crane for just such a contingency: Orlando Diaz.

We dug two tunnels beneath the chest, snaked lines through, and back up to the top. Then, with each of us holding an end, we gave a heave and it rocked slightly, but that was it. Orlando tied off my end to a nearby palm tree. Then he took his end in one hand, looped it over his shoulders and grabbed it with his other hand. He squatted like a weightlifter, took a deep breath and dead lifted. The chest came free with a crunching, sucking sound. The four of us managed to wrestle it up and out of the hole.

Three rusted hasps along the front held it closed. It took me a while to break them free with a hammer and screwdriver, but they finally yielded. I stood and turned to Ava.

'You have the honors.'

She grabbed my hammer and screwdriver and chiseled along around the lid until it loosened. She looked at me, took a deep breath, grabbed the lid and lifted. It opened with a squeal and fell back to reveal the long sought after treasure.

Rocks. Big ones, small ones, from top to bottom. Rocks.

Nobody said anything for a long while.

The laughter, when it came, was a high and shrieking whoop from off to our right.

'Like flies to honey, by God,' the old man shouted as he ran out of the shadows and into the moonlight, his snow white hair going in all directions, his short bandy legs scuttling like a crab's. Someone to laugh at, if it weren't for the .30 caliber Winchester rifle trained on us as steady as a snake staring you down. He stopped a short distance from us and cocked his head to one side.

'Mr. Riley,' I said. 'Put down that damned gun before you hurt somebody.'

He took a start, and then grinned as he recognized me. 'Sammy Carter, what the hell you doing down here, boy?'

Ava said, 'Who is he?'

'Mr. Riley is lighthouse keeper at Loggerhead.'

He sidled closer and lowered the rifle. 'I'm a lot more than that, Sammy-boy. How'd you like them rocks? Clever huh? You dug up that chest and what'd you get? Nothing!' He looked heavenward. 'Daddy, you were one clever man.'

He whooped and danced a little jig.

Ziggy said, 'This must be Ben Gunn's stuntman.'

I grabbed the old man by his shoulder. 'Where's the gold?'

'What gold?'

'The gold supposed to be in this chest.'

He grew instantly sober. 'Well, it ain't here, I can tell you that. But more than that...' He raised his rifle. 'You ain't never going to find it. Now clear out of here.'

Ava stepped forward until the barrel was touching her chest. 'That gold belongs to the Confederate States of America.'

Riley's eyes widened in surprise, and then narrowed. 'Maybe it do, and maybe it don't.'

She continued, her voice steady, soft and confident. 'In 1865 a group of sailors mutinied on the British blockade-runner *Mirabella*. They killed everyone on board and set sail through these straits, heading for the Gulf of Mexico - am I right, so far?'

Riley said nothing, but the rifle barrel wavered slightly. She stepped closer and continued.

'But a Yankee picket boat spotted them and set off in hot pursuit. A storm came up and they made good their escape. But being better mutineers than seamen, the *Mirabella* ran aground on the coral reef right over there and started breaking up. The mutineers made it onto this island with their chest of gold and they buried it. Right so far?'

Riley lowered the rifle. Ava tapped my shoulder

'Of course, the Key West wreckers, got word and raced out to salvage it. The mutineers waited on the key until the salvagers were swarming like locusts around the *Mirabella's* remains. Their plan was to set off in their longboat from shore and act the role of abandoned seamen. But a fight broke out, one of mutineers was shot and left for dead.'

She aimed her penlight at the spot where I'd re-covered the skeletal hand. I brushed away the dirt.

'This would be this gentleman here. The rest of the mutineers drowned when their boat overturned. But the man they left for dead didn't die until he told the story I'm telling you to your daddy who tried to save him.'

Riley went peered at the skeleton. 'I'll be damned. Daddy said he buried the man but I never believed him.'

'Your daddy also made a map,' Ava said. 'Recognize the handwriting?'

Riley put down his rifle and squinted while Ava played her penlight over its details, her voice soft and steady and relentless.

'Before the mutineer died, he said the gold was bound for Richmond to aid in the Confederate cause. Your daddy, being the good rebel he was, wrote down every word and sent this map to President Jeff Davis by secret messenger.'

'How'd you get hold of it?'

'That's my business, not yours.'

He drew himself up. 'Well, missy, that's a fine story you just spun, and not only that, it's a true one, down to the last detail. But here's something else that's true: that gold belongs to the Confederacy and always will. My Daddy was under direct orders from Richmond, and so am I. When I hear the call, the gold will be released, and not until. Especially to low-down, no-good, treasure hunters like you.'

'Your daddy ever tell you about General Longstreet visiting him?'

Riley smiled. 'You sure did your homework, little lady. As a matter of fact, the great general did come here in person a year after the wreck.' He spat on the sand. "Course, by then the war was a lost cause, so the general says to daddy, 'Patrick,' he says, 'this here order comes straight from General Robert E. Lee: you leave that gold where it lays. But if the day should ever come when the south needs to rise again to save this nation from its sorry self, you'll be…'

'Shown a sign,' Ava said.

She fished something out of her pocket. Moonlight gleamed off the gold coin in her open palm. She aimed her penlight on the robed figure engraved upon the coin, a flag-bearing 'Liberty' striding forward, sheaves of wheat behind her, bales of cotton alongside, clouds above and the words in a hopeful arc over her head.

CONFEDERATE STATES OF AMERICA

'Look familiar?' she said.

I said, 'The Confederacy never had its gold coins.'

'They did too. Had them struck in England and were bringing them back to aid the cause.'

'How'd you come by that one?'

'They made test strikes before they sent the over the dies. This one belonged to General Longstreet.'

She flipped it over to the reverse side: a linked chain forming a circle against a field of stars with the initials of each state inside each link. The letters 'CSA' in the center and '50 DOLLARS' underneath.

She smiled at the old man. 'Your daddy taught you what to do if the time should ever come. It has, Mister Riley. Do your duty, sir.'

Riley looked long and hard at her and then let out a snort. He dug into his vest pocket and slowly pulled out a small leather pouch. He opened it and shook a coin into his palm. Worn from eighty years of handling, but an exact copy of Ava's.

She said, 'This gold we hold in our hands, and the gold you hid away, will help the Sons of Liberty.'

Riley's face lit up. 'By God, they're back? You're telling the truth?'

'Would I lie to a patriot like you?'

He practically came to attention. 'What's the plan?'

'All I can tell you is that we're not taking neutrality lying down. The Yankees may think they can get along with the Nazis like they were some kind of business partners, but Johnny Reb knows better.'

'I'm one of them, by God!'

'I know you are, Mr. Riley and I am too. And here's something else I know: you're going to lead us to that gold because the time has come for the South to rise again, and with it the United States of America.'

Whatever enables us to go to war, secures our peace.
-Thomas Jefferson

Nobody could sleep. Too damn much excitement.

So we struck camp, piled into the plane and I step-taxied over to Bush Key, the site of Fort Jefferson and tied up near the East Coaling Dock. Just as dawn was breaking, Riley showed up in his Coast Guard-issued longboat. Together we set off for the fort, where he claimed his father had hidden the gold.

It had been twenty years since Orlando and I had raced through the abandoned gun rooms, pretending we were defending the Confederacy from the damned Yankees. But as our boat approached the landing pier, it seemed like we were doing it for real this time - at least according to Ava. Not the words she used when she spoke about taking action against the Nazis, although make no mistake they were dramatic. But way she held herself when she said them, like a regular Joan of Arc, only instead of armor she wore dirty khaki slacks and a sweat-soaked blouse.

I'd seen her in a lot of films, and while she played different characters each time, they were always the same: elegant, tough, self-sufficient. How much of this was true in real life and how much an act is hard to say. I guess that's what being a movie star is all about; fooling all the people all the time. If so, then she was sure fooling me.

'Ain't it the perfect spot?' old man Riley said as he pointed to the fort.

'Beats hiding it in the sand,' I said.

'Daddy was a'feared the key might go under and he was right. It was gone for about forty years. Then it came back.'

'Smart man.'

'And you thought lighthouse keepers were crazy. We're crazy like foxes.'

'You're sure Mr. Button's gone?'

'I seen the Key West supply ship head out last night. The man's off to feed his sins of the flesh. And while the cat's away the mice will play, yes sir.'

Ava shielded her eyes from the glare of the rising sun. 'Nobody else around?'

'Nobody but us chickens,' he cackled.

Most kids have haunted houses in their towns. Orlando and I had a haunted fort. Every time went fishing in the Tortugas with my dad, we'd beg him to let us poke around Fort Jeff, which by then had been abandoned for years. Once upon a time the tramp of soldiers' boots had boomed inside its vast, six-sided walls and endless corridors. Today they echoed to the screams of sea birds and the wind.

Riley led us across the beach and past the abandoned remains of the east coaling dock. Row after row of stone pilings and rusting turnbuckles poked up from the crystal clear, fish-filled water, hinting of a time gone by when all was glory and the Yankee flag snapped proudly in the breeze.

We followed him over a rickety bridge that spanned the moat surrounding the fort. Below us, angel fish and sergeant majors darted in a thousand directions, their bright blues and deep yellows like colorful comets.

We headed straight for the stone-columned main entrance, its massive doors long gone, their three-inch thick oak planks snatched away by some determined Key West wrecker.

Irony at its best: Fort Jeff had been designed to be a mighty engine of war. But in truth, that engine never turned over once. Made obsolete by rifled cannon, they made it a prison instead for unlucky Yankee deserters during the war. But plagued by malaria and other tropical illnesses, the army finally threw up its hands and walked away in the 1870s. And so it sat here for all these years, doing nothing but protecting the rebel treasure that Riley was supposedly leading us to.

We marched across the inner parade ground like we owned the place, thanks to Billy Button gone up to Key West to get his ashes hauled. No wind as yet to ruffle the palm trees scattered in clusters here and there, their drooping leaves making them look like sleeping soldiers. Most of the service buildings had crumbled away years ago, leaving only their foundations upon which to puzzle their purpose. The commandant's single two-story brick structure remained, used for Button's private quarters. The morning sun was just now striking the tops of the palm trees surrounding it.

'This-a-way.' Riley disappeared inside one of the arches. We followed him up a curving staircase leading to the parapets. Our footfalls echoed in the cool silence, as surprised lizards and other creatures darted into the shadows.

'You buried it up here?' I said.

'You'll see,' Riley answered.

Ava huffed and puffed alongside. "There'd better be gold at the end of this guy's crazy rainbow.'

The view from the parapets was as thrilling today as when I was a kid.

Back then Orlando and I would raise our pretend sabers and shout 'Ready...aim...FIRE!' and imaginary fleets of Yankee ships would explode in showers of flame and destruction. The brick parapets had a thick layer of soil on them and wild grasses grew in abundance. From here looking west, Riley's black and white lighthouse flashed its familiar beacon.

Ziggy saw it too. 'Aren't you supposed to turn that thing off during the daytime?'

"Course I am.' Riley said. He pulled out his pocket watch and regarded it for a moment. 'Watch how the experts do it.'

He cupped his hands to his mouth and shouted in a high pitched shriek, 'Turn off that light!'

It kept flashing.

'Takes time for my voice to travel from here to there,' he said casually.

The light winked out. He nodded approvingly. 'That's more like it.'

And he walked away.

Ziggy called out after his retreating figure, 'How'd you do that?'

Riley shrugged his shoulders but said nothing.

I said, 'My guess is that it's on some kind of timer.'

Ziggy couldn't help himself, he crowed, 'What a movie this is going to make! And what a comeback it'll be for you, darling. I even have the title.' He framed his hands against the sky and intoned, 'REBEL GOLD.'

We traversed two of the six sides of the fort and stopped by another tower. The morning wind had picked up, but from the looks of the cloudless sky the high pressure pattern was firmly in command, at least for a few days. Then all hell would break loose again. That's how it is down here in August.

Riley said, 'Here we are. Ladies first.'

And down we went on the stone steps, past the gun rooms, past the ammunition chambers, deeper and deeper until we finally arrived at the bottom level of the fort. Our flashlights swept back and forth over the moss-covered bricks, lost in the darkness for almost a hundred years.

Riley said, 'This-a-way.'

We arrived at a solid-looking wall. Riley pulled out a screwdriver and slid it along one of the mortar lines. But instead of hardened cement, packed sand trickled out. He removed the brick as easily as a rotten tooth. Minutes later, a pile of them lay on the floor and a hole in the wall, inside which lay a mound of moldy, gray cloth sacks.

'Daddy didn't want nobody finding this no how.'

'He did a good job,' I said.

Riley leaned back on his haunches and sighed. 'Well, like the man said, who ate a bad oyster, 'What goes down must come up.''

Ava stepped forward. 'Let me look, if you don't mind.'

She knelt down, dragged out one of the bags, untied it and reached inside. You could hear the soft clink of gold long before her flashlight revealed its splendor. The Confederate coins slipped through her slender fingers like water in Cleopatra's bath. Nobody said anything for a long moment. All you could hear was our breathing and the quiet drip of water on the walls.

'I can't believe it's really here,' she whispered.

Riley said, 'You had better put that gold to good use, hear?'

'We will.' She stood up and put out her hand. Her face was set and determined. 'Mr. Riley, on behalf of the Sons of Liberty, I want to thank you for your selfless devotion to the cause for which our fathers so proudly served. May we continue in their footsteps with bravery and courage.'

The old man refused to take her hand. He saluted her instead.

Each bag weighed at least forty pounds, and I counted fifty. We'd have a hell of a time getting them topside, but it had to be done. Orlando carried three in his arms like they were feathers, I managed two, but it killed me after the first few steps. The rest took what they could and we began the slow climb, knowing we'd have to repeat it many times before we were finished. Riley led the way, and then me, Ava and Ziggy. Orlando was our rear guard. Riley's stooped figure was silhouetted in the bright sunlight as he neared the top of the stairs. Wasn't our rear that needed guarding.

A voice said, 'Mr. Riley, just what in hell are you doing inside my fort?' Riley froze and the rest of us did too. Then, to his credit, he stepped forward. 'What in hell are you doing here? You're supposed to be in Key West with your ladies.'

'I made other arrangements.'

Riley whooped. 'You mean you brought one here?'

'None of your business, and what's in that bag?' Mr. Button stepped forward and looked down the staircase. 'And who are these people?'

'Morning, Billy,' I said cheerfully. 'Long time no see.' He peered into the darkness. 'That you, Sam?'

'Indeed it is.'

'Me too,' Orlando said.

We climbed up and out into the bright sunlight. Mr. Button kept adjusting and re-adjusting his suspenders over his ample belly as he struggled to comprehend our disruption of his quiet little world.

Riley said, 'How'd you know we were here?'

'Shouting at your damned lighthouse woke me up from a sound sleep.' Riley winked. 'Why didn't you just roll over and...'

'Look here, you're trespassing on government property. I'm going to have to report you.'

Ava said quietly, 'Mr. Button, you're a federal employee, correct?'

He nodded.

'And as such, you're entrusted to care for this national monument.'

He stood tall, his broad belly tight with importance. 'Ensuring that no harm befalls it by unauthorized visitors like you.'

'Exactly.'

'So, what if I were to tell you that a year from now, maybe sooner, you're going to be out of a job and this monument will be allowed to sink back into the sea. What would you say to that?'

He pulled at his suspenders and frowned, but said nothing.

Ava continued. 'You read the newspapers, you know what's going on in this country. America's in free fall because of the Nazis. The state of Florida's going to secede, right?'

'And why shouldn't it?'

He frowned. 'We Southerners are mighty particular about being trod upon.'

'I'm Louisiana-born.'

'Then your governor's saying the same thing. Nobody's in charge at the Federal level so he's taking the bull by the horns and taking care of Louisiana first, by God, and to hell with everybody else. Same is true for us Floridians.'

'You're all dead wrong,' Ava said.

'Why?'

'Because even though Abe Lincoln was a damned Yankee, he had it right; united we stand, divided we fall. And this…' She emptied her bag onto the ground. The coins sparkled and danced in the sunlight as they landed. 'This is going to make sure we do just that.'

While Button stared bug-eyed at the pile of coins, Ava knelt and began telling him about the Sons of Liberty while she stuffed them back into the bag. When she finished he said, 'I suppose you've got to start somewhere if you want to fight back.'

'We already have,' Ava said. 'And this gold is going to make things a lot easier.'

As he pondered her words, the sea birds cried out at something they'd spotted in the water. The wind gusted, blowing Riley's tousled hair. I felt like we were in some kind of tropical tableau, frozen in time.

Ava finally said, 'Now that you know the truth, you still going to report us?

Button considered this. 'I should… but I won't.'

Riley handed him a heavy bag of gold. 'Then lend us a hand, partner. We need all the help we can get.'

From the direction of Button's private quarters a woman's whiskey-rough voice shouted, 'Billy, where the GUT-damned hell you run off to?'

Riley cackled, 'Your lady friend can help us, too, if she's up for it.'

Button's face turned crimson. 'She can't. She's doing research.'

'Bet I know on what.'

While the others finished stacking the gold sacks on the coaling dock, Orlando sat in the cockpit calculating the plane's weights and balances. We had at least another thousand pounds to distribute evenly or we'd end up taxiing all the way back to Key West, which Orlando reminded me, would play hell on the engines and the airframe.

But I figured we'd already burned up enough fuel to yank her off the water, and if things got desperate maybe I could stay in ground effect, the cushion of air between the wings and the water that's saved many a seaplane pilot low on fuel and short on luck. We came to a cautious, uncomfortable agreement, as was often the case when engineers debate issues with pilots; they want the plane to function according to the book, pilots just want to fly.

I got up to do a pre-flight. Orlando put out a heavy paw and shoved me back in my seat. 'Ava said her and Riley's daddies served in the Civil war, right?'

'What about it?'

'Riley's an old geezer. Ava's young, maybe late twenties, tops. Her daddy would had to have been a baby back then. Babies can't make babies.'

'Agreed. Maybe she meant her grandfather.' Orlando frowned. 'That's not what she said.'

'She's an actress. Maybe it was all for show.'

'Maybe not.'

'Look, partner, let's just fly these folks back to Key West, send them on their way to their Sons of Liberty and we'll talk about it later, okay? We got us an airline to run.'

'Do you believe the stuff about the Sons of Liberty, or is she acting that too?'

'They're for real, but is she part of it? Don't know.'

Rumors of 'Sons of Liberty' militias springing up all over the country had started immediately after the Neutrality Act went into effect. Not surprising. Americans have a habit of creating organizations at the drop of hat to serve a need. And in this case the need was for action, even if it only meant moving your jaw up and down, arguing for America to wake up and smell the coffee instead of coasting along in the netherworld of neutrality. From what Ava hinted at, her group was doing a lot more than that.

Our loading went quickly, bucket-brigade style, with the bags being passed from Button to Riley, to Ava, to Ziggy and then to Orlando and I, who hoisted the first of them into the forward baggage compartment located in the S-38's long nose. We were careful to spread the weight evenly and make sure the bags wouldn't shift. We stacked the remainder on the passenger cabin floor. I did a final weights and balances and decided to play it safe and lose more fuel. We'd never get off the water otherwise. I reluctantly drained it out into five gallon jerry cans that Mr. Button gladly provided.

'I never turn down free gas. I'll use it in my generator.'

His whiskey-voiced friend never did join us. I figured she was content to sleep off their night's adventures. We made our goodbyes. Handshakes all around, Ziggy about to burst from excitement, Ava cool and determined. Me? I was just ready to move on.

Riley kept my hand after we shook. He leaned closer and whispered, 'You take care of that little lady, you hear?'

'She's a big lady, and doesn't need anybody's help, believe me.'

'Where she's bound, she will.'

I nodded, but thought instead of having supper in Key West and seeing Abby and Rosie and telling them about my big adventure.

'One more thing,' he said.

'Yes?'

'That gold? Don't spend it all in one place.' He cackled and bounced up and down on his heels, pleased with his little joke.

I've had my share of tricky takeoffs over the years. Hot, humid days in Rio de Janeiro, full load of passengers and luggage, all four engines in the S-42 firewalled, props at full pitch, and still took forever to unstick that fat Sikorsky from the glassy-smooth water.

Airplane designers and engineers can only do so much with lift ratios and power-to-thrust coefficients. There comes a point where the wings have enough lift to fly or they don't. And with a thousand pounds of gold and four passengers, the wings of our puny little S-38 were doing their best to lift us up, but I had my doubts.

I got us off twice, and each time lowered her nose to gain some airspeed but she settled back down onto the water like a tired Mallard duck. On the third attempt she rose about ten feet. I cranked in a touch of flaps which lowered my speed alarmingly, but the added wing surface ballooned us up another twenty feet. And so we went like a yo-yo; flaps down, nose down, more airspeed, flaps down, nose down, more airspeed until we achieved a positive rate-of-climb.

I patted my big round control wheel. 'Colonel Lindberg would be proud of you, old girl.'

Ava heard my remark. 'Lindberg?'

'He flew this very plane on Pan Am's first mail run to Rio back in '31.'

'The same Lindbergh who...''He's an advisor to Pan Am. He and Juan Trippe are drinking buddies —except neither one drinks.'

'Ever meet him?'

'Just in the newsreels.'

We leveled off at two thousand feet. The higher we went, the thinner the air and the less happy the wings would be in keeping us up. But right now Carter Air 45 seemed to be a happy airplane, and I was too. The instruments were in the green, visibility unlimited, and I was in the air, in command, and that was enough.

Other men want different pleasures I'm sure, and might sneer at my idea of contentment, preferring more earthly delights. You can have them, boys. Any day I can strap into a cockpit, start an engine and fly like a bird is a day in heaven for me. Feeling especially buoyed by this line of thinking, I turned to share it with Ava, who aimed a small, polished-nickel revolver straight at me.

'We're not going back to Key West, captain,' she said calmly.

'That thing real?'

'Want to find out?'

I laughed. 'Go ahead and shoot. Who's going to fly the - wait a second…'

She smiled. 'I'm multi-engine rated, remember?'

I kept my hands on the wheel. 'Why the Cagney bit with the gun?'

'Insurance that you'll do what I say. And what I'm saying is that we're flying to Lake Salvador, just south of New Orleans.'

'I've got barely enough juice to get us home. We'll never make it.'

'We'll refuel on the way.'

She shifted the gun from her right hand to her left, reached inside her jacket and pulled out a slip of paper.

'This is a list of airports, both land and water. Any one of them will have the gas we need.'

'You had this all figured out?'

'From start to finish, long before we met.'

'How are you going to pay for the gas? The gold?'

'That's not your concern. Set course for Lake Salvador.'

Something in her voice caught my attention. So I decided to take a risk and said, 'Cut the act, sister. You're not the type.' While staring at her half-lidded greenish-blue eyes, I slowly reached out and pressed down the gun barrel.

'Try talking to me instead.'

She shook my hand clear and raised the gun again, her eyebrows a single scowling line. But then she smiled, shrugged and dropped the gun in her lap.

'What gave me away?'

'That last part sounded like you were reading from a script. "Set course for Lake Salvador.' Like you were Captain Bligh on *Mutiny on the Bounty*.'

'I thought I sounded pretty damned good.'

'Why the gun?'

'I've got to get the gold - and you - to Lake Salvador. I knew you'd say no, so I jumped to act three and used the gun.'

I regarded the small, toy-like pistol. 'That's real? Not a prop?'

She slipped it into her purse. 'My mother taught me how to defend myself. After five years of living with Hollywood wolves, I'm glad she did.'

'Ever use it?'

She shrugged and then shook her head. 'Used my knee instead.'

'What's at Lake Salvador? And why me?'

'Because of what happened - to your wife and child, I mean.'

My face got hot and I heard a rushing sound in my ears that wasn't coming from the engines.

'That's nobody's business.'

'And because of what happened to thousands of other Americans who died that same day along with Estelle and Eddie.'

'How do you know their names?'

She hesitated, lost in thought. Then her eyebrows lowered and I could see it coming a mile away, so I said, 'Don't go for the gun. Just tell me the truth.'

Her full lips pressed into a thin line, then softened.

'Certain people want to offer you a chance to do something about what happened to your family, and what will happen to America if we don't take action.'

'The Sons of Liberty you mean.'

She nodded.

'What if I'm not interested?'

'Hear them out first.' I thought about Estelle and Baby Eddie and Abby and the empty hole inside me cracked open again. I wanted to pour whiskey down to fill it up like I did when it first happened. But whiskey wouldn't bring back what the Nazis had stolen from me. Maybe the gold would. But I doubted that too. Even so...

I tapped the fuel gauges; the needles were getting low.

'What airports you got on that list of yours?'

Like an airborne tiddlywink, we made the seven hundred-mile journey in a bunch of short hops. We'd take off, fly along the west coast of Florida for a while, get low on fuel and set down again. With such a heavy payload we had no choice. The plane's normal range was seven hundred miles, but with four passengers and a thousand pounds of gold, I could only carry half-full tanks with no reserve.

The laws of flight are few but immutable; exchange altitude for airspeed, and vice versa. Exchange weight for range; ditto. Flight rules are not bendable, which is a relief, because you never waste time figuring how to get around them, you just obey them or else.

We landed in Naples first, then Clearwater. From there I took a chance and leaped across the Gulf of Mexico to Apalachicola in a single hop. If we ran into engine trouble we were sunk, but if we didn't start cutting corners it would be dark before we got to Lake Salvador, and landing a seaplane in the dark without a lighted flight path is one those rules you never break. The only one who ever did and lived to tell the tale was my mentor Captain Fatt, and I was in the right hand seat when he did it.

I told Ava the story of how were on final approach in San Cristobal; a full load of passengers and cargo, ten o'clock at night, overcast with the ceiling about a thousand feet. Pan Am had spent tens of thousands of dollars rigging up a fancy underwater lighting system that would show pilots the outlines of the watery runway, including a flashing approach line, which was well and good when it worked.

Tonight it worked, and a more welcome sight I couldn't imagine after hand-flying the S-42 for the past two hours non-stop on instruments through heavy weather.

When I spotted the landing path, I wiggled the control column, relieved to surrender the plane to Captain Fatt for landing. Pan Am policy specified that the captain made landings when weather was at issue. But this time he waved his unlit cigar at me and said, 'Keep it kid, she's all yours.'

'You sure?'

'What'd I just say?'

'Yes, sir.'

My fatigue vanished, replaced by adrenaline as I scanned the instruments, made power adjustments, called for flaps and settled down to the business of landing a four-engine seaplane like I was easing a baby down on a pillow.

The S-42 was a handful. Her controls were stiff, reaction times sluggish, and just as I was approaching the threshold to begin my flare for landing, the path lights disappeared. I felt like I had been thrown into a black sack. I could see the distant lights of San Cristobal, but beneath a fathomless void. The water's surface could be fifty feet away or five. Impossible to tell. I had to abort the landing, go-around and figure out what to do next.

I started to shove the throttles to full power, but Fatt slapped my hand away.

'I've got the aircraft.'

To my amazement, he continued the descent, carrying just enough power to keep us above stall speed. The altimeter was no use. We were too close to the ground for it to register precisely. I held my breath, ready for the sudden slam that would signal we'd crashed into the rock-hard water. I ran the emergency drill: get the life rafts inflated, shove the passengers out and into them fast.

'I know you're there, sweetheart,' Fatt crooned. 'Come to daddy and give us a kiss.'

As if in answer, I heard a singing TWANG, then another, and another as the S-42's keel kissed the water surface. Fatt backed off the throttles and let her slowly decelerate until she finally settled safe and sound into San Cristobal Bay.

He had literally flown her onto the water, staying just above stall speed, ever descending until, with years of experience and thousands of flying hours under his belt, he sensed the nearness of the water and made a landing as smooth as if it had been the middle of the afternoon in a dead-calm sea.

'Home, Jeeves,' Fatt said and wiggled the control column, which meant I had the aircraft again. As I taxied toward the landing dock, Fatt lit up his cigar, which was strictly against Pan Am regulations as laid down by Dutchman Preister. But Fatt was an old-timer who did as he pleased. Had been with Pan Am from the start, worked shoulder to shoulder with Preister and Trippe in Key West, where I had first met him as a new-hire.

I began turning the S-42 in the wide arc that would lead us to the dock. As I did so, the water around me lit up and sparkled as the landing path lights came back on again.

'Nice, very nice,' Fatt said. 'Just when we needed them too.'

When I finished recounting my Captain Fatt story, Ava said, 'He still flying?'

My throat got thick for a second. 'He went down with the *Dixie Clipper* on a test flight right after Lufthansa took over. A Boeing 314, queen of the fleet.'

'The crew?'

'All hands lost without a trace somewhere fifty miles east of New York. They searched forever, but no luck. Like the *China Clipper* disappearing a few years back on its way to Manila; that one they're sure think was Japanese sabotage. My guess is that the Nazis did the same thing to Captain Fatt and the clipper.'

'Miss him?'

'Every day.'

We flew in silence. I tried not to think about that cigar-chomping, hell-for-leather man. The last of the breed. I was the type replacing him; cool, rational, no-nonsense professional, except for when I got pissed, or worse, pissed off; then I was more like my mentor.

Ava said, 'Miss flying with Pan Am?'

'Miss the big birds. But as for doing it for Trippe, no thanks, not with swastikas on their tails.'

'But that's just the clippers Lufthansa uses for their transatlantic flights.'

'And they use Pan Am crews to fly them, thanks to him. Traitor Trippe'll do anything to keep that precious airline of his alive.'

'I know.'

'How?'

A slight hesitation. 'I read the papers. Times like this, people do the damndest things to keep going. Like you and this airline of yours.'

I laughed at that. 'One bloody seaplane.'

'It's a start.'

She looked away, and then back at me. 'You were in Buenos Aires when they bombed us.'

The drone of the engines faded into the background.

'Who the hell are you, anyhow?'

'None of your business. You'd just gotten your Master Pilot's wings. No more First Officer Carter for you, no sir. Captain Carter would be at the controls. How'd it feel? To be the boss at last?'

'I can't remember.'

'Try.'

Instead I remembered Estelle's angry face, red with tears, and Baby Eddie crying in the crib the night I left for my first trip as captain.

'Sam, you promised,' she said. 'Can't you call in just this once? We've planned this forever.'

Her sister had just her first baby. All along the plan had been for us to fly to D.C. and visit her and Estelle's parents who lived there too. I glanced at the new wings pinned on my uniform chest: three small stars on them now, denoting full command.

'Captains can't call in. Especially on their first trip.'

Estelle marched over to the crib and lifted up Baby Eddy, who immediately began rooting for her breast. She deftly opened her nursing jacket, sat on the edge of our bed and fed him. She looked up at me, her face pale in the early morning light seeping into the room.

I had to go. I was late already. Still, I hesitated.

She said quietly, 'I understand more than you'll ever know. I've gone wherever your job took you. I've had babies and changed diapers when you were at ten thousand feet over God knows where. I've slept alone in this bed, wanting you beside me, on top of me, loving me, and I understood all along that this is what you love. And I love you. So, it stands to reason that I would love your job, too.'

She brushed away a strand of hair.

'Except today I don't love it anymore. I hate it. I don't understand why you can't be with Abby and me and the baby at such an important time in our lives. You'll be a captain forever. But your family will be grown up and gone before you know it. Is that what you want?'

I let the thought of cancelling the trip flicker through my mind, but it came to a dead halt.

'I never thought I'd get promoted like this. No warning, no nothing, just 'bang' here's your wings. Go.'

'That's the way Preister works. You of all people should know that.'

'It'll mean more money for us, more-'

Her furious look silenced me.

'You mean more climbing up from the bottom of the seniority list all over again. As first officer you were at the top, remember? All the choice trips. Welcome to just the opposite and you know it.'

She switched sides with the baby. 'Go ahead and go, Captain Carter. Your crew is waiting for you, but I promise you, your family is not.'

As things turned out, Abby came down with a fever the morning they were supposed to leave Miami for Washington. Rosie offered to drive up to Miami from Key West and take care of her, so that Estelle and the baby could head up to Washington and then on to heaven, too, I hoped and prayed.

Ava said, 'I'm waiting for your answer.'

'To what?'

'To how it felt to be a captain at last.'

I thought about her question. 'Ever read *Tale of Two Cities*?'

'Sure.'

'It was the best of times; it was the worst of times."

A huge hand holding a plate filled with food appeared between us and stopped everything.

Orlando said, 'Luncheon is served, madam. The same for you, captain?'

'Sure.'

'Make it two, Ziggy.'

'Coming right up.'

During one of our refueling stops, Orlando and Ziggy had raided a grocery store for lunch fixings. Right after takeoff, Ziggy began concocting a dizzying picnic lunch of thick corned beef sandwiches, cold chicken pieces, potato salad, pickles, olives, and cheese. He did it with flair; the sandwiches neatly quartered and pinned with festive toothpicks, the potato salad arranged just so alongside the pickles and olives. Even cloth napkins.

I said to him, 'Your wife must love having you around.'

'Don't have one.'

'Your girlfriend then.'

'No sir.' 'Those Hollywood ladies don't know what they're missing. Where'd you learn to cook?'

'At my mother's knee. God rest her soul.'

Ava said, 'She's still alive, and so's your father.'

'Pays to plan ahead.'

'That's morbid.'

'Better safe than sorry.'

I said, 'Where do they live?'

'Brooklyn, thank God. If it had been Manhattan, I'd be praying for real.'

'They survived, then.'

'Yes, which is more than I can say for my grandparents back in Germany. They're Jewish and it's a living hell for them. Yellow stars on their shoulders, friends getting arrested in the middle of the night, whole families disappearing without a trace. We're trying to get them over here, but they can't get visas.'

'Why not?'

He sighed. 'It's a long story that I don't want to tell.'

We finished the rest of the long water hop to Apalachicola in silence, each of us lost in thought and our ears numbed by the constant engine drone. I let Ava take the wheel to get some multi-engine hours in her log book, while I scanned the instrument panel for signs of mechanical trouble, and out the windows for Nazi compliance fighters. I doubted they'd be patrolling this far out in the Gulf of Mexico, but I wasn't taking any chances.

Fortunately, nature was on our side: puffy cumulus and high cirrus clouds were starting to pile up, created by a low pressure system sweeping in from the northwest. If trouble turned up we could duck inside the clouds and hide. By my calculations, we had a day or so more of decent flying before the high pressure system surrendered to the low, and the endless cycle of sun, clouds, and rain, would repeat itself.

I said, 'Be nice to have a chart instead of just a heading.'

'Ziggy, toss me my flight bag,' she shouted.

Moments later he handed up a thin tan briefcase.

'Look in the back,' Ava said. 'You'll find a New Orleans sectional. I use it a lot.'

'Why?'

'My family's from there, remember?'

I poked around inside. The normal pilot's tools: pencil, plotter, whiz wheel, log book, maps, and to my surprise, instrument approach plates too. It's one thing to be a fair weather flyer, but to be trapped inside the clouds, unable to see anything, relying completely on your plane's instruments to get you safely on the ground, that takes a true aviator.

'You got an instrument ticket?'

She laughed. 'Barely, but yes.'

I unfolded the map. 'Lady, you are full of surprises.'

Ava said, 'Lake Salvador's southwest of New Orleans. Got it?'

I located the kidney-shaped area of water easily.

'See that island about three quarters of the way up?' she said. 'That's Couba Island. Our destination.'

'No nightlife for you in the 'Big Easy,' huh?'

'Next time you visit New Orleans, I promise.'

'No thanks. Invitations at gunpoint aren't my style.'

'Sorry about that. I was afraid you'd refuse.'

'I still can.'

She shot me a look. I shrugged my shoulders. 'But I won't. Besides, I need to collect on the bonus you promised for finding the gold.'

'There's a lot more than a bonus waiting for you down there.'

'Like what?'

She pulled the pin from the control column and swung it over to me.

'You'll find out.'

We picked up a tailwind that increased our groundspeed. A relief because if we hadn't we would have had to land before nightfall. As it turned out, the lights of New Orleans were starting to come on as we passed over the city at three thousand feet. I reached to turn on my navigation lights to avoid collisions but thought better of it. I didn't want the Nazis sniffing my tail, especially with what we were carrying.

North of the city, Lake Pontchartrain was a vast, indigo blue nothingness in the gathering twilight. On the south side of New Orleans, Lake Salvador looked the same, only smaller. Couba Island sat crosswise near the top, its marshy surface laced with hundreds of glistening rivulets spread across the land like slug trails, filled with God knows what kind of critters, most of them more than happy to have you for dinner.

I'm no stranger to Louisiana, but to be honest, I've spent more time flying over it than being in it. Like Florida, it's got its share of heat, humidity and humanity, all bunched up together, itching, eating, laughing and loving. But where Floridians caper about, doing such things in the sunshine, I find Louisianans are much happier doing them at night. It's almost as if they can see in the dark better than we can. And what they see is blurry, with no sharp edges, soft and easy, and always filled with high drama and great romance.

I have a theory about that. Just a theory, mind you. While the east coast of Florida gets pounded by the Atlantic, by contrast, its west coast opens out to the glittering, quiet, Gulf of Mexico that just sits there in all its flat, watery glory. I think it's the Gulf itself that causes this relaxed spirit in Louisianans, who on the surface may appear sultry and stupid, but underneath sly and cunning creatures alert to the slightest sign of danger, but content in the meantime to loll about, toothpick in teeth, grits on the griddle until it turns up. Life's too short as it is, and if you're a Louisianan, you're not going to do anything to speed things up.

I said, 'You're from around here, right?'

'Born and bred. Momma was living in Georgia, but she moved back to be closer to her family after daddy died.'

'How old were you when that happened?'

'Oh, he died long before I was born.'

She cut off my question by with a quick laugh. 'I'm adopted. Momma never had kids with daddy. He was way too old for that when they married. Anyhow - look quick - at your nine o'clock and you'll see the top of our house.'

Too late. The failing light revealed only the trees and dense underbrush that covered the island, hiding the ground from view.

'Landing zone's on the south side,' she said. 'Make your base turn to the north at five hundred feet. When we turn final, I'll flash your landing lights - where's the switch? - never mind, got it.'

'Hang on back there,' I warned. 'We're heading down.'

I pulled the plane into a thirty degree bank to line us up for the crosswind leg.

'Light's fading fast,' I said. 'Got to put her down soon.'

'Don't worry, you'll be fine.'

'What do you know that I don't?'

'Turning final are we?'

'We are now.'

The island tilted to right as the plane tilted to the left. Just as I leveled the wings, Ava reached up and flicked the landing lights. Thanks to my Pan Am training, I'm as fluent in Morse code as I am Spanish, and quickly recognized her signal A...V...A, twice in quick succession.

In answer, the black void ahead blossomed into twin rows of underwater landing lights glowing just for us. Captain Fatt couldn't have done a better job himself.

'What the hell kind of setup have you got going down there?'

'We ain't whistling Dixie, I can tell you that.'

The moment we landed the underwater lights flickered out, replaced by the dark, hot gloom of a mangrove swamp, for that's what Couba Island was. Not an island with palm trees and volcanoes and pretty green hills with banana trees, but a series of narrow inlets, overhanging vines, marshy ground and mysterious figures darting here and there in the shadows of the approaching night.

'Taxi down that inlet to your right.'

'Can we fit?'

'Trust me.'

Moments later the S-38 was swallowed up in the narrow confines of a waterway that, once past the initial vegetation opened up to be about two hundred feet across. I slowly taxied along its meandering course for half a mile and then spotted the faint blue wavering dot of a flashlight held by somebody standing on a narrow dock projecting out into the water.

'Our tie-up?' I said.

'Follow the bouncing blue ball,' Ava said.

The closer we got the more people I could make out standing there waiting. But it wasn't easy. Dressed in dark grey uniforms and faces splotched with camouflage, they were more shadow-like than real.

'Some welcoming committee.'

'Don't mess with them. Let me do all the talking.'

I cut the engines; Orlando stuck his head out of the boarding hatch and threw a line to one of the waiting men. He pulled us to the dock and made it fast. Ava was out of her seat and out of the plane before I had a chance to shut everything down. She moved like a panther; here one instant, gone the next in a lithe twist of hips and legs.

Her voice rang out loud and clear. 'Unload the forward hold first, gentlemen. The rest is on the floor in the passenger compartment.'

'Yes, ma'am.'

'Where's Thompson?'

'Up with Miss Helen.'

'The general?'

'Due any minute.'

'Captain Carter, you come with me. Mr. Diaz will stay here and supervise the unloading. Mr. Siegel will assist, won't you Nathan?'

Ziggy saluted. 'Yes, boss.'

She turned to the guard. 'When you're finished, please escort these two gentlemen to the administration building.'

'Yes ma'am.'

'Any chow left?'

'Plenty.'

'Feed them well.'

She pointed into the darkness. 'Captain, if you please?'

I followed her along the dock that widened the closer we got an impenetrable wall of twisted swamp vegetation. We passed through a narrow opening, and I had the sudden sensation of being in some kind of a military camp; armed men bustling here and there; some singly, some in groups, all moving in absolute, highly-disciplined silence.

'Quite a setup you've got.'

Ava said nothing, just kept walking. We entered a grove of towering cottonwoods that dwarfed us.

'Daddy planted these himself when he first came here.'

'Must have had a lot of time on his hands.'

'After the war every Johnny Reb did.'

"But that was - I mean, your father fought in the Civil War?'

'Alongside Robert E. Lee at Gettysburg. He was second in command. General James Longstreet. Ever heard of him?' I stopped walking. 'You're his daughter?'

'One and the same.'

'But how could you-'

'I'm adopted, remember? Mamma didn't meet the general until thirty years after the war. She was thirty-four when they got married. Daddy was seventy-six. That was back in 1897.'

'Must have been some wedding.'

'Drove her family wild. But she did it anyhow. Daddy died seven years later. From happiness, I'm certain. Anyhow, that's when she adopted me. She always wanted a daughter and I always wanted a mom.'

'She must be something.'

'Eighty years old, and still packs a punch.'

The silvery-white columns of an antebellum mansion materialized in the middle of this mangrove-like island. Faint golden gleams of light glowed in the first floor windows.

'Home sweet home in the summertime when I was growing up,' Ava said. 'Forty rooms, fifteen bedrooms, never did know how many bathrooms.'

'I could use one right about now.'

She laughed and grabbed my hand. It was surprisingly warm and strong. 'Meet mamma first.'

Some people look old. Others look eternal. Helen Dortch Longstreet was in the second category: short, trim, grey hair pulled back in a no-nonsense bun, a black dress trimmed in white lace, crystal-clear blue eyes, and a wide, friendly smile wrapped around a small cigar.

'Smoke, Captain?'

'No thank you, ma'am.'

'Good for you. Nasty habit. Picked it up from the General and never put it down.'

'I'll have one momma, if you don't mind.'

'You know where they are, sugar.'

She waved in the direction of a bookcase that lined the entire side of a vast parlor and Ava went to fetch one from a humidor. What a place! Heavily draped windows, immense stuffed divans, chairs, and plaster-trimmed ceilings twenty feet high if they were a foot. I had lived in the south all my life, seen my share of plantation mansions from the outside, but never until this moment the insides of a real one, unless you count watching Gone with the Wind but that was just a movie set. This was the real thing.

Mrs. Longstreet crossed over to a dark mahogany breakfront and swung down a shelf to reveal at least thirty different bottles of liquor. The light from the chandelier sparkled off them like diamonds in a jewelry store.

'Something to wet your whistle, captain?'

'Bourbon if you've got it.'

She gave me a long look. 'It's about all I've got, son. Except for a little gin. The general likes his gin.'

Ava blew out a thin stream of smoke. 'Uncle Georgie's here?'

Her mother wearily closed her eyes. 'Two days so far. Feels like two weeks.'

'I need to see him.'

'He's on his way. Rest assured he knows the exact moment you arrived, down to the last second.'

She handed me my drink, we touched glasses and tasted.

'Nothing gets past the beady little eyes of General George S. Patton.'

'General Patton is here?'

Her eyes narrowed. 'After the Neutrality Act, he got tired of twiddling his thumbs at the Pentagon waiting for orders that he knew would never come, so he took a leave of absence.'

Ava said, 'To join the Sons of Liberty.'

Her mother laughed. 'George didn't exactly join them. He's a general, remember? He commands the whole lot of them now, and they love it.'

'How many?' I said.

She waved her cigar in the direction of the window. 'In Louisiana, maybe five or six thousand by the last count. Mississippi's somewhere near ten, Arkansas I can't recall, but whatever the number is, it's growing fast.'

'That's one hell of a militia.'

She laughed. 'Don't let the general hear you call it that. He prefers 'army.''

The tramp of heavy boots coming closer and closer, the door swung open and in marched General Patton. I had seen movie newsreels during the Louisiana War Games of 1940, when he outfoxed the 'enemy' forces invading the Gulf Coast. His armored tanks ran rings around the infantry, hitting hard and moving fast, with umpires scrambling in their wake, waving flags, calling soldiers 'dead.'

Ava flew into his arms. He embraced her quickly, but kept his eyes on me the whole time. When she let go he said, 'This the man?'

Ava mock saluted. 'Yes sir, Uncle George, sir. May I present Captain Sam Carter reporting for duty as ordered – at gunpoint.'

He strode over to me and we shook hands. I had expected Patton to be a short, Napoleonic sort of guy, but he was tall and had a commanding, patrician elegance, like a Roman senator, sort of.

'Glad to have you on board, son.'

'I don't know that I am, sir. I mean, what's going on around here?'

'We're at war. And we need you to help us win that war.'

He stared at me, waiting. All I could think to say was, 'Does the president know about all this?'

He regarded me in silence. Then a grim smile touched his lips. 'Let's just say that what you're about to see has her blessing.'

Ava and I followed him out into the darkness. She answered his terse questions as we made our way across an open field with camouflage netting draped from pole to pole to prevent prying eyes from seeing what was happening on the ground. An army truck roared by, and then another, headlights hooded to almost nothingness to preserve blackout conditions. Here a group of marching men, there a small gathering lined up, firing-squad style, shooting silenced rifles at dim targets. A muffled 'boom' sounded somewhere far in the distance.

'Mortar practice,' Patton said, and walked faster, leaving Ava behind.

She whispered, 'Uncle Georgie means business.'

'He's your uncle?'

'Dutch uncle. Mother's known him ever since he was a captain.' Patton's swagger stick swept to the right, 'This way. Watch your head.' Single file we entered a vine-covered path lined with white engineering tape. Its faint glow helped guide me along what otherwise would have been a walk inside a coal mine. Animals rustling here and there, frightened night feeders fleeing from our heavy footsteps. Something darted off to my left. I looked away and seconds later collided with Ava's nicely rounded backside. Flustered, I apologized, while at the same time felt a flash of guilty pleasure.

Patton's swagger stick aimed at an amorphous black blob in the distance that grew more distinct with every step.

'We're here.'

The first thing I recognized were the Clipper's impossibly long wings stretched out into the bayou darkness, then her four Wright Twin Cyclone radial engines towering overhead, then her eleven foot-high propellers with workmen clustered around them, the soft clink of tools drifting down like summer rain on a tin roof.

The hundred foot long, slab-sided Boeing 314 floated gently in the swamp water. Her aluminum-clad fuselage gleamed like a surfaced whale, her gracefully curved sides converged to a perfectly rounded, narrow nose. Darkness hid her graceful, triple-tail rudder, but countless photographs and endless newsreels about this beautiful airplane made it clear in my mind.

Like all the other Pan Am pilots I had been desperate to fly her. But right now, seeing her for real was enough.

'What in the hell is a clipper doing here?'

'Waiting for you,' Ava said. 'Now be a good captain, go with Uncle Georgie. See you later.'

She turned and walked away.

Patton was already crossing the boarding ramp connected to the stubby 'sea wing' or sponson, attached to the fuselage directly beneath the shoulder-mounted wing. The Clippers used them instead of wing floats, like most other seaplanes. Their broad surface and gentle slope doubled as boarding ramps.

As I followed Patton, the bright blue flash of an arc welder lit up one of the aft fuselage windows. I paused for a moment, just as the Plexiglas window slid open. The twelve-by-seventeen-inch square window had been retrofitted into a larger, aluminum panel of some sort that, when fully opened exposed a three by four-foot hole.

Seconds later a machine gun barrel swung outward, tracked right, left, up, down, and then pivoted back inside again. The modified window panel slid closed, leaving not a trace behind of its malevolent purpose.

I caught up with the general who, seeing what I had just witnessed, beamed like a kid about to eat an ice cream cone. 'This fat bird's got fifty-caliber teeth.'

He ducked through the sponson's boarding door and stepped down into the parlor compartment. Before I followed, I walked out to the edge of the sponson to see the name of the Clipper. But the angle was wrong so I turned back, only to see above the boarding hatch, where once the graceful lettering, Pan American Airways System' had proudly been, the blunt, block letters of LUFTHANSA.

'Trippe,' I whispered.

Patton's muffled voice sounded. 'You may have all day, captain, but I sure as hell do not. Get in here and meet somebody who's been waiting to see you.'

The parlor's plush-carpeted, Art Deco lights were dimmed to bare minimum, making it hard to negotiate the narrow space between the two sets of upholstered chairs that flanked the entrance hatch. Patton stood to my right, slapping his swagger stick against his leg. Framed in the doorway forward stood a man who waved his unlit cigar at me.

'Hiya,' kid. Took your sweet time getting here, din'cha'?'

It took me a moment to recognize him. His bushy black moustache was gone and his hair a washed-out blonde instead of dark brown. I had done my share of grieving for the man who had taught me how to be an airline pilot. I'd put him to rest, along with my wife and son, and had been trying to move on. But here stood a very different-looking but familiar-sounding Captain Fatt, smiling like I was the Prodigal Son.

'You went down with the *Dixie Clipper*,' I managed to say.

'I did indeed, with all hands. But it depends on what you mean by 'down. She's here and so am I."

I touched my upper lip. 'Your moustache, and... your hair, it's....'

'Different, ain't I?' Fatt ruffled it into a tangle and smoothed it out.

'Afraid the good Captain Fatt, rest his dearly departed soul, is no longer with us. Neither is the *Dixie Clipper*, leastwise how she used to be. Meet Captain C. Charles Adams in his stead, and welcome aboard our secret weapon.'

Patton stepped away and looked down the corridor toward the tail.

'Bring him up to speed captain. I'll join you later.' He touched the swagger stick to his uniform cap, 'You have the ship, sir.'

'Roger that.' Fatt saluted lazily, utterly unfazed by Patton's powerful presence.

'This is all a dream, right?' I said.

'It's real, kid, and it's a nightmare. America's in an inverted spin, no rudder or aileron to speak of and the ground's approaching fast.'

'You're one of these Sons of Liberty folks?'

'Hell no.' He lit his cigar and puffed contentedly. 'I'm a Brooklyn boy, born and bred, but I'm also a citizen who wants to lend a hand pulling this country of ours out of its God damned nose dive.'

I regarded the luxurious surroundings of the parlor compartment. 'You picked a fancy plane to do it in.'

He snorted. 'Look while you can, kid. This stuff be ripped out soon, just like they've already done back there. Stripping her bare for a special flight.'

I stepped through the doorway into what should have been Stateroom E and stopped cold. For years I had stared at photographs in magazines of the Boeing Clipper's luxurious passenger interiors, imagining what it would be like to see them in person. But where once cushioned seats upholstered in Miami Sand and elegant aisle carpeting in the Tango Rust pattern had greeted her privileged passengers, bare aluminum flooring with stacked metal boxes took their place.

A workman came by, his arms filled with rolled-up dark blue fabric that once had been the curtains the stewards used when they converted the passenger staterooms into Pullman-style sleeping compartments.

'Where's she headed?'

'You ask too many questions.'

'I'll damn well keep asking them until I get some answers that make sense.'

Fatt grinned. 'Always knew you'd be a good hire. Did you know that I personally told that asshole Preister that if they didn't take you as a pilot, I'd quit?'

'Yes, and you remind me of that every time we meet.'

'Well it's true, kid. You were one of the best, and that's hard for me to say because as we both know I am the absolute best and always will be.' He turned and led the way. 'Let me show you your office.'

'Wait a second, I don't know the first thing about 314's. I'm a Sikorsky captain. Was one, I mean.'

'Who taught you to fly seaplanes, kid?'

'You.'

'Back in thirty-one, who flew that dame with her lover-boy up to five thousand feet because they wanted to fuck above the clouds on their honeymoon?'

'You did.'

'Correction.' He poked me in the chest. 'We both did. And any man who learns to fly at the knee of James J. Fatt can and will fly any damn plane that comes his way, including this big, fat, sweet whale of a flying boat.'

He turned on his heel, marched through the Parlor Compartment and past the Steward's Galley and Men's Dressing Room. At least they hadn't stripped this part yet. I opened the door to the bathroom, tricked out in stylish maroon and beige, complete with art deco lights, polished aluminum sinks and even – astonishingly -- a urinal.

'Stripping down the men's room too?' I said.

'No way. A man's gotta' pee.'

Fatt swept aside the dark blue curtain that hid a turquoise-painted spiral staircase that led up to the control deck.

'Age before beauty, kid.'

I followed him as he darted up the narrow steps. For a big man in his mid-fifties, he moved like a jungle cat.

'Wait until you see what we've got for digs topside.'

Pan Am had publicized the Boeing Clipper like no other plane they'd ever flown before: newsreel clips, feature stories, Atlantic and Pacific route maps, profiles of the 'Masters of Ocean Flying Boats' - including Captain Fatt - every one of them a heroic aviation pioneer making history with the largest commercial flying boat in the world.

True, I had my Ocean Master's ticket, and it had taken me thirteen years to climb the seniority ladder to get it. But I had been flying the pokey, strut-filled S-42s when the Boeing 314 was born, and knew from the start I wouldn't get near her because of my low seniority.

I even considered surrendering command to fly right hand seat instead. But I knew Pan Am wouldn't let me. We were stretched too thin already in the South American Division, trying to meet our mail, cargo, and passenger commitments. I was strapped into the left seat for good. So I stared at photos and watched newsreels, instead.

Until now.

Fatt reached up, opened the kidney-shaped floor hatch and darkness gave way to bright light. He climbed up onto the flight deck and disappeared. I joined him seconds later.

'Secure the hatch, will you, Mr. Carter?' His voice had shifted ever so slightly, but I recognized it as the one I heard when I was his first officer.

'Some setup, huh?' he said.

I'd spent hundreds of hours inside cramped cockpits with barely enough room to move. But the flight deck of the Boeing was the size of a living room, including - believe it or not - real carpeting with stitched and padded soundproofing on the walls and ceiling.

A spacious, six foot-long navigator's chart table ran along the port side of the fuselage. Just behind it, and ahead of the rear bulkhead, two seats and a desk were reserved for the Master of the Bridge, and any crew member he wanted to grill like a hamburger for screwing up something during the flight. The radio operator's station was on the starboard side, directly behind the co-pilot. Its multiple transmitters, receivers and DF tuner were a far cry from the bulky stuff I'd first used in Key West.

Directly behind the radio operator's station was the Flight Engineer's station. Its plethora of dials, buttons and switches, some familiar, some not, controlled and regulated the hundreds of intricate electric, hydraulic and internal combustion systems that kept the enormous plane in the air.

Next to the engineer's station an oval-shaped hatch that opened into an access tunnel built inside the vast interior of the Boeing's wing. If needed during flight, the engineer could climb inside and perform limited repairs on her thundering engines.

And then the bridge, where the master and first officer presided.

Separated by a curtain at night to preserve their night vision, its spacious windows provided excellent visibility, including, at the moment, a workman perched outside on the nose, bent over, and scraping at something.

I automatically scanned the instrument panel the way a man scans an approaching woman to see if she has all the proper equipment. In a pilot's case, it's artificial horizon, turn and bank indicator, and airspeed indicator. Many more instruments of course. But these are the basics, just like the legs, breasts and a bottom are on a girl. If they're in good shape, anything is possible.

'How's she handle?' I finally said, trying to keep the awe out of my voice, but failing.

'You'll find out soon enough.'

'I repeat, how -'

'-like a big fat dream, ever since they extended her keel a few feet. Before then it was one bounce after another, trying to get her big butt to stay on the water.'

'Heard stories about that.'

'Boeing gave us this song and dance about it being a 'piloting issue' when all along it was their piss-poor design - like the single tail they had to make triple before she'd answer to the rudder.'

'Bugs ironed out?'

He puffed his cigar, considering my question. 'For normal flight conditions, yes. For what we plan on doing, that won't be answered until we take off.'

'When's that?'

He brightened. 'So, you're on board?'

'Don't fancy flying for Lufthansa.'

'Oh, that.' He shrugged.

'Why'd Trippe sell out to the Nazis? This airline was his baby. I was there when it got born. So were you.'

116

'The good old days, right?'

'They damn well were. Just you and Trippe and Preister, and a punk kid like me running the radio while you hauled drunks and gamblers back and forth to Havana.'

'A lot has happened in eleven years.'

'Including a war we never fought.'

'Listen, kid. You're sober, right?'

'Been ever since.'

He put a heavy hand on my shoulder and squinted at me, as if trying to focus. 'I never got a chance to tell you how sorry I was about Estelle and the baby. You were too drunk that day to even know your own name.'

'I should never have showed up for work.'

'Too late for that now.'

'I did it twice, drunk as a skunk. What was I thinking?'

'You weren't thinking, kid, you were on autopilot. Hell, after what happened, everybody was, especially you.'

I vaguely remembered Dutchman Preister's cold face staring at me. Even more vaguely, Captain Fatt standing there in his hot, cramped office in Miami. By then Fatt was Chief Pilot, South American Division, and had responsibility for the performance of his flight crews, including a drunk who stood there weaving in front of both him and Preister for the second time in a week.

'You haff disappointed us, Captain Carter.' Preister said in that damned Dutch accent of his with its tortured grammar. 'You, above all, the rules and regulations should know, having been with us so many yearssss.'

Preister and Fatt merged into one amorphous blob in my vision. I blinked to separate them, but they remained a single, foreboding presence.

'Under the circumstances, I haff no utter choice but to-' I held up my hand. 'Save your breath, Preister.'

I fumbled with my Pan Am Master Pilot's wings. They slipped off my uniform chest with surprising ease, considering how hard they had been to win in the first place. I held them in my open palm and slurred, 'For dereliction of duty, despite repeated warnings, your services to this airline are hereby terminated, effective immediately. Please surrender your wings, captain. Aye, aye, Mr. Preister, sir!'

I tried to casually flip them onto his neat-as-a-pin desk, but because I was falling down drunk they fell onto the carpet instead. As I bent over to pick them up, I lost my balance and fell to my knees. Fatt tried to help me

117

up, but I angrily shook free. This was my tragedy and I wasn't letting anybody steal my thunder.

I vaguely remember walking out the door, pleased with my performance, as if sacrificing my career would somehow compensate the sacrifice of my wife and son. All three of us were dead now, except I had to go on living.

Fatt's voice brought me back to the present. 'You dropped something back in Miami.'

He opened his hand, and there, in all its gold and blue-enameled glory gleamed my Pan Am Master Pilot wings, surrounded by a crown of laurel leaves and three stars in a center bar denoting the airline's highest rank. I'll give Trippe this; the man knew how to stir your heart.

Fatt shifted his weight from one foot to the other as he waited to see what I would do.

'No thanks,' I said. 'Water under the bridge can't come back.'

A familiar voice said softly. 'That doesn't sound like the man I hired thirteen years ago. Back then you would have given Jesus a run for his money and walked on water with him.'

Juan Trippe stood in the open hatch leading to the wing tunnel, a smile on his face and a gleam in his cold, calculating eye.

You may have to fight when there is no hope of victory, but better to perish than live as slaves.
-Winston S. Churchill

Horrow long my former boss had been standing there I couldn't tell.

Juan Trippe always had an unnerving stillness about him. Even when he was doing the talking, it felt like he was listening, gauging his delivery, calculating its effect on the victim. Of average height, black hair slicked back, eyes so dark they glittered like coal, his face, no matter how close-shaven, had the bluish- tint of whiskers waiting to jump out the instant the razor passed by.

Impeccably dressed as always - even on this hot, dark Louisiana night - in a grey suit, white shirt with enormous French cuffs so starched and bright they hurt your eyes, and a light purple silk tie, Tripp could have been a well-heeled banker on a business call. Since he had been my employer, I automatically felt like standing at attention, but at the same time wanted to slam my fist into his complacent, half-smiling face for doing business with the same enemy that had murdered my family.

I chose the safest path I could think of.

'Mr. Trippe.'

'Captain Carter.'

'Mr. Carter, now, if you don't mind.'

He nodded but said nothing, just stared at me, and by God, I refused to look away. Over the years, Trippe had destroyed more business enemies than I had friends with that relentless stare of his. Not only could he see into your soul, he was fully capable of reaching in and squeezing the life out of you unless you went along with his proposed deal. All of it done with a half-smile, of course, and a dry handshake when he won. And he always won.

Not this time, I promised myself. This time I was looking into his soul instead. After what felt like a lifetime of silence, I said, 'You son-of-a-bitch. I gave my life to Pan Am and you sold it like a whore to Berlin.'

119

He tilted his head to one side and smiled slightly: a master of the deal. Well, damn it, so was I, at least in flying boats. I swept my hand around the flight deck. 'And whatever you've got going on here can't be worth a damn because you're behind it. Am I right? You're the mastermind?'

He spread his hands slightly. 'I'm a tiny cog in a very large machine, Mr. Carter.'

'Bullshit, Mr. Trippe. I knew you when, and you've never, ever been a small cog.'

'May I explain?'

'No, because once you start talking you'll never stop until the other guy surrenders.'

He laughed, which was about as rare as snow in the desert. 'May I say one thing only? I promise to stop after that.'

A mistake, but I nodded for him to go ahead.

'It's good to see you again, Sam. And believe me, I'm sorry about what happened to you and your family.'

Without thinking, I hit him as hard as I could and he went down like a sack of rocks.

'Jesus Christ!' Fatt said.

'Get up you bastard,' I shouted.

Trippe rolled over onto an elbow and rubbed his jaw. 'If it's all the same, I'll stay put.' He spit some blood, turned to Fatt. 'You offer him his wings back?'

'Yes, sir.'

He shook his head. 'I thought that might help.' He ran his tongue across his teeth as if to count them. 'Apparently not.'

I was halfway down the stairway before Trippe shouted, 'Sam Carter, God damn it, at least hear me out!'

Never in all the years I'd known Juan Trippe had his RPM ever risen above a low idle. Nothing could get his emotions on the table, and yet, here he was cursing at me and I started laughing.

'What's so damn funny?' he said.

'You.'

There stood the president of Pan American Airways mouth bloody, looking down at me from the flight deck, his eyes bugged out like a Goo-Goo doll.

'Mr. Trippe, I didn't think you believed in God, let alone have him take the trouble to damn me.'

We ended up sitting at the Master's station, Trippe in the captain's chair - of course - me in the other, while Fatt leaned against the Navigator's table, silent as a library lion. To Trippe's credit he let me lay it on the line without saying a word, about how I'd let my work get between me and my family, about how I should have called in sick that day and saved Estelle and Eddie, and how Pan Am was a ruthless company run by ruthless men who were in cahoots with even more ruthless Nazis, and how I was good God-damned if I was EVER going to get mixed up with him or his company again.

When I finished Trippe sat there, for once not staring into my soul.

Instead he regarded his calmly folded hands as if they held the answer. Finally he said, 'You've been through some damned hard times, Sam, and I'm sorry you feel that Pan Am was the cause of it.'

'I don't think so, I know so.'

He nodded. 'Yes, of course you do. Decisiveness is the key to a captain's character. You've always displayed that, even when you were completely wrong. Like now.'

I could feel my face getting red and my hands curled into fists. Trippe instinctively put his hand on my forearm. 'Before you sock me again, hear me out.'

I looked at him and then Fatt, who said, 'Maintain your heading, kid. At least long enough to listen what the man's got to say.'

I nodded, not because I wanted to, but because, I confess, I wanted if only for a little while to be in the presence of these two men again. As a young man they had acted like bookends to support my dreams of conquering the sky and in doing so, conquering my fears along the way.

Trippe held up a neatly manicured finger. 'One, I didn't sell out to the Nazis. Just made it look like I did.'

'Those swastikas on the clippers' tails look pretty real to me,' I said sharply.

He gave me that blank look of his; no eyebrows raised in surprise, no furrowed brow to show emotion, just peaceful and still.

'Two.' He held up a second finger. 'When the Neutrality Act was declared, I knew the only chance America had to survive the coming darkness was to fight back, instead.'

'Against atomic bombs? Good luck.'

'You're right, it would seem hopeless. Except...' he hesitated, looked at Fatt and then back at me. 'Except, what if they're bluffing?' He leaned forward and held me with those dark eyes of his. 'What if they have no bombs left? What if they're using the shadow of a sword that no longer exists to conquer the world?'

'You'll find out when they drop the next one.'

'Precisely my point!'

He slapped his hand on the table. 'And why haven't they? Their famous *Blitzkrieg* has driven the Russians back across the Ural Mountains. Stalin's in hiding, they're like ripe apples on a tree ready to drop, but Hitler hesitates.' He sat back and held up his third finger.

'Hitler hesitates. Why do you think that is?'

'No idea.'

'I do.' He slapped the table again. 'That's why the *Dixie Clipper* is here. That's why my other clippers are flying back and forth to Europe with...' he held up his fourth finger, 'Pan American crews, including the good Captain Fatt here.'

'But Lufthansa owns them, right?'

He smiled. 'In time of war, businessmen circle their wagons like the pioneers did against marauding Indians. Krupp Steel has a long working relationship with United Steel. Farber chemical with DuPont. Lufthansa with Pan Am. We don't want to jeopardize those relationships when peace returns.'

'The good old boys club, right?'

'If you insist, yes. But in Pan Am's case, Klaus Heinemann of Lufthansa and I have an agreement; he gets the Boeing clippers, but we crew them. His pilots don't know the first thing about mastering the ocean in flying boats the way our crews do.'

'So, you have a deal with Lufthansa...'

'And because of it, we now have a way to further our plan of extricating a certain Very Important Person from Lisbon, Portugal.'

'Our first landfall on the southern Atlantic route.'

'Correct, captain, and it's there that our man will be waiting for us, forty-eight hours from now. And if we get him out successfully, he will help us change the course of history'

'One man?'

'Caesar did. So did Lincoln.'

'They were politicians. What's he?'

'A nuclear physicist.'

122

A long pause. Trippe turned to Fatt and said mildly, 'I just realized I've made a terrible mistake.'

'What's that, sir?'

'I've revealed top secret information to an outsider. What ARE we to do?'

He puffed meditatively on his cigar. 'We sure as hell can't let the good captain leave Couba Island now.'

'C'mon, you two…' I warned.

'Orlando Diaz too,' Fatt added.

Trippe said, 'We'll need to impound Captain Carter's plane.'

'Like hell you will!'

I turned to go, but was stopped by the rumble of boots pounding up the crew ladder. Seconds later, two armed men the size of Orlando burst onto the flight deck, weapons in hand, trained on me. Fatt smiled like the Cheshire cat and waved them a casual salute.

'Boys, please be so kind as to escort Captain Carter to the briefing room.'

You can argue with a Thompson submachine gun all you want, but you're never going to win. I spared myself the effort and followed Patton's goons out of the *Dixie Clipper* and onto the dock. Nobody paid us the slightest attention as we passed, as if men with weapons at the ready were the most common thing around. And the case of Couba Island, true.

Fatt caught up with me and we marched together in silence past barracks, a mess hall and then approached a two-story building with soldiers going in and out of it like a stream of ants.

'What are you people doing around here?' I said.

Fatt shook his head. 'Sorry. Need-to-know rules apply.'

'Well, I damn well need to know if I'm going to help you.' He chuckled. 'Joining the cause are you?'

I pointed to the two soldiers flanking me. 'What choice do I have?'

'Good point.'

'What Trippe said about the clippers and Lufthansa… he's on the level??'

'A carpenter could use him and the line would be true.'

'Everybody thinks he sold out.'

'Water off a duck's back. Besides, ever known him to get the short end of a business deal?'

'Grabbing a nuclear physicist doesn't sound like a business deal to me.'

'That's because you're not Juan Trippe. Even taking a crap is business to him.'

I laughed at this, but then remembered how my fist felt as it smacked against his face. 'I really popped him one.'

'Had your reasons. Just picked the wrong target. Now you're going to get the right one and send him to the moon.'

'The scientist?'

'Hell no, that's just part one of our little story.'

The guards hurried up the wooden steps. Two more soldiers stood at attention, barring our path. Fatt reached inside his uniform jacket and pulled out a laminated card and flashed it at them.

'Evening, boys. He's with me. Nice night, ain't it?'

They let us pass into a long, dimly-lit hallway. Our armed escort vanished into thin air, mission accomplished.

I said, 'You must have had your pick of the cream of the crop to fly this mission. Why me? '

'Because you're the best pilot Pan Am's got, next to me, remember?'

'But I don't work for you guys anymore, remember?'

'Figure of speech, kid. What's more important, you've got a chip on your shoulder that's going to keep you going when everybody else bails out, gets cold feet or runs screaming because they can't stand it anymore. You'll be there, kid, to even the score for Estelle and Baby Eddie.'

We climbed the stairs to the second floor and halfway down the hallway to another set of doors, guarded by two grim-looking soldiers. Fatt waved his ID and the doors swung open to a darkened room that had what looked like an illegal poker game going on. About fifteen people stood at a large round table lit by a single overhead light.

Fatt announced loudly for all to hear, 'The Prodigal Son returneth. At gunpoint, but hey, who cares, right?'

The gathered group turned as one to regard us as we entered, including Ava, Ziggy, General Patton and, to my stunned surprise, a determined-looking Orlando. Patton greeted us with a terse nod.

Fatt said, 'Captain Carter has kindly agreed to be our first officer, welcome aboard, captain.'

All heads swiveled to me, and to my surprise I nodded in agreement. Silence was the better part of valor right about now. Besides, I needed all my energy to keep from falling into the chasm I felt opening up beneath my feet, caused by voices shouting at me somewhere in the deep recesses of my mind. One was saying, 'Caution, danger ahead.' But the other one bellowed.

'Don't get mad, get even.'

I balanced myself between the two and listened to Fatt as he introduced me to the strangers in the group, including a group of men who I thought at first were a Pan Am flight crew, but upon closer inspection of their dark blue uniforms, gold stripes on their sleeves and distinctive gold wings, I realized they were U.S. Navy pilots.

Fatt must have seen the confusion on my face and said, 'Like you said, I had the cream of the crop to pick from. I figured navy guys can fly rings around us civilian fellas, can't you, boys?'

They smiled good-naturedly, but you could see they believed every word of it.

'Why not use a Pan Am crew?' I said.

Patton took over and snapped, 'Because this is a military mission, that's why.'

'Wearing navy uniforms?'

'Negative. You'll be wearing in Pan Am blue. And here's where you're heading.'

The general slapped his swagger stick on a large Mercator map spread out on the table and traced its tip along a red line as it left Baltimore and dropped two thousand miles southeast to a tiny dot representing the Portuguese island in the Azores named Horta, Pan Am's standard refueling stop. From there the line angled upwards northeast to Lisbon, Portugal. From there it went northwest via land-based planes to Marseilles, France. The three red lines on the map represented what used to be Pan Am's southern Atlantic route and now was Lufthansa's. A simple, clear route, but like all maps, not the full truth.

'We're flying the *Dixie Clipper*?' I said.

'Negative,' Patton said, 'She stays put for now. You'll be flying the *Yankee Clipper*. He swung his swagger stick to Fatt, who stepped closer to the map and said, 'Okay, boys and girls listen up. Here's what's going to happen.'

Ava's face was a study in complete absorption. She must have sensed my stare because she looked up, gave me a sly wink and a tiny smile.

Fatt borrowed Patton's swagger stick and used it as a pointer. 'Thanks to Adolf and company blowing Manhattan to smithereens, Pan Am's New York terminal is out of the picture. Instead, Lufthansa's using our Baltimore one for their ops and maintenance. The Yankee Clipper's there in turnaround at the moment, so we've got twenty-four hours...'

He checked his watch.

'...and twenty-two minutes before we lift off for Lisbon. We'll head out of Couba at dawn, be in Baltimore in time for the systems test flight, then board passengers and be off the water right on schedule.'

Patton said, 'Do you have the manifest yet?'

'Mr. Trippe will have it before we leave.'

'We need their names.'

'You'll have them, sir.'

I said, 'What's this guy's name?'

'*Herr Professor Doktor* Gunter Friedman.'

Fatt chuckled. 'Jerries sure love their titles.'

'Traveling alone?' I said.

Patton said, 'Married to his work. Makes it easier for us. Families tend to make things messy.' He glanced at me, then rolled onward like one of his tanks. 'Ava, you set with your stuff?'

'Yes, sir.'

She saw my look of surprise and said, 'Ziggy and I are the secret weapon, aren't we, partner?'

Her agent managed a weak smile and nodded, clearly wishing to be somewhere else instead of a smoke-filled room with soldiers and airmen hunkered over a map, planning a dangerous mission.

Ava continued. 'Thanks to Wally Westmore's makeup team, Ziggy and I are going to disguise the professor so that not even his mother would recognize him.'

She plopped a small case on the table and opened it. Bottles, brushes, pancake makeup, fake eyebrows, moustaches, beards, latex noses, and a host of unrecognizable objects filled every inch. She snapped it shut. 'That's our job.'

I said, 'What's your cover story?'

She swept her hand across her forehead in a theatrical, swooning gesture. 'I've just been offered the lead in Republic Picture's Lisbon Liaison. Haven't you heard the news?'

'No.'

'That's because Ziggy and I made it up.'

Ziggy raised his hand like a kid in a classroom, 'I'm there to seal the deal with the producers, providing Miss James agrees to the contract terms, of course.'

'Which I won't, of course' she said. 'And in flurry of anger and outrage, I'll walk out on the deal and leave on the clipper for America.'

'Along with the professor,' Ziggy said.

'Nice,' I said. 'Where's he staying?'

'The Aviz hotel. He and his scientist friends are having a conference there.'

I turned to Fatt. 'Pan Am still uses that place for crew overnights?'

Fatt smiled. 'Every last one of us, including Diaz here.'

'Doing what?'

Orlando started to answer but Trippe cut him off as he emerged from the shadows. 'Mr. Diaz will be our Chief of Engine Services, Atlantic Division on a maintenance inspection tour of our bases. Which came as no surprise to Mr. Diaz, considering he was doing essentially the same thing for our South American Division, before leaving us for opportunities...' he hesitated a beat. '...elsewhere.'

Orlando beamed, 'Don't worry, Sam, I'm still with Carter Aviation. This is just my cover story, right, Mr. Trippe?'

'Correct.'

'A nice one, too. Atlantic Division is a sweet place to be.'

Trippe raised a warning finger. 'Don't let Mr. Mulroney find out. He's the real Chief of Engine Services there.'

'From your mouth to God's ear, sir.'

I said to Orlando, 'You bought into all this?'

His smile vanished. 'The world's turned upside down. I'm doing my part to get it right side up again.'

I turned to Patton. 'How's this Kraut professor going to change the course of history?'

'Get him over here and you'll find out.'

'Why can't you tell me now?'

His patience was growing thin, but to his credit he said calmly, 'You've seen this base, you've seen how many people are involved in this operation. I can guarantee you only a handful know the score completely. I'm one of them.'

'And I'm not.'

127

'Affirmative. The walls have ears, captain. The more we limit knowledge, the better chance we've got of pulling this thing off.'

'And if we don't?'

In the ensuing silence, a night creature let out a shriek. Sounded like it was dying, or doing the killing.

'Ever read Machiavelli?' Patton said finally.

'No.'

'Fourteenth century fellow. Wrote a hell of book called *The Prince*. Filled with all sorts of good advice on how to rule a country without mercy and get away with it.'

'Hitler read it, I'm sure.'

'Probably did, the son of a bitch. But my point is this: Machiavelli warns his boss, a di Medici prince, never EVER let an outside nation inside his borders. Because no matter how peaceful they are when they first walk in, they'll eventually be up to no good.'

He tapped the map where Washington D.C. used to be.

'All those so-called Nazi 'compliance officers' they've got planted in our factories and military bases? It's only a matter of time before they get assistants, and more assistants, until we've got platoons of the bastards sticking their fingers into every pie America ever baked or will bake. All the time waving the atomic bomb over our heads, all the time warning us that we'd better toe the line and clean up our act and get rid of our Jews and Negroes and homosexuals and anybody else in our mixing pot that doesn't fit into their tight little Aryan skillet.'

'We're bugs in a bottle.'

'You got it.'

'The president knows about all this, right?'

'She does, but we've got an election in two months. She's running a distant third to the other two bastards who want that office. Who the hell are they, Juan?'

Trippe said. 'Senator Crawford from Pennsylvania.'

'Pacifist jerk.'

'And William Stanford from Nevada.'

'One of your businessman pals, right?'

Trippe shook his head. 'Not one of mine. But his many companies stand to benefit tremendously if we maintain our neutrality.'

'Got enough money to win the election?'

'He does. And as president, he'll guarantee we'll maintain the status quo.'

Patton's laugh came out as a snort. 'Status quo, my ass. I'm telling you, unless we turn things around, there's not going to be a United States five years from now. We'll be a world of little Machiavellian city-states, with governors banding together with some, warring against others, all because we let the Nazi bastards slip inside our doors when we weren't looking.'

'They didn't slip inside,' I said. 'They broke in with atomic bombs.'

'Figure of speech.'

He aimed his swagger stick at me. 'You get *Herr* Professor Doktor Gunter Freidman's sorry ass back here to Couba Island and I personally guarantee you the Sons of Liberty will turn this world right side up again.'

To be honest, I don't know what made me decide to stay instead of heading home to Key West where Abby and Rosie were waiting. Maybe what General Patton said about the states descending into warring principalities, or my surprise at Juan Trippe turning out to be a patriot instead of a traitor.

All I remember is that the moment I said 'yes,' the cold knot of bitterness and self-reproach I'd been carrying around in my gut since December 8, 1941, slowly began to loosen. Only a little, mind you, but when a prisoner feels the slightest weakness in his chains he feels the first stirrings of hope. I decided I go forward into the unknown in hopes those chains would loosen even more.

At dawn the following day, an ancient Ford Tri-motor transport, its engines turning over, sat on the makeshift runway the soldiers had carved out of the marsh.

As I started to board with the group, Trippe held me back for a moment.

'Glad you're with us,' he said simply.

'Abby's all I've got left. If something should happen to me...' I trailed off and then added, 'You'll make sure my message gets to Rosie?'

'I promise.'

'Just got my company up and running, and now I'm running away.'

'Your message said you were on a special charter.'

'Some charter.'

Tripped smiled. 'Look, I know a thing or two about the airline business. Allow me to take care of the details of Carter Aviation in your absence. I promise it will survive.'

'You won't absorb it?'

He laughed. 'That sorry little S-38 piece of shit?'

'You and Lindy loved it.'

'That was in the beginning.'

'Back when Pan Am took risks, you mean?'

He nodded soberly. 'Preister over-trained our crews, made them too obedient, like cattle, which is fine in peacetime, but in wartime we need bulls.'

'I'm a pretty damn skinny bull.'

It's not how big you are it's how sharp your horns are. You and Captain Fatt were always my biggest risk takers.'

'This is a hell of a risk, snatching a guy from beneath Hitler's funny little moustache.'

'It's only the beginning. There's much more to this than meets the eye. Here, you'll be needing these.'

He held out my Pan Am wings. I stiffened. Too many bad memories.

'I told you I'm my own man now.'

'But you'll be wearing a Pan American Airways uniform.'

'So will the Navy guys.'

'But they haven't earned these. You did.'

I took the wings. 'Consider it a loan.'

Tripped nodded.

'Then it's back to Abby and Key West and my charter jobs.'

'Really?' He looked at me for a long moment. 'What kind of world do you want your daughter to live in?'

'Not the one she's living in now, that's for sure.'

'Then stick around and help us change it for the better.'

The vast size of the Lufthansa's Baltimore maintenance hangar took my breath away. Two immense Boeing Clippers rested on their beaching cradles inside a cavernous structure the size of two football fields. Parked nose to nose, surrounded by three-story high metal scaffolding that moved on wheels, maintenance workers swarmed over the planes, each performing his appointed task.

One team serviced the engines and propellers while another clustered around the nose section cutting out what looked to be a bent stringer. Still another team, unseen, was busy cleaning the inside of the plane from tip to tail, vacuuming carpets, spot-cleaning upholstered seats, making the metal-clad flying hotel beautiful once again.

Pan Am's maintenance hangar in New York was still glowing with atomic radiation and unfit for humans, so Lufthansa had placed their Baltimore base on a 24-hour-a-day schedule to accommodate the high volume of passenger traffic shuttling back and forth across the Atlantic.

Most of the eastbound loads were high level German compliance officers heading home, while westbound wealthy European refugees managed to beg, borrow, steal or bribe German officials to let them escape Hitler's ever-widening grip of National Socialism on France, Czechoslovakia, Poland, the Netherlands and all points east.

The maintenance teams had just twenty-four hours to fully service a Boeing, get it out of the hangar and back into the air to make room for the next one to come trundling up out of the water on its beaching gear to repeat the process all over again.

Trippe had invested millions of dollars to create this stunning display of coordinated activity under one enormous roof with one thought in mind: maximize profits. A pity those profits were now flowing into Germany's bank account, instead.

When we first arrived in Baltimore, Ava, Ziggy and the Navy guys went directly to the crew hotel, while I followed Fatt and Orlando into the hangar, where, of all people, Chief of Engines, Atlantic, Jake Mulroney spotted us the instant we arrived. Fatt waved at him nervously and then headed for the men's room, leaving us to shake hands, clap each other on the back, renew our friendship and try to preserve our cover story.

If they ever have a St. Patrick's Day parade in New York again, Mulroney should lead it. By the grace of God he'd been in Baltimore the night the Nazis dropped the bomb on Manhattan. His friends and co-workers at the Pan Am hangers at LaGuardia field never knew what hit them.

But before we had a chance to start our lies about why we were here, a tall, spectral-like ghost of a man approached. His spotless white lab coat stood out in stark contrast to Mulroney's oil-stained coveralls.

'Cheese it,' Mulroney whispered. 'Hitler's brother.'

'*Herr* Mulroney,' the man said when he arrived. 'Who are these people?'

I stuck out my hand. 'Captain Carter, South American division, just got re-assigned.'

He took it. Like shaking hands with death.

'Brenner, Chief Shop Engineer, Lufthansa.'

'So you're the big boss around here.'

He nodded.

Orlando stuck out his hand. 'Orlando Diaz, Chief of Engines, South American Division. Just passing through.'

The man hesitated and Orlando grinned. 'I know what you're thinking. What's a colored boy like me tinkering around with the white man's engines, right?'

Brenner said nothing but his disapproving mouth said it all.

Orlando rolled onward. 'Engines don't care whether the hands that feed them oil or change their sparkplugs are black or white. All they want to do is run sweet as honey. Too bad folks like you don't feel the same way.'

Herr Brenner had nothing to say. He turned to me, as if Orlando didn't exist. 'You are crew?'

I turned on my happy-boy headlights. 'First officer on tomorrow's flight. Can't wait. Been flying S-42's up until now. Big Boeings, here I come.'

'I see. Well, we must make certain that your aircraft is ready for you in time. Correct, Mr. Mulroney?'

'Yes, sir!'

Herr Brenner turned on his heel and marched off like an SS trooper. We kept our faces blank until he disappeared into the scaffolding maze. Mulroney risked a smile, and then said softly, 'What in blue blazes are you two fellows really doing here? The truth, damn it. I heard you were running a charter outfit down in Key West.'

'Change of plans. Pan Am hired us back.'

'For certain?'

'Would I lie to you, Jake Mulroney?'

'You have done so in the past, Captain Carter, and by God I fully expect you to do so in the future.'

Nothing had changed with Jake since I first met him ten years ago, except he had more gray hairs. He had been Orlando's boss when they were stationed in Buenos Aires. On my turn-around days, we'd go out drinking together, where, if I didn't watch myself I'd end up under the table while Jake stayed sober as a judge and sang Gaelic songs.

I continued. 'All I can say for the record is that I'll be in the right seat tomorrow morning at eight o'clock sharp when the *Yankee Clipper* takes off for Lisbon.'

'I'm flying non-revenue,' Orlando added.

'As what?'

'Chief of Engines, Atlantic Division.'

'That's my job, damn it!'

Orlando lowered his voice. 'Not denying it. But unless you want to work for *Herr* Brenner and Lufthansa the rest of your born days, you'd best keep your wings folded and your beak shut.'

His eyes narrowed. 'What are two you up to? I can smell it.'

'Let it rest, brother.'

A long pause while he eyed us both. Then, 'Aye.' He lifted his grease-stained wrench. 'But if you need any help, say the word and Mulroney's monkeys will come running.'

I said, 'That day will come, but tomorrow comes first.'

Sometime around five, just as the sky began lightening with the promise of another hot August day, the Pan Am beaching crew hitched up their two caterpillar tractors to cables attached to the, 15-ton Kenworth beaching dolly upon which rested the refurbished and refreshed *Yankee Clipper*, looking like a bird perched on a fencepost. Not having landing gear, the clippers relied upon these wheeled devices to get them from A to B when out of the water.

The tractors slowly took up the slack, rolled forward and pivoted her around until her nose peeked out of the hangar. Perched precariously, she resembled an ungainly, beached whale with wings. Ava and the rest of the crew were still back at the hotel sound asleep, but I had risen early because I wanted to witness the transformation of this silver whale into a graceful swan and to think about the adventure to come.

Dressed in white coveralls, the crew bustled here and there, waving red flags that signaled the cat drivers when to go forward and when to stop. The men aligned the beaching dolly's wheels with the steel guide rails built into the concrete taxiway and locked them in place. The rails ran four hundred feet, arrow straight to the beaching ramp, and then gently sloped down and into the water.

Double plumes of black diesel smoke shot out of the cat's exhaust stacks as they took up the strain. Hard to believe that this land-bound aircraft would be soon be cruising at one hundred-forty miles-an-hour.

When the clipper reached the top of the ramp, the two front-end tractors pulled her forward to where the dolly began its downward slope. They swung clear, while the two rear tractors took up the slack on the cables to prevent her from rolling down the ramp. You could tell from the way her graceful nose leaned forward, that that was exactly what she wanted to do. Slowly, maybe a foot-a-second, the cats advanced, allowing the dolly to bear its impatient burden to the sea.

By now the sun had just opened its eye over Baltimore Harbor. The sea smells returned as if by magic and the surrounding buildings emerged from the misty night and back into hard focus. The immense maintenance hangar no longer carried the graceful words across its arched entrance proclaiming, PAN AMERICAN AIRWAYS. Instead, the blunt block letters of LUFTHANSA sat there like an uninvited guest that refuses to go home.

As the *Yankee Clipper's* nose touched the water I swear I saw her quiver with excitement. Foot by foot she settled deeper and deeper into her watery home until the float-equipped beaching dolly bobbed gently up and down. At that point, the dolly's internal flotation cells slowly deflated and it sank to the bottom to be retrieved later. The beautiful Boeing seaplane was officially free from land, but still on the water. Even so, she looked happier here than in the hangar.

A bleary-eyed Mulroney joined me on the patch of grass where I stood clear of the beaching crew but with a perfect view of the proceedings.

'Don't you ever go home?' I said.

'T'is my home, lad. For now at least. Those Lufthansa fellows are learning the ropes faster than I ever could.'

'And then what?'

He sighed and stretched. Faint sounds came from his shoulders as weary ligaments and sinews released their grip. 'Start looking for work, I suppose. Got any openings with that big charter fleet of your down in Key West?'

'I told you I'm flying with Pan Am now.'

'In a pig's foot.' He quickly held up his hand to ward off my response. 'Don't worry, I won't pursue my line of questioning, even though I could weasel it out of you in a jiffy. You never were good at keeping secrets, Sam Carter. Especially the big one you're trying to hide inside.'

We both watched in silence as the PanAir launch took over the job from the beaching crew and slowly towed the clipper over to the boarding dock where, in less than an hour, we would take her up for a shakedown flight before passenger boarding began at ten.

Mulroney cleared his throat. 'I fought in the Great War, y'know.'

'I know.'

'A miserable foot soldier I was, but I knew which end of the rifle to hold.' Another long pause. I knew what was coming but kept my mouth shut.

'Still do.' His bloodshot eyes were boring into me like a drill.

'Don't doubt it.'

'Militia's forming here and there. Every state it seems. Here in Maryland, Virginia. That true in Florida too?'

'Heard talk of it, yes.'

Mulroney thumped his narrow chest. 'We're not going to take this like a bunch of baby birds shivering in a nest, no sir. Mark my words, we are eagles about to fly, and I'm going to be one of them.'

'Me too.' I said without thinking.

He smacked his fists together and cackled, 'I knew it! You and Orlando both?'

I surrendered.

'Chief of engines, Atlantic, my flat foot. Wait until I get my hands on his sorry black hide.'

'Hope you're still good at keeping secrets. Especially this one.'

'With the best of them, providing...'

'Providing?'

'That one of these days I get to fly with you fellas.'

'Thought you were afraid of heights like Orlando.'

'Not if I've got a Messerschmitt in my crosshairs.'

The rising sun flashed off the *Yankee Clipper's* silver wings as she drifted at rest at the boarding dock. A set of slender lines held her fast. But not for long.

Our crew of ten boarded the clipper with no fanfare, no fuss, and no fancy uniforms. That would come three hours later when the passengers arrived. The 'Post Turn-around Check Flight' was Pan Am standard operating procedure. Much the same way you stretch and bend and touch your toes after a good night's sleep, that's what we were about to do from the tip of her nose to the tip of her tail, testing each flight system to be sure that whatever repairs that needed to be made had been made, whatever upgrades had got upgraded, that crew complaints, from master to engineer, to navigator to steward, had been satisfactorily resolved.

I for one had no complaints. The thrill of walking down the long wooden ramp, single file, Fatt leading the parade, with me and Orlando and the others trailing behind in a Vatican-like procession, made my missed hours of sleep fade away.

My footfalls sounded like a bass drum when I walked out onto her stubby sea wing. Instead of drag-producing wingtip floats, Boeing had borrowed the 'sea wing' concept from the Dornier flying boats and designed a broad, fuel filled, airfoil-shaped structure that not only allowed the plane to make water turns without tipping, but also provided additional lift, not to mention serving as a convenient boarding platform for passengers and crew.

I was careful not to skip like a boy, although I sure felt like it. Three days ago I was on my knees digging for buried treasure in the Dry Tortugas. Today I was the first officer getting ready to fly the biggest flying boat in the world.

For those of you who are pilots, right about now your eyebrows are rising, wondering if all this is on the level. Well, don't forget, I was a fully-rated Master of Flying Boats, I could handle four engines, a cranky crew, crappy weather, and still arrive on time with fuel to spare. Yes, I know what you're saying;

'That was the S-42, not the Boeing 314.'

I agree. And your question is valid: how could I confidently climb up the spiral staircase to the flight deck of an aircraft twice the size of anything I'd ever been in before, with half-again more horsepower and range and performance issues I hadn't a clue about, and instead of shaking in my boots I was whistling softly and smiling to myself?

Two words: Captain Fatt.

He wanted me in the right hand seat, and that was good enough for me. If it had been anyone else, trust me, I would have had my nose buried in every Boeing 314 manual ever printed. And believe me, there are hundreds of them. That said, and Fatt's confidence aside, I confess I did spend every second I had on the flight from Couba Island up to Baltimore thumbing through manuals that laid out the performance envelopes, power curves, handling characteristics, and so forth, that test pilots had compiled and that Pan Am captains had added to once they went into service. I might be dumb but I wasn't stupid, and I wasn't alone.

While Orlando and I were busy being thrown in jail by the Nazis down in D.C., the Navy crew was spending a solid week of crew training, So…. in the highly unlikely event I turned out to be a blithering idiot during the check flight, one of them could take over for me. But that wasn't going to happen. Not on my watch.

We settled in to our respective stations on the bridge: Fatt to my left in the red leather-cushioned pilot's seat, or 'Watch Officer's Station,' as Pan Am's Preister declared it to be in the manuals, while I sank happily into my co-pilot's seat to his right.

'This thing's like a sofa,' I said.

'The Dutchman thought of everything,' Fatt said, 'Including our sorry asses.'

Rightfully so. With overseas legs lasting eight and ten hours at a clip, our Pan Am asses could become sorry indeed. Preister might be a pain in the same place, but he understood ours all too well.

The smell of ozone joined the symphony of other smells on the bridge; leather, hydraulic fluid, warm oil, and the ever present smell of the ocean. The Naval officer acting as our radio operator, a skinny lieutenant who looked eighteen, sat hunched over his equipment at his station directly behind me. The crew staircase hatch between my seat and his led to the passenger compartment below.

The navigator, a somber, brooding lieutenant, swung the hatch closed and in doing so, gave us more square footage in a space that still amazed me as being big as a house.

'Hatch secure,' he said.

'Aye,' Fatt answered and turned to me. 'Let's find out if they glued her wings on tight.'

'Nothing better to do, I guess.'

'Oh, I could think of a few things. One of them is golf, the other a blonde met in New Orleans.' He sighed and keyed his microphone.

'Ready to cast off.'

The metallic-sounding intercom voice of our second officer, positioned forward in the nose said, 'Standing by, sir.' Then to me, 'Battery switch on.'

'Battery switch on.'

And just like that, we went from two men shooting the breeze to two serious cogs smoothly turning against each other in a vastly complicated machine designed to lift off from the water and fly across the ocean.

'Left generator.'

I flipped the proper switch. 'Set to forward battery.'

'Right generator.'

'Set to aft battery.'

'Trim tabs.'

'Neutral.'

'Altimeter set.'

'Set.'

'Prop pitch.'

A quick adjustment. 'Full increase.'

And so the ritualistic pre-flight checklist continued as we moved inexorably through the engine start procedure. As we did so, Lieutenant Mason, our flight engineer, a slight, sandy-haired man with ruddy cheeks, echoed us as he sat at his station next to the radio operator's.

Like the organist at Radio City Music Hall, Mason worked a vast array of instruments and levers in front of him that duplicated engine throttles, cowl flap controls, mixture levers, while all the time monitoring a maze of dials before him. Orlando sat next to him, watching his every move the way a lion watches an antelope, learning the ins and outs of the plane as fast as he could, just like me.

'Mixture,' Fatt said.

I confirmed the four levers. 'Full rich.'

'Master ignition.'

'On.'

'Turn number one.'

I reached for the engine start controls on the overhead panel between us, and mashed the start button marked '1.'

'Spinning one.'

The outermost left engine whined into life as the starter motor began turning its massive, fourteen-foot Hamilton Standard propeller. The pitch of the blades caught the morning sunlight and flashed over and over again, faster and faster as the cylinders began firing, one, two, then five, then twelve, but I kept my finger on the start button as more and more cylinders coughed and belched blue exhaust and chattered and stuttered until suddenly the clattering smoothed to a steady powerful roar as all of them joined in.

I released the button and checked the RPM to make sure it didn't exceed one thousand until the oil temperature gauges reached one hundred-four degrees, or so the checklist stated as I stared at its laminated surface and thought, if only we had checklists for life. I would make things a lot easier. But we don't. We just fly by the seat of our pants.

'Mason, watch your cylinder head temps,' Fatt said over the intercom to the flight engineer. 'These Wrights can run away from you fast.'

'Got my eye on them, skipper.'

'That's a good lad, and don't let Reverend Diaz touch any buttons. He might break something.'

'Hands in my lap, captain,' Orlando rumbled.

'Okay, let's get the rest of these sorry critters spinning.'

In quick succession engines four, two and three whined, groaned and then burst into smoky life. In less than a minute, four blurring discs spun the sunlight into silver buttons.

'Elevator trim five degrees positive,' Fatt said.

I cranked the small ridged wheel on the throttle quadrant beside me until the elevator trim tabs had five degrees up-angle. This was critical to getting our silver whale into the air because trim tabs added even more pitch angle to the aircraft's elevators as she sped through the water, which in turn increased the lift forces acting on the wing, and before you knew it, forty-two tons of airplane would be flying sweet as honey.

But at present we were just slowly taxiing from the boarding ramp out into the harbor to our takeoff lane. The Panair launch paced alongside usual, two men standing at the open stern, their binoculars trained on every inch of the clipper, making a visual check.

Soon a raspy voice came over the headphones; 'Launch reports looking good from here, captain. You're cleared for your check flight.'

'Roger.' He turned to me. 'Pray, Captain Carter, would you please let the Nazi assholes know we're ready for takeoff.'

I smiled and keyed the radio. 'Baltimore Harbor tower, Lufthansa zero-five requests permission for take-off.'

'Standby one,' the nearly accent-free voice said. 'Compliance traffic your area.'

Maybe a show of force, or just showing off, but in any event, four Me-109 fighters flashed past us at about two hundred feet in perfect wingtip-to-wingtip formation. As they reached the southern end of the bay the gleaming-white fighters split off, two each, and rose in a graceful climbing turn that ended with them re-joining formation at a thousand feet to continue their patrol of American airspace, guns at the ready.

Fatt watched the aerial performance without saying a word. Then he turned to me. 'Who would have thought we'd live to see the day.'

The radio crackled. 'Lufthansa zero-five, you are cleared for immediate take off, sea lane two. Wind zero-five-zero at fifteen, gusting to twenty. Observe altitude restrictions.'

Fatt rolled his shoulders, pulled out a cigar and lit it. 'Get us the hell out of here, kid, before I start goose-stepping and shouting '*Sieg heil.*'

'Not a chance. I'm still learning my way around this fat lady.'

'No time like the present.' Fatt lit his cigar, wiggled the control wheel and leaned back. 'You have the aircraft, captain. Full speed ahead.'

I took a deep breath and grabbed the control yoke.

'Your funeral,' I said.

'Always was, always will be,' Fatt said casually. 'Get her off at seventy knots, nose level until one-ten, then up we go to the heavens above, right, Reverend?'

'Affirmative and amen,' Orlando said.

I slowly advanced the throttles to full takeoff power and the engines answered with a confident roar. With only a partial fuel load and an empty plane we accelerated quickly across the open bay. Unlike a ground plane where its landing gear stays in firm contact with the earth until you lift off, a seaplane responds more like a sailing ship until you get some decent airspeed going.

Within seconds I could feel the effect of the reported fifteen-knot crosswind shoving against the immense slab-sided fuselage the same way it would against a ship, trying to make it weathercock. I instinctively applied more power to my left engines, turned the control wheel to the right and added a touch of right rudder, and the nose obediently swung back on course.

'Doing great, kid. Thirty on the dial.'

As the airspeed indicator needle touched the thirty-five knot mark, I called for ten degrees flaps. Fatt hit the toggle switch and her nose began rising as the additional wing area from the extending flaps made the Boeing lighter on her feet. Even though we sat high above the water, I could still hear the thrumming slap of her hull hitting the small wavelets. 40…45….the airspeed indicator needle continued climbing and the controls stiffened as the wind moved faster and faster across her ailerons and elevators. The rudder pedals tightened up as the Boeing awakened more and more to the idea that she was about to fly.

I relaxed back pressure on the wheel as I felt her lift up 'onto the step;' that carefully engineered spot midway along the fuselage where our seaplane's gracefully curving hull abruptly 'stepped up' up eighteen inches and then continued toward the tail. Without that design feature to break the glue-like, surface tension of the water, we'd be here until doomsday.

'All clear forward,' Fatt called out.

In a normal takeoff with Fatt at the wheel, the co-pilot's job was to keep a sharp lookout for potential water hazards. But for reasons known only to him, he had thrown me into the pool with every expectation that I knew how to swim. Time to show him - and myself and the crew - that I did.

'Here comes seventy,' Fatt crooned.

'Roger.'

I applied smooth back pressure to the wheel, but instead of feeling her leap into the air like most airplanes do at that magical instant, the Yankee Clipper rose like queen from her throne; slowly, elegantly, inexorably. And as she did I felt it square in my butt. Not too poetic, I know, but of all the instruments on the panel in front of me and the flight engineer, the best instrument a pilot can rely upon to tell him he's flying is the seat of his pants. Your rear-end never lets you down and it didn't then as the glittering waters of Baltimore Harbor fell away and I aimed her nose for the sky.

'Positive rate of climb,' Fatt intoned as the airspeed reached one hundred-ten knots. I throttled back to twenty-one hundred RPM and the thundering engines backed off from their frantic roar to a more reasonable rumble. Manipulating the four-levered throttle took a light touch, much in the same way a stagecoach driver holds the reins that lead to a team of galloping horses. But in my case, the 'reins' led to six thousand of them.

At five-hundred feet Fatt slowly raised the flaps while I re-trimmed for a steady climb to our operating altitude of two thousand feet. Once there I retarded the throttles to cruise setting, eased the prop pitch from full increase and leaned the fuel mixture.

'How we looking, gents?' Fatt said over the intercom.

One by one the various bridge stations reported in. Then he rang up the steward station located directly below us on the lower deck. 'How's the silverware, Nawrocki?'

The flight steward's voice crackled with mock anger. 'Who's flying this kite anyhow? A bunch of knives and forks fell into my pocket.'

'Put them back or else,' Fatt growled. 'It's company property.'

'Aye, aye, captain, sir.'

'And hurry the hell up with our coffee, I'm about to fall asleep.'

'Coming right up, oh mighty Lord and Master of the Boat.'

Fatt smiled and swung his bulk around in his seat and shouted, 'How we doing, boys?'

Thumbs up, 'OK' signs all around, and Fatt beamed. 'That's what I like; a well-oiled team doing what God put them on this good earth to do.'

For the next half hour we went through a meticulous systems checklist that, when finished, convinced us that the aircraft was ready to accept paying passengers, which when added to the crew count would be termed, 'souls on board,' a chivalrous naval term from ages past that signified both the dignity of our human cargo and of its frailty.

Fatt reached the end of the checklist. He turned to me and grinned.

'So, tell me, kid, how are you doing now?'

As I started to say that I felt pretty damn good about handling the Boeing, his hand shot out and yanked both port engines to idle.

'Fires in number one and two.'

The clipper sagged as if punched in the face and began falling off on her port wing. I quickly shoved her nose down to maintain airspeed.

'Got any plans?' Fatt pressed.

'Props full increase on three and four, mixture rich, throttles full,' I said as calmly as I could, and then added, 'Feather one and two.'

'Feathering one and two.'

Fatt's hand hit the switches that rotated the propeller blades parallel to the air stream to reduce them from wind-milling and creating flight-killing drag. The clipper could fly on two engines, but the control forces it took to maintain heading demanded powerful legs on the rudder pedals. I felt Fatt's legs helping mine as we struggled to keep her going in the right direction.

'Uh, oh,' he said. 'Number three doesn't look so good either. Losing oil pressure fast.'

'C'mon cap,' I said between gritted teeth. 'Aren't two dead engines enough for one day?'

'It happened to Eddie Musick in '34. Lost three, in a thunderstorm to boot, bless his heart, but he lived to tell the tale.'

'Okay, bring it on.'

Fatt retarded the throttle and number three engine's RPM needle slowly wound down. The choice was simple.

'Prepare for emergency landing,' I ordered.

'Got something more up my sleeve too.'

'Sweet Jesus.'

The radio operator said, 'Do I simulate transmitting a Mayday, sir?'

'Hell yes, and be sure about our position. We've got a load of scared passengers below who want to be picked up by a friendly ship the instant we hit the water – navigator, what's our position?'

A long pause.

'I repeat, where the hell are we?'

'Sir, I thought this was a shakedown flight for operating systems.' F

Fatt's voice tightened. 'You haven't been plotting our position?'

Another pause.

Fatt continued, 'Just been sharpening your pencils, checking the bubble in your octant, and staring out the window with your thumb up your Navy ass?'

'Yes, sir, I mean no, sir.'

'You'd better find out where we are fast, mister.'

A flash of bright light and sulfurous fumes shot up my nose from the burning match Fatt held directly in front of me.

'Fire just broke out in the cabin and we're going down fast.'

'Extinguishers forward!' I shouted.

'Aye, aye, sir,' Fatt crooned, and lit another match.

I tried to wave it away but he kept it in front of me, whispering, 'The day may come, kid…what are you going to do about it?'

'This never happened to Eddie Musick, damn it.'

'But it's happening to you. Three engines out, four hundred feet and closing fast, and you damn well better know what to do or we'll all be killed and I don't want to die, do you?'

My hands and eyes moved like a frantic marionette as I alternated between scanning the flight instruments and the sky outside tilting wildly to starboard as I banked hard to port. Only one chance to get her down, not enough power for a go-around.

The German-accented voice crackled cool and crisp in my headphones.

'Lufthansa Zero Five, Baltimore Harbor tower, are you declaring an emergency?'

Fatt said quickly, 'I'll handle this.'

He keyed his mike. 'Baltimore Harbor tower, disregard aircraft attitude, we are exploring flight performance envelope. Request landing clearance sea lane three.'

'Lane three approved, Lufthansa zero-five.'

'Some performance envelope,' I said.

He snorted, 'Bastards spying on us, as usual.'

The altimeter kept unwinding. No chance for flaps, too much drag and too little power. Had to be a straight-in approach. More matches, more sulfur and I had a coughing fit.

'C'mon, kid, you're almost home. Think of our passengers shitting bricks, praying you'll save their sorry hides.'

Two hundred feet, our diving turn ending, wings coming level, and the bobbing buoys of sea lane three swung into view. It took both Fatt and me shoving on the rudder pedals as hard as we could to keep her nose straight and still she yawed sideways. Who could blame her? A plane designed for four engines, dragging along on one made everything topsy-turvy.

'Hooray, the fire's out,' Fatt said.

'Roger, fire out.'

'No 'thank you' for my heroism beating back the flames?'

'Do you mind shutting up long enough for me to get us down?'

'Roger, wilco. One hundred feet...seventy-five...'

'Ready full left rudder...'

I yanked number four engine's throttle to idle.

The howling engine roar disappeared, replaced by the hiss of air passing over the wings of our powerless, behemoth glider sinking faster and faster.

'NOW!'

Free from the asymmetrical pull of a single engine, we shoved her nose back to center.

'Fifty feet...forty...'

'She's going to drop like a stone, damn it.'

'No she ain't. You're doing fine, kid. Nose up, nose up, you're still too hot. Stalls at seventy not eighty.'

I twisted and turned my control wheel in larger and larger arcs of motion as the ailerons and elevator grew mushy in the slower moving air. Baltimore harbor rose to meet us. Buildings, houses and factories appearing on both side in a blurring smear of brown, red and black. The airspeed indicator needle sank beneath seventy knots, and I waited for the dreaded sensation of falling out of the sky and slamming onto the water and bouncing up into the air again.

But instead, my rear end suddenly felt the distant 'thrum' of her hull kissing the waves once, twice, and then a steady rumble resonating throughout the entire aircraft as her fuselage settled deeper and deeper into the welcoming water.

I kept tracking in a straight line until she came to a stop, but not easy.

Once you're on a runway it's relatively easy to steer straight ahead. But the moment you land on water you become a sailing master, because the prevailing winds can shove the immense, slab-sided aircraft all over the place.

'Three engines still out?' I said.

'Behold, Reverend Diaz's prayers have been answered!'

Fatt unfeathered number one engine, flipped the magneto switch to 'Both On' and seconds later the propeller blades bit into the slipstream and the cylinders coughed into throaty life. With two fully operating engines on opposite wings, my sailing efforts eased because I was able to use the throttles to swing her around and head back to the boarding area. I kept my hands firmly on the wheel, because if I didn't, everyone would see how much they were shaking.

A bad peace is worse than war.
-Tacitus

'When are you and Uncle O coming home?' Abby said on the phone.

'What?'

She repeated her question, her voice hollow and far away. It had taken the operator forever to make the long distance connection to Key West and I could barely understand what she was saying.

'About a week. Maybe a little longer.'

'A man flew in on a Lockheed Electra. All polished up and pretty.'

'What man?'

'The man who talked to Grams about your charter job. He gave her some money.'

'Dark hair, short? A little pudgy?'

'Yes.'

Had to be Trippe. Holding up his end of the bargain. Time I did the same.

'What'd he do then?'

'He flew away. Where are you?'

'Baltimore.'

'Where after that?'

'A secret.'

'C'mon, where?'

'You know what Uncle O always says, if you tell, then it's not a secret.'

'I promise not to.'

'Maybe later – by the way, I found a nice stay-at-home present for you.'

'What is it?'

'A secret.'

'Daddy!'

'Gotta' go. Taking off soon. Uncle O sends you hugs and kisses. Me too, twice as many.'

Her voice faded as she said something else I couldn't understand and then disappeared. I hung up and left the phone booth, one of ten that lined the rotunda wall of Pan Am's Marine Air Terminal. Trippe's famous ten-foot high globe of the earth slowly revolved above the green marble service counter in the center of the rotunda. To show the airline's impressive international reach, glowing red lines inside the globe arced out in a spider's web of air routes connecting the various continents.

Pan American had come a long way from flying drunks to Havana.

Me too.

Orlando materialized out of the crowd; elegant grey fedora hat in hand, tan leather briefcase, highly polished shoes gleaming in the sunshine flooding down from the skylight. His dark grey business suit, white shirt and burgundy tie fit him like a second skin.

'You look like a banker,' I said. 'Where'd you get the rig?'

He brushed his lapels. 'What the well-dressed Chief of Engines, Atlantic Division wears on his inspection rounds.' He stifled a yawn. 'Delivered to my room at four this morning. What about your rig?'

He reached out and brushed the shoulder of my uniform jacket. 'Dandruff doesn't like dark blue.' He leaned forward and sniffed. 'Mothball smell's almost gone.'

To my astonishment, my original captain's uniform had been hanging in my hotel closet when I returned from the systems test flight. Coat, pants, hat, shirt, the works. At first I thought it was just a standard, off-the-rack outfit, but when I saw where Estelle had darned a worn spot on the right elbow years ago, I broke down and cried. To keep that from happening in front of Orlando, I said, 'Preister's people must have kept it in storage. What a cheapskate.'

'Aren't we all?' He hefted his briefcase. 'Time to meet my fellow passengers.'

'Where's your seat?'

'Compartment A, directly beneath the flight deck. Hopefully next to some nice, fat Nazi. Be fun watching him squirm, sitting next to a Schwarzie like me.'

'Where'd you pick that up?'

He grinned. 'One of the Lufthansa agents whispered it when I walked into the terminal.'

'Nazis got nerve, I'll give them that.'

'More than that, brother,' He gestured to the revolving globe. 'Almost got it all.'

'See you on the flight deck later. You've got to learn this big fat bird, same as me.'

'Plan on it.' He frowned and mock-growled. 'Chief of Engines, Atlantic Orlando Diaz is on the warpath about how Lufthansa's been mistreating his engines and he's going to get answers or get even, whichever comes first.'

'Nice cover story. Keep it up.'

Orlando strode confidently across the polished granite floor toward the passenger waiting lounge. Purser Nawrocki, passenger list in hand, stood guard by its hallowed double doors.

He took one look at the well-dressed, approaching mass of Orlando and swung open the door, smiled and saluted. Good thing Pan Am crews were still handling the pre-boarding details. Lufthansa would have had Orlando spread-eagled, searching for a spear and a bone in his nose.

The lounge door had barely closed before the polished brass terminal doors whooshed open and a cluster of men scurried in like swarm of ants. They took a few hurried steps, and swung around their, cameras held high, voices calling out,

'Over here, Miss James. Look here!'

Flashbulbs popped like mad as Ava appeared in a burst of scarlet and white, her red dress hugging every possible curve, her tiny white hat with huge feathers flowing from it like she was the lead swan in a formation flight. Ziggy scuttled along beside her, filled with importance as he rattled off answers to a reporter who matched him stride for stride. Two more reporters, a man and woman, notepads in hand, swooped down on Ava's left, their questions cancelling out each other.

Taking up the rear, two Pan Am porters wheeled a cart stacked with enough luggage for a round-the-world trip on an ocean liner. Ava, along with her entourage of five photographers, three newspaper reporters, Ziggy, her luggage, and the eyes of everybody in the terminal, headed straight for the ticket counter.

The Lufthansa agent braced himself for the assault, which was not long in coming.

'I'm ready to fly, darling,' Ava said to him. 'Which way's the plane?'

The agent nodded politely, 'And you are?'

The world's longest pause filled the terminal. Everyone could have shouted Ava's name, so familiar was her face to American audiences. But this poor German sap didn't have a clue. She nodded imperiously to Ziggy, who loudly proclaimed, 'Miss Ava James and Mr. Nathan Siegel for the Lisbon clipper.'

A wave of relief passed over the agent's face.

'Yes, of course. I have your tickets right here.' He fanned out impressive-looking, multi-colored engraved pieces of paper. Trippe believed in making Pan Am's tickets look ritzy to match the high prices they demanded. Round trips cost almost seven hundred bucks. Pretty steep considering most folks were damn lucky if they took home fifty a week.

The agent said, 'And your luggage, if any?'

Ava, looking bored, casually waved at the mountain of suitcases on the cart and the agent paled visibly. 'But I'm afraid that's entirely too much, Miss James. Passengers are limited to fifty-five pounds each.'

Another eternal silence. The agent nervously licked his lips and started to speak again, but Ava cut him off and turned to Ziggy. 'Tell your Lisbon friends the deal's off.'

She started walking away. Ziggy's eyes widened in shock.

'But the contract's been signed!'

'With your name, not mine.'

Ziggy caught up with her and skittered along like water in a hot skillet.

'But it's your career, darling. Principal photography starts in ten days.'

She stopped by the reporters. 'Now you've got a real story.' She framed her hands like an imaginary newspaper headline. 'Ava James a no-show in Lisbon because of a big baggage blow-up.' And you can quote me.'

Ziggy sidled back to the counter. 'What's the penalty?'

The agent eyed the pile. 'One percent of the fare for every two-point-two pounds over the limit. I'll have to weigh the items to get an accurate total.'

Ziggy sighed as he pulled out a blank check, signed it and handed it over. 'Fill out whatever it costs.' He lowered his voice to a whisper, 'And here's a little something for your trouble.' He slipped the man a folded bill and turned away before the surprised agent could hand it back. So he pocketed it instead.

'Done and done, darling,' Ziggy shouted. Then to the gathered retinue:

'Friends, last chance to photograph Miss James before we head to Portugal.' Like a trained ballerina, Ava glided over to an open space at the counter, swung around, lowered a shoulder, tossed her head back and let fly a dazzling smile that lit up the room. Flashbulbs popped, the crowd murmured its approval and I felt a tug at my sleeve.

Mason, the red-haired flight engineer said in awe, 'She's really something.'

'I'll say.'

'Way prettier in person than the movies.'

'Yep.'

'Taller too.'

'You two are about the same height. You'd make a perfect match.'

Mason blushed furiously. 'Cap wants you in ops. We're almost ready to board.'

I caught a last glimpse of Ava as she sailed past Purser Nawrocki and into the lounge. The brass-trimmed doors hissed shut upon the secrets of the very rich and the very well connected, now safely inside, protected from the rabble.

Nawrocki saw me approaching and grinned. 'All the chickens but one are in the hen house.'

'Let's see the manifest.'

A quick glance showed almost two-thirds of the passengers had German surnames. No surprise there. The higher-up compliance officers used the clippers the way New Yorkers used to use the subway to get from point A to point B. Which still ran, by the way, but only on lines running north of Ground Zero.

'Even got a priest on board,' Nawrocki said. 'So much for the vow of poverty, I guess.'

'Maybe the Pope's picking up the tab.'

'Don't make fun of my faith, cap.'

'Wouldn't dream of it - *Sprechen sie Deutsch?*

'*Natürlich, mein Kapitan.*'

'Good thing, because your tongue will be twisting plenty on this trip.'

He shrugged. 'These guys speak English pretty good.'

'They should, the bastards.'

A soft voice. 'Pardon me. May I go in please?'

The short, pudgy man wearing a long grey leather coat. He held his black leather briefcase against his chest as though it contained diamonds.

'I'm on the Lisbon flight.'

'Yes sir,' Nawrocki briefly consulted the manifest. 'You must be *Sturmbahnfüher* Bauer?'

The man smiled slightly.

'An impressive sounding title, but then, that's Germany for you; always trying to impress the world.'

He turned to me and said, 'I didn't recognize you in uniform, *Herr* Carter -- or should I say *Kapitan* Carter?' He clicked his heels slightly and nodded.

'Excuse me?'

'Last time we met, Mister Diaz and you were locked in a jail cell in Washington D.C. and not a bit happy about it either, as I recall.'

'You're the Gestapo guy at the airport?'

'Police inspector is more precise. But yes, I am he. And what about you?' His pale grey eyes regarded me calmly. 'You told me you were operating an aviation charter company in Florida, and yet here you are in uniform.'

I had to think fast or the game would be over before it got started. 'My plans didn't pan out. Lufthansa made an offer. I followed the money.'

'Still, you tried, and that's everything, isn't it?' He glanced toward the waiting room then back to me. 'You're involved with our clipper flight?'

'First officer.'

'Excellent.' His leather coat creaked as he shrugged his shoulders and suddenly looked sheepish. 'I confess I am deathly afraid of flying. But it's the only way I can get home to my family with any degree of convenience. Ships take forever, and I am prone to seasickness.'

Nawrocki said, 'We have Schnapps on board, if that's any help.'

He patted his briefcase. 'I have my own ammunition as well, but *danke schön* all the same.'

'*Gut reise*,' I said.

He brightened. 'You speak German?'

'Just enough to survive.'

He glanced around the teeming rotunda. 'The world grows smaller every day. *Nicht war?*'

'Bloodier too.'

'War is inevitable, *Herr Kapitan*. It is the nature of the beast.'

'Beasts maybe, but not men.' I pointed at the slowly revolving globe.

'There's room enough for everybody here. Why's Adolf grabbing what doesn't belong to him and killing innocent people to do it?'

'A candid question.'

'Well?'

'I am afraid it beyond my scope of knowledge to answer you.'

'You mean you're afraid somebody might be listening?'

He grinned suddenly. 'Yes, and that person might be you.'

'You've got to be kidding. Me?'

'How do I know you're not an SS undercover agent loyal to the Third Reich, on a mission to uproot traitors working the midst of one of our neutral nations?'

'Not a chance.'

'You are sailing under your own colors then?'

'Yes,' I lied, and then touched the gold wings on my chest. 'Pan Am circles the bloody earth - with Lufthansa's help of course.'

'Yet another topic for vigorous debate. Perhaps we can have it tonight during the flight? I will ask for the second sitting if you promise to join me.'

'My pleasure,' I lied again, but had no choice. Nazi or not, the customer is always right.

Pan Am's crew operations room was the exact opposite of the opulent Art Deco design of the passenger rotunda. Pitiless fluorescent light glared down upon the institutional gray tables, chairs, counters and battered map and weather boards that filled the small room. Here was where prior to the 'War-that-Wasn't,' Pan Am planned its Atlantic flights with precision born of long experience aided by a deep fear of the Dutchman's wrath if they got it wrong.

Not much had changed since Lufthansa took over. Pan Am meteorologists, flight dispatchers and maintenance workers still staffed the place, with only nominal supervision from the Germans, who acted like nervous new owners of a Kentucky Derby winner. At least that was my impression as I passed one of them on my way to join the crew gathered around Captain Fatt at the map table.

'Captain Carter,' Fatt boomed. 'Always a pleasure to have you join our happy family. We are a happy family, aren't we boys?'

The six naval officers, now disguised in their Pan Am uniforms, muttered their agreement. Not counting the stewards, a total of eight crewmen would staff the flight, each relieving the other during the endless hours of flying it would take us to make our way to Lisbon to snatch our prize.

'The good news is that we're ready to go,' Fatt continued. 'The bad news is that the seas are picking up at Horta. We may have to lay over there until the winds die down. If that happens, Captain Carter, here, will be in charge of humoring our dear, beloved VIP's.'

Nawrocki grinned at my unenviable assignment. Playing nanny to disgruntled passengers was not an easy job. He and Phillips, the steward, would bear the brunt of the social duties as was company custom, but passengers always liked it when an officer attended to them on a regular basis to keep their blood pressure down.

'How long's our first leg?' I said.

Fatt deferred to Stone, our navigator, who said in precise tones befitting his job, 'Fifteen hours, fifteen minutes.'

'How many seconds?' I said, and the others laughed. But Stone just looked at me and I regretted my bad joke.

Our laughter drew the attention of the Lufthansa flight supervisor, who edged closer. I sent Fatt a warning message with my eyebrows and he had Mason begin his litany of fuel estimates and go-no-go predictions, while I did my best to look serious and interested in the all-too-familiar pre-flight rituals that mark the beginning of the transition of eighty-four thousand pounds of engineered metal into a graceful figure of flight.

On paper it looked easy. Flying always does. From Baltimore we'd lift off and head southeast fifteen hours to a tiny speck of land in the Azores called Faial, where we'd refuel in Horta Bay, and with any luck - in short supply at the moment if you believed the meteorologist - we'd take off on our second and final leg to Lisbon, where we'd arrive six hours and forty-four minutes later, according to Stone, who'd changed his somewhat casual attitude ever since Fatt pulled the rug out from under him during our check flight. Now he was all business, so much so that he was already wearing his white uniform cap, squared away just right, covering his freshly-barbered scalp, whereas the rest of us were a bit more relaxed as we slouched over the map.

But despite the casual appearance I felt nervous as hell. About our crew, I mean. Flying for Pan Am was like climbing a long ladder where you begin as an apprentice pilot, work your way up through radio operator to flight engineer to junior pilot, senior pilot, and then to the hallowed 'Master Pilot Flying Boats' rating. If, for instance, the radio operator is disabled during a flight, seven other Pan Am crew members know exactly what dials to turn, what frequencies to use, and within seconds can be tapping out Morse code with the best of them.

Problem solved.

That said, other than Fatt and me, we had a bunch of flying sailors on our hands. While they were the best for security reasons and the most militarily inclined should the need arise, their cross-training was much weaker than ours. All the more reason for me to keep a sharp eye on Stone and Mason and all the others. Could they cover for each other like Pan Am crews? Maybe so, but I wasn't counting on it. The Navy worked with strict division of command. Pan Am worked the opposite. Even so, opposites attract, right? So maybe things would work out after all.

Fatt's finger landed on Portugal. 'What's Lisbon got on the table?'

Stone consulted his weather forecast notes. As he did, the German supervisor stepped in and said a bit too loudly, 'They are reporting mostly cloudy, twenty-seven degrees centigrade, winds two-six-zero at ten.'

'Thank you, sir,' Fatt said. 'Or should I say *danke*?'

'Either will suffice, kapitan.'

'Is that weather current or for our estimated arrival?' Fatt continued. A slight hesitation. 'That would be for now.'

Stone looked up from his weather notes. 'Low pressure system reported on its way out in the next twelve to fifteen hours.'

'My, my,' Fatt said. 'What a difference that will make, don't you think, *Herr* - sorry, I didn't catch your name.'

A slight nod. 'Weinacht.'

Fatt stuck out his huge hand and swallowed up the supervisor's. 'More than a pleasure, I'm sure, *Herr* Weinacht. So how do you like working this side of the pond?'

The man hesitated, trying to gauge Fatt's intentions. Good luck, I thought. Nobody ever knew what Fatt would do next, most of all himself.

Weinacht finally said, 'I find Lufthansa flight operations quite similar to yours.'

'Birds of a feather,' Fatt crooned.

'Except that I must approve your flight plan before you can depart.'

Fatt looked like somebody slapped him. 'Since when did that start?'

A thin smile. 'Regulations from our Berlin office.' He put out his pale white hand. 'May I see what you have prepared? That is, if you're ready for my review.'

Fatt's jaw muscles bulged but he held his tongue. Like watching a volcano get ready to pop, but then it doesn't. Weinacht pursed his lips and traced his manicured finger down the long list of items that made up our complicated flight: planned courses, winds aloft, fuel estimates, weights and balances, souls-on-board, and so on and so forth, while the rest of us stood like guilty schoolboys waiting for the master to grade our tests.

'*Alles ist in ordnung,*' he said finally.

'Whatever the hell that means,' Fatt snapped.

'It means that you have done adequate preparation for me to grant permission for you and your crew to safely transport the souls on board this Lufthansa flight to Lisbon, Portugal, and then return to this operating base.'

'Just 'adequate preparation'?'

'At the present time Pan American crews are the most qualified in operating Lufthansa's Boeing flying boats, but we will be replacing you with properly trained German personnel in the very near future.'

'How near's that future, pal?'

Weinacht said nothing. Just thin smile as he signed his name. When he finished he said, '*Gut reise, Kapitan.*'

Even with swastikas on her triple tail, the *Yankee Clipper* looked beautiful as she rubbed against the dock, her silver-painted metal skin a brightly polished sheen in the late morning sunlight. An impressive stack of rising cumulus in the east gave fair warning of a bumpy ride to come later on, but hopefully we could skirt around the more serious columns of rising air.

Just as flickering lights in a theater lobby signal the end of intermission, so did Pan Am's GONG resonating over the terminal loudspeakers declare that the Lisbon clipper was ready to depart.

'Okay, gentlemen, let's start the parade,' Fatt intoned as we prepared to leave the operations room. In reverse order of rank we proceeded down the curving, flower-lined sidewalk in perfect step; fourth officer, third officer, second officer, second radio officer, first radio officer, and so on up the hallowed seniority ladder through engineering and navigation officers until it reached me, just one car shy of the Grand Caboose himself, Master of Flying Boats James. J. Fatt commanding, whose footfalls sounded behind me like bass drums.

All for show? You bet. Andre Preister may have been a cold-hearted Dutchman with Baltic Sea water in his veins, but he knew how to put on a show for his paying customers. And with Trippe as his 'producer,' they made sure that before every flight Pan Am crews displayed an unparalleled measure of confidence, courage and safety for their passengers, who stood waiting for the second boarding bell that would let them share in the excitement, too.

It's fun to watch a circus parade, but much better if you get to march with the clowns - meaning us. Am I being cynical? Yes. Is it an unfair assessment? Perhaps, but after years of doing this 'March of the Confident Airmen' to ease passengers' fears, I believe that what we were actually doing was convincing ourselves too – at least a little.

The boarding crew, dressed in spotless white coveralls, saluted sharply as we passed. I noticed with a pang that LUFTHANSA had replaced the PAA letters formerly embroidered on the back. This sad truth was brought home even closer when I heard them calling out to each other in German. Even so, they seemed to know their job as one of them opened the passenger boarding door over the port sponson and waited at rigid attention for our crew parade to march across the aluminum boarding ramp that spanned the narrow space between the plane and the dock.

No hollow boom from our footsteps this time as we walked on the aluminum surface. The sponson's fuel tanks were topped off with over a thousand gallons of one hundred-octane aviation fuel. That, plus twelve hundred gallons in our wing tanks, gave us over five thousand gallons for our engines to gulp for our fifteen-hour leap to Horta.

One by one the flight crew stepped into the open hatch and then down inside the lounge where Nawrocki and his steward waited with beaming smiles.

Fatt touched my sleeve. 'Mind doing the honors with the passengers, kid?' I got work to do.'

He maneuvered his bulk into the hatch, momentarily filling it entirely with Pan Am uniform blue, his broad pants bottom, like mine, shiny-bright from hundreds of hours in the cockpit. I turned to the boarding crewman, a young man about the age I was when I first got started in the business. 'I'll take it from here, pal.'

He looked blank. I didn't know the word for 'Beat it' in German, so I tried using my thumb instead to show him where to go. That and a big smile did the trick. He scurried over to the edge of the sponson where it met the boarding ramp and resumed his stiff posture of attention. I had to admit, Lufthansa folks were no slouches when it came to style.

Old habits die hard: I re-checked my tie, fussed with my hat, and tugged at my uniform jacket to line up the buttons, Preister-style. My pants felt loose and I risked a quick five seconds to reach inside and tighten my belt another notch. I didn't feel thinner, but I must have lost weight since I handed my rig over to Pan Am stores. Going through hell does that to a person. I was no exception. With that thought, my mind sensed an opportunity to start re-hashing what I'd been through during the past six months, but blessedly, the faraway boarding bell distracted it the way a pretty toy distracts a weeping toddler.

The twin doors of the Marine Terminal swung open just as the last of the double GONGS echoed across the water. A phalanx of dark-suited, no-nonsense men led the passenger parade, hats square on their heads, steps firm, shoulders back, 'compliance officer' written all over their stern, well-fed faces. Each carried a small, light blue Pan Am overnight bag for his personal belongings, like pajamas and toothbrush, for when he turned in at night. Everything else was in baggage.

I'm not a religious man, but my few years spent as an altar boy taught me that pomp and ceremony are the sizzle on a steak. No matter how thin that steak is, or even if it's hamburger, if you've got enough candles, sweet-smelling incense, a decent choir and lots of stained glass windows, you can get most folks to believe in any damn thing you want. In Pan Am's case, we wanted our passengers to believe that flying over three thousand miles of ocean at six thousand feet with nothing between us and destruction but four engines and a thin-skinned flying boat was the most natural thing in the world to do.

Boarding GONGS helped. Overnight bags helped, attentive stewards with ready smiles and heaping plates of food and drink helped, not to mention flight officers like me with premature wrinkles around their eyes. We were the high priests they looked up to. All we had to do is look back at them with a calm, almost half-bored look that said in effect, 'This turbulent air that's got you bouncing up and down? Almost ready to vomit? Scared out of your wits? Not to worry, my friend, it's perfectly normal. You can tell by the way I'm looking at you with this half-smile on my face and a look of serene understanding that I know what I'm talking about. I'm a professional here to serve you, and everything is going to turn out just fine, you'll see.'

That's what I was keeping in mind I smartly saluted the first of the compliance officers to land on the sponson and make his way to the boarding door.

'*Willkommen, mein herr,*' I said with a happy grin.

He nodded curtly, grunted slightly, but said nothing as he heaved his fat legs up the small step stool and then squirmed inside. I kept my smile plastered on as the next group arrived, deep in discussion. They barely noticed my existence, so intent were they on some matter that, from the looks on their somber faces, must have been essential to the future of the Third Reich.

'Good afternoon, captain,' a gentle male voice said, and I turned to see a short, dark-haired, youngish man wearing a priest's collar.

'You must be Father Petrucelli,' I said, quickly remembering his name on the manifest.

His eyes danced, 'Please it's Father Dominic.'

'God's business in Lisbon?'

'Rome, actually.' He patted his breast pocket. 'Providing Mussolini lets me in.'

I started to say something, but the Nazi compliance officer behind the priest cleared his throat impatiently.

'Enjoy your flight, father.'

'How could I not?' He glanced up into the sky. 'I'll be with the angels.'

'And a few devils, too.'

And so the boarding continued; a few kind words when I thought they were needed, a smart salute when it fit the bill, a simple nod, a wave, each gesture calculated to fit the needs of the particular person. And rightfully so. Trans-oceanic clipper passengers were paying top dollar and expected service to equal it, and God help you if they didn't get it. But not all of them. In some cases companies were footing the bill, like The New York Times reporter for instance, who gave me a happy wink.

'Ava James on my flight. How lucky can a man get?'

'Not much more, I guess.'

'Maybe we'll be at the same seating.' He gave me a look. 'Think you could fix that up for me, captain? I'm a big fan.'‘

See what I can do.'

He glanced around, quickly. The next batch of passengers were far enough away for him to say quietly, 'What's it like flying a Kraut plane?'

'Boeing built her. The swastikas are just paint.'

He shook his head. 'Still can't believe it. You?'

I shrugged my shoulders but kept my big mouth shut.

Thirty-six names on the manifest. Thirty-four souls-on-board so far, including Inspector Bauer who looked like a kid on a holiday as he fairly skipped across the sponson and darted inside without saying a word, but not without raising his eyebrows in a silent message of shared excitement. I acknowledged his gesture with a smile and a small salute.

On the other side of the plane, engine number one groaned and spluttered into life. Fatt was getting down to business right on schedule. The boarding crew glanced at each other, readying themselves for the next step of their departure drill. I raised my hand and signaled the crew chief to wait. I pointed at the terminal and held up two fingers.

'*Zwei mehr*,' I said.

'*Jawohl, kapitan.*'

The whine of a generator overhead as the polished propeller blades of engine number four started turning. I grabbed my hat just as the cylinders caught and coughed a cloud of white smoke that quickly vanished in the brisk wind of the bay.

As if that were their entrance cue, Ava and Ziggy sailed from out of the Marine Terminal with two ticket agents on either side, chattering away but she shook her head dismissively and waved her hand in the air, holding a jeweled cigarette holder the way the Pope holds his crosier. The agents, ignored and vanquished, slowed to a stop while she sailed onward, victorious.

Naturally, Ziggy carried their overnight bags, leaving her free to glide along with imperial ease. Her left hand rose to guard her feathered hat as she encountered the slipstream from the idling engines. She nodded at the boarding crew who stood frozen at attention like white-uniformed Nutcrackers.

Ziggy darted across the boarding ramp to wait on the other side, his hand extended, as though Ava were about to alight from a Venetian gondola. She strode forward, shoulders back, face angled just so for the non-existent cameras, her smile the happiest of sunrises, and as her eyes found mine, I couldn't help but smile back.

'Anchors aweigh and all that,' she shouted to be heard above the clattering engine.

I saluted smartly. 'Welcome aboard, Miss James. I hope you enjoy the flight.'

Her hand on my sleeve was light as a feather but I felt it all the same.

She rose on her tiptoes and her lips brushed my ear as she whispered, 'Curtain up, my darling Sam.'

Open water looks the same no matter how high you fly. It's not like land, where you judge your altitude in relation to how things look down there. Flying over water is like crossing a featureless desert; interesting for about five minutes, but after that, you start looking everywhere else but down - unless you're a navigator like Stone, who had just used his Very pistol to shoot a flare down the tube next to his chart table. Now he was using a wind triangle to calculate our drift based on the smoke from the flare as it drifted down to the sea.

Pilots fly planes, but navigators tell them where to go. Stone was using dead reckoning to estimate where we were now in relation to a fixed point we had passed three hundred miles earlier. He used time, speed and distance to make his carefully calculated guess, but wind was critical to his calculations. So he hedged his bets by measuring how the smoke drifted in relation to the wind as it fell through the sky. He returned to his chart table, bent over and made some tiny pencil notations on the chart unrolled before him.

I turned in my seat and called out, 'Are we in Cleveland yet?'

He frowned at my lame joke as would any navigator worth his salt. I had been in his shoes years ago when, as a navigator, the fate of a clipper and her passengers often rested on my tired shoulders in the middle of a thunderstorm over Brazil when I wasn't sure of where I was, and hoped to God the course I had plotted on the chart was correct. If not we would be flying into the side of some nameless mountain.

Minutes later Stone came up to our flight station with a slip of paper. On it he had written the compass heading: 110.

I said, 'Can we take this to the bank?'

'You can cash it, while you're there,' Stone said sharply. Then turned and walked away.

Fatt's eyebrows rose marginally, but he said nothing. Neither did I, but we both noted the ring of absolute confidence in Stone's voice. When it's your job to tell people where they're going and when they'll arrive, you have to be as sure of yourself as you are that the sun will rise in the morning.

Especially when you're feeling just the opposite; that time, speed and distance be damned, something in your gut keeps saying, 'You're lost, pal, and there's nothing you can do about it.' That's when your voice has to strengthen, your eye sharpen, your shoulders square as you proclaim that this is the heading that will lead everyone home -- which made me wonder if Stone was selling us a bill of goods.

After letting that suspicion race through my carefully arranged list of possible actions to take if that were the case, I stuffed it away and dialed Stone's heading into our Sperry autopilot. Fatt looked away, pretending he wasn't watching but I knew he was. Masters of Flying Boats grow eyes in the back of their heads.

I unbuckled my seatbelt. 'Got to see a man about a horse.'

Fatt cocked his head to one side but said nothing. We both knew I didn't need to go to the head.

'Be nice.'

'I will. Unlike you.'

He grinned.

Before talking with Stone, I stopped briefly at the radio operator's station directly and marveled again at the immense size of the Boeing's flight deck. Because of my six foot three-plus height I had to duck slightly to keep my head from hitting the padded, soundproofed, six foot-high ceiling, but compared to the cramped cockpits of the Sikorsky and Douglas aircraft I'd flown in the past, hunched over double, this was like strolling along the deck of an ocean liner.

Allen, our radio operator, earphones clamped on his head, held court before two immense radios as he rapidly worked the Morse key. From long habit I mentally pictured the letters forming into words as he busily reported our position back to Baltimore. But the further we flew across the Atlantic, the weaker the signal would become, until finally silence would descend and he'd have to put his earphones down - for a little while at least - and we would be at the mercy of Stone's calculations.

When Allen finished sending his message I said casually, 'What kind of music you got, Sparks?'

He brightened and grinned. 'Some Benny Goodman. Want it on the speakers?'

'Nope, just give me a reverse bearing on it if you don't mind.'

'Sure thing, cap.'

He dialed up a radio station frequency on one of his receivers, and then slowly turned a small wheel located in the padded ceiling directly above us. The action, in turn, rotated the loop antenna located outside the fuselage. He smiled and rocked his shoulders back and forth to the beat as his earphones picked up swing music coming from some radio station three hundred miles behind us. We both watched the needle on the S-meter rise higher and higher, and then fall off to null as he turned the loop the other direction. He did it two times to confirm the exact bearing, jotted it down, and then found another radio station and did the same thing.

He made a face at what he heard in his earphones. 'They're saying Brylcreem helps you win the girl, and I'm using Wildroot.' He repeated the tuning action until he got another bearing.

I took the numbers and crossed over to Stone, who was acting like he was absorbed in his work all this time, but I knew for a fact he'd been watching my every move.

'Do me a favor,' I said quietly so that nobody else could hear.

'Sure.'

'Run these numbers for me.' I handed him the bearings.

He frowned and started to say something, but I lifted my hand slightly.

'No offense to the United States Navy, but something tells me we might be off course a tad.'

'We're absolutely not.'

'I know, you told me. But I disagree.'

'What makes you think so?'

'This.' I pointed to my gut. 'Plus, how confident you acted when you gave me the course.'

It happened fast: a flicker of doubt in his eyes. I smiled to make myself look friendly, even though I wanted to ream him out. But that would get me nothing but an enemy. We needed a navigator.

'Do me another favor,' I said.

He stared hard at me. A real cement-head in the making, if I didn't do this right.

'If you come up with a different number than the one you gave us, don't tell Fatt, okay? This is just between us navigators, okay?'

He hesitated and I continued, 'Look, it takes one to know one, okay? Remind me to tell you the time I almost sent a clipper into the side of a mountain because I was absolutely, positively sure we were right on course.'

I picked up his well-worn protractor and idly examined its etched numbers, waiting for him to respond.

'So, what happened?' he finally said.

I nodded in Fatt's direction. 'That man at the wheel is what happened.'

'What'd he do?'

I handed back the protractor. 'The same thing I'm doing to you. And I didn't like it either, but you know what? The son-of-a-bitch was right.'

And I was too, when five minutes later I dialed our adjusted course into the autopilot. Fatt made sure he was looking in the opposite direction when I did so.

'Something wrong?' he said casually as he stared out the window.

'Nope, just trying to get used to this autopilot. It's different than the S-42's.'

A soft chuckle. 'Was he mad as hell?'

'Oh, you bet.'

'You were too. That's when I knew you damn well weren't going to make that dumb ass mistake again. And you never did.'

'And I never did.'

'Of course you made others too numerous to mention.'

He returned to his thousand-yard stare at the cloud-filled horizon.

'Wake me in time for dinner. I'm starving.'

As 'Master of Ocean Boats,' Fatt's duty was to preside over the first dinner sitting in the Clipper's lounge, while I inherited his hallowed left-hand seat in the cockpit to pilot the clipper ever onward as 'Officer of the Watch.' I could picture him presiding over the crowd like an aerial Falstaff, slugging back club soda instead of scotch. No drinking on duty for flight crews, but we always made up for it later.

I checked the time: 8:16 pm. Fatt would be returning to the bridge soon, and according to Pan Am tradition it became my turn as first officer to host another 'Captain's Table' for the second sitting, so as not to overlook any VIP.

Most captains detested this social function as not being germane to their lofty title. But I enjoyed it. The secret was to let everybody else do the talking and just listen and nod. Never a shortage in that department. The amount of nervous energy contained in a flying boat six thousand feet above the water is an awesome thing to behold.

Passengers endure an alien environment where every bounce, every strange noise, can freeze them into immobility like defenseless jungle creatures trying to survive the night. No wonder their laughter is louder, arguments stronger, drinking heavier. Me? I was just putting in another day's work - at six thousand feet, true - but work all the same.

The last rays of the setting sun touched the high clouds gliding overhead. The ocean played occasional peek-a-boo through broken clouds as we sailed serenely in between, the engines a faraway roar, their noise muffled by thick insulation. I watched, fascinated, as our autopilot nudged the yoke slightly to starboard, and then a moment later, satisfied that the clipper was maintaining the correct heading, returned the yoke to center.

In order to preserve night vision, I reached for the curtain separating the cockpit from the rest of the flight deck. But just as I untied the hold-back loops, Orlando's laughter boomed out. My partner had arrived on the flight deck an hour ago and began peppering Mason our engineer with questions while they busily monitored the Yankee Clipper like hotel concierges pampering a favored guest, making sure everything is in perfect order.

Their talk was miles over my head. Sure, I understood basic things like fuel-mixture ratios, cylinder head temperatures and cowl flap settings. But when their conversation soared into the high atmosphere of potentiometer readings, pyrometers and thermocouple sensors, I left them to their sacred rituals and just flew the damn plane, or in my case, watched the autopilot do it for me.

A pounding sound on the floor and I became instantly alert. If I had been flying an S-42 or the S-38, I would have immediately known what was wrong. Planes are like people, each one has their own quirks. But the Boeing 347 was still new to me, and no matter how many hours I had as a pilot, no matter how confident I acted, new was still new and unfamiliar was unfamiliar, and I felt my chest tighten in a mixture of fear and dread like I was nineteen again and a novice.

By now Orlando was standing on top of the closed stairwell hatch, bent over, listening. Suddenly I understood, and felt relief as he unlocked the hatch and swung it open.

Fatt clumped up the stairs and onto the flight deck. 'Damned thing got stuck.'

I said, 'How was dinner?'

'Okay, if you like listening to everybody talk German.'

'That bad?'

'You'll find out. Now, scram out of here and let me get some peace and quiet.'

I stood and stretched. Fatt dropped into his seat with a contented grunt and pulled out his familiar baseball-bat-sized cigar. 'Yank that curtain before you go, willya' kid?'

I left him and the cigar smoke to follow Orlando down the staircase to the lounge, filled with sudden bursts of laughter, bright chatter, and the clink of glass and silverware.

Like aerial magicians, Nawrocki and his steward Addison had transformed the passenger lounge from what had been a stylish cocktail bar an hour ago into a formal dining room complete with white Irish linen tablecloths, flute-edged, Lufthansa-monogrammed china, Gorham sterling flatware, and fresh flowers. They had also reconfigured the tables and upholstered chairs for the passengers to sit in groupings of two, four and six.

Before entering the dining area, we stopped by the closet-sized galley where Addison, now dressed in a starched white waiter's jacket, was making up a tray of appetizers.

'What's on the menu?' I said.

He rattled away like a machine gun, 'Chilled Utah Celery, Consommé Madrilene, Grapefruit Supreme, Breast of Chicken with Peas *Francoise*, Parsley Spring Potatoes… '

'Lots of French-sounding food for a bunch of krauts.'

'Don't interrupt, sir. Followed by after dinner mints, Fresh Fruit, Brandied Dates, coffee, tea or milk, wine or beer as well.'

Orlando said, 'What, no *Wiener Schnitzel?*'

He rolled his eyes like a suffering saint, 'That's coming, I'm sure.'

As we entered the lounge I noticed that Nawrocki had made good his promise and I could have socked him, because sitting at the captain's table was my Gestapo buddy Bauer. Fortunately, Ava and Ziggy were there too, along with the New York Times reporter who – naturally – only had eyes for her. So did the other passengers too, only they studiously avoided looking our way, as if traveling with a famous movie star was par for the course on a clipper flight. And they were right.

Soaring across the Atlantic in a matter of hours instead of suffering days on an ocean liner represented the height of luxury, privilege and glamour. Not all of the diners exhibited that stylish quality, however. Only the Americans. The rest were dour-faced Nazis mercilessly plowing through their food the same way Hitler finished off Poland, counting the hours until they were back in Berlin for their bratwurst und bier und frauleins.

They did, however, bring their food assault to a momentary halt when Orlando and I made our entrance. And it wasn't me who caused it, I can tell you that. Not a first officer doing his duty but the sight of a Schwarzie standing in the same room with them, not dressed in a waiter's jacket and scraping and bowing, but instead sporting a stylish business suit and gracefully bowing to Ava before he took his seat beside me at the captain's table.

'What an honor it is, Miss James, to meet you at last,' Orlando said smoothly. His southern accent had a rolling, theatrical cadence that made you want to hear more.

Ava slid in, right on cue. 'Now tell me what it is you do, Mr. Diaz. I saw you going up to where they fly the plane. Something the matter?'

'Not a thing, Miss James.'

'Call me Ava unless you hear otherwise.'

'If you insist.'

'I do.'

'I work for Pan American Airways and I happen to know all there is to know about engines.'

A frown wrinkle touched her smooth brow. 'Something wrong with them?'

I said, 'If there were, we wouldn't be sitting here enjoying dinner.'

Ziggy waved a piece of celery. 'The menu doesn't look too bad this time.' He turned to Bauer, 'You like chicken, *Herr* Bauer?'

He shrugged. 'I can eat anything. And over the years I think I have.'

'I do hope the asparagus is fresh this time,' Ziggy lied away, playing the role of experienced world traveler. 'On my last crossing it was terribly overcooked. Like shoe leather.'

Bauer said, 'You travel often on these flying boats?'

'In my line of work it's one sleeping berth after another. Train, boat, plane, makes no difference.'

166

'You are Miss James' theatrical agent?'

He brightened. 'One and the same.'

Bauer sighed and turned to Ava. 'You seem to live such a glamorous life. Tell me, is it true?'

'Do you want it to be?' she said.

'Doesn't everyone?'

'Then it is. Every bit of it. Every champagne-filled moment of my life is filled with excitement, adventure, and lots and lots of money.'

As she spoke, Bauer contemplated his silverware as if seeing it for the first time. When she finished he looked up at her calmly. 'You are a great actress. I believed every word.'

She nodded her thanks.

'If I ever had to interrogate you, I don't believe I'd find out a thing.'

'Now, you're the bad actor. When the Gestapo wants answers, it gets them. Am I right?'

The soup course saved Bauer from responding. We ate in tortured silence, pretending we were hungry when in fact we didn't know where to go in the conversation, until the New York Times reporter, a thin, intense man named Nick Anston said bluntly to Bauer, 'So, what's next on Hitler's plate?'

The inspector took pains to daub his plump lips with his napkin before he said with a wink, 'The moon, I'm told.'

We smiled at his little joke and he nodded sheepishly. 'Mind you, a person could get arrested for saying a thing like that about our dear leader.'

'By the Gestapo, right?' I said.

'Yes. And I hereby announce that I place myself under arrest - after I finish this lovely dinner, that is.'

And so it went, this surface-level conversation, each of us with a different agenda, and none of us revealing what we were really thinking or feeling, but somewhere, deep down, all of us aware of our fragile setting; drinking wine and chatting merrily, six thousand feet above the ocean while Europe and Asia were going down in flames.

I had originally planned on making a graceful exit after coffee and mints impeccably served by Nawrocki and Addison, whose demeanor bore not a trace of impatience, even though they still had another dinner seating before making up everybody's sleeping berths for the night.

I started making 'excuse-me' noises, but Bauer touched my arm and said, 'I realize I am not your ordinary VIP passenger, but I understand you give tours of the flight deck. Do you think it might be possible...?' He let the question hang.

Ziggy chimed in. 'I've always wanted to see your guys' office. C'mon, show us around.'

Nick Anston piled on after the whistle. 'Make that three. I'll give you boys good ink in the paper if you do.'

I turned to Ava, who shook her head. 'Not my cup of tea, thanks.'

'Sure?'

'Count me out. This sounds like a toy store made in heaven for men.'

She stubbed out her cigarette and rose gracefully. On cue, we scrambled to our feet and the whole place watched as she snaked her way aft, acknowledging their admiring smiles with a dazzling one of her own and a delicate wave of her manicured hand.

Moments later I led the conga line of men up the spiral crew staircase, and swung the counterweighted hatch upward. The men entered the dim, instrument-lit space with the same awe and reverence of entering a church to witness high priests going about their sacred duties.

I made introductions all around: navigator, radio operator, flight engineer, and I must say that these navy guys had a flair for acting. They projected the epitome of lean- jawed, keen-eyed professionals, intent on their duties, yet graciously willing to acknowledge the men who stood before them in silent awe.

Fatt was the highest priest of all as he sat at his 'Master's Station,' the small office space against the rear bulkhead, head down, busily doing paperwork, which was actually part of his job. But the way he did it; with feigned officiousness and hunching of shoulders in concentration, was pure theater. And then, as if on cue, he lifted his noble head and regarded our visitors like Neptune would his loyal subjects.

'Welcome to the bridge, gentlemen. The heart and soul of this magnificent flying boat.'

For the next few minutes he regaled them as only Fatt could about the workings of his mighty airplane, interspersed with off-color anecdotes. But then, this was a gathering of male eagles in a nest six thousand feet above the ocean, was it not? A place where brave deeds and sex and excitement were the very things that kept the plane flying, aided now and then with one hundred-octane avgas, of course.

Ziggy, Bauer, and the newspaperman asked their share of questions, to which Fatt responded clearly and simply, with occasionally tosses to me when he felt so inclined. And then, as only Fatt could, he suddenly looked pre-occupied with the grave duties of leadership and nodded to me.

'Captain, would you please show these men the pilot station?'

'Gentlemen?' I said temptingly.

They beamed like puppies.

Fatt intoned, 'Reducing lights, stand by.'

With a turn of a dial, the golden yellow light on the flight bridge slowly faded to darkness, leaving only the dials and control panel lights gleaming like so many stars. I slid back the curtain to the cockpit. The relief pilot and first officer didn't acknowledge our presence at first; they were too busy adjusting dials and twisting knobs, but this too, was an act because the Sperry autopilot was flying the plane and their job was to sit there and watch. But no way would they do that for an admiring tour group, so they 'flew' instead.

Anston asked some questions about fuel consumption and range and got precise answers that he jotted down in his notebook. Bauer seemed content to just be in the presence of such an array of modern technology.

Ziggy turned to me, 'How do you park this thing once you land?'

'Excuse me?'

'Do you use an anchor or what?'

I explained how the fourth officer manned the mooring compartment and handled the lines.

Anston chimed in, 'What's it like for you Pan Am guys flying for Lufthansa?'

The pilot and first officer remained pointedly silent, so I said, 'We got into this business because we like to fly. Who we fly for doesn't matter as much as what we fly. And flying a beautiful big bird like this? Let's just say that up here, who owns her doesn't matter as much as who flies her.'

A silence fell over the group as the meditated upon my profundity, aided by moonlit clouds gliding past in a serene parade. The soundproofing reduced the engines to a hypnotic hum, which seemed to cast a spell on the group.

After a while, Bauer politely cleared his throat and said. 'I must say being up here on a night like this, it is hard to believe that we are a world at war.'

'America sure as hell is not,' I said without thinking.

'Not for now, perhaps. But your Uncle Sam will not sleep forever. Sooner or later he will wake up and fight.'

'Not with atom bombs hanging over his head.'

'Perhaps you are right.'

I stifled a yawn and Ziggy said, 'Is it the time or the company'?

'Neither. I need to rest before our shift goes back on watch.'

'Where do you sleep?'

I pointed to the baggage hatch on the bulkhead directly behind Captain Fatt. 'We've got crew cots back there past the luggage cages. Not as fancy as yours and a little cramped, but they do the job. Now then, may I escort you gentlemen back to your staterooms?'

Ziggy waved me off, 'Forget it. We know our way back, don't we, boys?'

They rumbled their thanks and threaded their way down the spiral staircase. I swung the hatch closed on their good natured chatter and the sound of their voices cut off like a knife. Freed from our gawking audience, the flight crew quickly resumed its state of calm teamwork.

Sparks handed Fatt the latest met report from Horta. Instead of the overcast breaking the way they had predicted during the night, it had worsened and so had the winds. Fatt groaned and got up from his station and stretched.

'Jeeves, would you mind turning down my bed?' he said to me.

'Let me draw your bath first, sir.'

He smiled and led the parade through the door leading to our cramped crew quarters. True to form, within minutes of hitting his narrow canvas cot, Fatt was snoring like a buzz saw. In contrast, I lay on my cot in the windowless dark, listening to each of the engines go slightly in and out of synchronization as the relief flight engineer ran through a ritualistic fine-tuning of fuel mixture and prop pitch that only he could appreciate. From the cot beside mine, Mason grumbled, 'Why doesn't he leave well enough alone? I left them running sweet.'

'Want me to tell him 'hands off'?' I said.

'A lot of good that would do. You know how flight engineers are.'

'Used to be one myself, briefly.'

'Why didn't you stay at it?'

'Pan Am's different than the navy. It's one long ladder you're always climbing from apprentice pilot to master of flying boats. Every other job you do along the way is just one more rung.'

'Hell of a way to run a business.'

'It is, but when everything starts going to hell, it's nice to know everybody on board can fly.'

'Too many cooks can spoil the broth,' he warned.

'That's for soup. Too many cooks can save a dying plane.'

He rolled over with a grunt and that was that. He had a point of course. Most companies and organizations hire specialists to achieve the greatest efficiencies. But Juan Tripp and Andre Preister embraced the apprentice-master approach from the very beginning. And they were right to do so. It's one thing for a Master of Flying Boats to call for more power from his engines, and quite another to know what that requires of the aircraft at that particular moment, unless he himself has sat and squirmed and sweated in the flight engineer's seat while staring at instrument readings that said what the captain was asking for was impossible – and found the courage to tell him.

Mason was right, too, though, about overly-fussing with the engines.

He had tuned the clipper's engines to a state of perfection that I'd rarely encountered in Pan Am flight engineers. These navy guys were meticulous specialists, or General Patton wouldn't have secured them for the mission. Too bad not all of them could fly, which put the pressure on Fatt and me and our relief pilots as the only qualified crew. But, I reminded myself again, this was no ordinary flight, and the weather seemed to sense it by going from bad to worse.

Two hours later, rested and refreshed, Fatt took over for landing at Horta. Instead of puffy cumulous clouds and blue skies bathing an azure-colored ocean as forecast, we slugged our way through dense cloud cover, glued to our instruments and putting more faith in what they indicated than any god up above who might help us.

'What are they reporting now?' Fatt said.

Sparks, his voice still heavy with sleep despite two cups of coffee said, 'Four hundred feet, visibility half-mile, winds two-two-zero at fifteen.'

'That won't last long,' he grumbled. 'And if the winds maroon us in Horta, our scientist pal will be in deep trouble. That conference only lasts three days. And it started yesterday.'

'So?'

'So, when the party's over, everybody goes straight home to Germany, including the good *Herr Doktor*, or they'll get suspicious.'

'The Gestapo, you mean?'

'They're watching those eggheads like a hawk. Portugal's neutral. Any one of them could hightail it to an embassy and defect.'

'They'd just storm the place and grab him.'

'Maybe yes, maybe no. The Nazis are dumb, but they aren't stupid. That would make egg-on-your-face headlines.'

'What's the plan if we don't make it in time?'

'None that I know of. But I sure hope there is one. They don't tell me everything, you know - Sparks, get me the latest.'

'Aye, cap.'

Fatt switched off the autopilot and took the yoke. 'Time to earn our pay.'

Then he wiggled it slightly. 'You have the aircraft, captain.'

'C'mon, don't you ever fly anymore?'

He grinned. 'Not if I can help it. Besides, you've got to learn how to make love to this fat lady.'

'I'm getting there.'

'Getting there is not the same thing as arriving, as we both know from long experience.'

'With planes or women?'

'Both. Get to work.'

And that was that, so I pulled back the throttles ever so slightly to begin a gradual descent, Then I reduced the manifold pressure slowly so as to avoid 'cold shocking' the engines, which would send Mason through the roof, and rightly so. Tens of thousands of carefully machined and lubricated engine parts had been doing their job perfectly well for the past fifteen hours. Chopping the throttles would be like choking a person to death.

I keyed the steward's intercom. Nawrocki answered instantly. The man never slept. 'Aye, sir?'

'Prepare passengers for landing.'

'Already doing so, sir.'

I keyed the navigator's station. 'Touchdown estimate?'

'Coming up on ten miles out,' Stone said.

'That was fast.' I retarded the throttles even more to increase our rate of descent.

'Tail winds picking up,' he explained.

Not good. Wind across a runway was one thing to worry about, but at least on the ground a runway stayed put. The wind made waves and the faster it blew, the higher the waves and deeper the swells, and onto that same water I had to plunk sixty-eight thousand pounds of flying metal filled with tired people.

'Watch your airspeed,' Fatt said quietly, his voice as steady as the rate-of-climb indicator showing us in a five hundred feet-per-minute descent.

'She loves it nice and steady, right up to the finish.'

'Don't they all?'

Fatt chuckled but said nothing.

I risked a quick glimpse out the window. Nothing but a dark grey void.

'Where's the bottom of this mud?' I said.

'Four hundred and dropping.'

The altimeter hands were unwinding to thirteen hundred feet. 'Cabeço Gordo's at a thousand feet,' I said to remind myself of the island's volcano. No need to smash into Horta's familiar landmark on the way down.

A lighter streak of grey, then another, and another as the overcast began thinning. I advanced the fuel mixture to full rich and banked slightly to enter the downwind leg of the landing pattern. So far so good. Because of the clipper's immense size, she was slow to respond to control input forces, but when she did, she did so solid and sure. The airspeed needle continued its slow retreat from one hundred-ten knots as I began a one-minute turn to port that would bring us onto final approach.

Still no sight of water or land or anything but milky grey. But the instruments told me I was on course and doing fine. Even so, I sure would have loved a little glimpse of ocean to let me know I was still on the planet earth and not in some dream world.

The curtain rings screeched as Fatt yanked them back and shouted,

'You boys gonna' love Horta. Any of you ever been there? '

'Do you mind?' I snapped.

'Sorry, got a little carried away.'

'Flaps ten.'

'Roger, flaps ten.'

I rolled in more nose-down trim to counteract the added lift, and kept my airspeed pegged at ninety knots, just as Fatt shouted, 'Land ho, mateys!'

The clouds surrendered their vice grip on my world to reveal the grey-green, white-capped tossed surface of the sea three hundred feet below. Land it wasn't but it felt great to see it nonetheless. Faial island lay two miles dead ahead and the striking difference in the water conditions of its wind-sheltered cove versus the open sea was striking as we drew nearer and nearer.

Pan Am had chosen this tiny speck of volcanic land in the middle of the southern Atlantic Ocean for the very feature I now observed. The city of Horta, located in the southeastern most part of the island, has a narrow spit of land curving up and around it like a fishhook that creates shelter from the wind and also functions as a perfect breakwater.

But not so much that I dared let her land by herself. The wind was coming from south and kicking up whitecaps and major swells. That same wind was blowing across the bay too, creating a smaller version of what I would call a less than ideal situation, but better than nothing.

I couldn't land into the wind like I normally would because that would slam her hull down across the wave crests and we'd end up cracking something, most likely our sponsons. Mike Kennedy had done that during a survey flight to Horta and caught hell from Preister and every Boeing engineer that had ever worked on the plane. And they were right to be angry. Every plane has its limits, and it's a captain's job to know exactly what that limit is, and exactly how far beyond he can press his luck. Kennedy's luck ran out. Would mine?

'Your rate of descent stinks,' Fatt said.

I applied throttle and she slowly ballooned up.

'Flaps thirty,' I said.

'Thirty you got.'

From then on things happened quickly, as they always do during those final seconds between being airborne and waterborne. Now at eighty knots, she was starting to be a real handful as the slower moving air made her control surfaces sluggish and I had to twist and tug the wheel in larger and larger motions as Fatt called out our altitude and airspeed, while I concentrated on the touchdown spot of two, brightly-painted buoys with flashing lights that marked the beginning of the seaway. The wave action bobbed and jerked them around, which helped me judge that perfect moment when the swell would pass and I could touch down her hull on the backside of the wave like a phonograph needle slipping into that first groove of a Benny Goodman record - without skipping, of course.

That's what I wanted to do. What she wanted to do was a different story, but one that had a happy ending, too. After two sharp, slapping skips over the waves her hull dug in and she became a ship again, wallowing in the swells as I taxied toward the boarding ramp.

Fatt peered out the window at the skies and growled something unintelligible.

'What do you think?' I said.

'Getting worse, I think.'

'Can we re-fuel and take off in time?'

He shook his head. 'Don't want to risk it. We're stuck here, damn it.'

Sparks handed him a slip of paper. He quickly scanned its contents and raised his bushy eyebrows. 'Kind of good news. Met says the front's moving fast. Conceivably we could get out of here first thing in the morning.'

'Conceivably.'

He crumpled the paper. 'Make that definitely, because I'll be at the wheel.'

'What about me?'

'You'll be too tired from playing nicey-nice with our Nazi storm troopers when they find out they ain't going nowhere and start stomping their hobnail boots on your pretty little toes.'

The backbone of surprise is fusing speed with secrecy.
- Carl von Clausewitz

Faial Island in the Azores is like a life preserver.

Without its bounty of food, water and supplies, countless clipper ships would have never made it across the South Atlantic. Today the Yankee Clipper's needs were much the same as the sailing ships of old, as the ground crew serviced her in Horta's sheltered harbor.

While this was taking place, passengers and crew, via a conga line of taxicabs, made their way up the steep hillside dotted with scrub trees and sparse vegetation, heading for what had been called the Pan Am Club, before Trippe's deal with Lufthansa.

Deplaning had gone off without a hitch. No broken bones on the bobbing and heaving sponson, but plenty of frowns and pursed lips from the compliance officers as they navigated the slippery walkway leading to shore. God only knows what kind of information those jokers were lugging around inside their black leather briefcases. But from the way Hitler had deployed these people to industries all across the United States, supposedly to 'observe, note and report' any deviations from the neutrality agreement, I figured they were doing a bang-up job of industrial espionage while they were at it.

And why not? On the surface, they were in America to make sure we weren't building bombers for Britain on the sly, or tanks for Russia on the cheap. But while they were doing so, it became the perfect opportunity to cherry-pick our latest manufacturing processes and haul them back to Germany. Forget about the fox being in the henhouse. These guys were wolves. And that guy Bauer? The more ordinary and simple he acted the more suspicious I got. I had to admire his easy-going, off-putting style, but I shudder to think how many poor suckers fell for it only to discover they were trapped in his sticky, Gestapo web.

I was having these thoughts for a good reason, because by luck of the taxi draw, the detective sat beside me, wet shoulder to wet shoulder, as our cab waited in line to let us out at the white painted, single-story club. Sheets of rain buffeted its arched glass entrance while scores of attentive, umbrella-toting doormen appeared as if by magic to escort the passengers and crew inside.

'Hear they've got a nice breakfast spread,' I said amiably as the rain thundered on our roof like gravel.

Bauer chuckled and patted his stomach. 'I am still full from last night.'

'How did you sleep?'

'Not a wink.'

'Sorry to hear that.'

He grinned like a little boy. 'Actually, I was too excited to sleep. I've never flown on a clipper before.'

'How do you normally travel?'

He closed his eyes and shuddered. 'They send me on catapult mail ships. One minute we're motionless, the next...BANG!' He smacked his hands together, 'We're in the air flying. It's miserable.'

'I thought they didn't use those anymore, now that you've got planes that can fly to America non-stop.'

'The Luftwaffe is using them for military operations. All that remains are those loathsome catapult planes and your beautiful Boeing clippers to do the job.' He shrugged. 'But, as Berlin reminds us all the time, compliance officers have priority seating over the Gestapo. We're just the sheep dogs, they're the owners.'

'And we're the sheep.'

He laughed. 'I'd hardly call Americans sheep. You have too many sharp teeth for that.'

'If so, then the Gestapo's the dentist.'

He sat back and gave me a long stare. 'Why this constant nipping at my heels? Why is it impossible for us to get along?'

'You tell me.'

He shook his head. 'The war is over, my friend. We won. Can we start from there?'

Our taxi pulled forward and stopped again. Other taxi doors ahead of us were opening and slamming shut, people getting out and dashing for shelter. I wanted to slug this guy so badly I could feel my fist itch. I scratched it instead.

'The war is not over, and you definitely haven't won yet.'

'A mere technicality. A few more weeks, a month at the most.' Again that gentle, maddening smile of his. The superior Nazi holding all the cards.

'Don't bet on it.'

'Is there something you know that could alter my position?'

My mouth got dry. This guy was damned good. 'Just a hunch, that's all.'

'I see. Well, time will tell, I suppose.'

Two taxis ahead of us and then our turn to make the dash through the rain.

I said, 'How come you managed to get a reserved seat on the flight?'

A slight hesitation. 'I thought I told you. I'm being summoned to Berlin.'

'On the carpet for something?'

He looked puzzled, and then brightened suddenly. 'Oh, nothing of the sort. Actually, they're giving me an award for some detective work I did in Warsaw.'

'The Iron Cross?'

'How did you guess?'

'You look the type.'

He laughed 'Tell my wife that when we reach Lisbon.'

'She's there?'

'Waiting for her conquering hero. We're taking a plane to Berlin. Just the two of us - like old times, before the children came along. You have family?'

My turn to hesitate. 'Some.'

'Then you understand completely what I am saying.'

The door opened and a gust of wind spattered rain inside. He held out his hand. 'A truce then?'

I shook it and smiled. 'Not on your life.'

Breakfast stretched into late morning, and the rain kept coming down. A few bored passengers played Ping-Pong in the game room while others played cards. Still others stood by the glass windows, staring morosely at the rain-soaked hydrangea and chrysanthemum blossoms shivering in the gusty wind.

Fatt, ever the schemer, had conveniently 'arranged' to remain dockside to supervise the refueling and provisioning operations, leaving me marooned with Nawrocki and Addison to appease and entertain the passengers during the unwanted weather delay. Our stewards were more than capable of handling the passengers during normal business hours in flight, but when things got strained, like travel delays, Pan Am wanted somebody with pilot's wings on his chest to soothe the savage beasts if they started rattling their cages.

I dreaded making the formal announcement that we'd be staying overnight, so I kept putting it off in hopes that the weather might miraculously change. This wasn't wishful thinking, however. The low pressure front was moving like a crack passenger train as high pressure shoved the isobars on the forecaster's map further and further east.

I decided to see if what I was imagining was actually taking place, and excused myself from the gathered crowd, five of whom swarmed around Ava who was holding court, Hollywood-style, laughing, smoking like a locomotive and dazzling them all.

I made my way over to the company's weather forecasting office located just off the main hallway. Minutes later I traced my finger over the freshly-inked isobar line and smudged it slightly.

The Pan Am meteorologist winced. 'I just spent five minutes plotting that thing.'

'Sorry. What's your best guess?'

He chewed his lips as he deliberated. 'I wouldn't pull the plug yet. You might make it out by late tonight.'

I thought of our scientist twisting in the wind in Lisbon while we twiddled our thumbs in Horta. 'Sure about that?'

He gave me that familiar, wearied look weather forecasters have been giving pilots ever since time began. I rephrased it to give him his proper due. 'What's your best estimate?'

He looked at the chart and then out the window.

'Maybe.'

To protect myself, I gave the passengers my, 'We're not going anywhere' speech and then, amidst their expected groans, I held out the same carrot the weather man had held out to me; a slight chance things could clear up, the seas grow calm enough, and we'd be on our way, so please have faith in God, Mother Nature and Lufthansa - in that order.

The crowd dispersed, Nawrocki and Addison scurrying after them like sheep dogs, nudging them toward the bar, the game rooms, and the restaurant, while peppering them with cheerful suggestions as to how to spend the next few hours on a tiny island in the middle of nowhere without going crazy.

The German contingent, led by Father Petrucelli, headed straight for the bar. Ziggy brought up the rear like a bobbing caboose.

A voice behind me whispered, 'What I wouldn't give to be a fly on that wall.'

I turned and there stood Ava.

'Got a light, darling Sam?'

I fished for a match. 'Didn't know you smoked.'

'I don't. Goes with the act.'

She held my hand to steady the flame, which unaccountably shook slightly.

'You okay?' she said.

'Never better.'

'Let's go for a walk.'

'In this?'

'The grandson of a Key West wrecker afraid of getting a little wet?'

'Not if you're not.'

Turned out to be more wind than rain, which was a good sign that the front was moving fast. But even so we had a time of it, wrestling with a hotel umbrella that was big enough for two, but kept threatening to turn itself inside out. I finally gave up and furled it, willing to risk getting wet instead.

Ava held out her palm and said, 'Where'd all the water go?'

'Towards Lisbon, I hope. And if we're lucky we'll leap frog over it tonight and get back on schedule. All depends on sea conditions.'

'Last time I checked we were flying in a seaplane. Why would water matter?'

'Our runways move up and down. If the waves get too high, we'll crash into them on takeoff, which is just like crashing into a brick wall.'

'Didn't think about that.'

'You're a land pilot, that's why.'

'When all this is over, maybe I'll get my seaplane rating. Mind showing me the ropes if I do?'

'I'm not Amelia Earhart.'

180

She took my arm. 'That makes two of us.'

We walked in silence down the long curving brick pathway from the club building to a sheltered overlook. No passengers in sight. Couldn't blame them. What is normally a delightful place to appreciate the flora and fauna of this little gem of an island was now a grey, gloomy foreboding place you couldn't wait to get away from.

I said, 'How did things go in Hollywood after I left last night?'

She sighed. 'The usual: grim Germans, nosy newspaper reporter, jovial priest, glamorous actress, weasely agent and an assorted cast of minor characters, all eager to be in Lisbon. Some of us slept, most of us didn't. How were things for you on the flight deck?'

'Just like you; trying to act the part. How am I doing?'

She gave me a long, calculated look. For the first time I had a chance to notice that her eyes were more violet than blue.

'Something the matter?' she said.

'Your eyes. Very interesting color.'

'Depends on the lighting. At night they're more blue.' She went on tiptoe to peer at my face. 'And yours are brown, I see.'

'Plain old brown.'

'Good, that's settled. Our eyes, I mean. It's been nagging both of us, I'm sure, ever since we met.'

We arrived at the sheltered overlook. Blossoming Wisteria vines jammed the pergola almost to bursting. Their weight made it creak in the wind.

Ava peered down into the sheltered harbor. 'Thar' she blows.'

The Yankee Clipper huddled on the water like a grounded sea bird. A crew member clambered over her rain-slicked wings, while a team of others worked on the starboard engines, their cowlings opened like clamshells for servicing. Even from this distance, I could make out Orlando's massive shape as one of the workers.

I pointed him out to Ava, 'Once a mechanic, always a mechanic.'

'He's acting the part great.'

'Not acting. Knows engines like you know movies.'

'All the better then.'

'So let's review our little movie, shall we?'

For the next ten minutes we went over the details of what would happen once we touched down in Lisbon; where we would go, what we would do. The experts back at Couba Island had figured out all the steps well in advance. But of course that meant everything except the plan would unfold because life is like that. Even so, people like to plan, mostly because it gives them something to do until it's time to actually do it and then all hell breaks out.

My job in Lisbon was to be - in Fatt's words - 'grease on the axle,' meaning my Pan Am uniform with its impressive 'Master of Flying Boats' gold wings would play a key part of the extrication plan for our good *Herr* Doktor, should something go wrong. Which it would, of course. I just didn't know what.

We finally ran out of words and stood there in silence looking out at the wind-tossed waters, each in our own thoughts.

I was so absorbed in mine that the touch of her hand on my arm startled me and I jumped.

'Sorry,' she said.

'That's okay.'

'Far away?'

'Thinking about Abbie. Want to get her one of those little carved monkeys I saw back at the club. She collects them.'

'I loved horses when I was her age.'

'Real or toys?'

'Are you kidding? Real.'

'Ever get one?'

'Not until I grew up. Had three, loved them all.'

We both turned to go at the same time and bumped shoulders.

'After you,' she said laughingly.

'Please, beauty before age.'

'Let's compromise.'

She took my arm and we made our way together up the curving walkway. I was about to say something about monkeys when she squeezed my arm and said, 'I'm so sorry about your family.'

I nodded stupidly, at a loss for words, and then finally said, 'How did you know?'

'It came up when they were talking about getting you for this mission.'

'"They"?'

'Uncle George, Captain Fatt, the other Sons of Liberty. Her name was Estelle, right? And Eddie?'

'Yes.'

'I can't imagine what it must have been like.'

182

'Me either.'

She stopped. 'So many people died that day. Washington and New York. People who had done nothing wrong. Slaughtered like...like...'

'Pigs.'

'Except they were innocent people. Your wife, your little baby boy.' She wiped away windblown wisps of hair across her face and with it tears. 'I'm just so sorry it happened, that's all.'

I stood there, waiting for the ache in my throat to loosen up. It didn't, so all I could do was nod my understanding.

We continued walking. Her grip tightened on my sleeve. 'I want to kill them all. The bastards.'

'We've got a whole planeload. Where do you want to start?'

'At the back and work my way forward, and save *Herr Inspektor* Bauer for last.'

'He's up to something but I don't know what.'

'Me either.'

'Think he's got wind of us?'

She frowned. 'I hope to God not.'

'He's one of those cops who's easy on the outside, but hard on the inside. Puts you at your ease and then pounces. At least that's what I think - but on second thought, why don't we ask him ourselves? Look.'

Bauer and Ziggy were weaving their way down the walkway, arm in arm, best of friends. And when I say weaving, I mean it. They were drunk as skunks.

'My God,' Ava said. 'A Nazi and a Jew, drinking buddies?'

Ziggy spotted us and waved merrily. 'Fancy meeting you here.'

Bauer smiled stupidly and bumbled along for the ride.

'Ziggy, you hardly every drink,' Ava said.

'Surprise!' he said.

They came to an inconclusive stop and regarded us with great benevolence.

'Let me guess,' Ava said. 'Bloody Mary's for breakfast.'

Ziggy stabbed the air with great authority. 'Correct as usual, Doctor Watson.'

Bauer looked puzzled.

I said, 'Ever heard of Sherlock Holmes?' He shook his head, but then suddenly brightened. 'Of course, the great British detective. Most excellent stories. 'The Hounds of something or other.''

'The Baskervilles.'

He snapped his fingers, or at least tried to, but he couldn't get it to happen. He stared at them like they'd let him down.

Ava said, 'This fresh air will do you boys a world of good.'

'As long as it doesn't sober us up, right *Herrrrrr* Bauer?' Ziggy rolled his 'r's' with great theatricality.

'Correct, *Herr* Siegel. There comes a time when the world is best viewed through the bottom of a glass.' He regarded at the gloomy overcast sky. 'This is one of them.'

He turned majestically on his heel and towed Ziggy along with him back to the bar.

Ava said softly, 'And the Lion shall lie down with the lamb.'

Despite everyone's desire to escape, the weather gods refused to cooperate until the following morning, when they quelled the waves long enough for us to lift off from Horta at 8:38am and never look back until when we touched down in Lisbon six hours and forty-four minutes later, after an uneventful flight with Fatt and me at the controls and a load of passengers ready to end their rain-soaked adventure in sunny Lisbon.

All I can say is, what a difference a war makes, not only on countries that are waging it, but on countries that are not, like Portugal. Unlike the United States, whose neutrality and distance from the battle left it like Noah's ark stuck on the top of Mount Ararat with not a drop of water in sight, Lisbon was awash in refugees trying to escape the madness of their native lands; Germans, Russians, Poles, Greeks, Jews, prostitutes, homosexuals, all of them desperately looking for a way out.

The ones with lots of money used it to beg, borrow or steal a clipper ticket. Few made it but most had to make do with a long ocean journey to a place where they wouldn't be persecuted. And those places were getting fewer and fewer.

During the flight, Sparks had tuned in on the latest of what was going on in Nazi-controlled England. Even more civilian restrictions had been placed upon the conquered nation. This latest one had to do with travel outside ones 'sector.' In short, if you didn't have written and stamped permission to travel to anyplace other than your immediate village, town or section of a city, you didn't move.

The Brits were not taking this laying down of course, and the news story focused on the protest groups marching from one village to the next in defiance of the Nazi decree. No one was harmed, but only a matter of time before the gloves came off and the hobnail boots started kicking. Not easy being trapped on an island with your conquerors breathing down your neck, just waiting for an opportunity to grab and twist it until you died.

Signs of the 'new order' were visible at Pan Am's ticket counter in Lisbon, with Lufthansa personnel replacing our Portuguese personnel. Sheer pandemonium greeted our crew after we cleared customs. Even though three in the afternoon and our return flight wasn't until the next morning, the place was jammed with refugees. They took one look at us and our uniforms, and the potential freedom we represented and surged toward the stone-faced Lufthansa ticket agents, who refused to yield.

Fatt nodded at us to keep moving, lest we get caught up in somebody's story. And it almost worked until a tall, haunted-eyed, neatly-bearded man stepped in front of Fatt and me and barred our way.

'Gentlemen, when is your return flight, please?'

I looked at Fatt who looked at me, so I said, 'Five-thirty tomorrow morning, weather permitting of course.'

The man's face tightened and he glanced over his shoulder at a woman and two children who sat perfectly still on the crowded bench, staring forward. But you could tell they were watching every move he made and listening to his every word. His desperate eyes locked with mine.

'Sir, I have reservations for this flight and now they are telling me they cannot locate them.'

'I'm sorry, but -'

'Forgive me for being so abrupt, sir, but our lives are at stake. If we do not get on that flight...' He blinked quickly, as if something had lodged in his eye but the enormity of what he just said made him choke up.

I looked at Fatt, who with the slightest twitch of his cheek muscle gave me the go-ahead.

'Your name, please?' I said quietly.

'Kreiser. Oscar Kreiser.'

While Fatt escorted the crew out of harm's way and to the taxis and the waiting hotel, I walked with the man back to the ticket counter. The crowd parted upon seeing my uniform like the Red Sea did to Moses, allowing us to move to the head of the line.

The ticket agent gave me a weary once- over. Even though I had shaved and cleaned up as best I could on the plane, I was still a little rough-looking around the edges. The agent was too, for that matter, but being a stolid German, he didn't show it nearly as much.

'Jawohl, kapitan?' Bored to death.

I sent him my most winning smile. 'Say, where's my friend Oscar's tickets?'

'Bitte?'

'Herr Kreiser's tickets for the Baltimore flight tomorrow morning.' I held up four fingers. 'Four of them. Hand them over. I need to check them against our manifest.'

He shook his head. 'We have no such record of that name.'

I smiled even more. 'Sure you do, you just misplaced it, that's all.'

'No, I am positive.'

I pulled out the manifest from our inbound flight, pretended to read it, and then tucked it away. 'Explain to me why the heck we're showing their names for the Tail Suite?'

A quick blink of surprise, and I knew exactly what was going on with this joker. Everybody in this room had money, some more than others. Hard cold cash was changing hands around here as fast as the refugees could shove it into someone's hands, who could pull enough strings to get them a space on the clipper. How much this clown had gotten from somebody to bump Kreiser and his family off the flight I don't know, but I was damned if I was going to let him get away with it.

'Let me see your manifest.' I said gruffly. 'I want to sort this out for my friend.'

He still hesitated, so I said, 'Where's your supervisor? I'm sure he can help me since it's obvious you can't.'

A quick eye-blink. 'That won't be necessary.' He fussed and fiddled with some paperwork, but I knew he was just killing time. I had tumbled this shark's racket and he knew it. No way was he going to slip off my gaff hook now. Time to flip him into the boat and sure enough, he reached under the counter and pulled up four slips of paper.

'Ach, someone has made a transposition error,' he said. 'It happens sometimes, especially with all the confusion lately. I am most sorry, *Herr* Kreiser. Here are your tickets. Be here at the terminal four o'clock tomorrow morning at the latest. Enjoy your flight, *danke schön* for flying

with Lufthansa, and please excuse me I have other customers who need my assistance.'

He couldn't wait to get away. Sure, he'd catch hell from whomever paid cash for Kreiser's seats, but that was his problem, not mine.

We cleared the crowd and came to a stop. 'How you doing, Oscar?'

He clutched his tickets like they were four sheets of gold. 'You have no idea...'

'I do. And three days from now you'll be in America.'

'America,' he said softly.

He made the word sound like music.

The scene at the Aviz hotel in downtown Lisbon was the exact opposite of the Lufthansa reservation desk. Instead of the strident, tense atmosphere and high-pitched voices filled with anxiety, the hotel lobby's three-story, gold-leafed walls was a vast space filled with elegantly-dressed guests strolling with a casual sense of purpose amidst towering potted palms, their countless conversations merged into a gentle, contented murmur. Somewhere in this glittering, palace-like place, two classical guitars tossed a piece of music back and forth like a silk-covered softball.

Portugal's declared neutrality kept it clear of the clutches of Nazi

Germany, and Lisbon had become the watering hole for spies, refugees and everybody in between that a global war attracts, including an improbable convention of prominent German scientists gathered for their annual meeting. Despite Europe being in flames, science apparently marched ever onward to the beat of a drum all its own.

From a quick scan of the fifty or so guests in the lobby, none of them seemed the scientist-type. Then I laughed at myself. What the heck did I know about what the well-dressed scientist was wearing that would distinguish him from - say, the two men standing by the potted palm, head-to-head in some intense discussion?

My orders were simple: Fatt and the crew would rest up at the hotel for a few hours, get some dinner, and then return to the Yankee Clipper early in the morning for the lengthy pre-flight procedures. Orlando and I were remain behind to help Ava and Ziggy, when, with scientist in tow, it came time for us to make a dash for the plane just before takeoff.

A scattered popping of flashbulbs lit up the lobby. Like some collective creature, everyone, myself included, swiveled our heads in the direction of the main desk where Ava leaned against the polished walnut and brass-trimmed counter, posing for pictures like she owned the joint.

Ziggy stood beside her, beaming and jabbering at the reporters and photographers in a repeat performance of the 'starlet' act they'd done in Baltimore, only this time a female Portuguese translator heightened the drama by jabbering Portuguese at the top of her lungs.

People love movie stars all over the world and react the same way when they're around them. What did it matter that Ava James didn't speak Portuguese? Everyone understood the international language of dazzling beauty, and in this she was fluent. Hard to imagine this elegantly dressed, highly made-up, glamorous woman wearing a dirty blouse and slacks, on her hands and knees digging for gold in the Florida Keys.

But I guess that's why she was a movie star. She could be anybody in the world she wanted, and still, somehow, stay Ava James.

She spotted me and gave me a quick wink before she brandished her cigarette holder in the air like a saber and shouted at me, 'Sam, darling!'

Right on cue, Ziggy frowned and tried to restrain her, as if not wanting this to happen, but she shrugged him off like an annoying fly and swept toward me. The photographers swiveled as one, following their favorite target.

'Where've you been hiding, you naughty, naughty, boy?'

I had no trouble acting sheepish and tongue-tied because I was, even though we'd rehearsed this routine a few times while we were stuck at Horta. There had to be a reason for our being together. This was it: movie-star-falls-in-love-with-dashing-pilot.

She twirled around to face the reporters, and as she gushed away in English, the translator rattled away in Portuguese.

'Captain Carter promised to show me Lisbon and I'm holding him to it. Aren't I, captain?'

I made a polite salute. 'Yes, ma'am.'

Her laugh was rich and deep, 'Get a load of this man's manners.' She took my arm and snuggled close. 'Stick around, I just might keep you.'

A burst of Portuguese. The translator said, 'He is your new boyfriend?' A sprinkle of appreciative laughter. Her lips brushed against my cheek then she turned to her admirers. 'What do you think, folks? Should I keep him?'

More flashbulbs.

Ziggy said sternly. 'Time for our meeting, darling.' She sighed. 'If you insist.'

She gave me a quick kiss. On my lips this time, and then twirled away to head for the elevator. The press followed her like a flock of bees, leaving me stripped of my thirty seconds of fame by being kissed by a movie star. What surprised me when she did was her smell. I had expected a tidal wave of heavy perfume to match her equally heavy makeup. But instead a fresh, light aroma that, for lack of a better word, smelled like happiness.

I left that mystery hanging because I had exactly ten minutes to get to my room, clean up and meet up with Orlando, and head for dinner. After that we were to lay low and wait like a pair of Al Capone's bodyguards until ten o'clock, when Ava would spirit the *Herr Doktor* to her room and the 'heist' would begin.

The word choice had been Ziggy's, who had, to everyone's surprise, gotten into the spirit of things ever since his drunken spree with Inspector Bauer back at Horta. Gone was the fretful, ever-worrying little nebbish. In its place was a brash, confident little Napoleon, intent on conquering the world. To watch him dismiss the reporters in the lobby with a confident wave of his imperious hand was to see Bonaparte himself standing at the gates of Moscow, demanding the Czar's immediate and unconditional surrender.

The very thought of such a thing made me wince. Where the French emperor had failed, a German one was about to succeed. Moscow, like Washington D.C. had a smoking bomb crater to mark the passing of the Nazi hobnail boot. But where the United States had signed a Neutrality agreement, Russia had remained defiant; content to let hundreds of thousands of its citizens fall under the rule and reign of Nazi warlords, and worse for many of them, suffer their butchery when the SS Death Squads laid waste to village after village.

Stalin and his Politburo had abandoned Moscow and hightailed to a hiding place beyond the Ural Mountains. And while the Nazis had pursued him, they had still not destroyed him. At least not yet, and Juan Trippe's words came back to me:

'Hitler hesitates... Why?'

The answer apparently lay somewhere deep inside the head of the *Herr Doktor* Professor, and our job was to get him out of Lisbon, back to Couba Island and find out.

I checked my watch for the millionth time, which was probably Orlando's limit, because he said, 'You're making time stand still by checking your watch all the time.'

'Nervous habit.'

'Pray instead?'

'No thanks.'

'Then I will, if you don't mind.'

He closed his eyes and together we sat in comfortable silence in my hotel room. The last time I checked my watch it had said, 11:28. I never got another chance because the phone rang and I jumped as if shot.

Orlando smiled, 'The power of prayer.'

Ava's voice was tight with excitement. 'He's here.'

'On our way.'

The original plan to have adjoining rooms hadn't worked out. We weren't even on the same floor. But a creaky elevator ride moments later and we were heading down a crowded corridor filled with Germans speaking in boisterous, unmodulated voices, edged here and there with insane giggles - your typical convention crowd doing its conventional, after-hours thing. We managed to dodge and weave our way past them without colliding with their wobbly trajectories, that is, until the last two, who plowed into us like we were flimsy roadblocks begging to be hit. Drunk? You bet. How else could they have misjudged someone Orlando's size, or been so stupid as to growl at him?

'Schwarzie, Raus!'

But to Orlando's credit, all he did was gently grab both men by their shoulders, turn them in the direction of their departing friends, said *'Auf Wiedersehen*, brothers' and nudged them on their way. They took one look at him and then staggered away in pursuit of the departing mob. The corridor quieted. The storm had passed.

'You're a better man than I am,' I said. 'I would have sent both of those bums to the moon for talking to me like that.'

'When hootch does the talking, I don't listen. And those two boys were talking up a storm.'

'Even so...'

Orlando's mitt landed on my shoulder. 'Brother Sam, I appreciate how you feel, but you don't live inside this skin like I do, and I manage all right with the Lord's help.'

He spun me around like a top. 'Let's go be heroes.'

'Welcome to the circus,' Ziggy said breathlessly, as he opened the door to Ava's room.

As befitting her star status, she had a luxury suite complete with a spacious sitting room, where she currently sat across from a short, fat man in his 60s wearing a black dress and a white towel draped over his shoulders. He had a look in his eyes of complete and absolute terror.

'Ready for this, professor?' Ava said.

He nodded without saying a word. Ava reached into a hatbox and pulled out a mannequin head upon which rested a grey wig done up in a matronly bob. She brushed it up a bit and then held it in both hands like a living creature.

'Head down,' she said.

He bent over and she deftly flipped it onto his balding head. A few tugs here and there, and the deed was done. When he raised his head, I saw an old woman.

'Now comes the fun part.'

Ava rummaged around in a wooden case beside her, its contents filled with tubes, cylinders, pencils and combs.

'Nice set up you've got,' I said.

'Wally Westmore's folks loaned it to me.'

'Who's he?'

'The king of Hollywood's makeup world, that's who – Professor Friedman, meet Sam Carter and Orlando Diaz. They're here to help us.'

'I am pleased to meet you both. I hope you succeed.' His voice was soft and high-pitched, which was good, considering he was looking more and more like a woman with every brushstroke and pencil line Ava applied to his pudgy face.

'You're good at this,' I said.

'Lots of practice - hold still, Professor, I need to line your eyes with this red stuff. You've been crying, don't forget.'

'Yes, I remember.'

'Quick, what's your husband's name?'

'Alfred Jäger.'

'And?'

'And he is vice-consul at the Compliance office in Denver, Colorado. He had a heart attack and is too ill to move. The doctors are afraid he might die. I am traveling to be by his bedside.'

She sat back. 'Excellent. I believed you. Almost'

'What did I do wrong?'

'You're words were okay, but...' She punched her fist into her palm. 'You need more oomph in your delivery.'

'What is meant by 'oomph.'?'

'This...' She leaned forward, eyes narrowed, fist stabbing the air for emphasis. 'You're going to be with Alfred come hell or high water because he's your husband, because he's the father of your four beautiful children, and because you will be good God-damned if anybody or ANYTHING is going to stand between you and the man you love, got that?'

Friedman watched like a man hypnotized; his chest rose and his fat-waddled chin jutted out and his tear-reddened eyes blazed. '*Ja*, I understand. *Vielen Danke*. This I can do.'

Orlando cleared his throat. 'I need your baggage stubs, sir.'

'Yes, of course.' Friedman motioned to Ziggy, who fetched his suit coat. The professor dug around for a moment before pulling out two tags and handed them over. 'Be careful. The trunks are extremely heavy.'

Orlando grinned. 'Nothing I can't handle.' Then his face grew somber. 'They're okay to move aren't they? I mean, in case they get dropped - not that I would, of course - but I don't want to break anything.'

'Not to worry.'

'What's inside?' I said.

Friedman shrugged his shoulders. 'I cannot tell you. That way, in case we are stopped and interrogated, you will be unable to divulge that information.'

'What about you?'

His matronly face hardened slightly. 'I have taken provisions to make sure that will never happen.'

I left it at that, and concerned myself with making sure Orlando and I were singing from the same choir book as far as getting this motley crew on board the clipper. The plan was to have Orlando head out to the plane early to load the professor's baggage. As a Pan Am crew member, he could do that without triggering any questions from the Lufthansa harpies.

'Where you going to stow it?' I said.

'Aft cargo hold, upper deck.'

'Will it fit?'

'I'll make it fit.'

'Make sure Fatt gets the additional weight for his COG calculations. Those things won't show on the manifest. And if he doesn't figure them in, then...'

He saluted. 'May I remind you that this is not my first day working the flight line?'

With that, he was gone.

Our side of the equation was a little more complicated.

'Where's the professor's ticket?' I said.

Ziggy pulled it out of an envelope and handed it over. Gone was the familiar blue Pan American Airways logo and flight information. In its place was a Lufthansa version printed in black and red, with their damned swastika taking up more space than necessary. This particular ticket was different than the other ones I'd seen, sporting a red band down the right hand side, signifying Frau Hilda Jäger was a high-priority passenger due all the rights and privileges contained therein, including preferential seating and additional baggage allowance.

'They did a good job on this,' I said.

Ziggy beamed. 'Those Couba Island counterfeiters could work in Hollywood any day. Take a look at what else they dreamed up.'

Not only had General Patton's gang of artists cobbled up the fake Lufthansa priority airline ticket, they had also created a 'letter of passage' from Heinrich Himmler's SS office that stated in almost hysterical terms that Frau Jäger was to be accorded every courtesy, given no restrictions, and afforded immediate passage through any and all ports of embarkation, without concern as to the inconvenience of others - so sayeth *Reichsführer* SS Heinrich Himmler himself, with all the official -looking stamps and seals to prove it.

Ziggy tapped the letter. 'This could get him into Hitler's bedroom, I bet.'

'I prefer America,' Professor Friedman said quietly.

'Speaking of which,' I said. 'Let's go through the drill again.'

We spent the next few minutes ticking off what I hoped would be the ordered, uneventful steps of making our way from the Aviz hotel to the clipper. As we went through the procedure, Ava stored her makeup back into the case, but not without pausing to carefully muss up her hair a bit and opening a button on her tight-fitting blouse.

When I finished, she said, 'How do I look?'

'Like you've been through the wringer.'

'Good,' she said.

'And how do I look?' Friedman said.

'The same. Only a bigger wringer.'

His laugh was dry, quick and nervous. 'I've never done anything like this in my life.'

'Then we're even,' I said, and stood and offered him my arm. '*Frau Jäger?*' May I escort you to the plane?'

She took my arm. 'Thank you, yes.'

Ava said, 'Curtain up.'

Even at this late hour people still jammed the hotel lobby, some talking, others laughing, and mixed with it the contagious beat of a swing orchestra in a faraway ballroom playing an American tune whose name I couldn't place to save my life. All of which made it easier for *Frau* Jäger and me to make our way to a relatively quiet corner, find two empty seats and wait for Ava's 'big entrance.'

Moments later she swept into the room, trailed by a bug-eyed Ziggy who bobbed and bounced like a tin can tied to a 'Just Married' car. But no happy bride and groom in sight, just one pissed-off actress about to explode.

'No, no, no, no NO!' she shrieked at Ziggy, and the lobby fell silent except for the faraway orchestra. 'I don't care who signed the contract. All I care about is getting the hell out of this dump and going home.'

She grabbed him by the collar and lifted him up onto his heels. 'And I mean now!'

'A deal's a deal, sweetheart.'

'Don't you sweetheart me, you little weasel.'

She brushed a stray wisp of hair out of her face and swayed slightly as if she had been drinking.

'They want good little Ava James to star in their shitty little movie?
Fine, they can start by kissing my little…'

Ziggy's hand clamped over her mouth and his eyes popped with terror
at coping with this unexpected Medusa, her snake hair squirming
everywhere and angry flashing eyes sending out death rays left and right.

I patted *Frau* Jäger's shoulder. 'You know what to do.'

He nodded and stood up and waited while I made my way through the
silent crowd that had gathered around Ava like she was a traffic accident.
With my height, she spotted me instantly and wailed, 'Sam, darling, it's you!
Oh, please, please, please take me away to your shiny bright plane right this
instant!'

She swept forward, the crowd parted and she fell into my arms in a
Hollywood swoon.

'What happened?' I said to Ziggy.

He played his part to perfection. 'They welshed on the movie deal.
Couldn't get the numbers to work. She blew up. Had one too many. Party's
over. Now she wants to go home.' He shrugged hopelessly. 'Can we,
captain?'

"Certainly." I made as if to ponder how to do it, and then said, 'I'm
returning to the plane with another passenger who needs assistance. I'd be
happy to help you as well.'

Ziggy's face melted with relief. Ava came out of her swoon and said
drunkenly, 'My big brave man promises he'll let me fly his shiny little plane
all around the sky?'

I extricated myself and smoothed my uniform jacket. 'We'll see what
can be arranged, Miss James.'

She grabbed me with one arm and swung her other one at Ziggy like a
major general. 'Check us out of here, you little twerp. And when we get
back to Hollywood you want to know something?'

'I know, I'm fired.'

'No, you're FIRED!'

I said, 'See you at the taxicab stand?'

Ziggy just nodded, but for the briefest of instants, his eyes flashed and
his face paled, as if he'd suddenly thought of something. But then he turned
resolutely to the reception desk to play his part in the drama that had
caused the lobby to fall silent and now waited see what would happen next.

I steered Ava over to Frau Jäger who stood there, demur and
sorrowful, her sheer black veil partially covering her face and blurring her

195

features. As we approached, the crowd murmured back to life again, buzzing about the bravura performance they'd just witnessed. How many understood English didn't matter. The way Ava acted made the place to buzz with excited gossip.

We made our way out through the polished brass doors that opened onto *Rua Duque de Palmela*. We stood there on the sidewalk, letting the rush and roar of Lisbon at night wash over us in a hot haze. In contrast to the rest of Europe being darkened by war, Lisbon blazed with the lights of a nation at peace. Not a thing to worry about. All was well - and to this day I don't know why that particular thought made me suddenly grab both women and steer them back inside the hotel, where we ran into Ziggy coming the other way.

His face stayed neutral, but his eyes didn't. 'What's the matter?'

'Change of plans.'

'But we've got to get to the plane.'

'Not this way. I smell trouble.'

Ziggy started to say something but Ava said quietly, 'Let's play follow the leader, shall we?'

I quickly led our parade back through the lobby, through the crowd and down a side corridor until I found an exit stairwell. There had to be more than one way to get out of this damned place and I was determined to find it. One flight down, and the clattering of our shoes on steel stairs ended when we arrived at a door that led to a side alley. Once outside, we hurried down the narrow, trash-can filled passage to a street running directly parallel to Rua Duque de Palmela.

'We need to gain some altitude,' I said.

'Huh?' Ziggy said.

'The *Santa Justa* elevator. This way.'

I had caught a glimpse of the famous Lisbon landmark on our drive to the hotel from the airport and prayed my memory served me as to its location. Built around the time of the Eiffel tower, the ornately designed, rectangular cast-iron elevator rose one hundred-twenty feet in the air like a gothic Jules Verne space rocket. Only instead of heading for the moon, the elevator lifted Lisbonites from *Baixa*, the lower town, to *Largo do Carmo*, the higher square, in a matter of minutes, bypassing the city's steep hills in one short vertical leap.

The elevator's lift cage doors were opening just as we arrived. A good omen. We piled inside, along with a crowd of laughing, singing, half-drunk

Lisbonites. The lift took off with a small lurch, everybody giggled, and then it settled down smoothly as the electric winches did their repetitive duty without complaint.

Ava squeezed my arm. 'What's next?'

I started to answer, but as I did, the lift cage cleared the street level and I could see down and across the jumble of rooftops to the flood-lit front entrance of the Aviz hotel where we had stood on the sidewalk moments before. My mouth dried up and I heard a ringing sound in my ears.

A cluster of policemen milled around the front doors, and from the midst of the swirling mass of dark-uniforms appeared the familiar Gestapo-grey leather coat worn by Max Bauer, who angrily pointed this way and that, sending the officers scurrying off like wolves in search of their prey.

'Bauer knows about us,' I said.

Ava watched in silence but said nothing.

The elevator climbed higher over the brightly-lit city. The faint touch of pre-dawn light threw the Lisbon skyline into crisp silhouette, including the Lisbon Castle, lights ablaze, a fairy princess's dream come true. Only in our case it wasn't a dream, but a nightmare if we showed up at the Pan Am terminal and tried to board the clipper. Bauer and his goons would be there waiting for us.

Ava said, 'What are we going to do?'

I said a prayer before reaching inside my small leather overnight bag and felt around until my fingers touched the smooth metal surface of the small pocket flashlight I always carried with me when I traveled. Under normal circumstances I would use it to light up my travel clock to see if it was time to get up for my trip. Tonight, with any luck - and I seriously wondered if we had any left after our narrow escape - this same flashlight just might save us from ending up in a Gestapo interrogation cell.

The lift cage was almost at the top.

I said to Ava, 'How much cash you have?'

'Enough.'

I checked my watch.

4:30a.m.

Fatt and the crew would be on board by now, going through the pre-flight checks. We had less than an hour before the plane took off. Whether we were on it or not, depended on what happened between now and then in a strange city filled with cops looking for us, led by our good old pal, Max Bauer.

Our cab driver wove his way down the steep hills like he was winning at in Le Mans. Ava's promise of doubling his fee helped, but I think he would have done it based on her smile alone when she first flagged him down and the four of us piled in shoulder to shoulder like sardines. She got him singing about half-way there, and he kept it up until we came to a stop on a deserted side street adjacent to Pan Am's maintenance building, about a quarter mile south of the main building, where the Lisbon-Baltimore passengers had most likely begun boarding. By now, Orlando must have loaded Frau Jäger's two steamer trunks on board, and was nervously awaiting our arrival.

But who had arrived instead, I'm sure, was a squad of Portuguese police, scouring the passengers for any trace of our little gang of thieves, who now waited in the shadows for mighty Captain Carter to make his next move. I tried to project that image by holding up my flashlight.

'I'm heading across the street to that shed by the dock. Everybody wait here. When you see me flash my light twice, like this...'

Their worried faces lit up briefly as I did so.

'Then come running - correction - walk casually across the street and onto the dock like it was the most natural thing in the world. Got it?'

Three heads nodded.

'Sure you don't need me?' Ava said. 'I've got more curves than you and a smile that can launch a thousand ships.'

I debated her offer for a moment but decided against it. If I got caught, the others would still have a chance of escaping. Although I didn't have a clue how, since Bauer had thrown a dragnet over Lisbon to find us. I bristled with anger at his lies and deceit, but repressed it and tried to make my voice sound confident and assured.

'Watch for my light.'

Three heads nodded and I was off.

If my calculations were right - and they had to be or we were screwed from the start - the PanAir launch crew had already deployed their boat to the seaway to check for any floating debris the clipper might strike during its takeoff run. As I drew closer to the shed I felt a wave of relief when I spotted the sweeping searchlight of the high-speed launch out on the water doing its official duties as it cruised along the pale green seaway lights bobbing in the waters of Lisbon Bay.

The most important moment was upon me. I squared my captain's cap, smoothed my uniform, briskly opened the door to the boat shed and felt my knees get weak at the beautiful sight of the other PanAir launch, not hanging from a dry-dock sling for repairs, but bobbing peacefully at anchor instead.

I looked around. Nobody in sight.

But then suddenly, '*Ja? Was ist los?*' A close-cropped, bullet-headed young mechanic walked purposefully toward me.

'You speak English?' I said.

He shook his head. I made a sign with my hands imitating an ignition key turning and pointed to the boat.

He frowned in ignorance.

'Key to the boat,' I said imperiously. 'Hand it over. Now.'

He suddenly understood because he glanced over his shoulder at the wall behind him and we both spotted the key hanging there at the same time. Then he turned back, his face quickly gathering into a dark cloud.

'*Nein.*'

I smiled as big a smile as I ever have in my life, and just as he started to smile back, as I knew he would - humans are like monkeys, we can't resist this reflex - I nailed him with a right cross that snapped his head back so hard I thought it would come off. Instead, the force of the blow knocked him back against a tool-filled wall, his head struck against a huge wrench and he dropped like a stone.

A quick search turned up some extension cords that served to bind his hands and feet. A few windings of electrical tape over his mouth to keep him quiet, and then I dragged him down into the launch and flopped him inside out of sight.

'Sleep tight, *kamerad.*'

PanAir motor launches are built for speed and can accelerate like a rocket when needed. But at the moment ours burbled sedately in the shadows of the shore, about a half-mile away from the *Yankee Clipper*. Ava had the wheel while I stood beside her, bracing myself against the windshield to keep steady while I used my flashlight to send my Morse code message.

'Any luck?' she said.

'Not yet.'

Ziggy said, 'What happens if they don't see it?'

'Party's over.'

'Are you sure it was Bauer back at the hotel?'

'Damn right. Stay down back there. The professor too.'

Sound carries across the water and I heard the *Yankee Clipper's* engines start before I saw the blades catch the silvery dawn light. Boarding was finished. She was getting ready to go. This was not looking good.

'C'mon, Fatt, don't let me down, old timer,' I said. 'Open your beady little eyes.'

Ava throttled up slightly. 'Maybe we need to get a little closer.'

'Okay, but go easy.'

The other PanAir launch was about a mile-and-a-half away, patrolling the takeoff lane, unaware that its sister launch was up to no good. One by one the clipper's three other engines caught and coughed into life. The red and green navigation lights on her wingtips gleamed softly, as if beckoning us. And then to my knee-buckling relief a light began flashing from the pilot's window, answering my dots dashes and with this message:

STBD HTCH WILL HIDE YOU FROM SHORE. FATT

The plane revved its engines and began taxiing toward the takeoff lane. I almost lost my cap in as Ava increased our speed in response.

'This is not going to be easy,' I warned. 'But if anybody can do it, you can.'

She didn't respond, so I said, 'I'll put out the fenders.'

'Roger, that. Make sure the bowline is coiled.'

'Aye, aye, captain.'

That got a smile out of her. Not a big one, but at least a smile.

'Can we sit up yet?' Ziggy said.

'No way. We're kicking up a wake and Bauer and his boys are watching. We're just two Pan Am workers doing their job.'

And that's what they saw, because every curve of Ava's body was temporarily lost in the voluminous folds of the Pan Am white coveralls she wore over her street clothes. Mine were a better fit, but not by much. We had grabbed what we could from the crew lockers before we left. At this distance, I hoped the police couldn't distinguish us other than being two white blobs in the morning light. The faint tendrils of morning fog here and there helped our cause, but lifting fast.

The clipper neared the takeoff lane, her bow wave a small white moustache curving gracefully as she parted the sea. We drew closer and closer, now pacing her, and then slowly catching up until we were gliding beneath her majestic triple tail towering high above us.

We drew alongside her hull, slewing and slicing as we bounced up and down in the wake. The prop wash buffeted us like a boxer in a ring. I climbed up onto the bow and crouched, line in hand. Just as I did so, the boarding door popped open and Purser Nawrocki's smiling face greeted me.

'About time,' he shouted to be heard above the engine roar.

Just then Fatt reduced power on number three engine to make things easier, wind-wise, but still a rocky ride. Faces filled the passenger windows, watching our every move. Great. All we needed was an audience. Ava sensed this too, but ever the actress, she tossed her cap off in response, shook her hair free and laughed like she was having the wild, drunken adventure of her life, this was just one more crazy Hollywood escapade that those who lived in tinsel town did all the time, so enjoy the show, brothers and sisters, I'm here to entertain you.

I used hand signals to guide her closer and closer to the sponson's edge. The tie down eyelet was tantalizingly close, but so small a target that it kept eluding my fumbling fingers as I tried to thread the line through.

'No use,' I shouted. 'Got to board.'

Line in hand, I judged the swells between our boat and the slab-like sponson and, at the right instant leaped and landed, but immediately began sliding off. I spread eagled as fast as I could to stop myself. Seconds later I made fast the line and began drawing the launch closer and closer, until directly alongside, its rubber fenders cushioning the boat's bobbing and bouncing motions as it kept perfect pace with the ever accelerating clipper.

I guided *Frau* Jäger across the slippery aluminum deck until she made it into Nawrocki's arms and he guided her inside. Ziggy followed next, giving a great WHOOP as he leaped onto the sponson.

Ava pointed to starboard and shouted, 'Here come the Indians!'

The foaming bow wave of a dark blue police launch was growing closer and closer. Its bright searchlight stabbed back and forth through the wisps of fog in search of its prey.

'You next,' I shouted.

Ava locked down the throttle, stepped out of her coveralls like a Broadway stripper, and gracefully hopped onto to the sponson and into my arms as though this was something she did every day of her life.

'Fancy meeting you here.' she yelled.

I handed her off to Nawrocki and leaped back into the launch. I had two minutes at the most before the police boat, with an angry Inspector Bauer on board, arrived to put an end to our game.

I waved at the figure leaning out the open co-pilot's window. Couldn't tell who, but he waved back. Then I motioned vigorously to starboard at the approaching police boat and he gave me a vigorous thumbs-up. They knew what to do and did it almost immediately, revving up the starboard engines even higher to swing the plane away from the intersecting track of the police boat.

Time for me to do my part as well. I went below to where the mechanic sat, hands still tied, tape over his mouth, but now wide awake and angry as hell.

I stripped off my coveralls, put on my captain's cap, yanked the man to his feet, knelt behind him and pressed the tip of my puny little penknife against his jugular vein. The best I could do for a weapon under the circumstances, and I prayed he would think it the tip of a menacing commando knife instead.

With my other hand, I reached around and ripped off the electrical tape covering his mouth. And even though he didn't understand English, my whisper in his ear made my intentions clear as I shoved him forward and hissed, 'Get moving Fritzie, and no funny stuff.'

Just before we got topside, I untied his hands, shoved hard and he went stumbling over to the wheel and flopped into the seat. I quickly pocketed my knife, not wanting the world to see what was happening. He sat there, stupefied. I smiled my winning smile and saluted him

'Auf wiedersehen.'

The WHOOP-WHOOP of the police boat siren drove me across to the sponson, where with two quick slashes of my knife, I cut the line that had been holding us. The launch lurched away to starboard as the Yankee Clipper continued its swooping turn to port. We were going at least thirty knots by now, and if I didn't watch it, Fatt would take off with me hanging on like a wing walker.

I crouched down and made my way toward the open hatch. Nawrocki was shouting something at me, but I couldn't hear him over the engine roar. His hands grabbed me, I was inside, the hatch slammed shut and the scream of the engines muted to a dull roar.

The PanAir boat arced away in the distance, and so did the police boat, now a dwindling speck of frustrated authority as the clipper reached her takeoff speed, and the drumming, slapping thrum of steel on water suddenly disappeared as she lifted off the water and flew.

I turned away from the window and was startled to see Ava and Ziggy and Frau Jäger standing there staring at me like I was the main attraction in a carnival side show.

Ava said, 'You sure know how to have a good time.'

I smiled weakly. 'It's not over yet.'

An Army lives, sleeps, eats, and fights as a team. This individual heroic stuff is a lot of crap
General George S. Patton, Jr.

The *Yankee Clipper's* flight deck felt like a church on Sunday.

Everybody calm and collected, engines humming, systems working perfectly. Mason and Stone, nodded their casual 'hello's' to me like I'd just returned from the bathroom instead of having barely escaped the jaws of the Gestapo. That's the Navy for you. Nothing impresses them but their own faces in the mirror when they shave. Fatt was no different. As I settled into the co-pilot's seat and he said, 'Long time no see, kid.'

Two could play that game. 'Figured I'd drop in and see how you and the boys were doing.'

'Oh, we're hunky-dory.'

'By the way, that hard left turn left you took left the Gestapo and the Portuguese cops in the dust.'

'Pleasure was all mine.' He grinned and wiggled the yoke. 'Time to do paperwork. You have the aircraft, captain.'

'Before you go...'

'Yes?'

'We got away okay, but we both know they've radioed ahead to Baltimore by now. They'll grab the professor the minute we land.'

'Ah, yes...' He eased his bulk back down. 'You have a point.'

'A big point.'

'But the Sons of Liberty have an even bigger point.'

'Which is?'

He shook his head. 'I've spent the past six months being strung along by Patton and his gun-toting, country boys, and I've learned the hard way that when it comes to dealing them they're like moonshiners; you find out what you need to find out when you need to and not a second sooner, less the revenuers find out and go after you. I guess that's rubbed off on me because now it's my turn to make like a moonshiner and zip my lip.'

'Well, somebody didn't because that Bauer damn well knew what we were up to at the hotel.' 'The kraut guy in the leather trench coat?'

'Waiting for us with open arms.'

'I wish I hadn't heard that.' Fatt sighed. 'Well, kid, we both know there's no such thing as a perfect secret. All you can do is do your best.'

'The Gestapo won't stop until they get him.'

'They can't catch him if they can't find him,' he crooned.

'But he's on this plane, and when we land in Baltimore they'll be waiting for him. Don't you understand?'

'That's what they're planning to do but that's not what's going to happen.'

'Because?'

He leaned over and punched me on the shoulder. 'Fly the plane. I'll be right back.'

'Before you go, Mr. Secret Agent, what the hell's in that guy's luggage?'

Fatt smiled. 'I haven't a clue.'

'C'mon!'

'Honest, I don't know. But I'll lay you odds it ain't underwear.'

I took the left seat as 'watch officer,' checked the autopilot and made a quick visual of the instruments while waiting for Allison, our third officer to take my co-pilot's seat.

The Purser's intercom light lit up.

'Flight deck, Carter here.'

'Chickens tucked into the henhouse, captain.'

'Where'd you put *Frau* Jäger?'

'She and Miss James are in the special compartment.'

'Perfect.'

The 'special compartment,' located just ahead of the VIP tail suite, could accommodate two overnight passengers, plus it had a privacy curtain to shield them from the prying eyes of their fellow passengers. If 'Frau' Friedman was careful, he might even be able to take off his wig and cool down a bit.

I said, 'So, who'd you kick out to make that happen?'

'Nobody. I lied on the original manifest. Even found a spot for Mr. Ziegler. Just ahead of them in Stateroom G.'

'Nawrocki, remind me to give you some kind of medal when we get home.'

'Scotch would be better.'

'Done.'

Instead of Lieutenant Allison, the massive bulk of Orlando flopped into the co-pilot's seat dressed in the 'Summer-whites' uniform worn by Pan Am station engineers. Lufthansa management in Lisbon didn't know from first base when it came to Pan Am hierarchy, and one sight of a man this big filling out a uniform that official-looking they must have locked their heels and saluted.

'All set with the luggage?' I said.

Orlando grunted. 'Heavy as hell, but easy as pie. You?'

'Piece of cake.'

He laughed. 'You are one crazy guy.'

'Only when I have to be.'

He leaned closer and said quietly, 'So, what went wrong back there?'

'Nothing on our side of the equation. We had the professor made-up perfectly and Ava played her exit scene in the lobby like a movie star.'

'So why the Keystone Cops? It doesn't make sense.'

Suddenly I felt a little woozy; the way you do when you're driving a car in the winter and you hit a stretch of black ice and suddenly your butt tells you that you're not in contact with the road anymore. Then the rest of your body chimes in as you start sliding sideways, like now, and I heard myself saying, 'Because somebody on our side must have tipped off Bauer.'

'How you figure?'

'This was no accidental meeting. Bauer and the cops were waiting for us outside the hotel. That stuff about him meeting his wife and getting an Iron Cross was a bullshit cover story. I think he's been onto us ever since we left Baltimore, maybe even before. In fact I'm sure of it. Why else would he have been on the damn plane in the first place?'

'Unless he really was getting a medal.'

'I'm telling you that's bullshit.'

'So who's feeding him the intel?'

I thought about it for a while but got nowhere. 'Could be anybody. Couba Island's a big place filled with lots of crazy people. All it takes is one rotten apple to be working for the bad guys while acting like a loyal Son of Liberty.'

We sat in silence. Nothing more to be said. But the equation had changed and the rules of the game too. When there's a Judas in your midst, you watch what you say and keep your eyes and ears twice as wide open.

Puffy cumulus clouds passed us in a serene procession, unconcerned with our plane or our dilemma as we made our way through a calm blue sky filled with nervous passengers eager to escape Europe at war.

Orlando said, 'What happens when we refuel at Horta?'

'Fatt's got something up his sleeve, but he's not saying.'

'Remind me again how we find ourselves at six thousand feet over the Atlantic Ocean with a nuclear physicist on board, instead of back in Key West, eating fried chicken at the Sugar Cane Club.'

'That day will come again, I promise.'

'When, do you suppose?'

'General Patton said Professor Friedman could change the course of history. The way things are going, we need to do just that.'

'Then the chicken.'

'Then a whole lot more than that.'

'What about Carter Aviation?'

'It'll be there when we're finished.'

'Finished with what?'

'Whatever it is they've got up their sleeve that made them put machine guns in the *Dixie Clipper*.'

We resumed our silence, lulled by the muffled roar of four powerful engines working in perfect synchrony.

'How's she handling?' Orlando said, moving to a place where there might be answers instead of questions.

'Slow, but steady as a rock.'

'I know someone just like that.'

'Jasmine?'

He scratched his head. 'You'd think her being a nightclub singer she'd be flighty and all, but she's just the opposite when she's not on stage.'

'You two really read scripture together?'

His eyebrows lowered in warning. 'Anything wrong with that?'

'Try to make a little love between the Gospels of St. Mark, why don't you?'

A long pause. 'We don't always read scripture.'

He grunted and levered his way out of the seat. The curtain slid back and he was gone. Seconds later Allison slid into the co-pilot's seat, fussed with the seatbelt, fiddled with the ventilation port, and finally sat back, hands folded in his lap and stared straight ahead. I did too. Horta was six hours away. Plenty of time to guess what the hell was going to happen once we landed.

The good news is that brilliant sunshine glared off Horta's small white buildings. The bad news was prevailing winds had shifted and it meant for a tricky landing, but one that Fatt pulled off like he was doing it in his sleep. I watched him out of the corner of my eye during those last few seconds before the plane lost flying speed. His hands and feet moved faster than I could follow, as he perfectly anticipated the right moment to let her have her head and stop flying.

As we began the slow, one-mile taxi to the shelter of the harbor, Fatt said matter-of-factly, 'Think you can handle a big girl like this all by yourself?'

'As pilot-in-command?'

'Indeed I do.' He killed the two inboard engines to save fuel. 'Well?'

I quickly compared the Boeing's performance characteristics with the four-engine Sikorsky, my previous command. While nowhere near the size of the Boeing, she was surprisingly the same in all the important categories. So much so that I ventured a cautious, 'I think I can do the job.'

'Think or know?'

'I know I can. Why?'

He pointed out the port window. 'That's why.'

I followed his gesture and saw the silvery shape of another Boeing 314 clipper tied up at the dock. At first glance I assumed the east-bound flight for Lisbon and said so. Fatt grinned and proceeded to light a cigar. He slid open the window to vent the smoke.

'That baby ain't going east, she's heading west just like we are.'

'I don't get it.'

'As far as Lufthansa's concerned, she's on a survey flight to - let me see if I remember this right - 'to explore alternate routing options that maximize service and minimize operating costs.' Trippe came up with the idea. A right clever man, even though he is our boss.'

'But Pan Am does that all the time.'

'Exactly. That's why none of the Nazis will give a damn that a non-revenue clipper is bobbing in their harbor, when in fact you're looking at Plan B waiting to happen.'

Then it dawned on me. 'That's the *Dixie Clipper*?'

'One in the same, flyboy, and you're flying her to Couba Island along with Ava, that little twerp of an agent, and the good *Herr Doktor* Professor too.'

'But it says *Atlantic Clipper* on the nose.'

'All part of the game, my friend. Ready to play?'

Passengers and crew jammed the reception room as they waited for the convoy of taxis to whisk them up to the Pan Am Club for some refreshments while maintenance refueled and serviced the *Yankee Clipper*. Ever the dutiful first officer, I mingled with the crowd, one eye peeled for the approach of a Gestapo agent to slap handcuffs on me, the other on Ava and *Frau* Jäger, who stood off to one side, chatting like old friends.

Ziggy circled the mob like a nervous bee flitting from flower to flower without bothering to taste the pollen. His confident attitude had vanished ever since we our Lisbon escape. I couldn't blame him. After all, as crazy as his show business world was, it had a certain stability to it compared to the unexpected twists and turns happening now.

Like when I felt a tug at my arm and Ava said just loud enough for me to hear, 'Head for that door over there.'

In the press of people, our absence went unnoticed as we slipped inside a darkened room. As soon as the door closed, somebody flicked on the light and I saw myself looking back at me. A dark-haired, brown-eyed man, exactly my height, same jaw line, same brow, same worry lines between his eyebrows. Almost the same smile as he grinned and saluted.

Like a scene from out of Alice in Wonderland, I saw Ava and Frau Jäger and Ziggy, too, like Alice in the Looking Glass staring at their exact doubles. Captain Fatt stood to one side, grinning like the cat who ate the canary.

The woman who dressed and acted exactly like Ava said, 'Hello, Miss James.'

'Peggy, you look divine - Sam, meet Peggy Page, she does all my stunts. Isn't she a gorgeous ringer?'

I nodded stupidly.

'And Tom Delaney here is playing you. Tommy, long time no-see, partner.'

He adjusted his Pan Am cap, smiled and snapped off a smart salute. 'Always wanted to play an airline pilot.'

Ava said, 'Enjoy it while you can. You'll be flying in a Gestapo holding cell after you reach Baltimore.'

He shrugged. 'Only until they figure out I'm Tom Delaney, not Sam Carter. Then it's back to Hollywood. By the way, you coming back after this gig?'

'Maybe, maybe not.'

'The gang misses you.'

'I miss the gang - Ida, is that you beneath all that makeup, darling?'

The *Frau* Jäger look-a-like nodded somberly, staying in character.

Ava swooped over and kissed her cheek. 'Ida taught me everything I know about movie acting. Including how to steal a scene.'

She punched Ida's shoulder lightly, turned and faced the group. 'Curtain up, kids. Break a leg, write if you get work, okay?'

She turned out the light, and one by one, our doubles slipped out into the crowd undetected and on their way to board the *Yankee Clipper*.

When the lights came back on I said, 'You were in on this all along?'

'Of course.'

'Why didn't you tell me?'

She examined one of her fingernails. 'Sam, be a good boy and shut up and listen to Captain Fatt, who has something to say.'

'Don't get sore, Sam. I told you the Sons of Liberty play their game close to the chest. Hell, even I wasn't sure what I'd see when I came in this room.' He laughed. 'Damnation, but they sure are spitting images of you folks. Especially the Professor. Don't you think so, doc?'

Friedman nodded. 'I was shocked and still am.'

'Well, you can relax and change back into a man again. You'll be flying to Couba Island without having to keep up your lady routine.'

'I am a poor actor, I'm afraid.'

Ava said, 'But you're a great scientist, and I'm glad you're working for our side now.'

He looked shocked and then recovered and grinned weakly. 'You are correct. I am no longer in the service of the Third Reich.'

Ziggy patted his shoulder. 'From now on you're in the service of the good old red, white and blue.'

Friedman looked puzzled. Ziggy stabbed the air as he spoke, as if pitching a film, 'The American flag, freedom of speech, equality, liberty, of thee I sing - all of that glorious stuff Americans celebrate when they love their country and aren't ashamed to let people know about it.'

'In Germany they do the same thing.'

Ziggy's exuberance disappeared. 'Like hell they do. They march around with hobnail boots, and use swastika's to ram Hitler's message down everybody's throats.'

Friedman accepted this assault calmly, as if observing a chemical reaction. 'You have family in Europe, *Ja?*'

'Damn right I do.'

'Not a good time to be separated from those you love.' Ava said softly, 'What about your family, professor?'

'My wife and children are in my luggage.'

My look of surprise made him add, 'A figure of speech, captain. I mean my life's work is in there.'

Fatt clapped his hands together. 'Cocktail party's over, kids. Sam, you've got a plane to fly, crew's waiting. I'll fly my mob to Baltimore and watch the Gestapo go nuts when they find out *Frau Jäger* is a real dame after all. I'll join up with you later at Couba.'

He swung his bulk in the professor's direction. 'In the meantime, Professor, you take good care of yourself, hear?'

'I will try.'

He nudged me playfully. 'Don't let this joker who thinks he's a pilot give you a bumpy ride.'

'I am confident we will arrive safely.'

He turned his happiness cannons on Ava. 'Those actor pals of yours are dead ringers. Great job.'

She gave a small salute. 'We aim to please.'

'Your mom will bust a button when she finds out you pulled this off without a hitch.'

'We aren't home yet. But thanks to Captain Carter...' She kissed my cheek, 'We're getting closer and closer.'

I leveled off the *Dixie Clipper* at three thousand feet. Any higher and the headwinds would start shoving us backwards, or so it seemed from the first set of performance numbers Duvall, my flight engineer, gave me. Like the others, he was a Navy guy. To be honest, they were all starting to look the

211

same to me. But I'll give them this; they were competent as hell, especially considering they had to learn the ins and outs of the Boeings so quickly.

I checked his numbers. 'She's on a drinking binge, isn't she?'

'And we're barely breaking one-ten as it is.'

'What's our ETA?'

'Next year, if we're lucky.'

'Seriously.'

Duvall leaned back and shouted back to the navigator, who wrote something on a piece of paper and handed it up.

'He's calling for a twenty-one-thirty hour landing on Lake Salvador.'

'We have the fuel?'

He raised his eyebrows. 'If we get better wind conditions, yes. If not, no dice.'

The last thing I wanted to do was to set down somewhere and re-fuel. A plane this size would cause a sensation with anybody who saw it, especially the Nazis. Even though Juan Trippe had arranged with his Luftwaffe buddies to grant us unrestricted airspace access with an 'open flight plan,' the compliance jerks would start asking questions and worse, come on board and poke around.

We had about eighteen hours before Fatt's Yankee Clipper landed in Baltimore and the Gestapo realized they'd been had. Between now and then I had to get us to Couba Island. I got up and theatrically dusted off the left hand seat.

'First officer Lewis, you have the aircraft. I'm making the rounds of the patients.'

'Aye, aye, doctor.' My co-pilot levered his wrestler-sized bulk out of his seat and took over mine. He and Orlando would make great dancing partners.

'What'd you fly before?' I said.

'Multi-engine patrol boats.'

'What do you think of the Boeing?'

'Love it.' He rolled his shoulders and stretched. 'First plane I ever fit in.'

When I arrived in her lounge the three of them huddled together like lost souls in a sea of empty seats. Frau Jäger minus her wig, but still wearing her dress, Ziggy staring tensely out the window while Ava casually leafed through a magazine.

I said, 'Sorry no steward service, Madam.'

Ava didn't even look up from her reading.

Ziggy stirred himself and said, 'That's okay, cap, I know my way around a galley. Here, help yourself.'

He gestured to a small tray on the table filled with neatly cut, crust-less sandwiches and a selection of relishes and freshly cut vegetables.

'You did all this?' I said.

'Busy hands are happy hands.'

'My compliments.'

'It wasn't easy. This plane may be pretty on the outside, but it sure isn't on the inside. It's like a flying basement.' He turned back to the window.

'Nothing but blue sky and pretty clouds out there.'

'Let's hope it stays that way.'

Friedman said quickly. 'Is there a chance we might be pursued?'

'I was referring to the weather, not the Gestapo.'

That seemed to calm him down, but no doubt about it, this was one troubled man. Maybe haunted is a better word for the way he was acting; as if he'd witnessed something horrible but had no words to express it. I sat down beside him and said, 'Look, it's over. You made it out. From now on you've got nothing to worry about, okay?'

He looked at me like I was five years old. In a kind way, but definitely as my superior.

'Someday that may be so. But not today, or tomorrow either. Not for a very long time.'

I risked the question. 'So tell me what it is you do, or did, that makes everybody and his brother want you, including the Gestapo.'

'And the SS,' he said and then fell silent.

'Well?'

He hesitated for a moment, looked at us one by one, and then said quickly, 'I was involved with the atomic bomb project.'

This was a man who helped kill my family. I waited for my anger to fade before I said slowly, 'Just how involved?'

He spread his hands and examined them instead of answering. 'I should have left with Einstein, Bohr, and the others. They knew Hitler was mad. They begged me to join them in America but no, I had my project and what's more, I was -' he pinched his fingers closed - 'this close to having it succeed. And besides, the SS had direct orders from Himmler to leave me alone.' He blinked behind his thick glasses. 'I'm Jewish, you see.'

Ziggy smiled and said, '*L'Chaim*, professor.'

'You as well?'

'Born and bred.'

He sighed. 'Your American world is much different than our German one.'

I said, 'Unless you're a nuclear physicist named *Herr Doktor* Friedman.'

'That was true once, but no longer. Once the uranium was successfully weaponized into bomb material and others could replicate my work, they had no use for an old Jew who knew too much. Before you rescued me I was days away from being sent to the camps.'

Ava said, 'Why'd they let you go to Lisbon?'

'Berlin keeps up appearances. If I hadn't shown up for the conference, my colleagues would have started asking questions, and sooner or later the newspapers would have started asking them too. But my days were numbered. I haven't been involved with the project for over a year. They cut me out long before they began dropping them on...on innocent people.

'And when I saw the newsreels, heard them bragging about how many thousands of Americans they destroyed, about how the next thousand years belonged to the Third Reich, I decided that I knew too much, and that what I did know must be put to use to help defeat these monsters. I had secret communications with my friends in America and...' he fingered the black material of his dress. 'And here I am.'

I said, 'What kind of man would build a bomb like that?'

'A man like me, and many others like me, although I assure you we never thought of it in those terms.'

'You damn well knew what the end result would be.'

He regarded me for a long while before answering. 'Some scientists never see the forest for the trees. I was one of them. And I am sorry.'

'Hindsight is always twenty-twenty.'

'Excuse me?'

'Never mind.'

He leaned forward. 'If it's any consolation, there will be no more bombs, at least for a little while.'

'Why?'

He sat back and his eyes became hooded. 'Let's just say that for once in my life I saw the forest.'

I pressed him for more details but, like Fatt, he turned into a sphinx. Still, if what he was saying was true, then maybe, just maybe, the nuclear threat hanging over Uncle Sam's neck like a guillotine could be turned into a penknife – at least for now.

Orlando entered the lounge, his eyes bright with excitement. Only two things got him going; the Lord and technology. I guessed the latter and said,

'Some setup, huh?'

'Have you seen what they did in the back?'

'I was too busy getting us the hell out of Horta.'

'C'mon, I'll show you around.'

Ziggy held up the tray. 'Have one for the road.'

I took one of the sandwiches and examined. 'Cucumber. Nice.'

'Don't knock it until you try it. Fresh, crisp, perfect for a summer getaway, and I do mean getaway.'

Going aft was like going from one world to another. When I first had seen the *Dixie Clipper* on Couba Island, the crew was stripping out her staterooms. That work was done. Where upholstered chairs and thick carpeting once comforted well-heeled passengers, anti-corrosion painted lime-green walls and bulkheads were all that remained. A narrow, perforated metal walkway allowed Orlando and me to move, single file, past what looked like oxygen canisters lined up like tin soldiers.

'They've finished the waist guns, too.'

Located over the 'step' of the hull, the fifty-caliber machine gun stations had been installed where Stateroom D use to be, including ammunition-feed chutes that looked like flattened metal snakes as they curved from the gun breeches to olive drab ammunition cans. The stateroom's original Plexiglas windows were still in place on the port and starboard sides, but were now part of a larger aluminum panel that slid back on rails to allow a waist gunner to swing out the barrel and shoot.

I followed Orlando into the next compartment. As I stepped through the bulkhead door, the outside noise grew louder. Long gone was the soundproofing that once sheltered passengers' ears from the output of four twelve-hundred horsepower engines. But the noise was even more pronounced because the work crews had knocked out the bulkhead between the 'special compartment' and the 'honeymoon suite,' creating one long, tapering compartment.

Orlando stood by the tail and shouted over the wind noise, 'Grab onto that stanchion. Want to show you something.'

I did so and he stabbed the intercom. 'Tail section to pilot. Permission to test release device.'

Lewis's voice rasped back, 'Make it quick.'

I looked up for the first time at an I-beam extending the length of the compartment. Claw-like clamps dotted its surface, sprung open, waiting to grasp an object.

And then I knew.

'Hanging on?' Orlando said.

'Affirmative.'

His face lit up and he hit a switch and shouted, 'Bomb's away!'

The fuselage floor split open along the centerline and swung down with a WHOOSH. The snakelike hiss of pneumatic pistons momentarily overpowered the combined roar of wind and engines. The whitecaps on the ocean's surface six thousand feet below moved serenely onward, unaware that our silver, luxurious flying boat had become an engine of war.

The moonlit waters of Lake Salvador tilted to the left as I began our final approach, the green luminescence of the underwater buoy lights marking the landing zone with perfect precision. A secret night arrival was essential. The less folks saw of this beautiful silver bird the better. The headwinds I had earlier feared never developed, and other than a brief scare over Atlanta with a compliance airspace air controller, our long flight had been uneventful.

The first thing I wanted to do after we landed was call Abby and my mother. It felt like old times, my being away on a trip, that is, but then a sudden sadness stabbed me like a knife.

'Watch your altitude, captain,' Lewis said quickly.

The twin green line of lights was widening too quickly and I made a quick throttle adjustment to slow our descent.

General Patton's voice crackled in my headphones, 'Carter, I want the professor's cargo offloaded right away, you copy?'

'Do you mind if I land first?' I snapped. 'Or do you want us to toss it out from up here?'

A brief pause. 'Negative.'

'By the way, general, mission accomplished.'

'That's what you think.'

We had been gone from Couba Island only a few days, but in that short time it seemed the base had doubled in size. Sons of Liberty soldiers marched across the open field in complete silence and with absolute precision. A convoy of covered trucks roared past Ava and Ziggy and me, kicking up clouds of red dust.

Ziggy said, 'What's with these guys' uniforms?'

'What about them?' Ava said.

'Regular army is olive drab. Theirs are grey.'

'Uncle Georgie's idea,' Ava said. 'His granddaddy served with the twenty-second Virginia during the war for Southern Independence.'

'You mean the civil war,' Ziggy said.

'We southerners prefer 'independence.' Uncle George thought it would be nice to resurrect the past to help America gain its future.'

Ziggy said, 'Let me get this straight, you're raising an army of Confederate soldiers?'

'Beats sitting on your hands and doing nothing, which is what you Yankees are doing.'

A squad passed, Ava waved gaily at them but they sternly refused to recognize her.

Ziggy twisted his hands. 'I'm afraid to ask what you're raising them for.'

She grinned wickedly. 'You'll find out soon enough.'

'Soon enough' came the following morning when I reported to General Patton, who had commandeered Mrs. Longstreet's massive greenhouse, removed the plants, and whitewashed the glass to make a bright and airy command post. He sat at the head of a long wooden table, flanked on both sides by subordinate officers, including a confident-looking Captain Fatt and his crew, just in from Baltimore.

I sent him a silent question as to how it went. He answered with wink and a breezy 'OK' sign, as if outwitting the Gestapo was an everyday kind of thing.

Professor Friedman and a civilian I didn't recognize sat next to the crew.

But I soon learned he was Professor Archibald – 'call me Archie' - Campbell. A permanent grin occupied the man's florid face and his bright, darting eyes constantly swept the place like a searchlight looking for something to land on. Five years ago, the British Government had detached him to America to work on a secret project that General Patton now proceeded to make public.

'Kill the lights,' he ordered.

Total darkness shifted to grainy black-and-white footage of Washington D.C. in ruins; capitol dome collapsed upon itself, Washington Monument broken in two, and somewhere in the dust and ash and devastation, what was left and tens of thousands of unsuspecting people who had breathed their last on the night of December 8, 1941, including my family.

Patton's high-pitched voice chattered like a machine gun. 'The war began and ended for America when the Nazis dropped their god-damned atomic bombs.'

Footage of an aerial view of what was left of Manhattan: the immense bomb crater carved a half-circle out of Battery Park as though bitten off by a monster. A cluster of deserted skyscrapers stood just outside ground zero, its inhabitants long gone, either dead from the blast or radiation sickness. Empty, rubble-filled streets, streetlamps tilted at impossible angles, automobiles tossed like crumpled bits of paper, and in the distance the occasional person standing perfectly still, as if contemplating Armageddon.

'We know what this weapon can do,' Patton continued. 'And thanks to Professor Friedman, here's what it looks like when it goes off – where exactly did you say this is?'

Friedman cleared his throat a few times before he found his voice.

'Moscow.'

Footage of a featureless plain at night. Moscow's lights twinkling in the distance. The darkness shifts to pure white as the bomb detonates. The flash recedes, and in its place a tumescent, glowing fireball blossoms outward and upward into massive proportions. And then, as the displaced air rushes back, a rising column of ash blooms into a mushroom-shaped cloud, climbing thirty-thousand feet into the still night air, carrying with it the remains of whoever and whatever once was alive.

The devastation footage afterwards was no different than Washington or New York. Broken gas lines burning out of control, featureless rubble where once buildings stood. Charred and shriveled lumps on the ground that once were human beings who had looked up at a bright light that exploded like the sun in the midnight sky.

Patton said, 'Berlin claimed these were rocket-delivered weapons and we believed them. And why not, with proof like this?'

Now came the familiar *Movietone* newsreel footage I'd seen along with millions of other Americans of the German's two-stage A9-A10 rocket rising majestically from its launch pad, balanced upon a column of fiery liquid oxygen and alcohol. Its first stage fell away a few minutes later, leaving only the winged second stage to arc across the thousands of miles separating Berlin from Washington to deliver the atomic bomb.

'Surprise number one,' Patton said. 'This rocket delivery method of theirs is pure Berlin bullshit.'

The room stirred like someone had slapped everyone.

'The footage is total fake. No way could that missile have carried that kind of payload that far. Thanks to the good professor, we've learned how the Heinie bastards really did it, and have film to prove it.'

I almost laughed when I saw the familiar profile of the Lufthansa 'catapult ship' *Friesenland* steaming at full speed in mid-ocean, with a *Blohm and Voss* four-engine seaplane perched on its stern-mounted catapult like an anxious bird. The very ship that Bauer claimed he sailed on back and forth to America? Not just Bauer could it carry, apparently.

The top-secret German navy footage showed destroyers escorting the *Friesenland* with guns bristling. Then an on-board view as a plume of steam billowed out from the catapult and the seaplane jerked forward and up into the air. Sailors pumped their fists, leaped and danced in celebration.

'They used their mail planes to drop the bombs?' I said.

'They damn well did, and we never knew.'

Lufthansa had beaten Pan Am to the punch with trans-Atlantic mail service back in 1937, long before Trippe's clippers arrived. The airline had fitted out ships with catapults to launch float-equipped mail planes that would take off for America while still in mid-Atlantic. I remembered newspapers and magazines touting their achievement, because it truly was. But that didn't compare with what those same planes had secretly done to America on December 8.

Animation replaced the newsreel footage. Maps of the eastern seaboard appeared. I stared numbly while Patton's voice pressed on relentlessly.

'The Friesenland launched both her aircraft about a thousand miles out. Two hundred miles off the coast they diverged to their respective targets.

They identified themselves to Coastal Air Defense Command as inbound Pan American flights.'

'They fell for that?' I said.

'They had all the correct flight identifications. Why wouldn't they?'

I bit my tongue but said nothing.

Patton continued. 'We estimate bomb release occurred at ten thousand feet.'

The bright red animated bomb tracks lit up on cue and glided inexorably toward their assigned targets. When they arrived, each city exploded into a brilliant star to signify a strike.

'The planes returned to their mother ship and beat it for Berlin. Case closed. Deal done. Lights, please.'

The lights came up. Friedman stared at his motionless hands curled on the table. He slowly flexed them into fists.

Patton said, 'Professor, you have the floor.'

He hesitated, looked at Archie who nudged him and said in a British accent, 'There's a good chap, Ernst. Time's wasting, remember?'

In a barely audible voice, Friedman spent the next ten minutes bringing everybody up to speed about Uranium-235, and how its atoms gave off incredible amounts of explosive energy when they split. Then he described how the Nazis had used fission bombs on our American cities as well as Moscow and London. But all of this was old hat to me. In the past six months I'd read hundreds of news stories that touted the Nazis so-called 'Super Weapon' and how the master race was going to rule the word.

I reached my limit and said, 'With all due respect, professor, just why the hell did we bring you here?'

He looked at me carefully, and then Patton, who nodded slowly for him to continue. Friedman cleared his throat and said softly, 'I am here to destroy the Genie's bottle.'

The room buzzed with everybody's puzzled reaction.

Archie Campbell slapped the table and took over.

'Gentlemen, for the past five years, in the greatest of secrecy, the United States of America, along with her staunch ally, Great Britain, have been racing to develop an atomic weapon as well. Unfortunately, *Herr* Hitler won and we lost - due in large part to *Herr* Professor Friedman's significant contributions, I might add. We, of course, tried to get him to cross over to us years ago, but...' Campbell patted Friedman's shoulder. 'At the time, my friend here believed he was doing the right thing for the right reason. But then again, we all go a bit mad now and then, don't we? And this time it was Ernst's turn, wasn't it?'

Friedman nodded curtly. 'I should have listened to you.'

Campbell brightened. 'Why don't you take up the baton and finish the race?' He promptly sat down, which was a signal for Friedman to struggle to his feet. He looked to Patton. 'General? The target please.'

The lights dimmed again. An aerial view of an industrial complex nestled in the wilderness alongside a winding river. Friedman's voice grew stronger, more authoritative. 'This is a United States government facility located in Hanford, Washington, situated along the Columbia River. Its sole purpose for being is to use a nuclear pile reactor to manufacture weapons-grade plutonium for atomic bombs. Next slide please.'

A complex diagram that took me a moment to recognize it as cross-section of a bomb. All the notations were in German.

'This is the design of the Nazi's current weapon. Note how the uranium core contains a tritium trigger that helps initiate the chain reaction. After long deliberation and great secrecy, I modified the triggers in their remaining weapons so that they would no longer cause a chain reaction. When detonated, the bombs - what is the word, Archie?'

'Fizzle.'

Ja, danke. And so it was in this way that Hitler's last two remaining bombs did not explode, they fizzled. As a result, the Third Reich is out of weaponized uranium to create further weapons for at least a year to eighteen months.'

Archie piped up. 'Out of material in the Fatherland, you mean.'

'Next slide, please.'

A blockhouse-shaped building surrounded by concertina wire and guardhouses.

'The only existing fissile material in the world is located at the Hanford facility. Berlin plans to seize it by force sometime in the next few days.'

An angry reaction rumbled up from the ranks, but a quick slap of Patton's riding crop on the table quieted them down. Friedman continued, his voice growing stronger.

'Whereas Germany has gained the ability to extract enriched uranium, American and British scientists have perfected the method by which plutonium is created and weaponized. While it is more difficult to fission, it is much more powerful. Berlin wants it, and whatever Berlin wants it takes.'

Fatt piped up. 'My ass.'

A supportive growl from the troops.

'Steady on, gentlemen,' Patton said. 'Let the professor finish.'

'If we can destroy the plutonium at the Hanford facility, we will gain valuable time.'

I said, 'To do what?'

Patton snapped, 'To get America back into the war.'

Patton nodded to his aide who, in turn, nodded to another aide, who opened the double doors leading into the potting shed, and motioned to someone waiting there. Seconds later two soldiers appeared, grunting and heaving Friedman's steamer trunks out of the room and then thumped them up onto the table. Patton held out a small key to the professor, who ceremoniously reached over, unlocked them and opened them in turn. Everyone at the table rose as one to see what was inside.

Inside the first steamer trunk, three grey, metallic, twelve-inch diameter cylinders, each about three feet long, lay side by side, tied down with strapping cords. In the second trunk, a series of thin collar-like objects with rivet holes, which I figured must be the mating couplers. Also two shoebox-sized instrument packages with thick bundles of wires neatly coiled in readiness, sat nestled at either end.

'Gentlemen,' Friedman said quietly, 'This is the only nuclear weapon left in the world.'

'Not very big,' I said.

Friedman said, 'It is a Plutonium 239 proof-of-concept version we built long ago.'

'Meaning?'

'Meaning it will only yield the equivalent of one hundred eighty-five thousand tons of TNT. But more than enough to destroy the plutonium and damage the reactor that makes it.'

'Lot of punch in a small package.'

'Nuclear energy is remarkable that way.'

Aided by a complicated-looking diagram, Friedman spent the next few minutes outlining how the bomb parts were assembled, how the fusing system worked - both proximity and barometric, how armed - manually by a weapons officer - and how aerodynamic fins and nose cap would give it enough stability to be dropped like an ordinary bomb.

'Who's the bombardier?' I said.

Patton said, 'Mr. Mason, here.'

To my surprise, our red-haired flight engineer grinned sheepishly at me and stood up.

'Sir, I've reviewed the basics with Doctor Friedman. It looks fairly straightforward. The only difference being that it's going to make a hell of a bigger bang than the ordnance I'm used to working with.'

The room chuckled at this, Fatt the loudest.

Patton singled him out, 'Captain Fatt, you've got the floor.'

He shot me a wink and stood up. 'While the Gestapo is still busy chasing its tail back in Baltimore trying to figure out what happened to the professor, the *Dixie Clipper* can be ready to go in forty-eight hours, if I can have the crew to myself.'

'You've got the crew,' Patton said. 'But you've only got twenty-four hours. The compliance people could move at any moment, and there's nothing we can do to stop them.'

I said, 'Why don't we just hide the plutonium somewhere else?'

Patton shook his head. 'The second we start, they'll make their move. Besides, I want that shit gone.' He slapped his riding crop into his palm. 'I promised President Perkins a level playing ground for America to go head to head with the Nazis using conventional weapons, and by God that's what we're going to do.'

'She approved the mission?'

He grinned. 'Let's just say she's looking the other way at the moment. If we fail, she'll blame it on those crazy Johnny Reb Sons of Liberty and leave it at that, but if we succeed, that's a different story.'

I said, 'A lot of governors are still running their states solo. What makes you think they'll sign on?'

'When our mission is accomplished, the president will blow the whistle on Berlin and call their bluff. Once the world finds out Hitler's bark is worse than his bite, mark my words, America will unite like never before and chew his ass to bits.'

'I hope you're right.'

He frowned and leaned forward, both palms flat on the table like a poker player. 'Let me ask you a question, captain. Would you go to war against these bastards if you knew you had a chance of winning?'

'Damn right.'

'That's exactly what the Sons of Liberty are going to do; give America and her people that chance.'

'But I'm not in the Sons of Liberty.'

'You are now.'

If you're doing nothing, twenty-four hours can be an eternity. But when you're planning a non-stop bombing mission that takes you over two thousand miles across the United States, those hours disappear faster than water drops in a hot skillet.

I spent the rest of the day dancing in that skillet, along with Fatt's crew in a hot, airless room with maps on every wall and performance charts spread out on the table. Our mission path would take us from Lake Salvador northwest into Texas, Colorado, west through Wyoming and Utah, further west into Idaho, Oregon, and finally due north into Washington State.

They had picked the Boeing because of her extraordinary range. Only a plane like ours could lift off, fly the mission and return halfway before we would need to land and refuel. Landing a seaplane requires water, however, so the Sons of Liberty had established a secret base on Lake Mead, Nevada where we would gas up for the flight home.

About two hours into the briefing, Fatt had two enlisted men bring in a sheet-covered table. He whisked it off like a magician to reveal the Hanford Facility painstakingly reproduced in miniature. In the late thirties, the government had made the barren landscape even more deserted by buying up the nearby small town of Hanford and relocated its unsuspecting citizens. Then private contractors built a string of concrete buildings nose-to-tail alongside a densely-wooded, deserted stretch of the Columbia River.

Their nuclear reactor bombarded uranium rods to create U-238. They sent the irradiated rods over to a building called 'PUREX,' the Plutonium Extraction Plant that ground them up into a liquid plutonium nitrate solution. The Plutonium Finishing Plant was the next stop, converting the solution into solid, disc-shaped objects nicknamed 'hockey pucks' which were stored in a top-secret vault that was safe from everything.

'Safe from everything except the *Dixie Clipper's* bomb,' Fatt added.

'Delivered right about here.' He touched his wooden pointer on the roof of the finishing plant.

I said, 'How accurate does your aim have to be?'

Fatt nodded to Mason who said casually, 'If this were a conventional pickle, I'd have to drop it right on the money. But from what they're telling me, if I can lob the damn thing within a mile or so, we're in good shape.'

I said, 'That powerful?'

'Let me put it this way.' Mason made a wide circle with his arms that embraced almost the entire Hanford complex. 'Boom, it's gone.'

According to Archie, the 'Manhattan Project' had proceeded excruciatingly slow for years. Apparently making this stuff was a lot easier on paper than in reality - not to mention the reactor 'going critical' and practically melting down before they could shove in the rods and shut it down.

But after two years of failure, they were finally achieving success. And while our scientists and technicians were working their butts off, FDR's White House was working equally hard to find out how far Nazis had come in the nuclear race. One advantage Hitler had over America's open society is that the he controlled information the way a greedy miser controls his money: nothing gets out unless he says so.

Was our security as good? Hard to say. But some claimed we had our share of spies happily sending - or selling - what we had learned about nuclear fission to the Berlin boys. But they hadn't bought it all, apparently, because from what Friedman claimed when he joined our briefing in the late afternoon, the German scientists still hadn't mastered the art of plutonium extraction beyond his small proof-of- concept weapon.

He and Archie tried explaining the gas diffusion process in detail, and how the Uranium 235 got converted to Plutonium 239, but they lost me and the crew early on. Sometimes too much information is too much, and I finally said so.

Friedman agreed with a faint smile. 'It is a highly complicated and time-consuming process to get a very small amount of product. Not to mention expensive too. The Third Reich almost went bankrupt at one point. But Hitler got Krupp and the other industrialists to make unrestricted loans.'

'What did he promise in return?'

'Their heads attached to the rest of their bodies.'

I studied the spaghetti-like diagram of the gas diffusion system with its paper-thin membranes mysteriously able to allow certain atoms of certain electrons to pass through while keeping others out. 'Ever think Mother Nature was telling you to stay the hell out of her back yard?'

'Wished we had.'

'Too late now.'

Archie said, 'But not too late for us to slow things down long enough to get America into the war and drive that madman out of Berlin.'

Fatt snapped, 'And into a pine box.'

Friedman nodded. 'Better him than the millions he's already killed and plans to kill; Jews, homosexuals, gypsies, the mentally disturbed, anybody who doesn't fit the Nazi idea of a superior race sees the inside of a gas chamber.'

'I thought that was just propaganda.'

Friedman's face grew still, like when the wind stops on a pond and everything becomes mirror-clear. 'Every day men, women and children are rounded up and put onto trains and sent to so-called labor camps. Except for the young, the old, and the feeble, there is no labor to do except to take off your clothing and go to the showers and never return. What kind of country would do this to its citizens?'

None of us had an answer.

Friedman continued, his voice quiet but relentless. 'I'll tell you what kind. One that has lost its way, one that believes in a nightmare named Adolf Hitler and is afraid to wake up for fear it will die along with the others he's already exterminated.' He leaned forward. 'That is why America must grab Germany by the shoulders and shake it until it awakens and sees the world – not as Hitler sees it – but as it truly is. Only then can it re-join the human race.'

The humid, August heat of the day had not dissipated with the sun going down. If anything it got worse. Professor Friedman and Mason assembled the bomb in the ordnance hut while Fatt, Orlando and I watched them work. Amazing how simple it is to create something so destructive:

'Insert flange A into groove B; twist until hand tight, then torque-wrench to seventy-five pounds, while maintaining proper alignment, etc...'

Drops of perspiration fell from Mason's reddened face – now the same shade as his hair - onto the bomb casing as he worked, staining its smooth gray surface with dark dots.

Orlando said softly, 'For such a deadly thing, it's beautiful to behold.'

Friedman said, 'Germans are elegant people. Unfortunately we practice it in the wrong places sometimes.'

226

A long silence followed while Mason fitted the nose-cap to the front unit with surgical precision.

Orlando whispered, 'Vengeance is mine, sayeth the Lord.'

Fatt said, 'Ours too.'

Orlando touched the bomb. 'Innocent people will die when this explodes.'

Fatt soothed, 'We've done our best to make sure that injuries will be minimized. Certain friends of our cause at the plant will scram the reactor about an hour before we arrive on target.'

He saw the blank look on my face, so he explained, 'They'll let the reactor reach critical levels by adjusting the carbon control rods so that it'll look like the core is going to melt down, even though it won't. They'll hit the alarm, the whole place will evacuate, and BOOM, we drop the bomb. It's a hell of a sweet idea.'

Orlando said, 'Providing it works.'

He shrugged. 'If it doesn't then too damn bad. You've got to break eggs to make omelets.'

'Easy for you to say at ten thousand feet.'

He gave him a long deadly look. 'You got any other bright ideas, reverend? We're dealing with the devil himself, not just one of his sinners.'

Orlando started to say something, but then shook his head.

Mason cleared his throat. 'Do you gentleman mind taking your moral dilemmas outside? We've got us a bomb to build.'

That silenced them.

Mason then showed us the bomb trigger: a cleverly-designed miniature radio altimeter that worked in concert with the more conventional barometric one; each cross-checking the other to get a mutually agreeable answer as to the proper height above ground wherein the contacts would close, the high-explosive spherical shell surrounding the plutonium would detonate, crushing the fissile material and triggering an uncontrolled chain reaction that released a violent burst of energy outward, consuming everything it its white-hot, radioactive fist.

Fatt said. 'Wouldn't mind having a warehouse full of these babies.'

Friedman said, 'This is the last one.'

'For now.'

He sighed. 'For a very long time, I hope.'

Fatt snorted. 'If we manage to pull this off and American enters the war, don't you think General Patton and his boys will want these weapons as fast as possible?'

'Wanting is not the same thing as having. America has the fissile material but Germany has the technology to construct bombs with it.'

'Then we'll steal your scientists the same way we got you.'

He smiled. 'After this, I am out of the bomb business, permanently.'

'What about the others?'

He shrugged. 'I cannot speak for them, but I am certain that they, like me, will pray that America will defeat Germany with conventional weapons long before enough plutonium is manufactured to construct more nuclear ones. If that happens, then we can put atomic energy to peaceful uses instead.'

Fatt laughed. 'You actually think you can tame this shit?'

'We have developed plans for nuclear power plants. And other civilian uses as well.'

Orlando said, 'The lion shall lie down with the lamb?' Friedman said, 'That is my fondest dream.'

Fatt pointed his cigar at the bomb. 'Dream on professor. I'm betting on the lion.'

The ordnance team transported the assembled bomb to the dock area, where the *Dixie Clipper* floated serenely beneath a canopy of camouflage netting hiding it from the prying eyes of compliance fighters droning overhead, heading east and west on their patrol missions in search of neutrality violators trying to slip through their tight little net along the Gulf Coast.

While Fatt and I watched from the shore, the team carefully winched the bomb onto a small barge and floated it out to the clipper's open bomb bay doors beneath its swooping tail.

Fatt puffed contentedly on his cigar. 'Who would have thought the day would come when that sweet bird would take off with an atomic bomb up her ass.'

'Providing we adjust for center of gravity. Otherwise she'll drag her tail until kingdom come and never get unstuck.'

'Then I suggest you damn well make sure we perform correct weights and balances, captain. I don't want to spend the rest of my life taxiing back and forth across Lake Salvador like a Mixmaster.'

With that, he spun on his heel and was gone. I checked my watch. Time to make the call.

'Hi, honey, it's daddy.'

Abby's voice mixed with the long distance rush of static. 'Where are you and when are you coming home?'

'A little tied up on the charter job. A few more days, sorry.'

'How many?'

'Don't know. A week maybe.'

'Daddy, you promised.'

'Sorry, honey. Really I am.'

A long pause.

'Abby?'

Rosie's voice came on the line instead. 'What did you say to her?'

'Nothing, Just that I was going to be gone a few more days than I thought.'

'We've got bills piling up here. You getting paid?'

'What about the money Trippe gave you?'

'Long gone. Hangar rental's due. Installment on the plane. Want the whole list?'

'I'll see if I can wire you some cash. That'll help.'

'It'll help your business, but not your daughter. You've got to make up your mind; you either save what's left of your family or watch that child drift off in between charters.'

'Let me talk to her again.'

'She's run off somewhere.'

'What's today? Tuesday? I'll be back Friday at the latest. Promise.'

'What exactly are you doing?'

'Can't tell you.'

A long pause. 'Samuel Carter, if you're involved with breaking the law, I swear I'll -'

'Mom, it's on the level, I promise. My client insists on confidentiality, that's all.'

'Still that Ava James woman?'

'Yes.'

'I knew it. You watch out for her, hear?'

'Thought you liked her.'

'I do. Just keep an eye out, that's all.'

'Promise.'

'Got to go find out where that child ran off to.'

'Tell her I'll be home Friday.'

'You'd better be.'

Minutes later I met up with Ava and Ziggy walking along the wooden dock that paralleled the *Dixie Clipper's* mooring. As I began making my case for more money, she touched my arm. 'I'll have Ziggy wire it from New Orleans. How much?'

'You promised me a thousand if we found the gold. Rosie said the bills were piling up and...'

'Done.'

She kissed Ziggy on his forehead. 'Be a dear, zip up to New Orleans and take care of this for me, will you?'

'But I thought I was invited to dinner.'

'You'll miss cocktail hour, that's all.'

'What am I doing, riding a skyrocket? New Orleans is a ways off.'

'You're taking Uncle Georgie's boat, silly.'

She pointed to a flat black, low-slung torpedo boat moored on the dock.

'In that?'

'It's a Higgins eighty-footer. Twelve-hundred horsepower Packard engines, top speed fifty knots. They're about to make a run to pick him up. You'll both be back in a jiffy. Now scoot.'

The boat's engines burbled softly into life, betraying the fact that they would soon be roaring like panthers as they hurtled the plywood craft across Lake Salvador to the Big Easy.

Ziggy gingerly climbed on board, made his way to the wheelhouse, and weakly saluted the captain. He clutched onto a fifty-caliber machine gun mount and hung on for dear life as the PT boat opened her engines wide and raced away, leaving a curving white arc of foaming water to mark her passage.

Ava took my arm. 'Doing anything?'

'Getting ready for tomorrow.'

'All caught up are you?'

'That'll never happen.'

'Then all the better to take a break and have dinner with us up at the house.'

'I'd rather not. Besides, I'm not dressed.'

She brushed her dust-covered khaki shirt and laughed, 'Who is?'

'What's the occasion?'

'Sort of a going-away party.'

'Wish it were a coming-home party instead.'

We walked in silence for a while, aware of the hustle and bustle going on around us, but content to not add to it with unnecessary chatter. The wooden sidewalk around the parade ground gave way to grass and then to the finely crushed gravel of the curving walkway lined with towering pines that led to the stately Longstreet mansion, its white columns glowing silver in the fading light.

I laughed. 'Looks like *Gone with the Wind.*'

'It does, doesn't it?'

'You'd have made a great Scarlett O'Hara.'

'I wish.'

'Try out for it?'

'Like everybody else in Hollywood. Paulette Goddard, Jeanie Arthur. Me.'

'Vivian Leigh's a brit. Doesn't make sense.'

'Viv's mad as a hatter. She deserved the part. And Selznick deserved her. They drove each other crazy.'

'You missed kissing Clark Gable.'

A long pause. 'Fine by me, I've got you instead.'

I stopped and looked at her. She looked back. 'Don't take that the wrong way.'

'How should I take it?'

'I meant that I admire you, that's all.'

'I see.'

'No you don't see, and please forget that I even said it. I feel like an idiot.'

'Join the club.'

She laughed and looked away. Then suddenly turned back, her eyes dancing, her mouth twisted in a puzzled smile. 'Keep a secret?'

'Shoot.'

'Uncle Georgie is not my uncle. He's my father. I just found out.'

'Excuse me?'

She grabbed my arm. The words came out in a happy rush. 'Mother came to my room last night, sat on the edge of the bed, held my hand and told me that after General Longstreet died, she decided she wanted a child, but not a husband to go with it. So she seduced General Patton when he was a young captain and that -'

'Wait a second, hold on -'

'Of course HE doesn't know I'm his daughter.' She laughed. 'Poor thing is happily married, has children, reads the Bible, pious as a damned saint.'

'Why are you telling me all this?'

'Because I'm happy. Deliriously happy."

She impulsively hugged me and I hugged her back.

'Not angry?' I said.

'Of course not. Mother always told me I was adopted. And my whole life I've wondered who my parents really were, where they lived, what they did. Now I know.'

'But she lied to you all those years.'

'Wake up, Sam. You're a southerner, you know what it's like down here. She had no choice. If anyone had found out her secret, Uncle Georgie's career would have been ruined; his family's too, not to mention the scandal of the wife of the high and mighty Confederate General James Longstreet having whored around with a soldier boy. And a Yankee at that.'

'How did she - I mean-'

She clapped her hands and laughed. 'It's better than a movie. It happened during the Civil War fiftieth anniversary celebration up in Gettysburg. Mother had volunteered to help out with her fellow southerners. My father - gosh, I like saying that - he was with an army detachment assigned to help the old timers get through day after day of ceremony and speeches. But the nights were all their own.

'Mother knew Patton from other social occasions. So it was only normal she would invite him to a nice quiet dinner at her hotel, and he, being far away from home, accepted. You may not know it to look at her, but mother is a perfect temptress. Even with her cigar - hell, probably because of it. Anyhow, Georgie-porgy took the bait, got good and soused, they did the delightful deed, and nine months later...' She gave a small curtsey. 'She gave birth to little old me.'

'You sure he doesn't know?'

'Positively and absolutely. If he did, he'd die from shame, but not before doing something noble and stupid. He's a King Lear in the making. All he needs is a bastard daughter to make him go nuts.'

'Doubt that would happen.'

'Mother said she wanted a child, not a husband, and he had to be worthy of someone as wonderful as her, and the child they created.'

'Why'd she decide to tell you now?'

Ava chuckled. 'I asked her that very thing and she simply said the time had come.'

'That's it?'

'Unlike my father, my mother is a woman of few words.'

'You'll still call him Uncle George?'

'You bet. But the next time I hug him, it'll mean so much more.'

We turned and kept walking. Trucks roared past, filled with Confederate soldiers, their faces grim, going who knows where. I had the sudden image of America as a sleeping giant, like Ava had been, and both being awakened from their dreams to a new awareness, where nothing would ever be the same again.

The issue is quite clear. It is between light and darkness and every one must choose his side.
— G.K. Chesterton

The dream was always the same.

Estelle and Baby Eddie huddled and helpless in the middle of the street while traffic zooms past them on either side. I try to save them but my feet won't move. Then a white flash, so brilliant that everything is a reversed black-and-white photograph and the air sizzles and crackles with heat and I can't breathe, can't move --

I awakened to the sounds of shouting and the 'POP-POP-POP' of small arms fire. My dream was gone, I could breathe again, but the gunfire continued. Where the hell was I? Lisbon? Buenos Aires? Key West? Different places clicked through my half-asleep brain like fruits in a slot machine as I groped in the darkness for the flashlight beneath my pillow where I always kept it and switched it on just as Orlando burst into the room, his face set and determined, the Thompson submachine gun in his hands all too real.

'Visitors,' he said.

'Who?'

'Doesn't matter. They're shooting up the place.'

I dressed as fast as I could. Orlando ran out, only to return seconds later with another submachine gun.

'Where the hell did you get that?'

'Off one of ours.'

'Jesus.'

'May he protect us and forgive us for what we are about to do.'

Head down, half-crouched, we made our way down to the first floor of the barracks, now empty of soldiers, long gone to defend Couba Island. Their tangled bedclothes and overturned cots mute proof of the attacker's complete surprise.

A sharp explosion somewhere to the right. Hand grenade maybe. Then rapid machine gun fire. Shouts.

Then I knew. 'They're going after the plane.' 'But how did they-'

I didn't hear the rest of O's sentence because I took off at a dead run, zigzagging as best I could through the 'ping' and 'zing' of ricocheting bullets clanging off trucks and metal buildings. Two trucks and a jeep were burning, their flames lighting my way to the Longstreet mansion, which by now was fully lit, front door open, and people running in and out. Where were Ava and her mother? I began angling off to the right, just as Orlando caught up with me and shoved me hard in the opposite direction.

'Head for the plane....I'll let you know.'

He ran toward the mansion, his menacing shadow soon swallowed up in other shadows laced with flashes of light. Only a few hours ago I had been sitting in the dining room with Ava, Patton, Ziggy and Mrs. Longstreet, enjoying a friendly meal, while trying to see if Ava resembled the general. I had decided, to her advantage, that she did not. Now I was running like crazy, my shoes untied, with a Tommy gun in my hands.

Off to my right a group of men approached in a half-crouch. I ducked behind a tree because their helmets gave them away. They weren't the familiar Wehrmacht iron pots. These were more rounded and had a thick ridge of cushioning around the circumference. I'd read some Nazi propaganda in a magazine - probably *Popular Mechanics* – about the German navy's elite waterborne commando units called *Kampfschwimmers*. These had to be the same guys, but in the flesh, not in a magazine, and firing real bullets.

The black-uniformed figures jogged past without making a sound. I waited a few seconds, and then took off in the opposite direction for the *Dixie Clipper*.

The dock was remarkably calm by comparison. Not a soul in sight, at least at first. But when I started cutting the ropes that held the camouflage netting, a figure staggered out of the darkness, his voice a muffled blur.

'Lemme' help, kid.'

Captain Fatt's right side was covered with blood. He made it as far as the boarding ramp before I caught up to him and lowered him to the ground.

'Jesus, Jesus, Jesus,' he said.

'What's going on?'

'Landed on the south shore, made their way into the camp. Nobody saw them coming. So much for our lookouts. They shot-'

A groan stopped him from talking. I scrabbled in the darkness to see if I could find the wound. No such luck. Just blood-soaked cloth. I smoothed back his hair like he was a little boy. He closed his eyes and breathed slowly, his mouth opened in a frozen grimace of pain.

More gunfire, closer this time. The horizon lit up from a tremendous explosion, and then darkness. The noise stirred Fatt from his stupor and he shouted, 'Kid, get the plane out of here.'

'Where's our crew?'

'Damned if I know. I ordered them down here, the professor too, then I got nailed. Look, if you don't, then-' He arched back as a wave of pain swept over him. I eased him down onto the ground, pulled off one of his shoes and used it as a pillow to cradle his head.

'Rest easy, sir. You'll be okay.'

'To hell with me. You got your orders. Now go.'

I sat back on my heels for a second. The *Dixie Clipper* loomed over me like a massive silver angel. But she would soon be a shot-up one if I didn't get her out of danger. Asking one man to fly a plane this size was impossible. Even so, I had to start down that path and see how far I could get. At least I could fire up her engines and taxi her out onto the lake. But what if they came after me?

I'd cross that bridge when I came to it - if I ever got that far.

My flashlight guided me through the clipper's silent, darkened interior. The strong smell of gas told me they had been fueling her for our morning mission. Where the hell had everybody gone, damn it? Out to defend the perimeter, probably. That was my only guess.

I tripped over a coil of rope someone had left in the stripped-down main lounge and staggered into the second compartment, more wary this time, not wanting to break my leg before I even got started. I raced up the spiral staircase and swung the door upward into the pitch black flight deck.

I hit the battery switches on the electrical panel and the gauges flickered once, and then glowed softly. Then I raced to the left-hand seat. Had to get the generators going. Funny to be sitting alone in such a huge plane trying to make it work. Like a kid would feel; overwhelmed by the immensity of it all.

But I was no kid and my fingers swiftly found the buttons and switches and dials and controls and within seconds, number two engine slowly turned, and then coughed blue-grey smoke and spun into life with a roar.

Number three engine followed suit. I adjusted the propeller pitch and opened the cowl flaps to keep them running as cool as possible. I had enough power to taxi the plane to safety. All I had to do was figure out how to cast her off without any help at all.

Seconds later - or so it seemed - I stood in the cramped bow compartment and opened the side hatch leading to the dock. I hopped out, untied the manila lines holding her fast until only the bow spring line was left. The pull of the engines was not too strong because of the propeller pitch, but even so I felt nervous standing out here while she was alive and straining at the leash with no one in the driver's seat.

Captain Fatt had somehow managed to raise himself up on an elbow and was pointed at something and shouting, but the engine noise drowned out his voice. A group of people coming toward me. Thank God, the crew at last. But it was only Ava and Ziggy, followed by Orlando and Professor Friedman, who had his arm around a staggering Mason, guiding him forward. Great. I had passengers, but no crew. Mason wasn't near enough to make this work. Fatt couldn't move. Now what?

The answer came with a sharp explosion, followed by someone shouting something in German, and the far end of the dock suddenly swarmed with soldiers making their way towards us.

I grabbed Ava and shoved her onto the sponson and into the open hatch. I turned to Orlando.

'Man the port fifty-caliber. See if you can train it back on the dock.'

Give me covering fire.'

'On my way.'

Mason was next. 'You and the professor get inside. Can you work your station?'

'Hell yes.'

'Then start the other two engines. Watch your cylinder head temps.'

'Aye, aye.'

I grabbed Ziggy by the shoulder and goose-stepped him toward the bow. 'Get inside and stand by to cast off that bow line. Can you do that?'

'D...damn right I can,' he said. 'What's 'cast off' mean?'

'Untie the rope when I say so.'

'Got it.'

Answering fire from the tree line slowed the commando's advance to a crawl. But they wanted the clipper and nothing was going to stop them, and they'd kill Fatt if I left him lying on the dock, and I would be good God damned if I would let that happen. The splinters jabbed my hands as I slithered across to him. But before I even got there I knew he was already

237

dead, his arms crossed over his chest, his head turned in the direction of the *Dixie Clipper*. His last sight on earth had been that big silver bird he loved. And I had loved him.

'Rest in peace, cap.'

Number two engine spluttered into life with a smoky roar. Darting shadows off to my right along the line of service shacks. Commandos coming fast. A muzzle flash and the deck around me splintered into pieces from enemy fire. I rolled over into a crouch just as the thundering crack of the *Dixie Clipper's* waist gun opened up over my head, its tracers arcing in the night air like molten globs of red.

Orlando had deflected the gun enough to give me covering fire and I took it, making it to the sponson, getting on board, securing the door and scrambling up to the flight deck where Mason at the engineer's station fussed with his controls like a pipe organist.

'Great job!' I pounded his back, and then turned to see a Friedman sitting at Captain Fatt's command table in the back, holding the chair handles in a death grip.

'Hang on professor, we'll get you out of here in one piece.'

I hurried past him to the left seat.

'Welcome aboard,' Ava said from the co-pilot's seat.

She laughed at the shocked look on my face. 'You don't expect to fly this tub of bolts by yourself, do you?'

'Got to try.'

'I'm multi-engine rated, remember?'

'But this is a Boeing clipper.'

'It's a plane, captain, now sit down and start giving orders.'

I keyed the microphone, 'Ziggy, you there?'

His voice tinny and tight. 'I'm here.'

'Cast off the line!'

'Aye, aye, sir.'

I advanced the throttles, but instead of pulling away from the dock, she slewed sideways, still pinned to shore by the bow line and began pivoting around on her nose, exposing her flank to fire. I cut power to minimize the swing.

'Damn it, I said cast off that line!' 'It's...it's tangled.'

'Cut it then. There's a hatchet to your right. Do it now!'

'Hang on, skipper. Wait...got it! We're free!' Ava shouted, 'Here they come!'

I couldn't see the dock from where I was, but the tracers streaking past us were proof enough. Because we were facing nose out to the lake, the clipper's port wing and engines overhung the dock, which gave me an idea. I shoved all four engines to full takeoff power. The resulting hurricane-like prop wash sent everything on the dock flying, including, I hoped, the enemy commandos.

From the sudden lack of tracers, it seemed to be working. Before we cleared the end of the dock we were moving at least fifteen knots into the dark, uncharted waters of Lake Salvador and picking up speed fast.

Gone were the lights that showed our runway, gone were the boats making sure no underwater obstructions waited to rip out her hull. We were on our own in the dark, but not quite; the first false light of dawn on the eastern horizon helped me orient myself enough to where I was. But where I wanted to go was another question.

Sure, we were free from the attacking forces, or so it seemed. But now what? I applied left rudder to keep her nose straight and realized that my left shoe was long gone, somewhere back on the dock. I kicked off my other shoe and flew barefoot, the cold metal of the rudder pedals oddly reassuring, reminding me that I was alive, the plane was safe and we were free.

But just then the plane shuddered from a long burst of fifty-caliber machine gun fire from the waist gun. Orlando's voice came over the intercom. 'We got company, brother. Two boats, converging port and starboard.'

I applied back pressure on the yoke to pull her up onto the step and then eased it off slightly.

'Flaps ten,' I called.

'Where, where?' Ava shouted.

I pointed to the flap control over her head. She found it and within seconds the plane shifted slightly from the increased wing area.

Orlando shouted, 'They're gaining on us, brother.'

Bullet strikes thumping into the plane...sixty-five knots, sixty eight, seventy and I rotated her nose and felt her slab-like wings bite the air and lift us up from the chattering, banging water surface and into the silky-smooth, pre-dawn air.

Now came the dangerous part; leveling out at fifty feet and holding her there until she built up more speed before climbing away. A big, fat, silver flying target to the boats below.

'Still taking fire,' Orlando said.

The fuselage shuddered and bucked from the bullet hits. The controls still worked fine, What about the engines?

'Four in the green?'

'So far,' Mason answered. 'But cylinder head temps are climbing fast.'

The airspeed indicator needle finally touched one hundred-five knots. I hauled back on the yoke to climb away from the enemy boats and away from the nightmare below. I made a slow climbing turn to starboard until we reached one thousand feet and flew over Couba Island. Fires still dotted the darkness and the occasional flashes of explosions meant they were still fighting down there while we were up here safe and sound.

What now?

My mind was a complete blank. For the past half hour I had run around like a demented monkey this way and that, dodging bullets, trying to make it safely to the clipper. Now that I was here, all I could think to do was continue climbing. That's it, nothing more in my head.

Ava said, 'What the hell happened?'

'Nazi commando unit.'

'How did they find out where we were?'

'Sixty-four dollar question.'

She shook her head. 'Can't believe it.'

'Believe it - how's your mother?'

'I left her in the cellar with a squad of troopers. She has some bourbon, plenty of cigars and if worse comes to worse the general's pistol.'

'Which general?'

She laughed. 'Longstreet.'

'A civil war pistol?'

'She fires it regularly - at people who ask too many questions, like you.' She glanced out the window. 'Now what, captain?'

We had reached two thousand feet. Instead of answering I leaned the fuel mixture and said. 'Maintain this rate-of-climb and heading until we reach five thousand feet. I need to check for damage. When I get back, I'll show you how to put her on autopilot.'

'I have the aircraft.'

'Make sure-'

'I repeat; I have the aircraft, captain.' Her frown prevented any further conversation, so I headed aft to count the bullet holes, both in the plane and in people, starting with Mason who had been grazed along his ribcage.

'This hurt?' I said as I probed the wound.

'Only when you do that.'

'Then I won't do that.'

He tried to grin but couldn't.

I broke out the first aid kit, folded up a gauze pad and tried to figure out how to apply the bandage. Moments later, Friedman arrived, alert and commanding. 'Let me help. I studied medicine early on.'

Mason said, 'What made you change your mind?'

He smiled. 'The sight of blood. Take a deep breath and hold it.' Together we wrapped Mason's wound with a compression bandage.

When Friedman tied it off, he said. 'Let us see to the others.'

'Okay, doc.'

We met Ziggy at the bottom of the spiral staircase. His clothes were disheveled and his shirt cuffs torn.

'You okay?' I said.

'Other than almost dying from fright, yes.'

'Think of it as a movie and you'll be fine.'

That didn't impress him. 'What happens now?'

I had the beginnings of an idea, but only said. 'I'll let you know.'

A beam of sunshine entered the compartment. For some reason it made me feel happy - happy to be alive to see its comforting warmth, instead of like Captain Fatt, gone to distant skies. I turned toward the door leading to the mooring compartment but Ziggy said, 'We're all set there, cap.'

'No bullet holes, no damage?'

He patted his chest. 'Just my heart attack. Other than that, we're tight as a drum.'

Friedman said, 'You are joking about your heart, yes?'

Ziggy shrugged. 'A figure of speech, doc, I'm fine, except for almost getting killed back there.'

It seemed impossible, but I couldn't find a single bullet hole in the fuselage except for a neatly-stitched line in what used to be Cabin F, leading from the window and then up the side. No way could I inspect our double-bottom hull. Surely we had taken fire there, too. But even so, small caliber stuff, and hopefully our bilge pumps could keep up with it long enough for us to dive down and plug them up when we landed. But with what, I wondered, and then dismissed the question. The answer would come when it needed to. Right now I needed to check on Orlando, who, when

241

Friedman and I reached Stateroom G, was sweeping up empty fifty-caliber cartridge shells.

'That monster packs a mighty punch,' Orlando said.

'Saved our lives – correction; you saved our lives.'

He patted the machine gun's breech. 'I'm calling him Joshua. And the walls of Jericho came tumbling down.'

Friedman was already heading aft and Orlando and I followed. We passed into the compartment the ground crew had converted into a bomb bay and came to a dead halt. The atomic bomb swayed gently from its mounting bracket, held by electro-pneumatic release clamps. The idea flickered through my cluttered mind again.

I said to Friedman, 'Do you know how to arm this thing?'

He looked shocked, but then recovered quickly. 'Regretfully, yes.'

'How complicated?'

He shrugged. 'A little, but from your line of questioning it would seem I will have many hours to figure it out.'

'Nineteen if the winds hold.'

Orlando cleared his throat. 'Are you saying what I'm thinking?'

'Yes.'

Friedman said, 'But where is your crew?'

Good point. I had no navigator, no radio operator, and no qualified relief pilot to spell me from what would be a nineteen-hour mission. Other than Mason, our twelve man rigorously trained crew was down on Couba Island, either dead like Fatt, or wounded, or in hiding.

'We'll figure out a way.'

Easy to say, not easy to do. Especially when I returned to the flight deck and announced my intentions. Ava would act as co-pilot, Professor Friedman would arm the bomb, Mason would be the bombardier, but only until he needed to do so. Until then, he'd double as flight engineer. Orlando would take over from him when needed, and Ziggy? When I announced my plan, he suggested he be the purser.

'I know where everything is in the galley, and we've got to eat, right?' I said, 'An army travels on its stomach.'

Mason interrupted, 'We're low on fuel.'

I knew he would say that, but even so it came as a shock, especially when I'd just announced we were flying clear across the United States to drop a bomb.

'Which tanks got filled?' I said.

He tapped the fuel gauges. 'Looks like they only did the wings. Must have been waiting until morning to top off the sponson tanks.'

Our wing tanks held six hundred gallons each. The sponsons over two thousand.

'There's worse news,' Mason said. 'The left wing tank must have taken a hit. We're losing fuel.'

'How bad?'

'Not the end of the world, but steady.'

'Any seaplane bases around here?' I said to Ava.

She thought for a moment. 'There's Creeley's Landing, about fifty miles from here.'

'How big?'

'LaGuardia field it is not.'

'Hundred Octane?'

'Unless Lester's been thinning it down to save money.'

'Who's he?'

'Fixed base operator. Old man Creeley is quite a character.'

'Time we pay him a visit.'

'You're kidding me. His marina's on a pond for God's sake.' She saw my frown and added quickly, 'Not a pond exactly, but you'll never set this thing down there.'

Turns out she was right. I didn't sit the *Dixie Clipper* down, I rammed her onto the still waters of the narrow inlet with all the teeth-chattering grace of a novice pilot. As soon as she hit I chopped the throttles and the clipper wallowed to a stately taxi as birds and wildlife exploded around us in shock and alarm.

The morning light had barely penetrated the overhanging cypress and cottonwoods at water's edge. At one point, their proximity made me certain at that our one hundred-fifty-foot wingspan would prove too much and our mission would end before it began. But by the grace of Orlando's direct line to God, we made it in one piece.

I checked the instrument panel clock: 5:17 a.m. Our entire world had changed in the space of an hour, and this was only the beginning.

I said, 'Think he'll be awake?'

'He will now.'

'Ziggy, can you handle the mooring?'

'I'm on it, captain,' He hurried up from the back where he'd been sitting with the professor. He opened the floor hatch and disappeared.

I turned to Ava. 'You've got the aircraft. Take us into the mooring.' I sat back and folded my arms.

She gulped but said nothing, then leaned forward to look over the nose of the plane to better judge her aiming point while I cut power to the inboard engines. To my surprise she smoothly worked the throttles of the two remaining engines back and forth to alter the track of the plane like she'd been doing it all her life.

'Lucky for you there's no wind,' I groused, realizing my little joke was backfiring.

'I can handle wind.'

'Sure you can.'

'Captain Carter, unless you have a legitimate reason for acting like the Wicked Witch of the West, do you mind letting me dock this beast?'

'*The Wizard of Oz*. Great movie. Abby loved it. Ever see it?'

'Mickey Rooney was my date at the premiere.'

'No kidding. How is he?'

'Short, now shut up.'

She advanced the port engine and the *Dixie Clipper* slowly swung around to line up with the orange and white mooring buoy. Ziggy's head poked out of the bow hatch, he turned, grinned and saluted, just as a small green dinghy pushed off from the dock and putt-putted straight for us. A bent over figure sat crouched in the back, his hand on the tiller and his jaw set.

'That would be Mr. Creeley?' I said.

'One and the same.'

Minutes later, Ziggy leaned out of the hatch, hands outstretched to snag the buoy line. He snagged it expertly and tied it off onto one of the bow bollards.

'Cut engines?' Ava asked.

'Affirmative.'

The Wright radials clattered into silence. A long beat before the surrounding trees and bushes came alive with the excited cries of birds and beasts staring astonished at a forty-ton flying boat floating in the midst of their quiet little world.

Ava said, 'Excuse me.'

Before I could react she plopped into my lap, slid open my side window, leaned out and shouted, 'Lester, you old buzzard, we need some gas and we need it fast.'

'Child, is that you?'

'Who'd you think it was? Some high falutin' movie star or something?'

'Hey, girl, that's what you is now, ain't you?'

'Sure am, and I'll give you an autograph to prove it, providing you gas up this big bird.'

Creeley took in the immense size of the clipper looming over him like an aluminum skyscraper. 'What in the God's green earth is this thing doing here?'

'Gas.'

He shook his head as if trying to wake up. 'Uh... how much you figure you need?'

'Fill 'er up.'

'You're joking.'

'C'mon Lester, don't be a pain.'

He gulped. 'Cash on the barrel then.'

'My credit's good here and you know it.'

'Not that good.' He folded his arms and stood there balancing easily in the bobbing dinghy.

I tapped Ava on the shoulder. 'My turn.'

She slid off my lap and I leaned out the window. 'Good morning, sir. Captain Samuel Carter, Pan American Airways at your service. Do you have any diving gear? Face masks, anything like that?'

'What the hell for?'

'Seems we got shot up by some Nazis an hour ago, and I want to check the damage.'

A slow smile spread across his leathery face like a hungry catfish spotting dinner. 'You don't say now.'

I thumbed in the direction of the tail where she'd been stitched with bullet holes. 'See for yourself.'

245

He examined the damage. 'One of them compliance fighters pounced you, huh?'

'Ground fire.'

'You don't say!'

He considered this new bit of information, adding it up like a miser stacking coins. He frowned and leaned forward for another look at the fuselage. 'Thought Looft-HAN-see was flying these big birds now.'

'They are.'

'Where's your swastikas?'

'What do you mean?'

He pointed to the side of the *Dixie Clipper's* fuselage. 'All I see is stars and bars.'

In the chaos of trying to escape, I never noticed what the Couba Island flight crew had done. Overnight they had painted over the loathsome triple-tail swastikas, and then scraped off the LUFTHANSA lettering to reveal the American flag that Trippe had painted on the sides of all the Pan Am planes in 1939, when war broke out in Europe to proclaim their American nationality.

Creeley said, 'Looks mighty pretty.'

'Be nice to see it flying over Berlin one of these days, don't you think?'

He considered this for a long minute. His jaw worked his tobacco like a cow's cud. Then he spat. 'This plane got something to do with that?'

'It might.'

'Secret mission?'

'Didn't say that.'

He nodded. 'No, sir, you didn't. But it could be, right?'

A long pause.

'About that gas,' I said.

He spat again. 'I'll damn well pump it for you myself.'

I left Mason to supervise the re-fueling while Orlando and I took turns diving under the clipper with Creeley's ancient gear, which was sketchy at best. But the sputtering air compressor and hose worked well enough to keep air flowing through the diving mask.

The water was clear enough for me to determine that the hull was basically sound, except for two rows of bullet holes near the nose that needed plugging. The clipper was built with a double hull for collision emergencies, but machine gun bullets weren't like floating logs. The slugs had torn through both the outer and inner hulls like a screwdriver jammed through a melon. Our bilge pumps couldn't keep up with that much water, so Orlando and I needed to fashion some kind of plugs of that would tide us over until the clipper could be properly repaired.

With Creeley's help we concocted a hybrid blend of bamboo plugs wrapped with oakum and hammered them into the holes. True, we had only half-solved the problem; the inner hull was still holed and held hundreds of gallons of water, but in theory the sump pumps could get rid of that water before we took off.

IF we took off.

I had been nervously kicking that can down the road the whole time we were working on the hull because I didn't want to do the math, which was this: a gallon of gasoline weighs five-point-eight pounds. Each of our topped-off sponson tanks now held two thousand gallons, which means we had taken on an additional twenty-three thousand pounds.

Not a problem when the Boeing 314 had nice long run to lug that kind of weight into the air. But in our case, Creeley's Landing was located on a narrow inlet with a decided hard left turn to the water's course about two miles downwind - make that no wind. The morning sun was well established, but it had brought no wind along with it. The water surface was like polished aluminum. When it came to the *Dixie Clipper* trying to break free of its tenacious surface tension, it might as well be glue.

My idea was a simple. Making it a reality would be the challenge. I explained it to Creeley and finished by saying, 'You got a boat with some muscle to it?'

'I might.'

'How much?'

He departed in his little green dinghy without saying another word. Minutes later the thundering roar of a diesel marine engine shattered the morning stillness as a massive, forty-foot long, low-slung symphony of polished mahogany and chrome burst from behind the landing and split the waters like a scalpel as it raced toward us. It slowed to a stop in a slew of spray that sparkled in the sunshine.

Over the contented burble of the massive engine, Creeley said, 'Will this do?'

I took in the immense size of the craft. 'What the hell is it?'

He patted the steering wheel and said slyly, 'I wasn't always in the aviation business.'

Ava said, 'Lester was a rum-runner. Made a fortune. Lost it, too, didn't you?'

Creeley bristled. 'Didn't lose the boat though.'

'Good thing, since Mother was one of your investors.'

'Your mother?' I said.

'She likes her bourbon, and didn't appreciate it when Prohibition came along. So she and some of her cronies ponied up a grubstake for Lester, who kept them in their cups, at least for a while.'

I said to Creeley, 'What you got for power?'

'Liberty Vee-twelve. Five hundred-twenty-five horses.' He revved it briefly as if to prove his claim and the birds screeched in complaint.

'Okay,' I said. 'Let's you and me go for a ride.'

I hopped into the rum-runner and Creeley took us down to the bend in the river. Once there, I measured the tree height and did some rough calculations. Didn't like the answers I came up with, but stayed with it until I finally found a set of numbers that didn't make my stomach sink with fear, just thrash around on the surface instead.

Creeley observed me in silence, and then said, 'Think we can make it, captain?'

'Got no choice.'

'My kind of odds. Count me in.'

Forty tons of airplane is a lot. If I had done my takeoff calculations right, and I knew I had because Fatt had been a good teacher, then I had roughly ten thousand feet of water 'runway' to lift eighty thousand pounds of aluminum and people into the air and clear a stand of cypress trees fifty-feet high. I had four radial engines putting out a total of six thousand eight hundred horsepower to do the job, which would have been child's play in open water where a flying boat's takeoff run is endless and her engines have plenty of time to develop full output.

On land I could have solved the problem a different way: stand on the brakes and bring the engines up to full power before starting my takeoff roll. I had done it hundreds of times in the past. But that was land, this was water, and while the laws of physics can't be beaten, they can be bent a bit.

With everybody strapped in and ready to go, we were going to try.

Think of a slingshot. I know it sounds preposterous, but I had no choice. Loaded with over twenty thousand additional pounds of avgas, no way in hell we were going anywhere but back and forth on this windless, calm water without a creative plan of action.

I keyed my intercom. 'All set, Ziggy?'

Back in his familiar station in the open nose hatch, he turned and saluted impressively. 'Standing by SIR!'

'You ever get sick of Hollywood, I'll get you a job with Pan Am.'

'No thank you, SIR!'

'Got your line release all figured out?'

He held up the end of a rope that led to a strange-looking knot tied across both bollards. I had originally planned on rigging a simple 'exploding knot' like a clove hitch, that would allow quick release when pulled, but Creeley had come up with something called a 'Double Carrick Bend' which was a ten times stronger knot. And considering what we were going to do, we would need it - at both ends of the plane.

'Pilot to waist gunner.'

Orlando's deep voice answered with a chuckle. 'That would be me, sir.'

'Your line all set?'

'In my hands waiting for your command.'

I leaned out the window and waved at Creeley, down and to the left of us, crouched over the wheel of his rum runner. He waved back, advanced the throttle and centered up on the plane. His maneuver took up the slack from the line that ran from our nose bollard to the rum-runner's stern cleats. He had wound the line around his gunwale cleats too, for good measure.

A haze of diesel smoke drifted across the still waters from his burbling engine. Those damn still waters. Why wasn't there any wind?

I ducked back inside. 'Stand by your flag.'

Ava unrolled the small American flag Pan Am co-pilots place outside on a stanchion after landing, after the tradition of a ship arriving in port. Only this time we weren't arriving, we were departing, and the flag would be Creeley's signal to hit full throttle.

I said to her, 'Things are going to get noisy real soon, so here's the deal, when-'

'When you call for flaps I keep my finger on the solenoid so they'll keep deploying without stopping, got it, got it, GOT IT. You told me that hundred times already.'

'Just want to be sure.'

She tapped the flag against her palm and then looked over at me.

'Didn't mean to yell at you like that.'

'That's okay, you're fired.' She grinned. 'Just like that?'

'It's the Pan Am way. No second chance with insubordination.'

'All along I thought Hollywood was bad.'

'Juan Trippe makes Jack Warner look like Mother Goose.' I said.

'That I'd like to see.'

'If we get through this in one piece, we will.'

Don't ask me why I said that, I just imagined the two of us doing something other than running for our lives, and I liked the thought. But it lasted about as long as a firefly's flash as the task at hand came rushing back.

'Pilot to crew, prepare for takeoff.'

Mason, Ziggy, Orlando and Ava dutifully answered in turn, and I almost laughed at my idea of a 'crew,' but it wasn't funny, it was scary.

Ava and I went through the engine sequence start, and two minutes later, with magneto checks accomplished, all four engines were turning over sweetly, sending a vibration through the plane much the same as a heartbeat does in a human being. Instruments in the green, pre-flight check done, I flexed my fingers for a brief second before closing them over the throttles.

'Stand by,' I said.

Ava sat up straight. 'Standing by.'

I slowly advanced the throttles. But instead of moving gracefully away from the dock, the clipper sat there, tied to it with the strong manila line leading back from Orlando's gun station to the dock.

'Waist gunner, line status,' I said over the increasing engine roar.

'Holding steady,' Orlando said.

'Ready close cowl flaps fifty.' Mason said. 'Standing by.'

The cylinder head temperatures were rising fast. The plane wasn't designed to be held back on a leash like a straining greyhound and her engines were showing the strain. The small flaps encircling the streamlined engine cowls were doing their best to let air in to cool down the cylinders. But once we started our takeoff run, they would add drag unless we closed them partway.

'Three degrees flaps.'

Ava answered, 'at three.'

I took a deep breath. 'Ready flag out.'

She knelt up on her. By now the clipper was vibrating like a tuning fork from the combined forces of four radial engines whirling eleven-foot propellers at full RPM.

Now or never.

'Flag out!'

Ava slid open the window and leaned out, waving and shouting but I couldn't hear her over the din of the engines, doubly loud because of the open window, not to mention the rum runner's engine soaring up into full power.

I shouted, 'Pilot to waist gunner, release the line!'

'Aye, aye.'

I can't exactly say we were shot from a cannon. After all, forty tons is forty tons, but for the first time since I'd been flying seaplanes, I literally felt myself shoved back into my seat from the force of motion as the *Dixie Clipper* surged forward so hard her nose began burying itself in the water. But the powerful rum-runner yanked it up before I could counteract it.

Creeley's boat was thirty yards ahead, pulling hard, the line connecting us as taut as a steel rod. Ziggy hunkered down in the mooring hatch, one hand on the line, the other clamped onto his intercom headphones.

We hadn't gone a thousand feet when the airspeed indicator ticked into life and was showing twenty-five knots already. So far so good. But forty-five more to go before we had the slightest chance of lifting off, and that bend in the river was getting closer and closer.

I found myself straining against my chest straps, as if that would make her go faster. Ava was doing the same thing.

'Thirty knots,' she called.

'C'mon old girl, you can do it.'

'C'mon darling Dixie, make us proud,'

'Thirty five.'

Her hull began slapping the water and I smiled. Creeley's boat was doing a lot more than pulling us with its five hundred horses, its marine propeller was churning up a roiling wake that broke up the glassy-still water and reduced its suction on the *Dixie Clipper's* hull, giving us a fighting chance.

'Fifty knots.'

One-third of the takeoff run left before the turn in the river. Needed seventy, but would chance it with sixty if we hand to. Felt a slight stiffening in the controls, as if she were flexing and stretching after a long nap, but not enough yet to wake up and fly.

Ava's hand moved up to the flaps control and hovered there, waiting for my call.

'Not yet,' I said.

'Sometime today I hope,' she said, and then, 'Fifty-five!'

'Ziggy, stand bye to release your line!'

'Standing by,' Ziggy's voice a buzzing blur.

The line to the rum-runner slackened as our increasing airspeed began to overtake her top speed. Creeley seemed to read my mind and nervously glanced over his shoulder. He pumped his fist hard.

'Pull the line!'

Ziggy tugged at it. Nothing. Again, this time more frantically. But the line held.

'Sixty!'

Controls firm, her wings biting into the morning air, she wanted to fly. Ziggy now halfway out of the mooring hatch, yanking on the line with both hands.

Nothing doing.

If I tried lifting her off now, we'd take the rumrunner along with us, and its weight would pull us back down.

'Ziggy!' Ava screamed.

Ziggy's arms flew up and he disappeared down through the hatch as though he were a puppet. A fraction of a second later Orlando popped up, grabbed the line, yanked it, and the double Carrick knot 'exploded' exactly the way it should have, and it slithered down and away like a manila snake.

'Sixty five.'

'Full flaps.'

I cranked in nose trim as fast as I could to counteract the wing flaps extending deeper and deeper into the slipstream, dramatically increasing lift. The approaching trees were a wall of green that filled the windscreen. Now or never.

I pulled back on the yoke.

The *Dixie Clipper* didn't take off so much as she ballooned off the surface of the water in perfect obedience to the rule of flight that allows you to exchange altitude for airspeed. And that's what we were doing as the airspeed needle dropped and the altimeter soared and we were clawing for just enough height to clear the trees that were suddenly upon us in a blurring rush of green and brown and a sudden banging, clanging, explosion of sound that came and went, and just like that we were clear of the trees.

Clear!

I lowered her nose and said a prayer we'd recover our airspeed before stalling. After that boost of height, the controls were mush, the wings wanted to stop working, but God bless the Wright Engine Company for saving our lives in that moment by having made machines that could be pushed past their limits and still keep working hard enough to shove the airspeed needle past the stall speed and into safe territory again.

When we finally reached one hundred-ten knots, I said, 'How we doing, Mason?'

He answered with forced casualness, 'Any time you want to cut RPM's would be fine by me.'

I did so carefully and put the plane into a gentle bank that would take us back over Creeley's Landing. Our last sight of him as we flew over at five hundred feet was a waving, dancing old man in a speedboat that had just helped us pull off a miracle. How many more we needed before this long, impossible day was over was anybody's guess.

The rising sun cast long shadows across the Louisiana bayou as we slowly climbed to our cruising altitude of six thousand feet. No way of knowing how strong the winds aloft would be until we got up there and I did some estimations. If they were not too strong, we could make it all the way to the target and then back to our refueling base in Nevada without additional fuel. Nineteen hours by Fatt's original flight plan, but no way of knowing how long now. Both he and the grand plan were out the window, flying among the stars.

Part of me understood my old friend was dead, but most of me felt he was still alive. The sheer momentum of his personality kept him talking and laughing inside me and I needed that, especially now.

One of the first lessons I learned from him was that it's easy to lift an airplane off the runway. A five year-old can do it. Airplanes are designed to fly. All they need is enough airspeed for the wings to counteract weight forces by lift forces and up you go. But landing an airplane is another story entirely; you must orchestrate the just the opposite: achieve that perfect meeting between your wheels and the ground by reducing power and airspeed enough to lose altitude, but not so much that you fall out of the sky like a stone.

I turned to Ava. 'Keep an eye on the store.'

'Where you going?'

'Try to raise Couba Island. See what's going on.'

I unbuckled my seat belt and made my way back to the empty radio operator station directly behind her.   It would have been nice to have a

'Sparks' on board, but I had to play with the cards the *Kampfschwimmers* had dealt us.

I stared at the transmitters and receivers but nothing made sense at first. It had been years since I sweated through a flight as the radio operator trying to locate distant radio stations on the RDF locator, or tapping out position reports to Pan Am ground control. Much had changed since I had done this kind of thing.

But then, like a picture coming into perfect focus, everything came back to me in a rush. I turned on all of the equipment, dialed in the correct frequency, grabbed the microphone and said,

'*Dixie Clipper* calling Couba Island. Come in Couba Island.'

Nothing but the rush of static in my headphones. I tried again but got the same thing.

'Any luck?' Ava called out over her shoulder.

'Either they're shot up or they're out of range.'

'Any other way to reach them?'

I stared at the Morse Key. Its well-thumbed black key brought back many memories of my first days with Pan Am. I slid it closer and began tapping away, slowly at first, and then faster as the familiar code came back to me.

DIXIE CLIPPER CALLING COUBA ISLAND

To my surprise, rapid DIT-DAH's instantly replied:

COUBA ISLAND, GO AHEAD.

'We got them!' My fingers flew, or at least I thought they did as I quickly tapped:

DIXIE CLIPPER ALOFT SIX THOUSAND FEET / SOULS ON BOARD AVA, MASON, FRIEDMAN, ZIEGLER, DIAZ AND SELF/ ENROUTE TO TARGET /ADVISE / CARTER

Another long wait. Then a terse,

RETURN TO BASE IMMEDIATELY /PATTON.

I started to reply but something made me stop. Why the hell would Patton want us to come back? Wasn't this mission the very thing the Sons of Liberty wanted?

Ava said, 'What's wrong?'

'Not sure. They may have been overrun.'

Ava twisted around in her seat. 'I don't believe it. We outnumbered them.'

'*Kampfschwimmers* are trained commandos. A big difference. Could have happened.'

'Never.'

'Say what you want but General Patton -- or somebody claiming to be him - just ordered us to return to base and I don't like it.'

I hit the key again:

AUTHENTICATE MESSAGE / AVA'S PET NAME FOR YOU

The long silence that followed was answer enough. I knew what Ava was thinking, so I said quickly, 'Look, he and your mother and the others most likely skedaddled into the bayou to regroup, and they're in hiding until they can make a counterattack.'

The Morse code began DIT-DAH'ing at me but I ignored it. Ava and I held each other's eyes until hers tightened slightly and we both came to a silent agreement. I switched off the transmitter.

Just then the wing inspection door behind Mason's engineering console banged opened and Orlando squeezed his way out. A frown on his face.

'What's wrong?' I said.

He exchanged a quick glance with Mason and then shrugged. 'Number four engine's running a little hotter than it should. Can't figure out why just yet.'

'Still in the green?'

'Yes, but I wanted to open the hood, just to be on the safe side.'

In order to make minor engine repairs in flight, Boeing engineers had designed a small passageway inside the massive wings and equipped the rear of each engine with clamshell-like firewall doors that opened onto the back of the engine's mysterious tangle of hydraulic, oil, and fuel lines available for inspection and possible repair. How Orlando had managed to get out onto the narrow inspection catwalk was a mystery. Especially the outboard engines that were furthest away and where the wing began to narrow.

'Couldn't find anything obvious,' he continued. 'But most likely we took a round or two.'

I held up the piece of paper with my scribbled words. 'They just ordered us to return to base.'

Orlando said, 'Who's 'they?''

'My point exactly. The Nazis are running the show - at least the radio shack part of it.'

Professor Friedman roused himself from the Master's conference chair, as if coming out of a deep sleep. 'What do you propose we do, captain?'

I glanced at my crew - minus Ziggy who was below decks - and realized that I was pilot-in-command of this harebrained flight and up to me to make the decision to obey or disobey orders. Not Fatt, not Patton, not Trippe. Me. A man in command of people whose frightened faces matched mine if I could only look into a mirror.

I finally said to Mason, 'Let's check out the bombsight, shall we?' He grinned and flexed his fingers. 'Thought you'd never ask.'

'Orlando, keep an eye on those engines.'

'Roger.'

'Ava, you have the aircraft. Got your bearing okay?'

She nodded silently, the perfect first officer. Even if it was just an act, a good one.

I opened the deck hatch and followed Mason down the crew staircase to the lower deck. We turned left and made our way forward past the galley where Ziggy was clattering and banging pans. He called out breezily as we passed by.

'Anybody else hungry but me? I missed breakfast by a country mile, what with all the bullets flying.'

I admired his coolness under fire, considering our harebrained takeoff.

'What you got?' I said.

He opened and closed a few stainless steel compartments, humming as he did so.

'Looks like Nawrocki stocked up pretty well. Eggs...bread...fruit...bacon - if you're not kosher, that is.'

'Are you?'

He looked pained. 'Of course I am.'

'You don't look it.'

He raised his eyebrows. 'Jews are very good at keeping secrets.'

I left him humming with his happy work and made my way forward into the mooring compartment in the nose of the plane, where by now Mason had already uncovered the bombsight stowed near the mooring anchor. Painted olive drab, about two feet high, the bombsight had a series of knobs and flat panels and a sighting eyepiece on top. Never having seen one before, and only having vaguely heard about it, I barely understood its function. Too many things had been happening too fast and I was bound to miss a few. This complicated device was one of them.

Mason grunted in pain and touched his bandaged side.

'You okay?'

'Fine, just need a hand. It's on the heavy side.'

We unfastened the retaining bolts and lifted the bombsight and slid it onto its mounting plate in the nose of the plane. The Couba Island crew had done a meticulous job of welding a series of cross braces that supported it so that its view plate rested just above a small, optically flat Plexiglas window fitted into the hull. They had also made a kneeling pad and backrest that Mason could use as he crouched over the device.

Mason patted the device. 'My Navy buddies would kill for this sweetheart.'

'It's that special?'

He looked at me disdainfully. 'A Norden bombsight can drop a pickle in a barrel from twenty-five thousand feet and do it every time. The Navy was just starting to get them when Adolf dropped the bomb. We could have won the war with this baby.'

'Sill can.'

He laughed, but he winced from the wound, and then patted the top of the device. 'This is the sighting head - the thing I look through. It's got an extended vision telescope that lets me acquire the target at an oblique angle. Once I've done that, the flight stabilizer down here locks on the target and keeps the plane flying on my heading.'

'It's connected to our autopilot?'

He grabbed a thick cable and slipped it into a waiting socket. 'It is now. You didn't know about that part?'

'I didn't know any of this stuff.'

'Captain Fatt sure knew how to keep his mouth shut. And he was right to do so. This thing is top secret. We have orders to protect it with our lives. Can't let it fall into enemy hands no matter what. See this thing here?'

He pulled out a small red knob near the bottom of the unit. 'If I leave that out, one minute from now this whole thing blows up. It's got a combination thermite and torpex charge inside. The thermite melts the mirrors, gear housing and anything that the enemy could make use of, and then the torpex takes over and blows it all to kingdom come.'

'Are you planning on pushing in that knob any time soon?'

He touched it but didn't. 'Plus, if for some reason you don't activate it - say you get shot up with anti-aircraft fire or something-'

'- or German commandos.'

'And the plane crashes, then this little baby goes into a booby-trap mode when it sustains over six impact G's. If a bad guy starts poking around the wreckage, spots it and touches it, BOOM, goodbye sight, goodbye bad guy. Those Norden folks thought of everything.'

'Times almost up.' I nervously reached over to push in the button but he beat me to it.

'Anyhow, so when I spot the Initial Point on the Columbia River and we start our final run, my baby and I are flying this bird from then on.' He gave me a salute. 'With your permission of course.'

I returned his salute. 'Granted.'

God grant me the courage not to give up what I think is right, even though I think it is hopeless.
Admiral Chester Nimitz

From six thousand feet, Oklahoma seems flat and featureless. But it's not.

For that matter, most of America west of the Mississippi and east of the Rockies looks that way at altitude. Hour after hour, nothing but endless plots of farmland laid out ruler-straight, filled with wheat, soybeans, alfalfa and corn.

It always puzzles me why people chose to tame our planet with perfectly laid-out borders separating farmhouse from forest, beets from sorghum, and neighbors from neighbors. Mother Nature works just the opposite: one thing flows into another, hills into valleys, rivers into streams, mountains into molehills in an unending sequence that carries with it animals, vegetables and minerals moving in the same effortless way in a perfect curve leading from birth to death. To hell with borders, give me Mother Nature's way every time.

A nineteen-hour flight leads to thoughts like these. So far we had been in the air seven hours: seven uneventful, engine-droning hours when pilots encounter all sorts of interesting thoughts prompted by being aloft with nothing to do but keep going straight across endless Oklahoma.

The autopilot was holding us on a steady course for our target, and my crew was in various states of readiness: Ava lay curled up beneath the navigator's table, sound asleep. Ziggy was prowling around the plane in search of some blankets, because even though it was August on the ground, air temperature decreases with altitude, and at six thousand feet things were on the chilly side. Orlando manned the engineering station while Friedman and Mason were aft, working on the bomb.

'Engineer to pilot,' Orlando said over the intercom.

'Go ahead.'

'Can you step into my office for a second?'

I didn't like the sound of that, and moments later I understood why when, with no amount of tapping the fuel gauges of our right sponson, the indicator needles on both tanks were not where they were supposed to be.

'How long's it been like this?'

'For the past half hour. Something must have finally worked its way loose in the tanks. Maybe we took a hit in a seam or something.'

'I don't remember seeing anything like that when we checked the plane at Creeley's. Do you?'

He swept his hands across the maze of indicators and gauges like he was blessing the congregation. 'Brother, we can agree all day on what we did or didn't see. But this tells me we are never going to make it to the target.'

'How much fuel have you transferred up to the wing tanks?'

'As much as I could. Any more and we'll be flying sideways.'

He was right. In a normal flight - which this one sure as hell wasn't - fuel pumps transferred the sponson's gas up to the wing tanks, which in turn fed it to the engines. But because the Nazis had already damaged our left wing tank at Couba Island, the right one had to do all the heavy lifting.

Orlando and I exchanged a long look.

He finally said, 'What's your plan B?'

'Actually, this was it.'

Even though useless, I rapped the fuel indicator gauges with my knuckles one last time in vain hopes of getting a different result. Then I headed for the navigation table where I unrolled the chart, took out my plotter, took a deep breath and got down to work.

Our line of progress so far was indicated with a series of my carefully drawn pencil lines leading from Couba Island to Creeley's landing, south of Baton Rouge, and then across into Texas, where we had passed well north of Dallas, not wanting to excite any interest in Nazi compliance fighters coming up for a look-see.

According to our Sons of Liberty contacts in Dallas, there weren't many planes around, but I figured far better to be safe than sorry. After all, we had no flight clearance and never would. As the world – including the Nazis - was concerned, the *Dixie Clipper* had gone down in the ocean months ago with all hands on board.

Yet here she was cruising at six thousand feet with an American flag painted on her nose, packing machine guns and an atomic bomb. With Texas long gone behind us, we were now about to leave the Oklahoma panhandle and cross over into Colorado. But if Orlando's fuel consumption calculations were correct, we'd crash somewhere in southern Idaho, probably skidding to a stop on some farmer's potato field, with a lot of explaining to do.

I felt a tug on my pants cuff and Ava's sleepy voice floated up beneath the chart table said, 'You're still barefoot, you know.'

'No shoe stores up here.'

She unwound herself and joined me. 'What's brewing?' I tapped the map. 'Ever been to Nevada?'

'Been over it many a time.'

'We're heading for the Sons of Liberty base there.'

'I thought that was supposed to be after we dropped the bomb.'

While I explained the fuel problem she casually unfastened her hair, held the hairpins in her teeth, ran a comb through it, and then tied it up neatly again, all the while staring intently at the map. I felt like I was in her bedroom for some reason. Not a bad feeling, by the way.

My 'Plan C' for what it's worth, was as simple as a stump: divert to the secret base before, not after the mission, as originally planned. Take on a full load of fuel, fly off again, leaking tanks and all, and lose it in a steady stream over Nevada, Oregon and Washington until we reached the target and dropped the bomb.

When I finished, Ava took my plotter, spent a couple of minutes working out some numbers of her own and then shook her head. 'Based on your calculations we can reach the target for sure, but we'll be running on fumes after that.'

'When that bomb goes off it will stir up a hornet's nest of compliance fighters and they'll spot us in no time. We've got to bury the murder weapon somewhere fast.'

'How?'

'I figure we'll have just enough fuel to reach the Pacific coast. We'll put her down a mile offshore, scuttle her and then take to the rafts.'

She winced, 'I wish there were some other way.'

'I'm open to suggestions.'

She stood there for a long minute, lost in thought, her finger tapping on Sentinel Island, a tiny speck of land in the middle of Lake Mead. Once an impressive mountain, now just the tip of it protruded from the waters of a lake created when they built Hoover Dam, re-named Boulder Dam because FDR didn't like our previous president, but was savvy enough not name it after another politician. Somewhere on that desolate-looking tip of land was the Sons of Liberty refueling base.

'Who runs this operation again?' I said.

'The McGraw brothers; Jacob and Esau. Own and operate a paddleboat, the *Desert Queen*. Give tours of the dam, the islands, that sort of thing.'

'Where the hell did they get a paddleboat?'

'A lake steamer they trucked in from somewhere on the Missouri River. Re-assembled it piece by piece. Company's based at Lake Mead Marina, and the refueling site is on Sentinel Island, about a half-mile away.'

She paused and made a face. 'I still can't see diverting there with the fuel leaking the way it is.'

'Like carrying a water bucket with a hole in it. Run fast enough, you'll make it to the sink in time.'

'We're showing about one-forty indicated. Why don't we descend and see if the winds are more favorable?'

'Air density will eat up our fuel even faster.'

She winced, 'You're right, I forgot about that.' She slapped the plotter on the map. 'Why can't something go right for a change?'

I returned to the radio operator's station. The clipper's autopilot was locked onto a radio frequency found by our RDF. I thumbed through a list of station frequencies more westerly than northwesterly and dialed the first three without any luck. But the fourth one, KNVN, Las Vegas, boomed out Glenn Miller's *Chattanooga Choo-Choo* so painfully loud that I had to yank off my headset.

I started to curse but then checked myself. Our situation was getting way too tense. The atmosphere thick with gloom and doom. Fatt had taught me long ago that a leader must appear greater than the problem or he was in deep trouble. How the hell was I supposed to do that? Then I had an idea. I flicked the switch that sent the swing music blaring over a set of speakers mounted in the ceiling of the flight deck.

At first nobody reacted; Orlando kept fussing with the potentiometers, Ava bent over the map. But then she started swaying to the beat, slowly at first and then more and more as the forceful beat of Miller's music turned the flight deck into a dance hall. Or at least it seemed like that to me and why not? Here I was, a shoeless captain flying a plane leaking like a sieve, with an impossible mission ahead. Why not at least act bigger than the problem at hand?

I made sure the autopilot was tracking the new station in Nevada, but instead of sitting down, I returned to the navigator's station and tapped Ava on the shoulder.

'Care to dance?'

Her surprised laughter was like a flash of happy lightning.

'Seriously?'

I led her into the small space between the navigation and engineering stations and did a scaled-down version of a jitterbug, while Orlando beamed with pleasure. My bare feet limited my moves, but I think I did a fairly good job, all things considered.

Halfway through our performance, Ziggy appeared with an armful of blankets. He leaned against the radio operator's table with a happy grin on his face. As the music ended I spun Ava around with a final flourish. We stood there staring at each other as Frank Sinatra began singing *Night and Day*.

'Thanks for the dance,' she said. 'I needed that.'

'You're welcome.'

'Like Sinatra?'

'He's okay, I guess. You?'

'Too skinny for my tastes.' She patted my shoulder. 'I like my fellas with a little more muscle.' She went back to the map while I went over and turned down the music.

Ziggy said, 'How'd you get the radio to play that?'

I briefly explained the Radio Direction Finder but lost him halfway through. Even so, he stayed with it, asking questions about the tuning amplifier, the Morse code key and the transmitters and receivers. I finally said, 'Thinking about changing professions?'

'Thought I maybe could help you guys out, but that radio stuff's too complicated.' He hefted the blankets and made a face at them. 'Looks like I'm stuck with being a glorified cook.'

'Don't sell yourself short, Zig. You make great food and you're a great scrounger, too.'

'Much rather shoot a machine gun.'

'Careful what you wish for.'

I left him to his brooding while I returned to the cockpit. After a careful check of the instruments, I keyed the microphone.

'Pilot to engineer.'

'Yes, sir' Orlando said.

'Let me know if our rate of fuel loss increases.'

'Roger, wilco, and by the way, all the years I've known you, I never saw you dance like that.'

'We all have our secrets.'

Four hours from touchdown, just as we were crossing the Jemez Mountains of New Mexico, I felt a faint shudder go through the plane. Up until that point I had been staring transfixed at the desolate mountain range below that marks the southernmost tip of the Rockies. From here the mountains climb northwest on a two thousand-mile majestic march across the United States and up into Canada.

The late afternoon sunlight cast indigo blue shadows on the unforgiving, waterless land below. But I no longer gave a damn about what was below, because the clipper had shuddered and I didn't know why.

'Pilot to engineer, which engine?'

Orlando said, 'Don't know yet.'

'Did you feel it?'

'Yes, but it happened so fast I couldn't spot it because - standby.'

Ava and I exchanged silent looks as we waited like two patients for the doctor's verdict.

'Number three,' Mason shortly announced.

Both men hunched over the control panel, their hands moving from instrument to instrument, like hypnotists trying to cast a spell, or break one.

'Magnetos okay?' I said.

'Affirmative,' Orlando said. 'But the cylinder head temps are through the roof.'

Mason added, 'Might be a frozen intake valve.'

'See if the cowl flaps can cool it down.'

'Roger.'

The floor hatch banged open and Ziggy practically flew out, his eyes bugged, his mouth moving but no sound came out. He finally managed to gasp, 'Oil everywhere! Coming from the wing!'

'Which side?'

He pointed to starboard. 'All around the front of an engine.'

As if on cue, the control wheel began vibrating like mad. I tried looking over Ava's shoulder to see the inboard engine, but couldn't get a clear view.

264

Orlando said, 'She's swallowed a valve for sure. Better feather before we blow a cylinder.'

Fortunately the clipper could fly easily on three engines, just not as high or as fast, which complicated my calculations. I had wanted to arrive at the refueling base before dark. Even now I was cutting it close, getting there around eight o'clock, when there'd still be enough light to sit her down. Now I wasn't so sure. As with everything else in flying, truth trumps dreams.

I stabbed the red 'feather' button to swivel number three's propeller blades into the airstream and keep them from spinning. I cut the fuel feed and the magneto, and that's when things went to hell faster than I could stop them. The plane began shuddering even worse.

'She's not feathering!' Orlando shouted.

I slammed the feather button again, and the pitch control too. Nothing. Halfway through the feathering cycle the blades had jammed in full increase takeoff pitch. Not enough oil pressure in the mechanism to rotate them further. She started pulling hard to the right from the drag. I applied left rudder to keep her from yawing.

'Help me on the pedals.'

Ava added her foot power to mine and the pressure eased slightly.

Then to Orlando, 'Try feathering from your end.'

A tense ten seconds as number three engine's tachometer climbed toward three thousand RPM; twice what it should be. At this speed, the propeller blades were spinning knives, and if that engine came apart, they'd slash through our fuselage like soft butter. I reduced speed as much as I dared to ease the RPMs to a mushy one-twenty-five knots.

Orlando said, 'No dice. Those blades are stuck for good.'

'Cross-feed oil?'

'Not on these.'

The Wright radial engines were beautiful to behold; compact, powerful, twenty-four-cylinder works of art designed to perform reliably and under strenuous conditions. But the good folks at Wright hadn't designed their engines to withstand Nazi machine gun bullets blasting through intricate wiring harnesses and complicated plumbing and ricocheting off piston heads. Which no doubt was the cause of this runaway propeller that we couldn't stop.

I didn't want to look at the altimeter because I already knew we had lost at least a thousand feet. And when I finally had to, even worse. I regarded at the rugged mountains below. Not a trace of water for hundreds of miles and we were in a flying boat.

'Sam?' Ava's voice was soft on the intercom, but insistent, nonetheless.

'We're going down,' I said.

'Here?'

'If I add power, the RPM will go up and the engine will eventually disintegrate. Twenty four pistons going every which way. Might take out the engine next to it, and the wing along with it.'

'There's no water.'

'Maybe I can find a level piece of ground.'

'For good, you mean.'

The rudder pedals dug painfully into my bare feet and my calf muscles were starting to cramp.

I shouted over my shoulder. 'Ziggy, cut up one of those blankets and make me some foot pads.'

'Coming up!'

The altimeter unwound through three thousand feet. Not the soaring Rockies but mountains just as threatening with low peaks, deep valleys and nowhere to land. We had five, maybe six minutes of flight time remaining. The engine was cycling in and out of sync with the others as the runaway propeller kept up its demonic spin and made the whole plane shiver and shake like a hard-run horse.

I hated to do it, but I keyed the intercom and announced, 'We are going to make an emergency landing. It would be nice if there were some water down there to do it on but there isn't so it's going to be a rough ride. Ziggy, strap in at the radio operator's station. Professor, you and Mason strap in at the commander's station.'

As they scrambled to do as ordered, Ava pointed out the window.

'Your eleven o'clock. What do you think?'

A patch of land looked to be level desert, half-hidden in the late afternoon shadows. I put the plane into left bank, which wasn't easy considering our starboard drag. Some kind of animal, a deer maybe, darted across the ground at the sound of our engines, and its movement helped me estimate the length of the field on which we were going to crash land.

Trying to gauge distance when you're higher than a couple thousand feet is tricky. The eye is fooled into thinking things are larger, longer, slower or faster than they really are. Only experience can save you in times like this. But in my case I had no experience trying to land a flying boat on the desert.

The altimeter kept unwinding. Two thousand feet now, and that bit of level land would never accommodate us unless I stood her on her wing and made a diving approach. But I wasn't sure of her performance envelope. Airplanes, like people, have limits, and unless you know them as sure as you know your own, you can exceed them and find yourself in a jam. In my case, a jam of broken metal and broken people scattered on the ground because I ended up stalling this big whale of a plane instead of bringing her down in one piece.

I dug back into my years of flying experience to see if I could bring anything to bear on our predicament. Had Fatt ever had something like this happen to him? Had anybody? People say pilots love to 'hangar fly' and spin yarns about their profession because it's fun. But it's only half true. The other half comes from sheer necessity.

We fly alone up here and it's our neck on the chopping block if something goes wrong. And believe me, something always goes wrong. And when it does, and if you survive, you tell other pilots what happened and how you solved it. Not for bragging rights, but to share the knowledge in hopes that the same thing won't kill the other guy if it ever happens to him.

A jabbing pain in my foot. 'Cramping up,' I said. 'Can you handle the rudder?'

'Both feet on it, go,' Ava said.

I bent over and dug my thumbs into my instep, trying to undo the locked-up muscle. To my surprise, my foot felt slippery, traces of oil on the rudder pedals or something.

Oil.

'Captain Ross!' I whispered as the answer came to me in rush. I applied full power and the plane nosed up and away from the approaching ground.

'Orlando, cut oil to number three!"

'It'll melt the pistons.'

'Do it!'

A slight hesitation, then, 'Wilco.'

Engines were like children to Orlando; complicated creations, each with a life of its own; thousands of interconnected, perfectly machined parts moving in perfect synchrony, bathed in soothing oil that I had just ordered cut off. But unlike humans who, when losing blood will simply die, a radial engine deprived of oil can die in a much more dramatic fashion, sending parts and pistons flying.

I was banking on that not happening, however.

For two reasons; one, I felt lucky. Two, my sudden memory of Captain Roscoe Ross, a flamboyant, highly-renowned Pan Am pilot who flew the Caribbean Division, once told me how his S-42 Sikorsky got a prop locked in coarse pitch, just like ours, and he had done what I was doing now; starving the engine of oil. But whether or not I'd get the same result as Roscoe depended on factors over which I had no control.

Vibration rippled through the plane like a tuning fork. Deprived of its oil, the engine screamed like a tortured banshee. Would it freeze gradually, piston by piston? Or would all twenty-four cylinders let loose like hand grenades ripping the plane to shreds and sending us spinning out of control?

Any second now.

I said to Ava, 'Help me get her into a left turn, so that when the engine blows the pieces will fly uphill.'

We no sooner heaved on the control yokes together when a tremendous shock rippled through the plane as the Wright radial seized, not with a trembling explosion but with a beautiful BANG. An instant later something flashed past us on the right, shining in the late afternoon sun. The radial had quit so suddenly that the drive shaft twisted in two, torn like a French baguette, sending the propeller rocketing off on its spinning journey to earth, and the plane, suddenly freed from the drag forces, became a dream to handle.

I began a slow, easy, vibration-free climb away from the rocks below and to the sky above. I took a deep breath and let it out slowly. 'Thank you Captain Ross, wherever you may be.'

The good news was that we were still flying instead of staring at a crumpled pile of aluminum in the desert. The bad news was that we only had three engines. The additional bad news was that we lost ten knots from our cruising speed. But the flip side of that coin was that we weren't burning as much fuel - still leaking like a sieve, mind you, but not as much if you worked the numbers, which was what everybody seemed to be doing during the remaining hours of flight we had before Sentinel Island was schedule to appear beneath our wings.

My numbers had to more to do with weather: isobars and barometer readings. So far we had been blessed. Other than a brief line of low-grade thunderstorm activity near Albuquerque, the gods had taken a high pressure broom and swept the skies clean from Louisiana to Northern Arizona, leaving only a stray cumulus cloud here and there to drift past in silent salute.

But their divine beneficence was not to be counted on when we reached the vicinity of Lake Mead. Large bodies of water are in a constant state of evaporation, which leads to clouds, and clouds lead to updrafts and minor weather patterns that can turn big and ugly before you know it.

Give me winter flying any day. There's snow and ice to deal with, but not the Wagnerian-like, hail and lightning-filled cumulo-nimbus monsters that can bloom sixty thousand feet or more before you know it, and to fly through one of those is to fly through hell itself.

I didn't anticipate that kind of weather, but in truth didn't know what might be waiting for us when we made our night landing. My mouth got a little dry thinking about it, but then I remembered Captain Fatt greasing us into Rio by flying the clipper right onto the water. If he could do it, then so could I, but a few more hours on the Boeing would have helped.

Time to spell Ava, who to her credit sat up straight and alert in the co-pilot's seat, monitoring the autopilot's heading as if she didn't trust it as far as she could throw it. Compared to my short sleeve shirt with a button missing and a torn pair of cotton pants, she looked surprisingly fresh and fit, considering what we'd been through since our escape from Couba Island.

'What's our ETA?' she said as I settled into the left hand seat.

'Two hours, five minutes.'

She tapped the quivering RDF indicator needle. 'We're about to lose the big band sound.'

I stifled a groan, heaved myself out of the seat and went back to the radio operator's station, where Ziggy sat listening to the headphones, bobbing his head to some unheard music.

I tapped him on the shoulder. 'Time to change stations, jazz boy. We're passing over this one.'

I flicked on the speakers, twisted the tuning dial up and down the frequencies in search of a radio station to the west of us on which I could get a bearing. Within seconds a fire-breathing, preacher with a Texas accent began warning me of 'The wiles of SAY-tan and his lowly MIN-yuns.'

'Let us pray,' I said as I locked in the frequency, entered it into our direction finder and watched the needle swing smartly fifteen degrees southwest to some small church where a cowboy minister sat thumping his bible. Once we locked onto the radio station, a piece of cake to enter our bearing to Lake Mead on the secondary needle.

'Got it?' I called out to Ava, who gave me a thumbs-up as she dialed it into the auto pilot.

I patted the receiver. 'May the good Lord carry us home,' I said. Ziggy didn't look very happy. 'Give me Tommy Dorsey any day.' Orlando said, 'Give the Lord a listen, brother. Couldn't harm you.'

'I'm Jewish, remember?'

'But we both believe in the same God.'

Back at the Master's station, Professor Friedman glanced up from his notebook and smiled. 'But not his son, I might add.'

Ziggy balled up his fists and punched the air playfully around Orlando's chin. 'Hear that, Reverend? The professor and me don't like being shoved around, you hear?'

Orlando raised his hands in silent surrender.

I said, 'That makes two of us,' and hit the speaker switch, cutting the preacher off in mid-scripture.

Professor Friedman held up his hand. 'When you have a moment, captain.'

When I sat down he said, 'Mr. Mason and I have concluded our examinations of both the arming mechanisms and the release device and we are confident that despite our unorthodox mission, with amateurs such as myself involved, the device will indeed operate as originally designed.'

'By 'device' you mean the bomb.'

'A euphemism. Yes, the bomb.'

'The atomic bomb to be more precise.'

He glanced at his neatly-drawn calculations. A muscle in his cheek twitched.

'What was it like?' I said.

He glanced up at me curiously.

'You saw one of these go off, right?'

'Never an operational weapon. Just the proof-of-concept ones. But they are remarkably the same. One is simply larger than the other.' He hesitated. 'Considerably larger.'

'So, what was it like?'

'It depends on where you are in relation to it.'

'How about ground zero.'

He looked shocked. 'You would see nothing but the face of God, or at least I would hope so.'

'Further back?'

'A towering cloud of destruction unlike anything you've ever seen before. Primeval in its power. Sacrilegious in a certain way.'

'Explain.'

'Splitting atoms, breaking apart what was brought together by God or nature or whatever higher power you believe in, is blasphemy of sorts.'

'But you loved every minute of it.'

He deliberated. 'The thinking part, yes. The end result, no.'

'Try telling that to the people who died because of your 'love of thinking.''

He blinked slowly behind his glasses but said nothing. Then finally, 'I regret we cannot put the Genie back in the bottle.'

'He's escaped for good.'

'But perhaps we can at least restrict his activities long enough to harness his powers in a more peaceful way.'

'Providing we get to the target in a plane that's becoming a rattling bucket of bolts.'

'At least we are still flying. You did a masterful job of solving an insoluble engine problem.'

'Thank Captain Ross, not me.'

After I recounted the story, Friedman said, 'We stand on the shoulders of giants.'

'Let's pray we don't fall off.'

I don't like to brag so I won't. But in honor of the late Captain Fatt, let me just say that I kissed the *Dixie Clipper* down onto the pitch-black waters of Lake Mead without a single ground reference.

Nobody on board including me quite believed we had touched down, so smooth had been our descent and final landing. But the answering rumble from the hull as we began skipping across the water and then finally settled in convinced everyone that after eighteen hours after taking off from Louisiana under hostile fire, we had safely arrived in Nevada.

Not ever having been here before, I was prepared for most anything.

But not the sight of a 1800s-era Mississippi-style side-wheel paddleboat sailing out to meet us, lit up like a Christmas tree to show off her snow-white superstructure trimmed in red, gold and shiny black. A shower of sparks flew from her twin black stacks.

'Those McGraw boys sure can put on a show,' Ava said.

The slap of the paddle wheels sounded sharp and crisp in the cool night air. And whichever brother was at the wheel knew his business as he brought the steamer smartly around in a tight arc and hove to, forty yards away. Seconds later a small launch lowered away and made its way toward us.

'Ziggy, you can handle the mooring station?'

He hitched up his pants and gave me a crisp salute. 'Just you watch.'

A minute later the launch bobbed alongside my open cockpit window. A tall, Stetson-wearing, six-gun toting figure stood motionless in the stern like George Washington crossing the Delaware.

He cupped his hands and shouted, 'Ahoy, *Dixie Clipper.*'

I leaned out the cockpit window. 'Captain Carter and crew reporting. Jacob or Esau?'

'Esau.' A long pause. 'A little early ain't you? And where's Captain Fatt?'

I had to say it. 'Killed in action. Nazi's attacked Couba Island. We got shot up on takeoff, started leaking fuel over Oklahoma and lost an engine somewhere over New Mexico.'

A long pause. 'You mean you haven't...'

'Affirmative. We haven't flown the mission yet.'

He rubbed his long jaw as he digested this. I pressed on with more important matters. 'Got any shoes? Lost mine during the attack. Been flying barefoot.'

'What size?'

'Twelve.'

'Got a pair of boots if you'd like.'

'Much obliged, and we'd also like two thousand gallons of one-hundred octane. Can you handle that, too?'

He looked insulted. 'Got a whole barge of it back at the base, just like the general ordered.' He looked up sharply. 'What about him? Is he okay?'

'Don't know. Most likely though.'

Another long pause. 'A tough nut. Served with him in the Great War. Just a young captain back then, but even so I knew he was bound for general's stars one day.'

'What do you say we help him win a few more?'

One of the first rules of airline command is to have confidence in yourself and your ability to succeed no matter the challenge. Like a stone thrown into a still pond, this feeling ripples out, touches your crew, and gives them confidence too. But it's a hard rule to follow when you only have three engines. The fact of which Orlando quietly reminded me as he and Ava and I observed McGraw's crew pulling camouflage netting over the *Dixie Clipper*, now tied up at the refueling barge.

From the air, Sentinel Island seemed desolate and deserted; just one more lonely mountain top surrounded by a man-made lake. With clever use of camouflage nets and painted paneling, the McGraw brothers made the fuel barge and the *Dixie Clipper* vanish into the pale brown and ochre landscape, devoid of greenery of any sort, leaving only the Desert Queen to rest majestically at her mooring, her lights blazing as she exercised her rightful claim as queen of Lake Mead.

I countered Orlando's caution with airline captain-like confidence. 'We can do it with three engines. We're not that heavily loaded.'

'We will be with full tanks.'

'Look, we've got miles and miles of takeoff space. This lake goes on forever.'

Orlando shook his head. 'Didn't you notice? We're surrounded by mountains on all sides. You may get off the water, but by the time you get positive rate of climb, you'll plow into a rock wall, guaranteed.'

'Oh, that.'

'Yes, that.'

Ava cleared her throat, but didn't say anything. I bristled a bit, thinking she was criticizing my piloting skills.

273

'Any bright ideas, Miss James?'

'A few.'

'Such as?'

'Take off with half the fuel. Find a place like Creeley's, land, take on more fuel, and keep on going, like we've been doing so far.'

'We're already a flying circus. If we do that everybody and their brother will know we're here, and sooner or later, so will the Nazis.'

A heavy-set man lumbered down the dock towards us, all smiles, dressed in the dark blue uniform of an ocean liner captain, complete with four gold stripes on his cuffs, polished brass buttons and a master's cap sitting smartly on his big fat head.

'Captain Carter?' he said in a high tenor voice. 'Captain Jacob McGraw. Welcome to Sentinel Island.'

I took his surprisingly firm handshake and then made introductions all around. He saluted Ava and Orlando as fellow officers.

Ava said, 'I heard you and your brother were twins.'

'Indeed we are. Fraternal.'

Orlando said, 'Are you on better terms with Esau than your Bible namesake?'

His eyes disappeared in a smile. 'Not when we were growing up. But a different story now. Esau manages the passenger side of the business, I handle the *Desert Queen* - now then, captain....' His jovial attitude vanished as though he'd thrown a switch somewhere inside that huge head of his. 'I understand you haven't completed your mission yet. What are your plans and how can we help?'

As I laid out my somewhat sketchy plan of refueling and taking off after a long run across the lake, my mouth got drier and drier, because I realized that Orlando was right, we couldn't clear those damned mountains with only three engines, so I said, 'You know what? My idea stinks. Anybody got any ideas?'

The four of us stood in uneasy silence for a long while.

Captain McGraw finally said, 'Considering you do manage to take off successfully, what's time to target?'

I did some quick figuring. 'Six hours or so, depending on the winds.' I turned to Ava. 'What do you think?'

'The winds would have to be pretty damn good.'

'We've been lucky so far.'

She nodded in affirmation. 'Six it is, then.'

McGraw said, 'Time over target?'

'Three a.m. Minimum folks on site. That's always been the plan.'

Jacob pulled out an enormous pocket watch and studied it. 'So you'd have to take off from here in about thirty minutes, to make this work, correct?'

'Affirmative.'

'A very tight turnaround. But as you said, you can't get your plane off the water if it's completely fueled.'

'Affirmative.'

'We have a dilemma.' He paused for a moment. 'I'm not a pilot, but I think there might be a way out of this, depending on how adventuresome you folks are.'

My past adventures came to mind: digging for gold in the Florida Keys, flying to Lisbon, giving the slip to Bauer and the Gestapo, escaping from Couba Island.

'I'd say we know how to take a chance or two.'

'You'll have to delay your mission twenty-four hours. I need time to set up a few things, including a scouting mission.'

I opened my mouth to protest, but nothing came out. So I listened to what he had to say. When he finished describing his harebrained scheme, I compared it to what we'd done so far and decided if the mission was going to happen at all, it would have to be his way.

'Breakfast at seven,' Jacob said. 'We pick up our first trip at 9a.m. sharp, over at the landing.'

'Any chance we can get something to eat? 'All we've had are Ziggy's sandwiches.'

Ziggy looked pained, so I added, 'Not that they weren't great. It's just that...'

Jacob intervened with a sweeping gesture of his four-striped sleeve,

'Your timing is perfect, my dear lady and gentlemen, my brother and I were just about to sit down to dinner when you made your dramatic entrance.' He extended his arm to Ava. 'May I escort you to the dining room, Miss James?'

She looked faintly surprised.

Jacob continued smoothly, 'Only a fool wouldn't recognize one of Hollywood's greatest actresses.'

She fingered her wrinkled blouse. 'Dressed like this?'

He patted her hand with his dimpled fingers. 'A princess in rags is still a princess.'

We learned during dinner that the *Desert Queen* made three trips around the lake every day and overnight trips on Wednesdays and Saturdays. The lake's one hundred-fifty-mile shoreline allowed plenty of sightseeing opportunities, although what everybody really wanted to see was only a few miles downstream from Sentinel Island: Boulder Dam; the world's highest dam that had created Lake Mead in the first place.

Jacob lifted a cut-crystal glass of red wine. 'Here's to Boulder Dam. Without it we wouldn't be here.'

'Neither would we,' I added.

The *Desert Queen's* dining room was surprisingly spacious and extended across the entire deck. Candlelight reflected off the darkened windows like a thousand stars. I was glad I didn't have to plot a course using them, because I was already feeling the effects of the wine, and could barely keep my head from falling into the soup.

Ava, by contrast, seemed to gather fresh energy as each course was served, while Orlando sat across from me, a calm and silent port in a storm. The professor ate small bites, but never seemed to stop. Mason was still on the plane, standing first watch, and Ziggy couldn't seem to shut up. He cornered Esau early in the meal and wouldn't let him go. But the man didn't seem to mind, watching the Hollywood agent like he would watch a snake oil salesman, with his money safe in his pocket.

I did my best to rouse myself from the effects of the wine and start a conversation with Jacob about how back east some of the states were planning to secede from the union.

The captain smiled and shook his head. 'Not out west. Am I right, Esau? Anybody here care that America's gone neutral?'

Esau swung away from Ziggy. 'Depends on who you talk to. After they dropped the bombs, the governor appointed all his cronies, every one of them a businessman who believes the status quo is the way to go. Don't rock the boat. That sort of thing.'

'But you're a businessman, right?'

'I am, but those boys are all hat and no horse. My brother and I are different. We dragged a steamboat down here from Wyoming and turned it into a money-making business.'

Ava said, 'You not only rocked the boat, you took it apart and put it together again.'

Esau managed a smile at that.

I said, 'Who's running for congress in the November elections? Any candidates with guts?'

Esau worried a piece of food in his teeth, oblivious to table manners.

'It's ain't guts they need, it's another part of the anatomy.'

Ava said, 'Don't be coy on my account. You mean balls.'

The candlelight made Esau's blush even brighter. He nodded. 'Yes, ma'am, that's exactly what I mean.'

Jacob moved smoothly into the conversation. 'Compliance officers are coming to survey Boulder Dam next week.'

Ava said, 'What for? It's just a dam.'

'Hydroelectricity,' he said. 'Two point-eight million kilowatts. Nothing like it in the world, and nothing like Boulder Dam either. That's why they're snooping around.'

I said, 'What are they going to do? Take it apart and ship it back to Berlin? That's a hell of a lot of concrete.'

Jacob snapped, 'They'll steal our technology and that's just as good, the bastards - excuse me ma'am.'

Ava said shook her head in frustration. 'I can't believe we let those people get away with stuff like this.'

Friedman cleared his throat. 'Because people like me invented the atomic bomb.'

Ava leveled her finger at him. 'But because a person like you is sitting here in this room, that's going to stop, right?'

Friedman nodded briskly, almost like he was in school.

'And what if it does?' Jacob said, his eyes bright with hope. 'Let's assume your mission succeeds.'

'It will,' I said quickly.

'What happens next is my question.'

I countered. 'What do you gentlemen think?'

Esau's face slowly darkened. 'Nothing will happen. America keeps moving along, head down, letting Europe go up in flames and Japan rule China's roost. All of that destruction can go ahead and happen just as long as good old dad can take good old mom and the kids out to good old Lake Mead and have a nice tour of the dam, maybe even have lunch, and shake their heads and cluck about what an awful state of affairs the world is in, not counting America, of course.'

He paused for breath.

Jacob grinned at his brother. 'Don't hold back, Esau. Tell them what you really think.'

Esau fussed with his wine and then gulped it down. 'It just confounds me sometimes what people will put up with.'

'You're not putting up with it,' I said.

'I'm not the majority.'

Ava leaned forward on her elbows. 'Mark my words, you may be right about men wanting the status quo, but you're overlooking a simple fact.' She paused. 'We have a woman president.'

'But only until November. And right now she's trailing what's-his-name...'

'Stanford,' I prompted. 'William Stanford.'

'William my ass,' Esau snorted. ''Stinky' Stanford is Nevada's biggest success story; silver mines, railroads, steamship lines, you name it; whatever Stinky wants Stinky gets, including the White House when they rebuild it, that is.'

Ava said, 'A lot can happen between now and November.'

'Like what?'

'Like declaring war against Germany.'

He stared at her, his mouth half-open. 'You're kidding, right?'

'War tends to focus the mind, don't you think? And who wants to change horses when we're in mid-stream fighting the enemy? My vote goes to the person already in the Oval Office, President Perkins, who had the balls to order this mission, not some rich kid named Stinky Stanford.'

Esau's face eased up at the thought. 'Do you really think we'll get in the fight?'

She touched my arm lightly. 'The *Dixie Clipper* has to fight first. And then? Yes I believe we will. I don't know how or when; that's something people a lot smarter than me are working on day and night to make happen. All we've got to do is destroy that plutonium and the machinery that makes it. The rest is up to them.'

I said, 'We've got to get off the lake first.' Captain McGraw said, 'You leave that to me.'

Esau raised his glass. The rest of us did the same. He carefully looked at each of us before he quietly said, 'To the Sons of Liberty.'

'Daughters, too,' Ava said.

With Ava leading the way, we made our way along the carpeted passageway to our staterooms on board the *Desert Queen*.

As much as I wanted to feel fresh sheets and a soft pillow, I said to Orlando, 'I'll go relieve Mason. When he gets here, show him his room.'

Orlando nodded. 'I'll relieve you at four.'

Ziggy said, 'Let me take your watch, captain.'

'That won't be necessary, I'll...'

'It's necessary for me, damn it.' He took a step forward and seemed to grow a foot taller. 'I'm sick and tired of being nothing more than a glorified short order cook around here. I'm part of the team and I'm standing watch whether you like it or not.'

'We have guards outside the plane, and...'

'Two men stationed at the nose and two at the tail. I know that. And nobody is allowed on board except crew. Nobody.'

'And make damned sure my orders are carried out. We've got valuable cargo on board.'

He nodded sternly, all business. 'Affirmative. And I'm to tell Lieutenant Mason that Orlando will show him his room, correct?'

'Affirmative.'

Ziggy saluted and turned to Orlando. 'See you at four, Mr. Diaz.'

Orlando, God bless him, saluted back. 'Roger that, Mr. Ziegler.'

Ziggy pivoted on his heel and half-marched, half-ran down the hallway.

As tired as I was, and as cool and fresh-smelling the sheets and pillow were, I didn't want to close my eyes because while I know babies can't talk, in dreams they sometimes can. I didn't want to hear Eddie's cry again, and I didn't want to see Estelle's sweet face again, or her angry face, or anybody's face, shouting at me about how much they needed me and why couldn't I reach out and help them?

No use. I was asleep before I even took my clothes off, and this time Eddie's voice sounded just like Abby's, only a little higher in pitch. And for some bizarre reason he was at Couba Island, and he could walk, even though he was only six months old and his little legs were bowed like a cowboy's.

I knew I was dreaming, but I couldn't wake up. At one point I succeeded and stared at the ceiling of the dimly lit stateroom, only to hear somebody breathing.

Estelle.

Sitting on the edge of my bed, staring at me with the sweetest smile, like when we first met, and I was so happy until I realized I was still dreaming because I awakened with my hands reaching out to nothing but thin air and all I could hear was the sound of my own breathing.

2:20a.m. by my watch.

Enough.

I got up, dressed, left the stateroom, and minutes later was nodding 'hello' to a grizzled old cowboy of a guard by the loading ramp next to the plane.

'Heading on board.'

'Okay, captain.'

'Everything all right?'

He patted his Winchester carbine. 'Oh, you bet.'

I glanced up at the flight deck windows, dimly lit from within, and a shadow flitted past. Good old Ziggy on the job. Would probably give him a heart attack, showing up out of the blue like this, but better to deal with a hysterical man in this world than a walking baby in a nightmare.

From force of habit I climbed the crew stairs smoothly, quietly, acting the part of the confident captain should a nervous passenger happen to see me. The flight deck hatch was open, and as my head cleared the hatch, the first thing I saw were Ziggy's legs bouncing up and down as he sat at the radio operator's station. The unmistakable smell of ozone told me the radios were up and running.

Annoyed, I crouched, planning to pounce on him as I would any novice crew member who wasn't performing up to Pan Am's rigid standards. I took the last two steps in a bound, landed with a thump on the flight deck.

'Having fun, Mr. Ziegler?'

He shot up like a rocket, headphones flying one way, a half-eaten sandwich on a plate sailing the other, staring at me like I was the Ghost of Christmas Past.

'Jesus Christ, ever heard of knocking?'

'Ever heard of standing watch?'

The tinny sounds of music vibrated the headphones on the desk. I looked at them the same time he did.

'What the hell are you doing?'

'Listening to music.'

'You figured out how to operate the radios?'

He shrugged. 'I watched you do it.'

I lifted up the Morse key. 'Played around with this too, I see.' He looked ashamed. 'A little bit.'

The transmitter was humming away. I reached up and switched it off.

'That thing eats up electricity. We're on batteries.'

'I didn't know - look, captain, I'm sorry. I was just bored to death.'

'And hungry too. Wasn't dinner enough?' He patted his stomach. 'I'm a growing boy.'

I pointed to the crew hatch. 'Go grow in your stateroom. I'll take the rest of the watch.'

A quick flash of concern in his eyes. Fear, maybe, or was it anger? Hard to say.

'You're the captain,' he said stiffly, and turned to go.

'Ziggy, look, didn't mean to blow my top. Thanks for helping out. I mean that.'

'I let you down.'

'That's okay. You never stood watch before. How were you to know?'

'No.' He waved me away. 'I screwed up and I apologize.'

'Apology accepted.'

He gave me a level stare. 'Just no dancing from now on, right?'

I laughed. 'Right.'

He got halfway down the crew stairs, his head sticking out above the hatch. His eyes different now, almost sad. 'I'm sorry, Sam.'

And then he was gone.

I switched off the work light and sat in the dark. Part of my mind decided it was time to get to work on the problem of lifting the *Dixie Clipper* off Lake Mead with a full tank of gas. But another part of my mind overruled it with the argument that Captain McGraw had his own idea and to just shut up and do nothing for once instead. And so I did.

Before long I could hear in the headphones, a faraway Frank Sinatra singing There Are Such Things. I reached over to turn it off to save our batteries, but decided instead to flick it to the speakers. Sinatra's light but mellow voice filled the flight deck:

A dream for two, there are such things.
Someone to whisper
'Darling you're my guiding star,
Not caring what you own
But just what you are.

'May I have this dance?' Ava said.

Startled, I switched on the light. Only her head was visible in the crew stairway. She answered the questioning look on my face. 'You left the *Desert Queen* like an express train leaving town. Woke me up.'

'Couldn't sleep.'

'What'd you say to Ziggy? He looked terrible.'

'Caught him goofing off instead of standing watch.'

She arched her eyebrows. 'You mean listening to the radio like you're doing?'

Embarrassed, I turned it off.

She came over and stood by the radio operator's table. 'Turn it back on. I like Sinatra.'

Back he came and light smile played across her face. 'That kid sure can get inside a lyric.'

'He's no kid. He's almost thirty.'

'Twenty-seven, same as me. But, you're right, he's no pup.'

I felt embarrassed. 'I didn't mean you were old.'

She patted my shoulder. 'Don't worry, Grandpa, I can handle it.'

'Since when is thirty-eight a grandpa?'

'You're getting gray hair.'

'Like hell I am.'

'Your joints creak, you can't even dance.'

I started to say something but she took my hand, pulled me to my feet and placed her arms in a dancing position.

'Prove it, grandpa.'

And so we began; not much at first, just two people moving to the slow rhythm of Sinatra's music. We hadn't taken but a few steps when she leaned back and switched off the work light.

'Let's not put on a show for the guards. They've got itchy trigger fingers.'

And so we danced by the light of the radio dials. I held her lightly, as if she would break, which was absurd. Ava had single-handedly shanghaied me and Orlando into an adventure I never dreamed possible - or probable for that matter.

After a while I said, 'How am I doing?'

Her mouth was close to my ear. 'Not bad. And in pointy-toed cowboy boots too. I'm impressed.'

We bumped into the navigator's table and rebounded into the center of the bridge. Not much room to maneuver, but enough to feel like we were dancing. When we jitterbugged earlier I had played the role of the confident captain boosting the morale of his crew. This time I was just dancing.

The song ended and we stood there staring at each other. Ava made a small curtsey and said, 'Thank you, captain. Been a long time since I've been in a man's arms.'

'Quit kidding.'

'It's true. Romance on camera is like buying a quart of milk at the grocery store; all in a day's work.'

'Really?'

'Let me show you.' She leaned back, her lips slightly parted, her eyes dreamy. Then she leaned forward and pressed her mouth against mine. Flat, uninteresting, almost cold. I leaned back, a little shocked.

'See what I mean?' she said. 'On film that would have looked romantic as hell.'

'If you say so.'

'I know so. Now get load of this.'

She kissed me again, but this time her lips were soft and warm. They nestled and twisted against mine the way a cat purrs and rubs up against you. By reflex I kissed her back. But it became much more than a reflex in the seconds that followed as I kept on kissing her and she kept kissing me. Then she stopped and looked straight at me. I could barely see her face in the dark, but her gleaming eyes were wide and clear.

'Now that's what I call real kissing,' she said. 'How long's it been for you?'

'A while.'

'Me too.'

I couldn't think of anything to say. Fortunately the music saved me. Another slow tune. This time Bing Crosby singing Irving Berlin:

Be careful, it's my heart.
It's not my watch you're holding, it's my heart.
It's not the note I sent you that you quickly burned.
It's not the book I lent you that you never returned.
Remember it's my heart.

We danced back toward the hatch that led to the cargo compartment and the relief crew bunks. It had been left half-opened, so I kicked it shut with the heel of my cowboy boots.

'A regular Fred Astaire,' Ava said.

'A good captain is always on duty.'

She began humming along with Crosby's crooning. Not a great voice. Sweet was more like it.

'What about Bing?' I said.

'I like him. He sang this in *Holiday Inn*. Ever see it?'

'Took Abby last month for her birthday. She liked it a lot.'

'You?'

'It was okay.'

A few more steps, she nestled closer and sighed. 'I was up for a part but Ginny Dale got it instead.'

'Sorry.'

'It's all right. Besides, she's a nice kid. Her big break. She'll go far.'

'So will you.'

She chuckled. 'When the war's over, maybe.'

'It's not even started.'

'It will soon.'

The music stopped. We let go of each other at the same time, which was good. I didn't want to be caught hanging onto her, even though a part of me wanted to do just that.

She yawned.

'Keeping you up?'

'Not anymore. I'm heading for the sack.' She brushed my cheek with quick kiss. 'Thanks for the dance, Sam. You're a sweet man.'

And she was gone.

I followed her a half-hour later, after Orlando came on board and relieved me. By then I had the lights on and everything looking shipshape. Enough that Ava had twisted my feelings around in circles, I didn't want to broadcast it to the world. Especially not Orlando. He'd be sure to weave the Bible into it somehow, and I'd just as soon keep God out of it for the present, and have this be between just Ava and me.

I got back to my room. I had two hours left to sleep if I wanted. But not daring to take a chance on any more nightmares, I kicked off my cowboy boots, lay back on my rumpled sheets and began to think instead.

Let your plans be dark and impenetrable as night, and when you move, fall like a thunderbolt.
- Sun Tzu, The Art of War

The *Desert Queen* cast off at nine o'clock on the dot.

The full load of summer sightseers laughed and clapped their hands over their ears when Captain McGraw blew the steam whistle in a shrieking farewell.

From Ava's and my vantage point in the wheelhouse, we had a commanding view of the forward section of the riverboat. What a tourist draw. After all, how many people have read Mark Twain? Millions, I guess, and here was their chance to experience the genteel pleasures of the South by sailing on a genuine side-wheel, Mississippi-style riverboat, albeit not down the mighty river itself.

But water is water, and the *Desert Queen's* paddles churned it vigorously as McGraw eased her out onto Lake Mead. The short, stocky captain handled the helm with easy confidence. The polished oak wheel, almost as tall as he was, was trimmed in brass with mother-of-pearl inlays weaving around its circumference. The binnacle containing the ship's compass was mirror-bright brass as well. In fact, every metal object in the wheelhouse seemed either polished brass or plated nickel. Boeing engineers could have taken lessons in style from the old-timers who had built this monument to Mark Twain's *Life on the Mississippi.*

I mentioned this to McGraw, who said, 'They didn't skimp when it came to final touches. 'Course she was in sorry shape when we found her up on the Missouri, hauling freight and lumber. But a lot of tender loving care put her on the right side of beautiful.' He patted the wheel. 'Didn't it old girl? Go ahead, tell the world what you think.'

He yanked the steam whistle rope to let out a long warbling cry. A flock of birds shifted their flight pattern in alarm.

'Folks sure love to hear her sing.'

Ava stood by the front window. 'And not a sandbar in sight.'

McGraw chuckled. 'Nothing but nice deep water. Only a little thing called Boulder Dam to contend with. Wouldn't want to run into that.'

I went over to the chart table on the back wall of the wheelhouse to study our destination. As noted on the chart, Sentinel Island lay northeast of the dam; a small oval in an otherwise open lake, dotted here and there with smaller outcroppings indicating lesser mountains that had suffered the same watery fate. According to the map the water narrowed considerably as it flowed southwest down Black Canyon toward the dam.

During its construction during the 1930s, Boulder Dam had captured newsreel and newspaper headlines almost every week. Thousands of men, out of work because of the Depression, found dust-filled, hard-scrabble jobs in Black Canyon, the construction site. But that's about all I knew about it, until now when Captain McGraw unlocked his encyclopedic mind and let loose.

'It's an arch gravity dam,' he intoned. 'Meaning it curves upstream and directs most of the water against the canyon walls, thus providing the force needed to compress the dam and keep it in its place.'

'That a fact?' Ava said, her eyes already slightly glazed.

'Indeed.'

She and I exchanged a quick glance. We both seemed to sense what was coming. When people start saying 'thus' you're in for a long, hard ride.

'And did you know that one hundred-thirteen workers died during its construction?' he continued, almost breathlessly, as though it were breaking news. 'The first was J.G. Tierney, a surveyor who drowned while searching for the original dam site. Thirteen years later to the day, his son Patrick was the last man to die. Imagine that.'

Ava and I both shook our heads in sympathy, like trained monkeys.

'Guess how many cubic yards of concrete?' I said, 'Couldn't begin to.'

'Guess.'

Ava said, 'A ga-zillion?'

'Very funny. In point of fact, three million, two hundred-fifty thousand cubic yards. One bucket at a time. Eight cubic yards a load. And you may not know this but when concrete cures it throws off a lot of heat. Want to know how long it would have taken for three million cubic yards to cool down if they had done it in a single pour? Don't bother, I'll tell you how long. One hundred twenty-five years! And that's a fact.'

'Captain,' I began. 'As much as I like learning about new things, we've got a bomb to drop. So do you mind coming to the point of this river cruise?'

'But I'm already at the point, captain.'

'How so?'

'Boulder Dam. You're flying over it to get out of here.'

A long pause. His face shining with happiness.

'That's your idea?' I finally managed to say, trying to keep my anger in check.

'It's more than an idea, it's a fact. You told me you can't get off the lake carrying a full load of fuel with only three engines, correct?'

'Yes.'

'You can do it if you fly in this direction.'

He pointed out the window at the approaching low-profile shape of the upstream side of Boulder Dam. Two cylindrical, art-deco styled intake towers rose out of the water like skyscrapers flanking our approach. He skillfully guided the riverboat to a dock carved out of rock near the right spillway. The ground rose in a gentle slope to a level ground. The passengers quickly disembarked to go swarming up to the dam for a series of guided tours. McGraw, Ava and I followed them soon after, but headed for the top of the dam instead.

'It's hard to appreciate the size of this thing from upriver,' McGraw said as we kicked up dust along the walkway. 'It's just water, water, everywhere, and these intake towers and the spillways. Hardly worth your time, if that's all there is to it.'

'But there's more to it, right?' Ava said wearily.

McGraw literally rubbed his hands with glee. 'Oh, SO much more.'

The passengers were long gone, swallowed up inside a doorway leading to a set of elevators that would whisk them down into the bowels of the dam to gaze in wonder at the gigantic spinning hydro-electric generators arranged single-file in a long vaulted hallway.

A two-lane paved roadway ran across the top of the dam, linking Nevada with Arizona. Cars occasionally drifted by slowly, nervous drivers gingerly aware that they were high above the ground and should take care. And they were right. I'd seen photos of downriver of Boulder Dam, but standing here looking down into the shaded depths of Black Canyon, I felt a touch of vertigo.

To McGraw's credit, he refrained from babbling statistics - at least for a while - and allowed us to take in the majesty of this breathtaking point-of-view made possible by man.

The dam wall dropped gracefully downward hundreds of feet until its light grey, smooth as glass concrete surface merged into the canyon's craggy, jagged stone sides and rocky bottom. Much like the human body hides immense complexities; the bland, almost blank surface of the dam face hid hundreds of the original building blocks of cement that had been meticulously poured one at a time, and cooled with piped-in refrigerant before pouring another block on top of it.

The cooling part I didn't know about, but Captain McGraw did, of course, including the type of refrigerant used, so I let him go on and on about this, but simply stopped listening. I felt the wind instead. Brisk, maybe ten knots or so as it swept up the canyon. I held up my hand to judge it better.

McGraw noticed my gesture and said. 'This is the prevailing direction. Always blows like this, even at night. It'll lessen your takeoff run a little, I should think.'

'My takeoff run…'

'Yes.'

'Do you fly airplanes, by any chance?'

His batted away my question away with an embarrassed flutter of his pudgy hands. 'Not a bit. But I read a lot, and that's how I came up with this idea.' He pointed to the bottom of the canyon. 'It's seven hundred-ten feet to the bottom. If you can crest the dam here you've automatically gained seven hundred feet in altitude.'

'I'd lose half of it just maintaining airspeed.'

He looked crestfallen. 'I didn't realize that.'

'That's because you're a riverboat captain, not a pilot,' I snapped.

He looked hurt and Ava said, 'What are you, 'Mr. No' all of a sudden? Let's talk this through. We got out of Creeley's marina by jacking the flaps, why not do the same thing here?'

'With four engines and a speedboat to break the suction, not with three engines and a side wheeler riverboat.'

'Creeley's trees were at least seventy-feet high. Here it's looks to be about thirty feet from the water to the top of the dam.'

'Thirty-two feet,' McGraw added quickly.

'I bet we could do a short field takeoff on three engines.'

289

'I'm not a betting man.'

'I'm a betting woman, and I'm positive we can. An idiot could do it. Even Captain McGraw could if he knew how to fly. No offense, sir. I didn't mean to imply you were an idiot.'

'None taken, Miss James.'

I raised my hands to silence them. 'We sound like the Marx brothers doing a routine.'

'Like hell we are.' Ava's voice rose half a stop. 'We've got a mission to fly and we're going to do it or... or...'

'Or die trying, which is probably what'll happen.'

'Not if you're at the controls, captain.'

I turned away and analyzed the canyon again. I had to admit the idea was clever. The walls were more than wide enough to accommodate the *Dixie Clipper's* wingspan as she swooped down into the canyon. That didn't worry me. But the left hand turn the river took about a half-mile away did for sure. Just like back at Creeley's, only worse. We'd still be inside the canyon walls at that point, clawing for enough airspeed to climb out, and I'd have to stand her on her wing to make that turn, and lose even more airspeed in doing so.

I said, 'We'd have do this tonight for us to make it over the target at the scheduled time.'

McGraw rose on his tiptoes, excited at finding a chink in my armor.

'This is your lucky day, captain - or night, I should say. The full moon rises around 8:30. It'll light up this place like daytime.'

'That'll help.'

'The good news isn't finished. I've got a tour scheduled for tonight. Charlie Macomb, he manages the dam, always lights up the place like a Christmas tree as a favor to me. 'Course I grease his palm a bit too, to do it. No sir, there's nothing more beautiful than Boulder Dam at night.'

Ava said, 'Except for the *Dixie Clipper* flying over it.'

McGraw smiled. 'If we time it right, we can give our passengers an unexpected treat.'

'Heart attacks, you mean,' I said. 'We'll be blasting down the river like there's no tomorrow.'

He clapped his hands. 'You'll do it then?'

'Yes.'

The leaking avgas from our ruptured sponson tank cast a rainbow-like sheen on the lake waters as I taxied the *Dixie Clipper* away from her mooring. It felt like she was bleeding to death. But nothing we could do about it now. While we were on our scouting mission at the dam, the Sentinel Island crew, under Orlando's supervision, had managed to find bullet holes in the right sponson that we had missed. But like our battle damage to the hull, not just the outer duralumin skin the Nazi bullets punctured, but the fuel tanks themselves had been hit.

If only we had the self-sealing tanks like the fighter planes we had been building before the Neutrality Act. I remembered movie newsreels showing row after row of twin-engine, supercharged Lockheed P-38 *Lightning* fighter planes moving down assembly lines, out onto the tarmac and then zooming into the air, guns blazing, on their way to Britain and France. But now those same assembly lines were gearing up to make refrigerators instead, while we were stuck with a bleeding seaplane.

The crew briefing had been surprisingly quick and issue-free. When I announced our intentions I had expected objections, but to a person they agreed that we had come this far together, and if we had a chance to continue, we should take it, no matter how risky, no matter how farfetched.

When they finished I said, 'Fair enough. But let me say one more time, if you want out, that's fine too. There's no guarantee we're going to make it out of here in one piece, let alone get to the target.'

I paused. For sure I thought Ziggy would want to bail and I couldn't blame him. Of all the crew, his was the least important position. We could easily do this without him. But from his stony silence and stern features, it became clear to me that he felt just the opposite.

Captain McGraw was right about the moon, just as he was right about a lot of other things; it rose bright and clear in the night sky. The barrenness of the surrounding rock outcroppings, empty of vegetation, reflected the light and became a silvery, craggy landscape almost as barren the moon and just as unforgiving. How anything managed to survive in these dry, dusty conditions was a mystery to me. But that was a thought to consider only while calmly cruising at eight thousand feet on autopilot on a starry night. We had to get up there first.

'Flaps five,' I said.

'Flaps five.'

I slid back the cockpit window and leaned out to catch a glimpse of the slowly receding dock. The tall figure of Esau McGraw stood silently watching. I waved at him. He took off his Stetson and waved it in return. The moonlight made it look white as snow.

I said to Ava, 'What an odd pair those two are.'

'I'm sure they feel the same about our crew.'

All of whom were now at their assigned stations. But since we weren't anticipating armed resistance at this point, Orlando had exchanged his waist gun position for the radio operator's station. He sat facing the engineering panel, watching Mason's every move.

The noise on the flight deck was slightly less because we only had three engines. A mixed blessing to be sure. I would gladly have traded quiet for power. Even so, we still needed our intercoms to communicate normally.

'Captain to crew, station report.'

'Engineering, check.'

'Co-pilot check.'

'Ziggy? Professor?' The two were strapped in at the captain's station next to the navigator's table.

'Doing fine back here,' Ziggy said, his voice pitched higher than I'd ever heard. 'Telling each other Bar Mitzvah jokes.'

And that was it for my 'crew.' I wanted to laugh but it wasn't funny.

'Channel buoy,' Ava called out.

The red beacon marking Black Canyon's channel shone brightly in the darkness. I throttled up our port engines for a differential turn to starboard. The buoy dutifully slid away in the opposite direction as I came into the wind. Sure enough, the starboard wing dipped slightly as the force of the air struck it. But our taxi speed was just below ten knots, so we were spared the embarrassment of weathercocking. Instead of the wind hitting us sideways as it had been all the way from the dock, we now faced it head on, making it much easier to taxi.

'So far so good,' Ava said.

'...said the man falling off the cliff.'

'Funny.'

'But true, in about five minutes.'

A mixture of fear, anger and excitement, all rolled up into one, flickered across her dimly-lit face.

'Fasten your seatbelt,' I said. 'And keep your eye on the head temps.'

She flicked her eyes to the gauges. 'That's not the only temperature rising. I'm sweating bullets.'

Dead ahead of us the night sky was getting brighter. I could only assume the lights coming from Boulder Dam. No time like the present. I flexed my fingers over the throttle quadrant, gripped three of the four rounded knobs and shoved them forward. The engines responded smoothly and we began accelerating. To them, just one more flight. To me it might damn well be their last. The airspeed needle quivered past twenty, then thirty knots. The nose felt heavier than usual. I cranked in more elevator trim and that seemed to help.

'Forty,' Ava called.

'Flaps ten.'

The first faraway slap of water against the hull as she started skipping along. A slender string of stars appeared on the horizon, then grew larger and larger until they became lights, hundreds of them it seemed, ringing the upstream edge of Boulder Dam. Off to starboard, the *Desert Queen*, lit up like a Christmas tree, sailed full speed for the dam.

'Sixty knots,' she called.

Too slow, way too slow. Rudder stiffening, adding more trim to keep her from pulling toward the dead engine.

'Ready flaps forty.'

'Standing by.'

I could read the engine instruments, but wanted confirmation.

'Engineering, how we doing?'

'In the red, but go, go, GO!' Orlando shouted.

I risked some back pressure on the yoke and felt her rise up onto the step momentarily, fall off, then rise again and stay there. The wallowing motion instantly disappeared as the hull rode higher and higher and the thrumming sound increased as the wavelets began spanking her bottom. How much room left before the dam? Half mile? Less? Hard to tell. Never tried taking off into a concrete wall that rose higher and higher the closer we got. All we needed was thirty-five feet to clear it.

Ava stroked the instrument panel, 'C'mon, darling, you can do it.'

I wasn't so sure, but I liked her confidence. Sometimes it adds lift to your wings when you need it most.

And then suddenly I was flying down a tunnel; that familiar place where nothing exists but the task at hand, and knew the time had come. Nothing on either side of me, just the dam ahead. No engine sound, no outside noise, just my own breathing and my hands feeling the warmth of the yoke and my feet on the stiffening rudder pedals as the *Dixie Clipper* merged with me into one creature with metal wings and engines and a human heart and mind rushing across the water faster and faster, and slowly lifting off the water surface, getting her nose down, gaining airspeed.

Needle touching seventy, intake towers skyscraper-tall flashing past on both sides.

'Full flaps!'

The wings broadened with added lift just as the *Desert Queen* flashed past to starboard, a gush of steam coming from her whistle, but I didn't hear it, and I pulled back on the yoke and up we rose, higher and higher and cleared the top of the dam with nothing but stars above and clear sky. But the stall horn was sounding, control yoke softening, and I shoved it forward and we nosed down, losing the sky, and the dark canyon walls rushed in on both sides, reaching out to rip off our wings.

Gone was the wide expanse of water behind us. Now just the narrow, winding river below that curved to the left and I kept the throttles at full power as we dropped further and further, gaining airspeed but losing altitude. Ava shouted something but I couldn't make it out.

All I could think about was the airspeed building fast enough to let me pull back on the yoke and level us out from the seven hundred-foot circus dive we made off the edge of a cliff, and that damned canyon wall was straight ahead, velvet black, unyielding and coming fast.

'Landing lights!'

Twin cones of white split the darkness, turning the black canyon walls brown and dark red. They slid to starboard as I banked into a tight turn that instantly stole the precious airspeed we had gained from the drop, only to lose it as I tried to escape the stone walls. By how much I don't know. All I know is that we were still here, not a tangled wreck, and Black Canyon opened out ahead of us, its river sparkling in the moonlight as we flew below the ridge like some gigantic, prehistoric bird in search of its prey.

The iron band around my head slowly began to ease and my tunnel vision melted outward until I could see more to my left and right and the cockpit noise rushed back like a rising tide and I heard Ava's voice, 'We're losing number two if you don't throttle back.'

I gently eased back on the power, even though my instincts told me to push her even more. We still needed to climb out of the canyon, but we were too heavy to do it unless we had at least one hundred-ten knots

294

indicated, which we did not. And so instead, I continued flying a weaving, sinuous path that followed the river as it coursed down the canyon toward God knows where.

Slowly, ever so slowly, the canyon walls grew wider, maybe three or four hundred feet, which greatly reduced the chances of losing a wingtip or worse. But it couldn't last forever. Sooner or later the walls would start narrowing again and this time it would be too tight a fit.

'Sure would love to see some sky,' Ava said.

'Ten more knots and we will. Keep your eyes peeled on these walls. If they start squeezing in, holler.'

'I'll scream my head off.'

I had been slowly milking up the flaps the whole time, and by now they were fully retracted. The lessened drag would give us a few more much-needed knots. What else could help? Then I remembered.

'Cowl flaps closed?' I said.

Orlando said, 'Been closed.'

'Damn, so much for that idea - where's Mason?'

'Beside me.'

'How's our fuel?'

Mason chimed in. 'Too soon to tell. Give me an hour into the flight and I'll have a chart ready for you.'

'Let Orlando do it. You've got a bomb to drop, remember.'

A chuckle. 'Forgot that little detail.'

Ava shouted, 'We've got positive rate of climb!'

I started pulling back the yoke before she even finished her sentence, so anxious was I to escape the brooding depths of the dark canyon. The clipper climbed slowly, an aluminum whale in search of the surface to take a breath of air. The night sky slid into place, complete with countless, comforting star while the altimeter continued its clockwise journey, five hundred feet...seven-fifty... one thousand...

When we reached cruising altitude, we flew in silence for a long minute, while I tried to loosen the iron grip I had on the yoke, as if somebody had welded my fingers to its Bakelite surface. But finger by finger, I finally succeeded.

Ava voice was shaky but calm. 'That was a first.'

'And a last.'

'Had to close my eyes toward the end.'

'Don't blame you.'

'Glad you didn't.'

I wiggled the control wheel. 'Need to dial up an RDF station.'

Ava took over. 'Find something good to listen to. No preachers, okay?'
I saluted her and made for the radio operator's table. From long habit I was
flicking power switches on the transmitter and receiver before I even sat
down. I started tuning the radio direction finder, but then noticed its big
round dial wasn't lit. Neither were the frequency dials and indicator lights
on the transmitter and receiver. Tried again.

Nothing.

To Orlando and Mason, 'Check your radio breakers.'

They flicked them on and off. Nothing. Without power the transmitter
and receiver were useless boxes. Ditto the RDF. And without RDF we
couldn't fly the frequency to our target. Futile, I know, but just to be sure I
checked the cable connections by pulling on them one by one, especially
those leading to the power supplies. I almost overlooked the one curled
around a lower stanchion then disappeared into the fuselage wall.

I got down on my hands and knees and squirmed underneath the table
to reach it. I gave it a quick tug, expecting the same resistance, but it came
free from its socket like a rotten tooth.

One look at the tangled mass of torn and stripped wires and I felt like
somebody had punched me in the head with a brick. What should have
been a tightly-bound bundle of color-coded wiring carefully soldered into a
large multi-pin, screw-on connector, was nothing but a tangled mess. The
connector was still screwed into place, minus the cable that somebody had
intentionally yanked out and then stuffed back to make them look okay.

After Orlando examined it he said, 'No way can we fix it.'

'What if we had the wiring diagram?'

'Something like is a division-level repair item. They'd just swap it out.'

'Can we guess where the wires go?'

His silent stare made me regret my stupid comment. Then he said,
'Look, even if we did have the diagram, we've got no soldering tools.'

'Can't we just wedge them in somehow?'

'Sam, stop it.' He shook his head. 'The radios are dead. Either move on
to a Plan B or turn this girl around.'

I couldn't let go just yet. 'Were the radios okay when you stood watch
last night?'

He shrugged. 'They were turned off, but they looked okay to me.'

'And they were working when I was there. And when Ziggy was there too.' I dropped my voice to a whisper. 'Who the hell did this?' He shrugged. 'Bad guys for sure.'

'But who?'

'You're asking the wrong person.'

Before I could stop, my mind took off like a bloodhound, sniffing with suspicion at everything; the Sentinel Island crew working around the clipper, the old-timer guard I'd talked to before I came on board last night, any one of them could have ripped the wires out and disabled the radios.

But whoever it was, he'd done a good job. Gone was simply finding a radio station's frequency and homing in on it. Had we been flying with a full crew and lost our radios, this would not have been the end of the world. Our navigator could have plotted our position with a combination of dead reckoning and celestial navigation.

Orlando nudged me. 'Got that plan yet?'

'Getting there.'

I unwound myself from underneath the radio operator's table. Ziggy stood there with his hands on his hips like a sidewalk superintendent.

'Problems?' he said.

I decided not to feed the flames. 'Radio's not working.'

'But we need it to find the target, right?'

'Not anymore.'

He looked pained. 'You mean the mission's off?'

I didn't answer him because I didn't have an answer... yet.

Seconds later, with a prayer running thorough my head, I rummaged around the drawers beneath the navigator's plotting table. Had this been anything but a Pan Am plane I wouldn't have bothered doing this, but Dutchman Preister was good at training his crews to be prepared for any and all contingencies.

Since Pan Am flew over empty oceans and seas, this included a fat-barreled flare pistol and eighteen flares clipped to the wall for firing downwards towards the water to determine wind drift. Was it in there?

Check.

Add to this, the more prosaic navigator's tools: parallel rulers, sight reduction tables, plotting sheets, dividers, sharpened pencils and a stopwatch. Were they there?

Check.

And in the third drawer beneath the long chart table, a thick blue book lettered in gold: 1942 *Air Almanac*. I breathed a sigh of relief. Fine to have a church, but this was the bible. Even so, we needed the 'preacher' or we were sunk. I took a deep breath, opened the next drawer, and for a moment saw nothing and my heart sank.

Then I reached further back and my fingers brushed against a wooden box with a hinged lid. I pulled it out, held my breath, and opened the lid. The *Spencer, Browning and Rust Company* bubble octant rested peacefully in its blue-velvet home. The polished brass instrument felt cool in my hands as I carefully lifted it out of its resting place. It would warm up when I put it to use.

Ziggy said, 'What the heck is that?'

I turned it over in my hands and silently thanked our navigator Stone, back on Couba Island, either dead or alive, for following Preister's rules to the letter.

'Something we need.'

I left him and went forward to bring Ava up to speed. I had her make a timed turn over a fixed point on the ground so that I could get to work.

'Can you plot our course with dead reckoning?' she said.

'Not as accurate by itself. Washington's too far a reach and besides, the weather's never going to hold long enough. Look out there.'

The moonlight lit up a faraway, soft silver wall of clouds to the northwest.

'Maybe we can climb above it.'

'Doubt it. That's why I want a star fix right now.'

I fished around inside my pocket and pulled out a slip of paper upon which I had scribbled something I always automatically did as a captain:

33°03'23.00' N 114°44'44.09' W

From long Pan Am habit I had noted the latitude and longitude of Sentinel Island from the chart in the *Desert Queen*. It's not that I didn't trust my navigator to get it right, but because in my early career I had spent many a bullet-sweating hour as a navigator trying find out where the hell we were in time and space. I knew how important that first fix can be.

Written beneath our starting latitude and longitude, I had written that of our target in Hanford, Washington:

Two small dots on a map, eight hundred-twelve miles apart as the crow flies. All I had to do was connect them.

Ziggy jumped out his seat when he saw me open the rear door of the flight deck bulkhead leading to the astrodome.

'Where you going?'

'To get a star fix.'

He scurried over. His face reminded me of a boy scout 'Mind if I watch? This kind of stuff really interests me.'

'So I've noticed.'

He winked. 'You'd be surprised what strange things you need to know in my business.'

'What exactly is your business?'

'Two words.' He raised one finger, then another as he chanted,

'Make....believe.'

The navigator's astrodome was a multi-windowed, streamlined teardrop housing protruding eighteen inches above the fuselage surface. And by standing on an aluminum stepstool in the baggage passageway, I had just enough room to fit my head, hands and bubble octant.

Ava held us on a steady course, but the occasional light chop made it difficult to work the instrument and keep my balance at the same time.

'Grab my belt in the back and steady me,' I said.

'Wilco.'

'And when I say go, start the stopwatch.'

'Roger.' A brief pause. 'I know this sounds ridiculous, but I'm really having fun.'

I swung up the octant and centered the bubble on the night sky. The moon was long gone behind a high bank of clouds to the east, making it useless as a sighting target. So I turned my attention to the western sky which remained clear. An infinity of stars to choose from. At first just a confused jumble of pinpricks of light; some clustered, others as separate and alone up there as I was down here.

But then, the way you suddenly recognize a lover's face in the midst of a crowd, I spotted the Orion constellation. Named the 'Hunter' for the way its stars suggest a hunter stalking his prey, I quickly found the three that make up his belt, the two his bow, the four his club, and finally at the top, the bright star Betelgeuse, his 'shoulder.'

But I was hunting bigger prey tonight; the Big Dipper, in particular its bottommost star that makes the dipper's cup because it points directly to the gleaming friend of navigators throughout the western hemisphere: Polaris, the North Star.

It took only seconds to rotate the octant's mirror to 'pull' the reflected image of Polaris to the horizon. The ease with which I did, a miracle in a way, seeing as how I hadn't done any hard navigation in years. That's what RDF's can do to you; make you forget how to find your way around the sky when they go belly up and you're far from home.

The mirror image of the star swam around at first, but then steadied on the horizon.

'Start your stopwatch.'

I quickly climbed down and played the flashlight on the face of the chronometer installed on a rack next to the astrodome.

'Stop your watch.'

Surrendering to Ziggy's questions, I explained how the chronometer was set to Greenwich Mean Time, and I would compare its exact time to tables in the Nautical Almanac that listed the position of each heavenly body for every minute of every day of the year. From that I could determine the *Dixie Clipper's* position along a fixed continuum.

'And then you'll know where we are?'

'More or less.'

He shook his head. 'Amazing. So that means we're still doing the mission?'

'Unless something else happens.'

I played my flashlight past the mail cages to the relief crew sleeping quarters. Behind them lay the baggage compartments. Kind of creepy seeing the space empty like this. On a normal clipper flight it would be packed to the gills with expensive luggage and steamer trunks, along with the snores of crew members blending in with the engine roar.

'Ziggy, when you were on watch last night did you check back here?'

'Checked the whole plane. Why?'

'See anything out of the ordinary? Hatches loose? Anything?'

'Just this. A big dark nothing.'

'Think I'll check again.'

He grabbed my flashlight. 'Go plot your course, captain. Leave this to me.

His Boy Scout enthusiasm made me laugh.

'Okay, but be careful.'

He stuck out his chest. 'I may be small but I pack a big punch.'

I gave Ava the new heading and she dialed it into the autopilot like she'd been doing it for years.

'You're a quick study,' I said.

'It's all an act.'

'Don't believe you.'

'That's what good acting's all about.' Her toothy smile gleamed red from the cockpit's night lighting. She adjusted rudder trim and her smile disappeared. 'I've ridden horses that pulled this hard for the barn.'

'You've got five thousand of them now.'

Because we were flying on three engines, the combined propeller torque from the two engines on our port wing kept pulling us in their direction. The rudder trim tab skewed us straight, but even so, we were still flying slightly sideways through the air, the way a car with a bent frame does on a highway.

Ava said, 'Time to target?'

I laughed. 'You sound like you're in a war movie.'

'Wish to hell I was.'

'A little under seven hours if the wind and weather hold.'

'Neither of which we know much about, correct?'

'Roger. We're flying blind in that department.'

'And the radio department too. Any idea what happened?'

I told her what I thought, which wasn't much beyond the obvious. But what seemed worse, as I spoke, is that I realized that the protective little bubble we seemed to have been floating inside of had burst the instant I yanked on that damned cable.

Ava heard me out, thought about it for a while, and then said, 'I wonder if they know where we're going.'

'Could be.'

'If so, that means they'll be waiting for us. The surprise factor will be gone.'

'Then we'll have to figure out a way to surprise them.'

'Such as?'

'I don't know yet, but I'll think of something.'

301

She grinned. 'That's what I like about you, Sam. Even though you don't have a clue, you always act like you do.'

'I've been hanging around a pretty good acting teacher for a while now.' She drew a sharp breath and her eyes widened. 'I just had another thought: what if it's somebody on the plane?'

'Are you kidding? Who?'

'Mason, maybe?'

'Forget it.'

'I'm just trying to consider all the possibilities.'

'As long as they're reasonable, yes. But Mason? Not a chance.'

'How about Ziggy?'

We both burst out laughing, but to our chagrin, Ziggy leaned in between us and said, 'Let me in on the joke, you two.'

I said, 'Where'd you come from?'

'Checked in the back like you said. Coast is clear.' He handed me the flashlight and leaned in, interested and alert. 'So, like I said, what's the joke?' Ava casually lied to spare his feelings, 'I was just trying to break the tension with one your Harpo Marx stories.'

'Which one?'

'The time he ate the ladies' menu at the restaurant.'

'Yeah, that was funny, all right. But what about the time I played golf with him and George Burns?'

'That never happened. You hate golf.'

'When two movie stars like them invite you to play, you love it.'

Ava surrendered with a wave of her hand. 'Tell the story. True or false, it's still funny.'

Ziggy dove right in. 'Hot as hell that day, so the three of us show up on the course, take off our shirts to cool down and then proceed to play eighteen holes. Harpo shoots a seventy-five as I recall. I'm in triple digits, don't ask. Burns is somewhere in between. Game over, back to the clubhouse we go for a drink or two or three. Manager comes up and says, 'Sorry, boys, club members gotta' wear shirts. Rules are rules.'

'Fine, we say. Will do. Next day we show up wearing shirts like the man said. Even so, he throws us off the course before we even reach the second hole.'

'Why?' I said.

Ziggy shrugged. 'The rules didn't say anything about having to wear pants, so we left those at home.'

'You showed up in your underwear?'

'George and me, but Harpo doesn't believe in wearing underwear.'

As I tried to imagine this, Ziggy raised his right hand. 'Every word true. Swear to God.'

After he left, we flew in silence for a while, lost in our thoughts. If you spend endless hours in a cockpit, you tend to become introspective. It doesn't matter if you're the life of the party when you're on the ground, when you're up here at the mercy of Mother Nature who can clobber you in the time it takes to go from blue sky to thunderhead, you tend to think a lot.

My thoughts were centered on our sabotaged radio and who the hell did it. I tried to imagine just how he had managed to pull it off in a plane as closely guarded as ours. But I gave up on the particulars because it was getting me nowhere but angry.

More importantly, how reliable was my navigation as a substitute for the broken RDF? And even more important, how bad was our leaking fuel situation? We really were like a man running from the well to the kitchen with a water bucket full of holes. How much water would be left when we got there? If we got there at all. Mason and Orlando insisted that we could make it to the target with about an hour reserve to head for the coast and scuttle her.

The mathematics involved in these calculations was crippling. Not that I didn't trust their fuel consumption numbers. It's just that I would feel better if I could confirm them myself. I pulled out the slip of paper with their estimates and went to work again with my pencil.

'Doing the fuel numbers?' Ava said.

'Yes. But my math looks shaky.'

She reached out her hand. 'May I?'

'Help yourself.'

I surrendered my notations and she bent over them, lips pursed, her pencil lightly tracing the agonizing path of my calculations. A slight shake of her head, followed by a quick nod. In less than a minute she handed back the paper.

'They look fine to me.'

'You know how to do this kind of thing?'

'Look, my friend, I may fly a small plane but it still burns fuel like the big ones, and from there it's just a matter of bumping up the numbers to see if they jive. And yours do.'

She looked out at the night sky, then back to me. 'Not that I especially like the numbers I saw. It's going to be a squeaker, but they're spot on.'

'Wind and weather permitting.'

We both laughed at that.

The clear weather held for three more hours, which got us out of Nevada and into southern Idaho. I managed two more star fixes before a line of cumulus clouds began rolling in from the west. After wasting time and fuel trying to climb above them, we failed at twelve-thousand feet and had to head for the bottom, which varied between two and three thousand above the ground. All I could do was hope that the position I got from my final star fix would last long enough for this stuff to break up. If not, it would be dead reckoning the rest of the way to the target.

It would have been much easier flying if we were doing it along the eastern seaboard. Clusters of lights from small towns coupled with the occasional airport beacon would have made it easier to keep one's orientation to the ground in proper perspective. But out in the middle of

'Nowhere Idaho,' with the moonlight blocked by a thick ceiling of clouds,

nothing but velvet darkness on the ground, occasionally interrupted by a pinprick of light here and there, coming from the porch of a some ranch or farm house. I imagined husbands and wives, children and animals tossing and turning on this hot, dry August night, waking to the insistent drone of our engines as we flew high above and then falling back to sleep again. If only I could have done the same.

But instead, I hunched over the navigation chart table, lost in my calculations. The small gooseneck light cast a golden circle on the pencil line that stretched from Sentinel Island to our present location. Along the way, I had made tiny, precise pencil tics that represented each star sighting. After comparing relative airspeed to true airspeed and computing possible wind drift I confidently marked the most recent spot where I prayed we were.

Confidence is everything. Especially when it weakens, as mine did without warning.

It happened because I had made the mistake of thinking about what had happened so far, when instead, I should have been thinking about what was to come. The instant I got lost in the past a dark, silent rush of fear came at me from the depths like a man-eating shark bent on its prey. I took a deep breath, but that didn't help. I bit my lip to break the hold, but no use.

My pencil snapped in my hand, its broken edge hurt, and I almost laughed out loud as I heard Fatt's booming voice in my head shouting at me across time and space,

'Action leads to discovery, God damn it, kid. Thinking just leads to more thinking.'

So I took a deep breath and took action by sharpening my pencil as fast as I could. It wasn't much by Fatt's standards, but at least it was action.

Two hours later, getting close to the state of Washington, my eyes burned from nonstop staring at the instruments, not trusting our autopilot to hold us on course, even though it was doing it without the slightest deviation.

The impenetrable two-thousand foot ceiling had remained monotonously the same, save for the occasional distant flicker of lightning to remind me of the danger that awaited us inside that soft billowy nothingness.

During the past few minutes I sensed the ceiling lowering even more.

Not a good sign. Time to find out how much. I disengaged the autopilot, advanced the throttles slightly and began a slow climb.

Ava, who had nodded off, stirred at the change in engine sound. She stretched and said, 'Are we there yet, daddy?'

I was about to say something clever in return when a dark object flashed across our nose about a half mile ahead. It happened so fast that I barely registered it at first.

'We got company.'

I flicked the intercom to 'All' to warn the crew. I continued our steady climb and the clouds drew closer and closer. After what seemed forever, but probably less than a minute, I began to think I had imagined it.

But just then a green navigation light appeared off the port wing and removed all doubt. I dialed down the cockpit lights to see well. A flash of lightning in the far off cloudbank outlined the crisp silhouette of the Me-109 compliance fighter. The Luftwaffe pilot had turned his cockpit lights all the way up so that I could see him vigorously gesturing downward with his thumb.

I hit the intercom. 'Orlando, standby the waist gun.'

'On my way.'

Ava let out a curse that would peel paint. 'This is not an airplane ride, this is one damn thing after another.'

I waved back at the pilot and smiled like I was out for a Sunday stroll.

The pilot gestured to his headphones. He was obviously trying to contact us by radio. I pointed at my headset and shook my head. I doubt he understood my futile pantomime. But seconds later he removed all doubt by lowering his landing gear and I knew we were sunk.

I hit the intercom. 'Listen up folks. We've got about two minutes before this guy starts shooting at us. Here's what I want everybody to do.'

It took about thirty seconds of those two short minutes to get across my plan of action. As I did so, the fighter's navigation lights slid out of sight as he took up position on our tail. Seconds later the night sky lit up with the bright reddish-gold blobs of twenty millimeter cannon fire across our nose and into the clouds that swallowed up their menacing light.

Orlando said over the intercom. 'He means business.'

'So do we, I said.

To keep him happy, I began a slow descent like a docile lamb, and he soon drifted back to his original position, but now further off our port wing, his mission proudly accomplished.

Everybody ready?' I said.

Ava, Mason, Ziggy and Orlando reported in. I risked a quick look over my shoulder to confirm their positions. Ava crouched by the navigator's table, Ziggy to her left, his hand on the window latch. Mason at his engineering station, hand hovering over the emergency fuel dump valves. I couldn't see the professor, but I knew he was strapped in.

'Hang on tight, here we go,' I said.

I shoved the throttles to takeoff power and dropped my left wing into a steep diving turn. The fighter vanished from sight, but I knew he would be after me like angry yellow jacket with a twenty millimeter sting.

Pitch black outside, no ground reference, my artificial horizon the only

thing keeping me upright as I quickly leveled my wings but continued my dive, building up as much airspeed as I possibly could to escape the Great White Shark on our tail.

130...140...150...the airspeed indicator kept climbing. I knew my time was up. The fighter must be on top of us by now, the pilot smiling, almost laughing at our big, lumbering plane centered square in his gun sight.

'Stand by,' I shouted.

The first string of tracers lobbed past us on both sides. He would soon have our range.

'Dump fuel!'

'Dumping!' Mason said.

A heavy jet of AVGAS jetted out of the dump valve, an L-shaped, two-inch diameter pipe located beneath our left wing, just aft of the number two engine.

'Go, Ava!'

A rush of air and roaring engine noise erupted behind me as Ziggy slid open the navigator's window and Ava and fired the flare pistol into the vaporizing avgas. The popping sound of the pistol going off was buried in the engine noise that quickly vanished as Ziggy slammed the window shut.

'Missed,' Ava screamed.

Again the blast of sound. Again she fired the flare pistol, sending the burning phosphorous shell into the slipstream.

'Got it!'

A blossoming golden glare of burning fuel lit up our world as it streamed backward in a long flickering tongue, making it appear as though we'd been mortally hit by gunfire. At any second the flames could shoot back up inside the fuel tank, explode, and the mission - and us along with it - would be over. To keep that from happening, I had to keep her going at a high rate of speed to atomize the fuel properly. Problem was I had to lose speed right now and I didn't know what was going happen when I did.

'Hang on, everybody, going up.'

I yanked back on the controls as hard as I could. The clipper began reaching for the clouds, exchanging precious airspeed for equally precious altitude. Another burst of enemy tracer fire streaked past us, but the rounds curved harmlessly away beneath us as we clawed for the sky.

'Got a deflection shot?' I said.

'Worth a try.'

I glanced at the altimeter and the approaching cloud bank.

'Six hundred more feet and we're home free. Can you do it?'

In answer the plane shuddered from the vibration of the fifty-caliber machine gun. Two short bursts, and then a sustained one. I couldn't see what was happening, but Ava, had a clear view to the rear.

'He's hit! No wait, he's not. He's turning away.' I said. 'He'll be back.'

Orlando chuckled. 'Come to Joshua you sinner.'

The first welcoming wisps of cloud streaked past the windscreen.

'We're almost there. C'mon baby, you can do it.'

'Permission to cut fuel?' Mason said nervously.

'Not yet. He's got to see us go into the clouds on fire. Otherwise he'll call out the dogs.'

More clouds, even more, and then bumpy darkness as we entered the vapor-filled sanctuary at last. I kept us climbing while I counted slowly to ten, and then ordered the fuel dump valve closed. He wouldn't follow us in, fearing a collision. By now I imagined him on the radio, crowing about how he attacked us and sent us into the clouds, a shot-up, flaming wreck about to crash.

'Mr. Mason, when you get a second,' I said, trying to make my voice calm and composed like just another flight to Buenos Aires. 'Work me up some new fuel numbers, will you? I don't think what we lost will affect our overall range, but I want to be sure.'

His voice was on the high and on the tight side, but to his credit, still calm cool and collected. 'Not a problem, captain.'

'Thanks.'

'And captain?'

'Yes?'

'Nice idea, sir.'

'Thanks. Nice execution. Let's hope it worked.'

Ava dropped into the right-hand seat, with Ziggy close behind who fluttered around us, flushed and excited, recounting blow by blow what had just happened, as if we hadn't been there. But he eventually ran out of adjectives and adverbs and stood there panting.

'Do me a favor, Ziggy.'

'Name it, captain.'

'Take this flashlight. Make a complete tour of the plane and check for damage. Check the fuselage walls, the wings, stop at every compartment window and look out. I think we made it out in one piece. But find out for sure and report back to me, okay?'

'Aye, aye, captain.'

He dashed off and we both let out a sigh of relief at his absence.

'Busy hands are happy hands,' Ava said finally.

We spent the next five minutes re-establishing cockpit discipline. Ava, as always, was precise and focused as she dialed in the autopilot heading, re-trimmed the controls, replaced pencils in their proper place, folded bits of paper and stowed them away, tightened her flight harness and sat there looking at the instrument panel, alert for the slightest deviation from the norm.

I couldn't resist. 'Too bad Pan Am doesn't hire female pilots.'

'They will one day. Good ideas have a way of happening.'

'Like this one?'

She laughed.

We flew on instruments through the murky blackness for another half-hour; the compass, turn-and-bank indicator, altimeter, and artificial horizon the only trustworthy friends standing between us and flying upside down and spinning out of control. Instruments are like good friends: you have to trust them implicitly, sometimes even more than you trust yourself.

At first I thought I was imagining the cloud layer might be thinning out, so I kept my mouth shut.

But a few minutes later Ava said, 'Is it me, or are we getting out of this soup?'

A few more endless minutes passed. The wings started bumping and flexing more and more, which meant were encountering small, individual cloud formations floating inside the general murk. Then a wave of silvery moonlight washed into the cockpit as we broke free from the clouds like breaking free from the water.

But instead of sparkling waves, a smooth, undulating sea of cloud vapor glided beneath us, stretching out as far as the eye could see. No way to tell how long this respite would last, so I left Ava in charge and hurried back to get a star fix. By now Orlando had returned to the engineering station and he smiled at me as I passed by.

'Nice job back there,' I said.

'All in a day's work, brother.'

I looked at his beaming face and said, 'We've come a long way from that jail cell.'

He frowned. 'But not much further to go before the walls of Jericho come tumbling down.'

I left him to his Bible-world and went to the astrodome, with Ziggy once again tagging along as my official mascot. Once done, I peeled him off, returned to the chart table and made the necessary calculations. That last run-in had cost us time and fuel for sure, but surprisingly we had not drifted too far off course. Numbers are to a navigator what instruments are to a pilot: at some point you either trust them or you don't. So I did.

Professor Friedman's voice pulled me out of my calculations. 'Captain, a minute of your time, please?' As always, his smooth, pudgy face was drawn and concerned as he stood next to me.

'What's cooking?' I said.

'Pardon me?'

'I mean, what's on your mind?'

'Oh, yes, I see. English is not the easiest language, *Ja?*'

'*Jawohl.*'

He leaned closer and pitched his voice low. 'It's about the device.' My heart sank. 'Problems?'

He fluttered his hands soothingly. 'Not really. It's just that I am going to need more time than I planned to arm it. For some reason the fusing mechanism is proving stubborn.'

'How so?' I said, as if I had a clue what he was talking about. But sometimes feigned interest gives the other person confidence to solve the problem by talking about it out loud, and I wanted to give this guy every bit of confidence I could.

He clasped his hands together as if praying. 'As you know, to be doubly sure of success, the fusing mechanism operates on a combination of factors; barometric pressure and radio proximity being the primary ones.'

'Uh, huh.'

'And when the output signal from the amplifier reaches the required amplitude to fire the thyratron, and the barometric reading confirms it, the device will explode.'

'You lost me after 'thyratron.''

He smiled. 'The details are not important. What is important is that working on it under these conditions is especially trying. I'm used to a quiet laboratory.' 'And I'm used to quiet flights to Buenos Aires. Maybe when all this is over, we both can go back to what we're used to do.'

He considered this in silence. I had never met a man who paid such close attention to what you said and then deliberated forever before answering. As if my words had to pass through some complicated

310

mechanism inside his head that took apart every syllable, turned it this way and that, analyzed alternative meanings, averaged out possible interpretations and then finally arrived at a response suitable for the moment.

'That is highly unlikely,' he finally said. 'As General Patton said, now that the Genie is out of the bottle, it is our task to smash the bottle and slow him down.'

'I wish we could kill him instead.'

'Impossible, I'm afraid. Because the genie, you see, is people like me, like Einstein, Niels, Szlislárd, and Bohr - scientists who looked too far, probed too deeply and as a result, got what we prayed for.'

'You prayed for this shit?'

'Pardon me?'

'Scheisse.'

He winced slightly, and I felt sorry for him. But not for long. Anger returned and I tried to stop myself but couldn't. 'Didn't any of you bastards ever think that splitting atoms wasn't the brightest thing in the world to do?'

'I don't understand.'

'You don't know this, but the bomb they dropped on Washington D.C. killed my wife and kid.'

He looked at me like I'd hit him with a baseball bat and that's just what I wanted. I was convinced he'd never answer me after this, and for that matter I didn't want to hear what he had to say, so I turned away and pretended to continue with my navigational computations. But what I was really trying to do was scramble back into the present and out of the past which was burning me up inside. They says time heals all wounds, but it takes a hell of a lot longer when they're radioactive.

After a while I got so absorbed in my fuel calculations that I actually managed to forget about the professor. That's why I jumped slightly when he finally spoke.

'I am deeply sorry for your loss.'

'Thank you. I got work to do. Excuse me.'

'May I say something more?'

I nodded carefully.

He bit his lip, his eyes bright with tears.

'I cannot hope you will understand my world any more than I can understand yours.' He waved his hand around the flight deck. 'All of this work by so many people to create a piece of machinery that can fly through the air. It is a miracle, nicht war? But tell me, where are the men who dreamed of flying? I do not mean the Wright brothers, they were the builders. I mean the dreamers: Icarus, Daedalus, Archimedes, Leonardo Da Vinci, and the ancient Chinese. Those are the ones who set all of this into motion.'

'They wanted to fly. What did you guys want?'

'A new form of energy. And we found it. But Hitler wanted power and he took it from us.'

'They're the same damned thing.'

'No they are not. One gives life, the other death. Controlled energy release from atomic fission creates heat, from which we can make steam to make electricity. But when that same energy is released uncontrolled as explosive, raw power it brings destruction to unfortunate, innocent people, including your family.'

'And now we're about to do the same thing.'

'If I am successful in my task and the bomb works properly, we will kill people in a few hours. How many I am not sure. But if General Patton is to be believed, the storage facility will be deserted and perhaps no one needs to die. I hope so. There has been too much death and so little life, that...'

He fell silent. We looked at each other for a brief moment. Then he looked away, unable to face me. He turned to leave but I placed my hand on his shoulder.

'I'll do my best to get us there, professor. You do your best too, okay?'

'Jawohl, Yes, okay.'

'Tell me something; if we manage to destroy the plutonium, then what?'

He already had his answer on the shelf, waiting for someone like me to ask the sixty-four dollar question:

'If we dreamers were smart enough to split the atom, we are smart enough to build a new bottle to put the Genie back inside, so that he can work peacefully. But we need time to do it. And that is something only America can give us.'

Courage, above all things, is the first quality of a warrior.

- Carl von Clausewitz

We left Oregon and crossed over into Washington State at 1:46 a.m.

My charts indicated the state boundary line on paper, but Nature doesn't work that way. It's all one piece, one planet, all connected and interdependent. It's people who are the holdouts. Some worse than others, but all of us laboring under the illusion that something as complicated and diverse as the world can be corralled, subjugated, and bent to our will.

Hitler believed he could do it in a global way. Goering, Himmler, Mussolini, Tojo and the rest of their other toadies were riding on the same hateful bandwagon. And us? God willing and nature permitting, we were going to run that damned bandwagon off the road and into a ditch.

Despite being jumped by the compliance fighter, the Dixie *Clipper*, wounded and battered bird that she was, remained on course and on target. Time to 'Initial Point' was just under ninety minutes. Engines running smoothly. Rate of fuel loss not increasing. Our gamble of leaving Boulder Dam with full tanks was paying off.

Mason was now stationed forward at the bombardier station in the nose, while Professor Friedman continued working on arming the bomb in the tail. I would leave them alone for now. They had enough to do without my looking over their shoulders. But by the same token, I didn't want them to feel isolated from the crew. As small as we were, we were still a team.

Ava said, 'What if it's socked in?'

'Weather forecast calls for clear skies.'

'What's the temperature spread?'

Then it clicked in my mind. 'You're thinking fog?'

'Could happen if the dew point's against us.'

'We'll go in fast and low and use the chute delivery.'

'That's dangerous.'

'Mind telling me what isn't dangerous about any of this?'

'You're right.' She bit her fingernail.

313

'Don't worry. The chute will work just fine if we need to use it.'

'Quit being the mighty captain with me, okay? You're such a lousy actor sometimes.'

'The others don't seem to notice.'

'That's because they don't do it for a living. I do.'

She was right, of course. The idea of strapping a parachute onto an atomic bomb and lobbing it out at low altitude seemed farfetched as hell. Yet Patton and his team were confident of a workable alternative delivery method, and during the briefings had shown us films of successful trial drops. Instead of the bomb falling at terminal velocity from ten thousand feet, we'd roar in at about one thousand feet, drop the bomb and its large chute would slow its fall to a crawl, and delay detonation long enough for us to escape major effects of the blast. The chute was compact, easy to attach and, with luck, it would do what it was designed to do: save our lives while taking a minimum of others.

The plan was for the Sons of Liberty insiders to scram the reactor around 1:00 am. The McGraw brothers were supposed to have radioed them of our change of planes right after we took off. Had the message been acknowledged? Were they out of harm's way? No way to know for sure. And besides, I already had too many fish to fry and couldn't add that one to the skillet.

I unfastened my seatbelt and stretched. 'Time for Captain Courageous to make his rounds. You okay up here?'

Ava patted the autopilot. 'Mr. Sperry and I are doing just fine. Go look after your boys. Who's first?'

'Mason.'

I swung open the crew hatch, climbed down the spiral staircase to the dimly-lit deck and then forward to the mooring compartment. Mason had switched over to red lights to preserve his night vision, so the effect was eerie. He knelt over the Norden bombsight, fiddling with the knobs like some ancient priest performing a mysterious ritual. The combination of stabilizing gyroscopes, motors, gears and bearings inside the compact device reminded me of a mechanical brain humming with perfection but missing its body. An eerie green glow came from the sighting eyepiece and spilled onto Mason's red-lit face.

I spoke quietly, so as not to startle him. 'Greetings from the flight deck.'

He spun around, the whites of his eyes and his smiling teeth blood-red. Reminded me of a vampire, and I wondered if Ava was right. Maybe he was the spy-guy who ripped out the cables.

'How's it going?' I said.

He patted the bombsight. 'Open for business. You?'

'The same.'

We talked for a while, mostly generalities about what had happened so far, how he was feeling, the normal kind of temperature-taking a captain needs to do. And when I felt things were on an even keel, I slipped the problem onto the table to see how he'd react.

'Look, we're forecasting clear weather,' I began. 'But seeing as how the target's on the Columbia River there may be a chance of ground fog. From what you told me, the Norden needs a strong visual to work properly.'

He shrugged. 'Unless they've torn down the boiler plant's smokestack - which I doubt - I've got a two hundred foot-high aiming point, complete with anti-collision lights. It'll look like a flashing red pencil sticking out of a foggy sea, and that's all this baby needs.'

He patted the bombsight like a trick pony, and I decided Ava was wrong. It couldn't be him, I just knew it. It had to have been somebody back at Sentinel Island. But then again, what did I know about this guy, other than he had red hair, freckles and seemed like an all-American boy - which would be the perfect cover if - wait a minute, was it a coincidence that he was the only crew member to escape the Couba Island attack, or something carefully arranged? I had to step on the brakes of my suspicions, otherwise I'd head off the cliff.

'Is the parachute hard to attach?' I managed to say.

'Less than a minute if you know what you're doing.'

'Something the professor could do?'

Mason smiled. 'He's a nuclear physicist, what do you think?'

'Right.'

I decided that if we ran into fog, Orlando would help him out. I didn't want to abandon our engineering station in the middle of a bomb run, but I had to play with the cards I was dealt, and at this point I was barely holding two pair.

I got on the intercom and told Orlando to meet me at the bomb bay to practice installing the parachute. I hoped Ava was wrong about the ground fog, but something told me she could be right. The weather patterns on the eastern slope of the Cascades were generally on the dry side. But if the ground temperature got close enough to the dew point, fog would roll in like a grey blanket.

I passed from one dimly-lit compartment to the next, each stripped of its long-ago, luxurious fittings. Missing too, were the wealthy, spoiled, overwrought, anxious, demanding, and often imperious passengers who occupied these berths. In their place was a haunted, three-engine, flying machine, leaking gas, and filled with a handful of frightened but determined people, led by an equally frightened and determined captain who was 99.999% sure everybody on board was on the up and up.

I stopped midway and peered out the starboard window to examine the trailing edge of the starboard sponson. My flashlight beam played over the duralumin trailing edge. Impossible to see the steadily escaping fuel.

Orlando's voice startled me. 'Don't worry, Sam, we got enough to make it.'

'To the target, maybe, but we've still have to cross the Cascades and make it to the ocean.'

'You're really going to scuttle her?'

'Got another way to hide the murder weapon?'

He shook his head. 'Lots of moving pieces in this puzzle, that's for sure.'

'Too many.'

'Not for a Master of Flying Boats like you.'

I laughed at the thought. 'Wearing cowboy boots.'

Moments later, we came upon the professor, as occupied with his bomb as Mason had been with his bombsight. A small, flat red leather roll-out tool kit filled with hex wrenches was spread out beside him. An oscilloscope and some other kind of strange electrical measuring device rested on a small shelf built into the fuselage wall. A bundled cable snaked out from the instruments to a point midpoint on the bomb where it was plugged in. A continuously moving line squiggled across the oscilloscope's single green eye, accompanied by a small beeping sound, almost like a heartbeat.

Beads of sweat covered the professor's bald head, but his hands moved with calm deliberation as he continued attaching the bomb's nose housing. He glanced up briefly, noted our presence with a tight nod, and then returned to his labors.

Nothing I had to say at the moment could match the importance of what he was doing, so I kept my big mouth shut and let him finish the job in silence. The roar of the engines seemed louder back here, when the opposite should have been true, seeing as how we were in the next to the last compartment of the plane. It may have been because the bomb bay doors were not a perfect fit.

The professor finished tightening the last screw, stood up, checked the monitoring instruments one last time, and wiped his sweaty hands on his pants.

'It is ready to deploy.'

I waited until he disconnected the monitoring cable before introducing the idea of the parachute delivery option. His eyes glazed over early on at the specifics, so I kept it short and sweet.

'If we need to do it, Orlando will install it. Won't take but a minute or so, right?'

'Easy as pie.'

The professor nodded. 'I will need to re-calibrate the device.'

'How long will that take?'

'It's merely a matter of changing the impact data and re-loading it into the device with this.' He lifted the monitoring cable like a rattlesnake. I was about to say something positive to promote crew solidarity when the small loudspeaker on the bulkhead came to life.

'Sam, get back here right now.' Ava's voice sounded calm, collected, but ominous, too.

I keyed the talk switch. 'What's wrong?'

'Bring everybody. Hurry.'

'Everybody?'

'You heard me.'

As the three of us hurried back through the plane, my mind tried to land on a specific problem so as to deal with it in advance: engine trouble? No, they sounded fine. Control problem? No, flying straight and level. Why'd she say 'all' of us? I took the crew stairs two at a time, Orlando pounding right behind me. Around and up and through the already opened hatch, and I instinctively turned toward the cockpit and saw Ava's angry face staring not at me but at something behind me.

Orlando and the professor obscured my vision for a brief moment, but when they moved, there sat a wide-eyed Mason at his Engineer station, Ziggy next to him, equally wide-eyed, and two other men standing on either side of the opened rear bulkhead door.

I recognized Bauer, wearing his long, grey leather jacket. The other I didn't know by name, but had seen trained apes like him wearing the black *Kampfschwimmer* uniforms the night they attacked Couba Island.

'Inspector,' I said. 'Of all places.'

He nodded slightly and smiled. 'Nicely put, captain.'

'Who's your goon friend?'

The soldier swung around his sub-machine gun and aimed it at my chest. 'You will be silent.'

I took a step forward. 'Like hell I will. I'm the captain of this aircraft. Put that gun down now, that's an order!'

Bauer shook his fat little head. '*Hauptman* Eiger and I do not contest your leadership position. In fact, we commend you on how masterfully you have performed your duties thus far.'

'What the hell are you doing on my aircraft?' I finally managed to get out. 'And how did you get here?'

Silence. Just the muted roar of the engines and the hiss of the slipstream outside the navigation window.

Bauer finally spoke. 'We are here to recover stolen property that rightfully belongs to the Third Reich. And to apprehend the man who perpetrated the theft; namely *Herr Doktor Professor* Friedman.' He clicked his heels slightly and said,' *Gruss Gott, Herr Doktor.'*

Friedman took a step backwards, Orlando half-hid him with his bulk.

'It's a pity we didn't succeed in Lisbon,' Bauer continued. 'You could have been spared...' he waved a pudgy hand around the flight deck. 'All this adventuresome effort.'

I said, 'Where the hell were you hiding?'

'Thanks to Mr. Ziegler, we have been enjoying excellent accommodations in your crew relief quarters ever since you left Couba Island.'

'Ziggy!' Ava shouted.

The little weasel, his face a mixture of defiance and fear took a half-step towards Bauer.

'I had to.'

'You slimy bastard.' Her voice broke slightly. 'You've been in on this all along?'

He hunched his shoulders as if struck. 'I'm sorry. I really I am.'

Bauer intervened. 'He's telling the truth, Miss James. We have benefitted from Mr. Ziegler's information ever since Key West. Or course,

318

I had already met Captain Carter earlier in Washington D.C. and learned of the Sons of Liberty's interest in retaining his services for this mission of yours, ill-starred as it now has become. In fact...'

Without warning, Mason lunged toward the German commando, hands clawing for his machine gun.

Orlando moved almost as quickly, but Bauer beat them both to the punch with a swift parrying move and a sharp, vicious karate chop on Mason's neck. He crumpled to the floor, unconscious.

The *Kampfschwimmer* buried the gun barrel into Orlando's chest. 'Move and die,' he said, his eyes coal-black and empty.

'Trust me, you will indeed,' Bauer said, unperturbed and calm, as if nothing had happened. 'As I was saying before your crewmember's heroic gesture - oh don't worry, he'll wake up with a sore neck, but not much else - anyhow, let me come directly to the point, Captain Carter.'

He drew himself up to seem more officious than he already was. 'As a sworn agent of the Third Reich, I hereby order you to fly this plane to the designated target area and thereupon land on the Columbia River. We will take *Doktor* Friedman and his bomb into custody, and then the rest of you are free to go.'

I considered his statement. 'And if I refuse?'

'You have no choice in this matter.'

'The hell I don't. This is my airplane, and I'm the captain.'

'I'm not debating that, I'm simply telling you your new orders. Now get on with them.'

Ava's voice was sad. 'Why'd you do it, Ziggy?'

He looked down, unable to speak. At least the little shit had the common decency to be ashamed. Then he said softly, 'They know all about me.'

'You mean...'

He nodded. 'And if I didn't tell them what they wanted, they'd tell the world about...about...' he faltered.

Bauer slid in smoothly. 'As you well know, Miss James, but I assure you Hollywood does not - as yet, Mr. Ziegler is a bona fide, full time, practicing homosexual. Should your town of tinsel find out that dark little fact, his job prospects would be ruined. Am I correct, Mr. Ziegler?'

Ziggy barely nodded.

'I believe the expression is, 'You'll never work in this town again,' correct?'

Ziggy glanced at me, then away.

Bauer wouldn't let up. 'Of course, if he had this same 'condition' in Germany, the consequences would be far more dire. *Der Führer* frowns on those who do not fit his Aryan ideal. So, all in all, consider yourself lucky, *Herr* Ziegler. Because of your loyal service to the Third Reich, your deep dark secret remains safe with us, and with your friends here, too, of course.'

Ava said coldly. 'You sold us out to keep your damn JOB?'

Ziggy shook his head. 'My grandparents. Trying to get out of Germany. They said they'd throw them in the concentration camps if I didn't cooperate.'

Bauer looked oddly pleased at this revelation. 'To use one of your flying expressions, captain, this was our 'alternate runway.' Had *Herr* Ziegler decided not to cooperate with us, I assured him that his grandparents would die in the camps. But if he did assist us, Berlin would issue them exit visas. I don't want to boast, but I think the double threat worked out quite well. So much so that I have already processed the paperwork for their visas. I should think they will be arriving safe and sound in American in two weeks' time to reunite with their loving grandson.'

I said to Ziggy, 'When you two were together in Horta. You were in on it then, right?'

Ziggy nodded.

I turned to Bauer. 'I assume your people at Hanford know we're coming.'

He smiled. 'Of course they do. While *Herr* Ziegler was on watch last night on Lake Mead, *Hauptman* Eiger used your radio to send the alert before he ripped out the cables - with his bare hands incidentally. Quite a feat.'

I said, 'You know, for a fat, dumpy, harmless-looking Gestapo detective, you are one hardworking, heartless son-of-a-bitch.'

'Only when on duty, when I'm chopping heroes like Lieutenant Mason on their necks or threatening little queers like Mr. Ziegler. Off duty, I am a family man, much like you.'

I had already made up my mind what I wanted to say, but somehow what he just said was the icing on a cake that I wanted to throw in his face.

'Mister, you can stuff this whole game of yours up your ass with peanuts on it.'

Bauer's ever-placid face twitched slightly. 'By that you mean...'

'I mean you can't land this plane without me. And I refuse to do so. You can shoot me, but you'll still be out of luck. Nobody here can get this bucket of bolts down in one piece. We'll all die. I'll just be dead a little sooner, that's all.'

'But Miss James...'

She laughed. 'Are you kidding? I can handle straight and level, pal, but landing this monster? Find somebody else.'

I said, 'Now, this is the part in the movie where your Nazi goon says, 'I am multi-engine rated on seaplanes, *Herr* Bauer, stand aside.' Right? Go ahead and say it, Hauptmann.'

A long silence. Both men looked like idiots. Ava said softly, 'Mexican Standoff anybody?'

Bauer smiled. 'It seems we have reached one indeed. You have your 'gun,' so to speak, captain, and I have mine thanks to *Herr* Ziegler. And *Hauptmann*? He has a real one. None of us wants to surrender. So what shall we do?'

'You tell me.'

He reached inside his leather coat pocket, I tensed and he paused.

'Don't worry, it's not a gun.' He took out an envelope and handed it to me.

'Please open it. I will be interested in your reaction.'

Two small black-and-white photographs: Abby sitting in a chair in an empty room, hair tousled, and lips pressed in a thin line of worry and her frightened eyes as big as saucers. The other photo, she and my mother, Rosie on a shabby couch, arms around each other, their knees touching, and their wide eyes staring at something just beyond camera range.

'As you can see, your family misses you,' Bauer said. 'Land this plane, let us have Doctor Friedman and the bomb, and you can have your family back.'

'Where are they, damn it?'

'Safe and sound in Key West. But if you don't cooperate, I can't be held responsible for what will happen next.'

'What do you mean?'

'They'll be killed, of course.'

'You bastard...'

'Orders, captain. I have mine and you have yours. Mine are to stop this plane from completing its mission, no matter the cost. I suggest you help me by complying. The choice is yours, of course. But I should think losing your wife and infant son was hard enough. To lose little Abby and your mother would be tragic beyond belief - at least to me.

'But perhaps I have overestimated you all along. Perhaps you are not a sensitive family man trying to put his broken family back together again. *Nein*, you are made of much sterner stuff, *Ja?* Willing to let innocent people die for the sake of principle. I salute your iron will. As does *Der Führer.*'

I handed the photographs to Orlando, who shook his head slowly, like an ox bemoaning something unspeakable.

Bauer stood there, leather jacket and all, with his bullet-headed henchman beside him, master of the situation, every contingency planned, every 'i' dotted, every 't' crossed.

I felt like I did when Pop used to beat me in chess; that painful moment where after evaluating every conceivable escape route for my king, I was forced to reach out and tip my king to the board in defeat.

'Deal,' I finally managed to say, then turned and slowly walked toward the cockpit.

Bauer called out after me, 'A wise choice, captain. Not a pleasant one I'm sure, what with your patriotism and desire to right the wrong with your comrades in arms here. But Abby will thank you one day when she is all grown up and has a family of her own. She will thank you for her life.'

I turned around and came back. 'No she won't. She'll ask me why I didn't keep my word. Why I didn't act on my beliefs, why I didn't fight you and your Nazi goons to the very end.'

He seemed amused at this. 'And what will be your answer?'

I exchanged a quick glance with Orlando. He nodded imperceptibly.

'Well?' Bauer pressed.

'I will tell her that I failed her, failed my friends, and failed my country.'

He made a face. 'A most painful confession.'

'Could you do the same if you were in my place?'

He deliberated for a while. 'I don't think I could.'

'Well, you know something? Neither can I.'

I slammed my fist into Bauer's stomach as hard as I could. The fat gave way to bone and I felt something crunch, and a sharp pain in my wrist, but Bauer's explosive grunt made it worthwhile. At the same instant, Orlando ripped Hauptman's gun away, but not before it went off in a spray of bullets, and the flight deck filled with the haze of gunpowder.

I wrestled Bauer to the floor, Ziggy beside me, pounding on Bauer's face, half-crying, half-shouting, 'Bastard, bastard, bastard' while the detective squirmed and twisted, trying to get at something inside his coat.

I tried to shove Ziggy out of the way and pin down Bauer's arms but got tangled up and somehow Ziggy got between me and him.

Two quick shots.

Ziggy's body jerked as he screamed. I dove for Bauer's Luger as it swung toward me. My hands closed around his thick wrist, stunned at his strength. Iron muscle beneath that fat and fighting me hard, his breath hot on my face as I rolled on top of him.

Shouting sounds. Orlando's booming roar, the thump of bodies falling as Bauer and I fought for control of the gun. He twisted around and rolled on top of me. I clamped my hands on the barrel pointed straight at me, his face contorted in rage, teeth bared like an animal, eyes slits, and then from out of nowhere Ava's arm snaked around his neck and yanked back.

The pistol wavered in momentary surprise, I twisted it up and backwards until the barrel dug into Bauer's double chin. My thumb scrabbled on top of his trigger finger and yanked. Ava screamed and ducked as the top of Bauer's skull left the rest of his head in a spray of blood and brains and hopes and dreams.

The steady drone of the engines returned. Orlando, machine gun in hand, stood over the *Kampfschwimmer's* body, his legs awkwardly twisted like a rag doll dropped on the floor. Professor Friedman slumped in the captain's conference chair, a stunned witness to what had just happened.

Mason rose up on one elbow and said, 'Jesus.'

Orlando kicked the *Kampfschwimmer's* body and said, 'Amen to that.'

Ava cradled Ziggy's head in her lap, while stroking his forehead as he struggled to breathe.

'I was wrong,' he moaned.

'Shut up, and live, okay?'

He shook his head. 'Doesn't hurt. Bad sign, right?'

'Why didn't you tell me? I could have helped.'

'Wanted to, but…. too late.'

'Ziggy, I'm so sorry. About everything.'

He smiled. 'That's okay, we got even… with them in the end… didn't we?'

'We sure did.'

A long pause. His eyes closed. A sense of calm settled over his face. In between breaths, 'Do me... a favor... sweetheart.'

'Name it.'

'Don't tell my folks about... about me being.... Tell them that...that...'

'You were a hero.'

'Yeah, something like that. You'll know how to say it. You're a great actress.'

'I won't have to act.'

He smiled and then he died.

Orlando and I dragged the dead Germans into the baggage storage compartment to get them out of sight. I didn't care how we handled them, I just wanted them gone. We flopped down Bauer's body first and tossed the *Kampfschwimmer* on top of him like so much cordwood. But when it came to Ziggy, I changed my mind and we laid him out alongside the others and folded his hands across his motionless chest.

'Rest in peace, you little shit,' I said.

Orlando chuckled. 'I'll give Brother Ziggy credit, he almost pulled it off.'

'Not 'almost.' He did pull it off. They know we're coming. The surprise element's out the window.'

'But we still have the bomb.'

'Correct.' I said. 'And how exactly do you suggest we drop it?'

'Mason's going to say, 'Bombs away?''

'Don't get wise with me. You know what I mean.'

Orlando paused to gather his thoughts. I never hurried the man because it was always worth the wait.

The plane hit more turbulence and Ziggy's hands slid off his chest. I put them back again.

He finally said, 'If McGraw's warning got through, they've scrammed the reactor and skedaddled. That means there's nobody there to help the compliance folks.'

'To do what?'

'Grab the plutonium and head for high ground. And they can't because it's radioactive. They'll need all sorts of protection and that takes time. So they've got to try another way to keep us away. Compliance fighters, most likely.'

'What do you want to be the sky will be filled with them within the hour?'

Orlando frowned. 'I'm not a betting man. Besides, even if I was, I'd lose that one.'

Turns out, I was about right. Approximately twenty minutes from the target, the Messerschmitt's jumped us. 'Jump' isn't the right word; the squadron of Me109's surrounded us like an inescapable escort; above, behind, side to side and below. The lead aircraft, probably the squadron commander, floated just off our starboard wing, his cockpit lights up full, like always.

'Déjà vu,' Ava said.

I waved at the pilot and said through my frozen smile. 'Ready back there, Orlando?'

Orlando said, 'Whenever you are.'

I turned up the flight deck lights full so that the Luftwaffe pilot could see *Herr* Inspector Bauer and *Hauptman* Eiger leaning over the navigator's chart table, heads down, seeming to examine the maps. Propping up the dead *Kampfschwimmer* had been relatively easy. Mason, an experienced sailor, lashed the body's arms, trunk and hips to the table so that he appeared natural standing there. Bauer's body was the problem. Half of his skull was gone, but thank God for his snap brim fedora. Pulled just right over his right eyebrow, it hid the exit wound perfectly.

Making the dead man move had been Orlando's bright idea. I expressed doubts he could pull it off but he said, 'The blind shall see and the dead shall walk.'

After we had secured Bauer's body, Orlando cut a slit in the right shoulder of the leather jacket and slid his arm in and up alongside. That, plus using his left hand to move Bauer's head, Orlando, kneeling behind him, was ready to become a macabre puppeteer.

I said, 'Do it.'

Orlando said, 'Lazarus, I say unto thee, arise!'

Bauer looked up and around and out at the pilot. He raised his arm in a Nazi salute and held it. The pilot hesitated a moment, and then snapped off a smart, conventional salute in return.

He drifted back to a more distant position, assured that we were complying with *Herr* Bauer's orders. I slowly lowered the flight deck lights as Orlando moved his puppet a bit more for good measure, and then stopped.

We held our breaths forever it seemed. But nothing happened. Just a squadron of German warplanes peacefully escorting us to our final destination.

'My God, I think they bought it,' Ava said. 'But what happens when we start the bomb run? The instant they see that, they'll shoot us down.'

'Not with Bauer on board.'

'Don't kid yourself, he's expendable and you know it.'

'I do, but I'm counting on their getting official permission before they start shooting. Nazis love their little rules and they follow them to the letter.'

'They'll get permission sooner or later, I promise you that.'

'Yeah, but by then maybe we'll have dropped the bomb.'

'And maybe not.'

'Got any other ideas, First Officer James?'

She laughed. 'I'm not the resident pessimist, just trying to make sure you cover all your bases.'

'Yeah, we'll if you're going to steal second base, sooner or later you've got to start running.'

I throttled back the engines.

'What are you doing?'

'Beginning our initial descent. They're expecting us to land peacefully, remember? Just watch how they follow.'

I made the rate-of-descent as slow as I could. I needed to buy time.

'Orlando, head back to and start rigging the chute on the bomb.'

'On my way.'

Pilot to bombardier.'

'Bombardier, go ahead.'

'We're using the chute. Can you comply?'

A slight pause, then 'Doing the numbers now. I'll take control of the aircraft in about...five minutes.'

'Roger. Professor Friedman, can you recalibrate in time?'

His voice in my headsets tinny and tight. 'Jawohl, I can do this.'

Ava touched my arm 'The instant that bomb goes off, they'll shoot us down like a mad dog.'

'Wrong. The instant they see our bomb bay doors open they'll start shooting.'

'How long will they stay open?'

'Probably a minute or so, maybe longer, from what Mason said.'

She winced and said, 'I guess at this point, we really don't have much a choice.'

The pre-dawn light turned the eastern horizon soft rose. I had witnessed countless sunrises over countless oceans while flying with Pan Am and the sight always brought the feeling of relief; daylight had won once again won over the darkness. But this time, when I saw the first shades of a new day coming to America, I felt frightened, but then happy, proud, and most of all determined as hell.

Ava placed her hand over my hand that still gripped the throttles. The gesture wasn't as a co-pilot backing up the pilot, but as a friend as the both of us watched the altimeter unwind the way you watch a clock ticking off the final seconds before Happy New Year. Only we had nothing to celebrate.

I tried to judge the ground conditions but darkness still ruled the land. Then the faint gleam of a river, which could have been the Yakima that flows due south of the target. Was that a sprinkle of lights too? If so, Benton City. And what's more, if I could see the ground then the fog wasn't there as we had feared.

The government had built the Hanford Site in the middle of nowhere on purpose. And accordingly, nothing could be seen, no landmarks, no city lights, nothing but scrub grass, shallow arroyos, low rolling hills and then finally, somewhere dead ahead, the blocky shape of the nuclear reactor and the plutonium storage site.

The altimeter reached two thousand feet and I slowly leveled out. The compliance fighters obediently followed like pilot fish. They wouldn't wonder - just yet - why I stopped my descent. But if I didn't resume it soon, they'd start to worry. The squadron leader seemed to read my mind, because he sidled up alongside me and waved. I waved back.

Mason said, 'Coming up on the I.P. Got the smokestack. I am taking the aircraft.'

'She's all yours.'

I turned on the autopilot, felt the control column shudder momentarily and then smooth out as the Norden bombsight system began feeding it input signals. From now on I was just a spectator. I put my hands in my lap and stared at the slight motions of the wheel moving without me.

'Look ma, no hands,' I whispered to myself. Mason said, 'Four minutes to drop.'

The squadron leader slowly drifted away again. He might be on the radio already, voicing his concerns. No way to tell. How Mason managed to see the smokestack was a mystery. All I could see was the pre-dawn sky ahead and velvet black below.

'Orlando, all set back there?'

'Chute's on, ready to drop.'

Mason said, 'Opening bomb bay doors.'

My control panel indicator light switched from green to red as the doors in the plane's tail opened, creating a slight buffeting as the airstream flowed up and into the open space where the bomb hung on its cradle. Outside, the compliance fighters flew steadily onward. Who would be the first to notice?

'Three minutes to drop,' Mason said.

Ahead, a tiny red pinprick in the black velvet. Then two more dots, winking softly: the smokestack's anti-collision lights slowly drifting toward us. The throttles advanced back and forth automatically, driven by the Norden's dispassionate, mechanical calculations of wind drift, airspeed and outside air temperature.

'Input data complete,' Friedman said briskly. 'Device armed.'

The atomic bomb was finally free from its coaxial umbilical cord. No more messages from its master. The malevolent child was alive at last, its plutonium core waiting to be squeezed to death and born again into a full-blown, radioactive, Frankenstein fireball.

And still, miraculously, the Nazi fighters maintained their position. Maybe the darkness kept them from seeing the open bomb bay doors. Or laziness. Didn't matter. The *Dixie Clipper* keep flying and the clock keep ticking.

'Sixty seconds.' Mason said.

I stared at my hands in my lap; useless, motionless. I clenched and unclenched them for lack of anything else to do. After days and nights of action, pressure, worry and concern it came down to this; motionless hands, staring straight ahead, acting like the obedient captain carefully calculating my landing as ordered by *Herr* Bauer.

'Thirty seconds.'

All hell broke loose, or at least that's what it seemed like. A meteor shower of bright red tracers laced the sky above and below us and into us too.

'Hang on everybody,' I said. 'Orlando, get ready!'

'I'm there, brother.'

'Fifteen seconds to drop.'

A line of twenty millimeter cannon shells struck our left wing, followed by the swooping rush of the attacking fighter, directly over us. The clipper absorbed it without a shudder, but within seconds, our number one engine began throwing a thin finger of flame back from its cowling. I feathered the prop, killed the engine and hit the extinguisher, but with no confidence it would work.

'Ten seconds!' Mason shouted. 'Help me hold this bearing, cap, we're drifting.'

'Wilco,' I grabbed the controls.

The Norden wasn't compensating enough for the dead engines. I applied rudder to help. An explosion of noise from behind me as cannon shells shattered the navigation windows and ripped through the radio operator's station. Soundproofing gone, the engine roar suddenly deafening, my headphones useless.

All I could do was stare at the bomb release indicator on the instrument panel and pray for it to light up. Seeing that would somehow make all this chaos worth all the pain, all the suffering, all the work by so many people who wanted to be left alone to live their lives until they died of old age, but were up here in a shot-up plane trying to drop a bomb and start a war instead.

The light flashed red. Mason must have shouted 'Bomb's away' but I didn't hear him, so I pointed at the indicator light and bellowed, 'Bomb's away!'

I turned to Ava, expecting her marvelous grin, but she sat slumped to the right, motionless, her head on her chest. I tried to reach out to her, but another wave of cannon fire, this time into our right wing, kept me in my seat. All I could do was wrestle this slow-moving giant of a plane out of the line of fire.

Intermittent blasts of fifty-caliber fire from Orlando's waist gun. Doing his best, but against these sharks, we didn't stand a chance.

Somewhere behind us, the bomb continued its silent descent, its fusing systems clicking away, waiting for the final moment. With every second it fell, the further we escaped from the blast. But the irony of the moment suddenly struck me: with Nazi fighters chopping us up into bits, we weren't escaping after all.

I scrabbled around and found my smoked-glass blast goggles, and managed to get them on just as brilliant greenish-white light flooded the cockpit, so intense and overwhelming that it banished all sound.

Silent, cold and impossibly bright, it faded seconds later, and I ripped off my goggles to see what I was doing. And just in time, because the shock wave hit us and flipped the plane almost completely on her back like a bathtub toy. Debris showered down from everywhere. Momentarily disoriented, I firewalled the remaining engines, applied cross controls, and fought her to the horizontal. But barely. With only two functioning engines we going down whether we liked it or not.

Where were the tracers? Where were the fighters? Nothing but rosy sky ahead and a towering mushroom cloud to my right rising higher and higher with greenish lightning bolts flashing deep inside its grey billows like a monster's heartbeat. All I could think of was that the light from the explosion had temporarily blinded them. But that wouldn't last long.

Someone grabbed my shoulder. Mason shouted, 'On the BUTTON, skipper. We did it!'

I nodded, and pointed to Ava, 'She's hit. Check for a neck pulse'

He crouched over Ava, his hands probing and poking. As he worked, to my relief she stirred and tried to straighten up.

'Stay still,' Mason said. 'Found it.'

'Bad?'

'Can't tell. Lots of blood. Upper arm and shoulder. Bleeding.'

'Artery?'

'Maybe.'

'Use your belt for a tourniquet. High up as you can get it.'

'Yes, sir.'

He stripped off his leather belt and wrapped it around her arm. As he worked to stop the flow of blood, his trousers slowly slid down around his ankles. His boxer shorts white sails in the reddish light.

'Jesus Christ, skipper. Help me out here.'

Ava smiled and said weakly. 'That's okay, I won't look.'

The *Dixie Clipper* was dying, and I didn't need warning bells and horns to tell me. She had been through too much, too long, and just wanted to lie down and die and I understood. Still no pursuing fighters, but how long could that last? How long could I keep her flying? Half the instruments were either shot up or their sensors destroyed, but the altimeter still worked; three hundred lousy feet and descending.

'I'm putting her down. Professor. Orlando, up here as fast as you can.'

'Roger.'

'Mason, break out the life raft.'

Off to my right a quick shimmer of reflected light. Water. Had to be the western leg of the Columbia River. If I put her on land she'd grind herself up to bits and take us along with her. Better to let her die on the water. But I had to reach it first and it didn't look like I could.

Dawn light just brushed the tops of the distant Cascade Mountains off to my left. Beyond that, the Pacific Ocean that we would never see like we'd originally planned. Not now, and not ever unless I flew this dying plane like I'd never flown it before.

Outboard engine number four backfired flames out its exhaust. Whatever had struck its intricate world of pistons, crankshafts and valves had finally done its deadly work. Two hundred feet...one hundred eighty…....

Orlando and the Professor on the flight deck.

'Brace for a crash landing.'

Orlando clapped me on the shoulder. 'Lead us to the Promised Land, not into it, you hear?'

Controls beyond sluggish now, almost useless, making huge motions just to keep her nose level and the river approaching, but perpendicular to our flight path. Had to slew her around to the left to line up for the final approach but the airspeed was so low she would stall and drop off on a wing.

Tracer fire lancing across the sky. Fighters finally found us, game over, but a plane to land no matter what. I lowered the flaps but the starboard wing rose, trying to flip us over. Flaps only working on the right side, the left side shot out. Great. Too late now, water coming up sideways, raise the nose, raise the nose, bleed off airspeed, kick left rudder as hard as you can, line up, line up, stall warning horn, flare, flare, FLARE.

The *Dixie Clipper* struck the water like a skipping stone and bounced back into the air. I fought to keep her wings level as she sagged down lest a wingtip nick the water and sending us cartwheeling nose over tail. We hit again and stayed down for good, skidding slightly sideways but not so bad as the keel dug in and the airspeed bled off and the engines, God bless them, were still pounding away, but with dying, broken hearts.

Tracers stitched the water off to starboard in an explosion of spray.

Two compliance fighters roared overhead. We were sitting ducks. I killed the engines and climbed out of my seat. Ava was conscious but barely.

'Hang on, kid, we're getting out of here.'

She nodded and managed a weak smile. 'Nice landing, skipper.'

'Could have used your help.'

'Next time.'

The crew life raft rested on the debris-filled flight deck like a long yellow, tubular sausage. But when inflated would hold ten people. I did a head count. Only four.

'Orlando?'

Mason jerked his thumb aft. 'Below.'

The sudden hammering of the fifty-caliber answered my next question.

'Shove the raft through the nose, we'll hand Ava down.'

'I don't need any help. I'm fine.'

Ava stood by her seat, weaving slightly, holding her blood-soaked, wounded arm. Then she fainted, but the professor broke her fall by grabbing her shoulders in time.

More tracer fire, more planes.

'Go, go, GO!'

Mason tossed the raft down the crew spiral staircase and followed. I grabbed Ava's feet, Friedman her shoulders and we half-walked, half-stumbled after him.

Roaring engines and cannon fire as the fighters made another strafing pass. The clipper shuddered from hits up on the flight deck. Had we stayed any longer we would have been mincemeat.

I steered our small group forward into the cramped mooring compartment, where Mason had dropped the bomb. It took only seconds to unlatch the boarding door and swing it open.

We manhandled the raft up and over the hatch coaming and let it drop into the water. As it fell I yanked the cord releasing the CO_2 cartridge and the compressed yellow sausage hissed and twisted and swelled into our instrument of escape.

'Mason, you go and I'll hand Ava down.'

'Got to set the charge.'

Satisfied, he straightened up from the Norden bombsight and patted it affectionately. 'Bye, bye baby.'

He dropped into the raft and steadied it. Ava came to as she landed and Mason propped her up to one side. The Professor went next. The wind had picked up and the water was getting choppy. He had trouble getting his feet planted on the raft's rubbery floor.

Mason shouted, 'C'mon, doc, c'mon, she's gonna blow.'

I ended his indecisiveness by grabbing a pair of short-handled oars, and half-jumping, half-climbing, got into the raft and pulled him down with me. I heard the roar of flames before I saw them.

Sheltered in the lee of the clipper's bow, right wing was now ablaze.

The Luftwaffe pilots knew their work and were busy exacting revenge on the perpetrator of the crime, the evidence of which still loomed in the distance, a slowly rising smoke column at least forty-thousand feet high by now. The sun made it a rose-colored thing of beauty, but it was a beast.

Another fighter pass, more machine gun fire that Orlando returned with his waist gun. His tracers followed the departing fighter in a futile gesture. He barely had a deflection angle to be a serious threat. But even so, machine gun fire coming from our dying plane must have made them a little nervous. But not enough to make them leave. They wanted the plane and they wanted us.

Mason and I paddled down along the fuselage, diverted around the port sponson and arrived at Orlando's gun position. The gun barrel swung hard left as he began firing again.

The Messerschmitt's cannon fire steadily marched across the water towards us in a splash of white spray, and then struck the starboard wing and danced across it, each shell shattering metal into pieces and engines into wrecks. The wing tanks exploded and the shock and heat wave rocked us up against the fuselage and back again. As I watched, half of the wing drooped into the water like the broken wing of a bird.

'Abandon ship!' I shouted.

'Go ahead,' Orlando bellowed. I'll give you covering fire.'

'And die a hero? Like hell you will. We need you to fight another day.'

'I said GO.'

'This is not a god-damned war movie. I order you out of that airplane, or I'm coming in there and pulling you out.'

Orlando frowned his displeasure, but then moved like a cat. Seconds later he was beside me paddling for all he was worth, so hard that I could barely keep up with him. I managed to say in between struggles for breath,

'It's a good thing... I didn't have to come in... and get your sorry ass.'

'You needed covering fire. Out here they'll shoot us like fish in a barrel.'

Just enough daylight to make out the dark outline of the river bank about a quarter mile away. It may as well have been a hundred miles. Paddling the rubber raft was slow going, and the fighters were making passes like a training mission, except we were the target.

The *Dixie Clipper* gave us a brief head start by dying like the fighter she had been. The Norden bombsight detonated as promised, ripping her nose off in a white-hot flash of light. As if on cue, the fire on the starboard wing reached the fuel tanks and exploded, which drove burning metal shards into the sponson's fuel tanks, which in turn sealed the deal in a tremendous blast of reddish-yellow fire and roiling black smoke that blossomed into a small mushroom cloud over the Columbia River and she sank almost instantly.

All those miles, all those ports, only to end up on a river bottom in the middle of nowhere. And we would follow soon if we didn't get the hell to shore.

Fat chance. The lead fighter had spotted us and zoomed in for the final kill. The cannon fire from his first attempt landed to starboard, but each towering white column of water was grim proof of what would happen on his next pass.

Orlando and I paddled even harder. Mason and the Professor leaned out of the edge and used their hands. Ava stared at me, her pain-drawn face a mix of hope and despair. The familiar approaching snarl of the Messerschmitt again, and I unconsciously bunched up my shoulders in preparation for the bullet strike.

The distant POP-POP-POP from his nose cannon as he roared over us and Ava screaming, me screaming, cannon fire striking to the left, but close enough to drench us.

Suddenly a new engine sound: not the Messerschmitt's distinctive howl but a deeper, double-throated, turbocharged roar, and a flash of olive drab and chattering nose guns as a Lockheed P-38 twin-engine *Lightning* flashed overhead in hot pursuit of its prey.

The Messerschmitt climbed in a frantic chandelle to escape its larger, heavier opponent, but the P-38's twin engines gave it superior climbing and turning power and it kept narrowing the gap, its fifty-caliber tracers reaching out like a spider's web to trap its victim. Black smoke began streaming from the enemy's engine just as I lost sight of it in the glare of the rising sun.

Mason said, 'More of ours over there, look.'

Ten or fifteen fighters, both Nazi and American, this time, swirling and swooping across the pale blue sky in a graceful yet deadly dance with only one outcome.

The meleé lasted less than five minutes, with two Me-109's shot down and the rest escaping. One of ours got chewed up pretty badly, with its pilot hightailing for home, one engine feathered and his wingman flying alongside like a worried mother hen. The remaining squadron of P-38's made a low pass over us and waggled their wings in salute. We waved and cheered back. The throaty roar of their engines faded long after they disappeared in the dim morning light.

Ava said, 'Uncle Georgie saves the day!'

'He called them up?' I said.

'Had to be. He's an old cavalry guy, and in the movies they always show up in the nick of time.'

'Ziggy was right,' I said. 'This would make a great movie.'

Less than five minutes later, two P-38's escorted a U.S. Navy PBY *Catalina* seaplane, flying low and slow up the river. The pilot spotted our yellow raft and landed. Five minutes later we lifted off from the scene of the crime while a medical corpsman worked on Ava's wound. Professor Friedman assisted with calm assurance, instructing the young sailor as if the two of them were in an operating theater.

Ava floated in the peaceful embrace of morphine as she murmured to Friedman, 'I thought you said you couldn't stand the sight of blood.'

'For you I make an exception.'

A lot happened in the next eighteen hours, nine of which were spent by Orlando, Mason, the professor and me collapsed in sleep, wedged in the cramped seats of an Army C-47 transport that had picked us up in Seattle after our Catalina landed. Ava was with us, too, lashed to an army stretcher rigged into the fuselage, her bandaged arm snugged into a sling, wounded artery neatly sutured, a blood transfusion to make up for what she had lost, and an army nurse to grant her every wish.

I slept through refueling stops in Oklahoma and Iowa, and finally woke up somewhere over Lake Michigan, or so I guessed from its familiar shape. I went to check on Ava. The nurse spotted me coming and rose to protect her charge. But she needn't have bothered. Ava lay there like Sleeping Beauty, hands folded peacefully, her chest slowly rising and falling.

I said quietly, 'She's really something.'

'All of you are.'

Ava was right about 'Uncle Georgie.' He had foreseen the problems of our flight and ordered Sons of Liberty fighter planes scrambled in case they were needed, which they most certainly were.

I learned this and a lot more during Patton's and my conversation in Seattle on a military telephone connection that made him sound like he was in inside a sheet metal shed in a hailstorm. I briefed him about Inspector Bauer tailing us and how Ziggy was the inside man and how that explained the attack on Couba Island.

'I never did trust that little prick,' he said.

'We did.'

'He's dead and you're alive. That's all that matters.'

'How bad was the attack?'

A brief pause. 'A hell of a lot more Nazi sons-of-bitches died for their country than ours.'

'Captain Fatt...'

'May he rest in peace and may we avenge all their noble deaths.'

I had been holding the photos of Abby and Rosie as he was saying this and told him about Bauer's threat to my family.

'Don't worry, captain. Key West ain't that big a town. We will turn it upside down and shake it until they drop out safe and sound.'

Those words rang in my ears as I stood staring down at Ava, unable to do anything but wait for this flight to come to an end. Where exactly remained a mystery. They had refused to tell us before we took off, citing 'security' reasons.

Fine. Well and good. But now time to use a little muscle. I headed up to the cockpit.

'Mind a visit, fellas?'

The two officers turned to me. The pilot a first lieutenant, the co-pilot a smooth-faced second looie.

336

The pilot said, 'Thought you were going to sleep all the way home.'

'Mind telling me where exactly 'home' is? Pretty closed-mouthed about it back in Seattle.'

He smiled. 'You know how those MI boys can be.'

'You're not one of them. Spill the beans.'

He tapped the compass. 'Right on course. ETA in about three hours, barring some dicey weather in western Pennsylvania. It can be tricky this time of year.'

'Where exactly are we arriving?'

He exchanged raised eyebrows with his co-pilot, and then shot me a grin. 'Can you keep a secret, sir?'

'With the best of them.'

'Well, seeing how you folks managed to pull off a miracle, somebody high up on the totem pole wants to have a little chat with you and hear all about it.'

He paused for effect.

I played along and said, 'And that person would be...?'

'President Perkins, of course.'

'Baloney.'

The four of us sat in reverential silence upon plush-cushioned Chippendale chairs arranged in a neat row along a dark-blue carpeted hallway, with Ava in a wheelchair beside me.

The complicated millwork on the white walls and ceiling a testament to the Philadelphia craftsmen who had first built Independence Hall back in the 1700s. Today, the temporary seat of the Federal Government until Washington D.C. was finished re-building. And, true to that army pilot's word, we really were here to meet the president.

Raining heavily when we arrived. And when we piled out of the limousines, our armed escort put up a black forest of umbrellas that blocked the view of the Liberty Bell and George Washington's statue in the courtyard square. But I already knew what the man looked like. That, plus the fact that I was about to meet his direct successor kept me more than occupied.

I sat closest to the double doors leading into the president's office.

From inside came muted voices, sometimes sharp and questioning, other times low with laughter. I couldn't make out the words, so I finally gave up and leaned my head back against the wainscoting.

Ava patted my hand. 'Hang in there, my darling, we're almost home. Mother says she killed the fatted calf and she can't wait to start carving.'

'Need a rain check. Heading for Key West.'

'Any word yet?'

'I would have heard.'

She held my hand but said nothing.

The murmuring voices crew louder, more distinct, the double doors swung open, and a naval aide-de-camp decked out in full dress blues and a gold-braided aiguillette bowed slightly.

'The president will see you now.'

The army nurse reached for the wheelchair but Ava stopped her.

'That's no way for an actress to make an entrance.'

She rose a shakily, took my arm and steadied herself.

'Co-pilot to pilot; ready for takeoff.'

I led our small entourage into the spacious office. The floor-to-ceiling windows transformed the grey rainy day into silvery lightness. From behind a massive oak desk, President Perkins stood up, came around and joined a beaming General Patton on the other side.

Perkins's familiar, stern, no-nonsense face melted into a radiant smile as she opened her arms as if to embrace us all. 'Home are the sailors, home from the sea! And what an honor for me to thank you for the great service you have done for our country.'

What followed was a slightly awkward version of a receiving line, and I marveled at how pointed her questions were, no detail too small to have been overlooked. Perkins had seen many of Ava's films and complimented her on her acting skills; she knew of Professor Friedman's earlier work in nuclear physics and was gravely attendant when he expressed his gratitude for being granted asylum in the United States. She had a mutual friend in Lieutenant Mason's home town and they shared a brief reminiscence. As for Orlando and me, she a Pan Am loyal customer and knew our Caribbean routes as well as I did, or so it seemed.

I'm sure Perkins had been briefed on our backgrounds long before we arrived. Presidents can't possibly know these things in advance. But how they handle the information makes all the difference. Perkins made you feel like you were the only person in the world who really mattered, and that everything you had to say was important, worthwhile and grand. I told her she had my vote in the fall elections. America needed leaders like her if we were to get out of the mess we were in.

'One vote at a time, Captain. That's my plan.'

After the pleasantries had concluded, two butlers rolled in an heirloom silver tea service that looked like Paul Revere had finished it just before he made his famous ride. Over sips of the best coffee I have ever tasted in my life and delicate cookies that disappeared in my mouth before I even chewed them, Perkins conducted the debriefing as well if not better than General Patton.

From what we told her and what her sources on the ground confirmed, the Columbia River target had been destroyed, the plutonium neutralized, and the nuclear weapons clock reset to zero as far as she was concerned. Professor Friedman was confident it would take the Nazis twelve to eighteen to weaponize enough uranium to start making bombs again.

The president said grimly, 'They'll never get the chance.'

Patton grunted his stern approval.

The briefing concluded, she rose gracefully. With Ava holding my arm, we stood there looking at each other the way you do when the party's over and it's time to go home. I was anxious to do just that.

'My friends,' the president began. 'I want to thank you for your bravery, your courage, and your absolute refusal to quit until the job was done. It's an admirable trait that Americans will strive for in the days to come.'

She took a step toward me. 'Mr. Carter, you have a commission waiting for you as a full colonel in the Army Air Corps, should you choose to accept it.' Before I could say anything, she turned to Orlando. 'The same holds true for you, Major Diaz. If ever we needed help from experienced people like you, we need it now.'

Mason got promoted to lieutenant commander and Friedman was heading directly to a top research job at the Pentagon.

'Miss James, I'm afraid I can't offer you anything but a promise to watch all of your movies with the greatest of pleasure.'

Ava smiled. 'I appreciate that, Madame President, but I'm taking a break from make-believe until this is over.'

'What will you do?'

She glanced at General Patton. 'Oh, I think Uncle George will find something interesting.'

He smiled and rubbed his hands together. 'Don't worry, I will. But we need to celebrate your safe return first - all of you, for that matter - including you, Madam President. When Helen puts on a feed, she doesn't spare the horses.'

'I appreciate the offer, general, but pressing business keeps me from accepting.'

'Me too,' I said. 'But thanks all the same.'

Patton was instantly grave. 'I know what you mean, Carter. I'd do the same thing if I were you. Unless...'

He and the president exchanged a quick look. She pressed a button on the desk top. Seconds later the double doors swung open and there stood Rosie and Abby.

'Daddy!'

She ran to me and I scooped her up in my arms, a skinny, trembling, frightened, crying kid who I kissed and hugged and went weak in the knees and had to sit down. Rosie's calming hand on my shoulder, her familiar voice, and Ava's too, and nothing left to do but rub my kid's hair, tell her that I loved her and cry.

Patton was right. Ava too. Helen Dortch Longstreet hadn't actually killed a fatted calf, but the food, drink, music and conversation at her antebellum mansion on Couba Island was of biblical proportions. Helen, cigar and all, made the rounds of rooms filled with happy guests, making sure everyone we felt welcomed, especially Abby and my mother, who had stared at a Gestapo kidnapper's gun barrel for days.

According to the general, the battle for Couba Island had gone pretty much as I had figured. Caught flat-footed by the Kampfschwimmer, his men had been beaten back soundly. But after we flew the *Dixie Clipper* out of harm's way, he rallied his men and mounted a counterattack that eventually drove the enemy to the beach and those who survived back into their assault rafts for a ragtag escape

In my wanderings through the mansions many side rooms, I came upon Juan Trippe sitting quietly by himself, taking in the celebratory activity with those piercing black eyes of his that never missed a trick, or an opportunity to advance his airline across the chessboard of big business. He spotted me, and with a fractional nod of his head motioned to the empty chair beside him.

We sat in silence, each absorbed with the conversational buzz and excitement that comes when a hundred people are jammed inside a mansion filled with strong drink and even stronger feelings.

Trippe cleared his throat and I fastened my seatbelt.

'Captain Carter, I want you to know that you will always have a place with Pan American Airways.'

'Thanks, sir. But when I quit, I quit for good.'

'We need experienced captains like you.'

'My daughter needs a father.'

Another stretch of silence. Somebody somewhere started singing *Dixie*, and others whistled and joined in. Soon a fiddle took up the tune.

Trippe said. 'I still can't believe you pulled it off.'

'Makes two of us.'

He chuckled. 'Who would have thought the *Dixie Clipper* could be a bomber.'

'Not me that's for sure.'

He cleared his throat. 'I understand that the President offered you a commission in the Army Air Corps. A full colonel, no less. Congratulations.'

'Thank you.'

'Never made more than lieutenant back when I was in the navy.'

'That's okay, you're a general of industry now.'

He laughed and then stood up. 'My offer still holds. Abby will be grown up all too soon. When that day comes, the captain's seat is yours, should you ever want it.'

I thanked him, but wanted outside instead.

Except for the blackened tree stump here and there, the deepening twilight revealed no trace of the Nazi attack. I made my way down to the dock to check up on my beat-up little S-38, now moored in the same spot as the late, great *Dixie Clipper*. She looked like a bathtub toy by comparison, but she was all mine - and the bank's too, of course.

The aircraft mechanics had neatly repaired the twenty or so bullet holes she suffered during the attack. I ran my fingers over the cotton fabric patches but felt no rough edges that would catch in the wind stream and rip them off. This kind of craftsmanship was a fading art, but on Couba Island, alive and well.

Ava's voice startled me. 'We've got mighty good boys.'

'They'll be needed elsewhere soon enough.'

'How soon?'

'We'll find out at eight o'clock.'

President Perkins was scheduled to make a radio address to the nation before a joint session of congress. It wouldn't be about the budget.

Ava shifted her arm sling and flexed her wrist. 'They told me to keep exercising without fail.'

'Still hurt?'

'Only when I do this.'

'Don't do that.'

Her smile was a crescent moon in the shadow of the wing. 'So, do I call you colonel or Sam?'

'Either will do.'

'You accepted the commission?'

'Surprised?'

She shrugged. 'I know how much Abby means to you. And you've done more than enough for your country, I should think.'

I pretended to examine a fabric patch on the fuselage, but I was really buying time to collect my thoughts.

'I took that Buenos Aires trip for the sake of my career. I'm taking this commission for the sake of America. Abby will understand the difference. Maybe not today, but one day, I hope.'

Ava touched my arm. 'I can help her understand if you'd like.'

I took a quick breath and she said quickly, 'It's not what you think. I mean as a friend of the family. Nothing more. 'Aunt Ava,' if you will. Whatever you want, Sam, I'm happy to do it.'

'That's kind of you.'

'Thanks.'

'But that's not what I need.'

'What do you need?'

'This.'

I took her in my arms.

Where were you the night President Perkins made her speech? My guess is that you were among the tens of millions of Americans across the nation listening to their radios, waiting to hear the 'swoosh' of her fiery torch. Me too, except instead of being stuck in Buenos Aires, I was here on Couba Island, with Abby, Rosie, and Ava by my side in the midst of a crowd of determined people long past surrender, determined to fight instead.

Two minutes past eight o'clock, after a breathless introduction by a radio announcer who could have used a stiff drink to calm himself down, the network broadcast shifted to Independence Hall in Philadelphia, where President Perkins addressed a joint session of congress to finish what FDR had begun eight months ago. Her voice was clear, calm, insistent and firm:

'December 7, 1941 - a date that will live in infamy - the United States was suddenly and deliberately attacked by naval and air forces of the Empire of Japan.

'December 8, 1941 – a date that will live in far more infamy, our nation's political and financial capitals were deliberately attacked and destroyed by Germany.

'As your president, confronted with Adolf Hitler's threat to attack even more cities, I declared a state of neutrality to exist between the United States and the Axis powers.

'I did so to spare tens of thousands of innocent American lives. But in doing so, we nearly lost the very soul of our Constitution. That is why I come to you tonight to announce that the time of sacrifice has ended, the soul of our Constitution is alive and well, and the time for retribution has come!'

Shouting, cheering, applause, all across America I figured. When it finally subsided, Perkins continued:

'Because of the heroic action of a brave group of American citizens, supported by members of an organization called the Sons of Liberty, and our own armed forces, I come to you tonight to declare that the imminent danger of nuclear attack on our soil has ended.

'And while I can announce tonight that our nation is safe from the Damoclean sword of nuclear destruction, never before has there been a greater challenge to life, liberty and the pursuit of happiness, not only for

America but for our allies around the world, who at this very hour struggle against the dark forces of fascist dictatorship.

'Any delay on our part to join the fight guarantees the victory of savagery and barbarism over peace and prosperity.

'Therefore, tonight, as your president, I ask members of congress to declare a state of war to exist between the United States and Germany, Italy, and the Empire of Japan.

'No matter how long it may take to overcome this invasion of evil upon righteousness, the American people will win through to absolute victory and ensure that this form of treachery shall never endanger the world again.

'There can be no blinking at the fact that by declaring war, our people, our territory, and our interests are in grave danger. But with the unbounding determination of the American people, we shall gain the inevitable triumph - so help us God.'

Paul Lally is an Emmy award-winning, television and film writer/producer/director. He lives in New Hampshire.

His previous novel is **SILK**

Find out what's coming next at:

www.paul-lally.com

or

Write him at:

paul@paul-lally.com

Made in the USA
Charleston, SC
10 March 2015